P9-DJL-265

ALSO BY WIL HAYGOOD

Showdown: Thurgood Marshall
and the Supreme Court Nomination that Changed America

The Butler: A Witness to History

Sweet Thunder: The Life and Times of Sugar Ray Robinson

In Black and White: the Life of Sammy Davis Jr.

The Haygoods of Columbus: A Family Memoir

King of the Cats: The Life and Times of Adam Clayton Powell Jr.

Two on the River (photography by Stan Grossfeld)

TIGERLAND

TIGERLAND

· 1968–1969 ·

A City Divided, a Nation Torn Apart,
and a Magical Season of Healing

Wil Haygood

 ALFRED A. KNOPF · NEW YORK · 2018

Henderson County Public Library

THIS IS A BORZOI BOOK
PUBLISHED BY ALFRED A. KNOPF

Copyright © 2018 by Wil Haygood

All rights reserved.

Published in the United States by Alfred A. Knopf,
a division of Penguin Random House LLC, New York, and distributed
in Canada by Random House of Canada,
a division of Penguin Random House Canada Limited, Toronto.

www.aaknopf.com

Knopf, Borzoi Books, and the colophon
are registered trademarks of Penguin Random House LLC.

Library of Congress Cataloging-in-Publication Data

Names: Haygood, Wil, author.
Title: Tigerland : 1968-1969, a city divided, a nation torn apart, and a magical season of healing /
by Wil Haygood.
Description: First edition. | New York : Alfred A. Knopf, 2018. | Includes bibliographical references.
Identifiers: LCCN 2018002138 | ISBN 9781524731861 (hardback) | ISBN 9781524731878 (ebook)
Subjects: LCSH: Basketball—Ohio—Columbus—History. | Baseball—Ohio—Columbus—History.
| East High School (Columbus, Ohio)—History | Race relations—Ohio—Columbus—History.
| Columbus (Ohio)—Biography. | BISAC: SPORTS & RECREATION / Baseball / General. |
SPORTS & RECREATION / Basketball.
Classification: LCC GV885.73.C65 H68 2018 | DDC 796.32309771/57—dc23
LC record available at https://lccn.loc.gov/2018002138

Book design by Maggie Hinders
Jacket design by Tyler Comrie

Manufactured in the United States of America

First Edition

Henderson County Public Library

For Phyllis Callahan, and Paul Pennell

& in memory of Jack Gibbs and Bob Hart

Contents

TIGERLAND

Prologue

1968

Reverend King Passed This Way

They were poor boys wedged into the turmoil of a nation at war and in the midst of unrest. They were the sons of maids and dishwashers and cafeteria workers, poor as pennies and too proud to beg, but not to ask or borrow. Their mothers were among the large waves of those who had come from the Deep South, a sojourn begun in the early part of the twentieth century known as the Great Migration. The Pacific coast and the Midwest were favored destinations. Families had fled by train or bus, escaping all those cotton fields and scenes of raw injustice. Columbus, Ohio, was a stop on the above-ground railroad where families had come praying for new opportunities. The boys' fathers were mostly absent. Garnett Davis, the gifted third baseman on the baseball team, had a father, but he was stuck down in South Carolina, on a damn chain gang. Nick Conner, the pogo-jumping basketball player, had a father too, but one who had abandoned the family for another life in Cleveland. Basketball player Robert Wright's father had murdered a man. Kenny Mizelle, who played second base, sometimes dreamed about his dead father. At least that's what he had been told all these years, that his dad was dead. But he wasn't. Boys will be boys, and blood rolls thick, and when it comes to fathers, it often rolls backward. Their mothers could only implore them to look ahead, especially so because it was a tricky and dangerous time.

The year 1968 began convulsing and flaming its way toward 1969. There was deep tumult on the streets of America. Martin Luther King Jr. and Robert F. Kennedy had tried to do something about it all—the poverty, the absence of fathers that cut to the bone of despair, the pitiful condition of black men and the uneven social fabric of America. But these boys were athletes—sinewy, quick, and agile basketball and baseball players—blessed with a unique talent that, with the start of 1968, they were hoping could ward off the darkness that seemed to be engulfing their community. They were the Tigers of East High School.

Some of them lived in single-family homes that fronted a fertilizer plant—and the obligatory railroad tracks—just off Leonard Avenue. Some lived in Poindexter Village, the government-funded public housing project, one of the first of its kind in the nation. (President Franklin D. Roosevelt had even come to the city for the dedication. Crowds had lined the streets as he cruised by in a convertible.) Still others lived in old apartment buildings behind Mount Vernon Avenue, where the bars and speakeasies were, where the gamblers sauntered about like roosters. Laws and boundaries had been drawn against their families long before they were born, consigning them to a segregated world on the East Side of this midwestern city. They were black boys in a white world, running, jumping, and excelling inside that world.

They played most of their basketball games through that cold winter in a converted rodeo cow palace on the Ohio State Fairgrounds, where you could still get whiffs of the horse manure, but no one seemed to mind as the East High Tigers couldn't stop winning. The gym at the high school couldn't accommodate the thousands who wanted to see them play. Their games were often broadcast on radio, an uncommon occurrence at the time for any high school basketball team. Come baseball season the crowds vanished. At the away baseball games, there would sometimes be only one fan in the bleachers rooting for the Tigers, and that was the coach's wife. The boys actually didn't mind playing their baseball games away, in and around rural Ohio, because the baseball diamonds were better at the other schools. They simply set about swinging their bats and blasting the ball into the cornfields. They looked like figures out of Negro league baseball, that professional and segregated league which was by now almost two decades removed from existence. The umpires—white men raised in segregation—sometimes would gawk at the East High players with awe. They were so proud at game's end, tired and smiling as the farmland receded into view on the ride back home. The proud black boys never complained about the well-to-do schools and all their fancy equipment. They realized they didn't have the luxury of escaping the crazy and murderous times. They were in the center of it all.

Martin Luther King Jr.'s presence hovers over that season. Rev. Phale Hale was the unofficial minister of the East High basketball and baseball teams. He had known King from his own Georgia days and was the first to bring the prophet of black America to Columbus. The gunning down of King in Memphis on April 4, 1968, was an awful deed that unleashed riot and rebellion from Los Angeles all the way to the east coast itself. Small pockets of Columbus burned on the city's East Side. In nearby Indianapolis, 168 miles west of Columbus, Bobby Kennedy spoke movingly of King's death, and blacks and whites were weeping around him like a gospel chorus. Then, like King, Kennedy also fell after being shot by a crazed assassin. Hale had counseled these East High athletes with King-like optimism. He had told them to hold on. He had told them change was going to come. Now, with King's death, Hale, who had given the citywide eulogy for King, was himself emotionally spent. King and his wife, Coretta, had slept in Rev. Hale's home. It seemed, at ground level, that a nation was unraveling.

It was a year of endless apocalypse. King and Kennedy had warned that black and white must come together, though King long before and with much more passion than Kennedy. But now the question loomed: What integration? East High, in the 1968–69 school year, and in spite of integration laws, remained an all-black school. In the fall of 1968 when Jack Gibbs—the first black principal at East High—opened the doors to the cavernous school, he did not know what to expect. It had been a hellish summer. He confided to his wife, Ruth, that he was worried that

some returning students might think of the all-black school as a laboratory now for dissension and protest. He vowed not to let that happen.
The air was uneasy and unpredictable when the doors swung open and
the school bells rang out.

Gibbs had his own tortured story. He had escaped Harlan, Kentucky,
a dangerous coal mining town where he had seen murderous deeds on
the dirt streets. In Columbus he worked nights, finished high school,
and got into Ohio State University, where he played football. He was a
benchwarmer, but had gotten into a very important game (Michigan,
of course) and made the play that turned the game around. In time he
found himself on East Broad Street, at East High School, on the fault
lines of rise or ruin, depending on which side of the street you stood.

The basketball and baseball players of 1968–69 at East High had their
own narrative arc to create. They would brush away the fires of discon-
tent and neighborhood pain, replacing it all with a far more glorious
timepiece: They would become statewide champions and even heroes
amid the upheaval. They would give the citizenry something to remember from that year other than fire and death and haunted dreams.

Both teams had white coaches, Bob Hart in basketball and Paul Pennell in baseball, big-hearted men who had a social conscience. Hart was
a product of rural Ohio and had survived the landing at Normandy during World War II. He came home from the war with medals. And also
with a sickening feeling about all he had seen in the military but particularly how badly blacks were treated. In the mid-1950s he took a job at
all-black East High. Other white teachers cried their way out of assignments there; he exulted in the posting. "Basketball in the '60s became
a place where the black kid could show off his talent," is how Bob Hart
put it regarding the social and political forces at play. "And there was a
different breed of kid. They were hungry." Pennell, the baseball coach,
hailed from the West Side of Columbus, known as the most inhospitable
part of town when it came to integration. He was in his early twenties
and given the baseball job almost as an afterthought. What he aimed
to do was prove to the outside world—anyone beyond this segregated
neighborhood—that black boys could play baseball. Because there were
so many people who needed reminding.

Amid all the pain—the martyred deaths, the glass-strewn streets, the military tanks patrolling the neighborhoods, the city's intermittent juvenile curfew—change was indeed coming. And some of it came in the form of two statewide athletic championships happening just sixty days apart. Blacks, especially, had never witnessed such a collective and back-to-back example of athletic prowess. In a city without a professional major league sports team of any kind, a high school could take on a feverish dimension—not to mention a cult following. Blacks held no political strength in the city, but they did now have athletic strength. The nation may have been on fire, and those embers still burning, but these championships were both undeniable and fortifying. They seemed, in their own unique way, to say to those who needed uplifting: Hold on.

It was here, through the fall, winter, and spring of 1968 and 1969, when a season of glory unfolded that would make national history. It was here, in the storefronts up and down Mount Vernon Avenue, that the salesmen and saleswomen began, at first, pinning those portraits of the slain Martin Luther King Jr. to the storefront windows. Then a short while later—to the same walls and windows—they began pinning up portraits of those basketball and baseball players from the neighborhood. A dreamer was shot down, but the prophet had left more than just anguish behind. Twenty-seven limber black boys across two sports would rise up through the smoke. They had something to prove to the world.

This is the story of how it all happened.

PART I

Down to the River

He was born in 1924 in Columbus, Ohio, in a tight-knit community on the city's South Side. It may have been the Roaring Twenties, but Columbus, located in the middle of the state, was a relatively quiet state capital. Cleveland, at the time, had genuine gangsters. Cincinnati had inept gangsters. In Newport, Kentucky, however—just across the river from Cincinnati—the gangsters really gained a foothold during the Prohibition era. Bootlegging, gambling, and prostitution were rampant. Frank Sinatra was just one of the Hollywood stars who popped in for a visit. As for Columbus, it had Republicans, state office workers, and farmland extending in all directions from the center of town. (The Columbus gangsters would, however, make a bit of noise in the late 1960s because of illicit gambling.) It was the annexation of suburban land in succeeding years that would be the cause of the city's noticeable growth.

His given name was James Robert Hart, but he would always go by Bob. Families at the time tended to have multiple children, the better to keep the engine of family life humming. Children created hope and a belief that the times would surely get better. As well, children, in time, meant more family earning power. But Jimmy Hart and his wife, Mirza Mae, stopped having children after their little Bob was born. Friends and relatives wondered if the child would be spoiled, such was the attention that his mother, Mirza, heaped on him. But little Bob never complained about being an only child, and he never took on an air of entitlement just because he had his parents all to himself. As the years rolled on, he acquired an independent streak. Other children on the South Side—a brew of whites and blacks who mostly got along—marveled at his sense of discipline. Teachers thought young Bob Hart wise beyond his years. Being an only child, he learned to do for himself when Mom or Dad wasn't around. He found camaraderie in sports, honing decent enough skills in basketball, baseball, and football.

Jimmy Hart worked at Union Station, the downtown railway station. Sometimes he'd take little Bobby down there, and his son would gawk at all the Negroes, as they were often called then, bunching about: They had just arrived from southern states. Jimmy Hart's most common trip was the St. Louis run. On one of those runs Jimmy met famed actress Mae West. He could hardly contain his excitement. "He said she was the most beautiful girl in the world," Jimmy's granddaughter, Sherri, remembers. Money was tight during the Depression, and the times were hard for most everyone. Bob's mother, Mirza Mae, worked as a waitress. She was sweet, loud, and exuberant. Neighbors whispered behind her back about her shameless loudness. She chuckled their snickering away. The Hart parents were respectful of the local black citizenry. Jimmy Hart had worked alongside black Pullman porters on all those railway runs; Mirza Mae's fun-loving manner seemed to preclude meanness toward others, no matter their racial identity. If the Harts doted on their only son, his affection for them was deep as well. Dinner conversations were full of spirited talk about train travel and the outside world.

At South High, young Bob began to appreciate basketball more than the other sports he played. He liked the nuance of talent, the comraderie on the court, the mechanics of the game and how fast it moved. He noted that selfishness could disrupt a team of gifted athletes as quickly as could an injury.

After graduating from South High School in 1942—when the nation was jittery and mired in war—Bob Hart enrolled at Ohio Wesleyan University, a small Methodist school in Delaware, Ohio, a rural community only thirty miles from his home. He arrived at the school with a continuing interest in sports—as well as a social conscience—and made both the basketball and baseball teams. He wrote letters to his girlfriend, Jean Woodyard, back in Columbus. During his occasional visits home to see his parents, he and Jean went on picnics and snuck away to the homes of friends to drink beer. She was attracted to his focus and his dependability. Bob Hart was no ladies' man and didn't try to be. He wore thick glasses and was already a little larger than the average high school boy. He was also serene, fastidious, exact, and particular about his likes and dislikes—sometimes to the point of annoyance—but these were traits that Jean found appealing. The letters he wrote to her were more flowery than her letters to him; he saw the difference, and it only heightened his doubts about her love for him. "Hi Sweetheart," he wrote her while on a fishing getaway to Buckeye Lake. "I am having a swell time . . . Have been missing you a lot. Wish you were here. Are you missing me? I love you, Bob." At times he was so insecure that his mother felt the depths of that insecurity. She'd write Jean telling her how much Bob loved her, and imploring Jean not to tell Bob she had written.

When the Japanese dropped bombs on Pearl Harbor, Bob Hart, like other young men at the time, found his life upended by World War II. His parents were shattered when in the summer of 1943 their only son enlisted in the army, stalling his education, at least for now.

He was first sent to Camp Sibert in Alabama. He wound up being assigned to the very first chemical warfare attack company the army had formed. The battalion's expertise was the firing of mortars, tube-shaped pieces of artillery that shoot bombs, sending them spiraling toward the enemy. During World War I, mortars were used to unleash gas shells that were poisonous. The effectiveness of the mortar as artillery became especially effective during the Civil War.

The Alabama heat proved wicked for Hart and his fellow recruits; one member of the unit, Philip Francis, died of heat stroke during training.

Being an only child seemed to have fortified Bob Hart; he was not used to whining. He forged his way through boot camp with nary a complaint, not that grumbling would have done any good anyway.

When his furlough came, he hustled home to Columbus, up the steps of the family home and into the arms of his mother and father. He regaled them with stories of boot camp, the food and the heat, the customs of southerners: Alabama was brutally segregated, and, unlike in Columbus, there was an edge to the segregation, fierce laws behind it. His return home was written up in a local newspaper ("James Robert Hart, son of Mr. and Mrs. J.H. Hart, 974 Heyl Av, is home on furlough. He is a South High School graduate. . . ."). He got spiffed up and went out with Jean. She was very happy to see him—her soldier boy home from the army! They kissed and drank beer and fooled around. He asked her questions about local basketball games, telling her how much he missed watching the games. He begged her to wait for him while he served his army stint, and promised her he would take care of himself. He did not want her thinking about Hitler and the Nazis and the unknown.

But he returned to Camp Sibert still unsure of Jean's eternal love. The uncertainty bothered him. He couldn't shake thoughts of her. He sent her more letters in his unmistakable handwriting, which was as beautiful as calligraphy. "My Dearly Beloved . . . I rather suppose that you've guessed it by now that I'm headed overseas but how soon I don't know. Everyone seems to think that it will be within the next month . . . I want you to know that I love you with all my heart and even though it won't do any good, I want to ask you to wait for me because after this damn thing is over I have a few plans in line for you and I." He was a soldier in love and facing peril. He felt no reason to mince words: "As far as we know we're headed for England and going as heavy weapons . . . I love you and I miss you more than I can put on paper." He feared she was being wooed by other young men on the homefront. She confided she was thinking of joining the military because she had her own patriotic urges. She wanted to defeat Hitler! In a subsequent letter, he begged her not to, told her she wouldn't like army life. She read his letter and thought he had some nerve. She had actually already made up her mind.

.   .   .

The 87th Chemical Mortar Battalion embarked for Europe from New York aboard the luxury liner the *Queen Elizabeth*. The army commandeered the ship for troop movement. During the week-long journey, the ship—bound for Scotland—often zigzagged in the water to elude Nazi U-boats. From Scotland the soldiers traveled by train to London. It wasn't long before Bob Hart, college student from Columbus, Ohio, found himself in the raw madness of war. In December his battalion was encamped in the biting cold of Sadzot, Belgium, seeking warmth in a few of the houses. The unit had stationed guards on the outskirts of town, but an approaching panzer division found an opening and slipped through. In the middle of the night, several German soldiers silently crept into one house and slit the throats of several American GIs. German paratroopers began invading the area. Corporal Bill Cummings spotted some approaching Germans and bolted to warn his fellow GIs. "Get up, there's Krauts all over the place!" he yelled upon reaching the first of two houses. The Germans spotted Cummings and hit him with a burst of gunfire; he dropped dead on the snow-covered ground. At another house, several soldiers—among them James Hosmer, William Breuer, and Bob Hart, who was the squad's gunner—quickly realized they were badly outnumbered. They had to escape. They raced for the kitchen and dived through windows. Some of them left their outerwear and raced through the cold coatless. Hosmer stopped, whirled, and tossed a grenade in the direction of the Germans, killing two. First Lt. Ralph Walker—who had happily bragged to the unit in recent days about the birth of his son back home—spotted an SS crew of four kneeling in the street, propping up a machine gun. Walker slyly positioned himself and fired at the German crew. In seconds the Germans lay dead.

Hart's mortar battalion continued fighting in Germany, France, and across Belgium. Their landing on Utah Beach on D-day had been as brutal as they had imagined it might be. "The approximately 62 hours spent . . . in the English Channel was a rather miserable, never-to-be-forgotten experience," a history of Hart's battalion reveals. "Salt spray fell across the craft at all times and the decks had from one-half to an inch of water washing about at all times." They marched and rode through Aachen, and into the Hürtgen forest, which is where Lt. Col. Bob Hart got frostbite.

There were more than four thousand Allied casualties on D-Day. Hart's battalion lost 2nd Lt. Harold Shouse, Pvt. Herman Richey, Cpl. James Montgomery, and Cpl. William Trent. In the days ahead they would lose many more: Pvt. Francis Plubell, Cpl. Frank Stubb, Cpl. William St. Clair, Pvt. Tom Fowler, Pvt. Adolph Miller, Pvt. Fred Berry, Sgt. John Albright, 2nd Lt. William Cable. It was grim and harrowing. Bob Hart knew how lucky he was simply to survive. There were days he thought the noise would never stop, men yelling and blood spraying. "There has never been any rest for the . . . chemical mortar company for when the infantry to which it is attached gains its objective," a field report noted. "The heavy mortar company is transferred to another unit which jumps several hours later. The wear and tear on our men and material is terrific."

Bob Hart's hometown girl, Jean, did join the army, becoming part of the WAVES. Bob admonished her from Europe about the drop-off in her letter writing.

The men of the 87th Chemical Mortar Battalion moved far and wide across Europe. From Poland, Hart wrote yet another letter to Jean: "This might sound funny to you but you came awful close to becoming a mother yesterday. We ran into some Polish refugees and in the group there [were] two of the cutest twins you ever saw. Both were girls, Danut and Sophie. They were nine years old and honest if I had some way to get them home I'd have taken them with me. We gave them chocolate and all kinds of candy and gum . . . Honey, it sure made me homesick. I was holding one of them on my lap and thinking that if this damn war hadn't come along maybe I'd be home with you holding our Baby Jean on my lap. That's all I want, just to come home to you and raise a family. What do you think of that idea?" So he was professing his love. But it didn't seem to matter all that much to Jean, because her letter writing tapered off and the romance lost its heat.

When it was all over, Bob Hart had his health, some war medals, and a broken heart. He made his way back to America at war's end, back to the Ohio Wesleyan campus in 1946. He really didn't talk much about the war. There was the time he had marched a couple of captured German soldiers back to base and realized, once there, putting his rifle down, checking it, that he had had no bullets in the chamber during the entire march. He could chuckle at the memory of that episode. But not about much else: There were just too many soldier buddies, too many friends, who had been lost. Dead in the snow, dead in the mud, dead in the tall grass of some battlefield. Gone forever.

There was something that seemed to stay on Bob Hart's mind after his return from the war. It was inequality. He had witnessed the mistreatment of blacks in the Deep South and then overseas. The disenfranchisement of blacks began to bother him. He told his college English teacher he was going to write a paper on black Americans and their plight. He got the *Encyclopaedia Britannica* citation of "American Negro" and pored over it for hours, for days. He became familiar with the teachings of Booker T. Washington, the poetry of Paul Laurence Dunbar, the singing of Paul Robeson, the writings of Carter G. Woodson. He felt energized and enlightened as he pursued this course of study. This is what the home-from-war soldier with a social conscience wrote in his paper, handed in to his professor on February 18, 1946:

> I am convinced that the Negro has possibilities for development equal to anything we whites have. I am convinced that if given the chance the whole Negro race can become one of our greatest assets. To do anything to deprive them of this possibility is to deprive the world of some of its greatest culture. I am convinced that the only answer to the race problem, the only hope for an undivided America, the only possible program from a cultural viewpoint is equal rights for black and white, and the opening up of our institutions to the development of the Negro.

It was certainly a progressive piece of writing for a twenty-two-year-old white midwesterner. Bob Hart finally graduated from Ohio Wesleyan in 1949. He decided he wanted to teach and to coach. His mother fretted about his emotional state of mind because of the breakup with Jean, but he assured her he would be fine.

Shortly after graduation Hart got a lucky break and was offered a head basketball coaching job at Manchester High School in rural Adams County, nestled along the Ohio River. Hart was a quiet, methodical coach and considered himself a student of the sport. He realized the talent pool would be limited in such a small school. Nevertheless, he coached his team to a 26–4 record and a county championship. The victories did not ease his loneliness. Jane Breeze was a cheerleader. She thought the head basketball coach was worldly. They spent time together, away from the eyes of others in hopes of avoiding any meddlesome gossip. On September 8, 1950—she was eighteen years old—they went over to a justice of the peace and got married. The couple did not think it a good idea to remain in Manchester.

Bob Hart was soon in the trenches of journeyman coaching, bouncing around rural Ohio with his young bride. There was a two-year stay at Peebles High School, where he won a county championship. In 1952 he landed a coaching job at Junction City, Ohio, another all-white rural community. He would sometimes joke that he was out in the sticks, but he was also learning how to coach, how to draw up defenses and analyze an opposing team's strengths and weaknesses. His teams at Junction City had admirable success, going 44–29 over a three-year period. He was happy to have a job, even if the kids were smallish, and even if he was sometimes pulled into coaching football as well. His wife, Jane, occasionally complained that he was never home.

Hart began to go to basketball clinics. He cornered veteran coaches, getting as much insight as he could. When he landed at Watkins Memorial High School in Pataskala, Ohio, in 1956, he was a little giddy because he was getting closer to his hometown. Pataskala was just a short distance from the state capital of Columbus, which is where he wanted to coach because the schools were larger and, as he knew, the talent pool would be more wide-ranging. He also reminded Jane that they would be nearer his parents, who could help out with their young brood, Sherri and Bobbi. Later they would have one more daughter, Lynne.

A year later, in 1957, Bob Hart's desires came true. He was offered a job as the reserve basketball coach at Columbus East High School. Jack Moore was head basketball coach at the time; Hart and Moore had been roommates at Ohio Wesleyan. Hart told his wife he had to take the job, that there would be a chance for advancement if he did well.

East High sat on the city's mostly black and segregated East Side of town. (City fathers didn't seem to pay any attention to the landmark *Brown v. Board of Education* ruling three years earlier, in 1954, which had called for the desegregation of public schools. And the protestations by black teachers about equality of education, for the time being, fell on deaf ears.) In 1951 East High won its first state basketball championship. Romeo Watkins was a star guard on that team. Watkins enjoyed being an East High Tiger and all the neighborhood celebrity that came with it. But there was an individual at the school he didn't like: Helen Bartow, the vice principal. Every day, or often enough that she put a wicked fear into the black students, she would admonish any of them who dared come through the East Broad Street entrance—the front doors—of the school. She insisted they enter the school through a side door. It was tantamount to the backdoor policy that was customary in the South. It may have been an unwritten rule in Columbus, but Watkins and the other black students at the school felt the impact of it. "She was the one who related everything to the students," Watkins recalls years later. Watkins played alongside three other blacks on that championship team, and one white player, Dick Linson. Linson had grown up on the East Side of the city, alongside Italians and blacks. He was a kindhearted soul. His fellow players thought so highly of him they voted him team captain, an honor usually reserved for one of the team's stars. As team captain, he was the representative face of the team at the beginning of every game. Whether it was fair or not, some black parents wondered why one of the black stars hadn't been named team captain; they wondered if the fix had been in for Linson to be named captain. At season's end, the only player on that championship team to receive a scholarship offer was Dick Linson. He went to the University of Kentucky. All of his fellow athletes there were white. He hated the place, hated the segregation, thought the school was downright racist.

Close friends and acquaintances suggested to Bob Hart that he might want to live anyplace but the East Side of town. They referred to the area as alien, unknowable, even dangerous. But those people didn't really know Bob Hart, how he viewed the racial dynamics of America. Bob Hart didn't blink and moved his wife and daughters straight to the East Side of town.

Once they were settled, the Harts enrolled their daughters in the local public school. The girls did not mind that they were among the few whites in their school because they lived in a neighborhood where black faces were all around them.

Bob Hart was quite delighted about being back in Columbus. He began going to the black playgrounds of the East Side: Franklin Junior High, Champion Junior High, and—later—Monroe Junior High. These were the all-black feeder schools that served East High. And Bob Hart, hanging out around the playgrounds that abutted those schools, introducing himself to players, could hardly believe what he was see-ing: Good basketball players were everywhere! He saw tall players and lightning quick players. He saw players who could jump higher than he had ever seen at this level. And they all wanted to play, hard, every day, no matter the heat. This was a new kind of athlete to Bob Hart. These were also the players who would make up Bob Hart's East High reserve team in the upcoming 1957–58 season. The reserves usually comprised a team of first-year high school players. They had their own coach and schedule of games.

That season, after tryouts, he winnowed the reserve team down to thirteen players. More than half the team was over six feet tall. They won their first three games, then the next two, then three more after that, leaving them undefeated as the mid-season approached. They kept win-ning into the second half of the season, their record going to 12–0. And when the season had ended, they had won the city championship with an undefeated record of sixteen straight victories. East High officials suddenly had to take a good long look at their new coach and his coaching abilities. Athletic school administrators tend to have a conservative bent. The East High decision-makers were not going to jump on Bob Hart's bandwagon because the reserve players had one impressive season and won a championship. So he kept on coaching the reserve teams, year after year, piling up fine seasons. No other school tried to poach him, nor did school officials promote him. He thought they were overlooking his talent, even as they, in their own manner, continued to make mental notes on the coach with the crew cut and thick eyeglasses who seemed to have a rapport with his players.

In 1961 East High had a head coaching vacancy in basketball. Of course Bob Hart wanted the job; he believed he had proven himself after years of coaching the reserve teams to winning records. But the job went to Mark Whitaker. Hart was disappointed. "Bob should have gotten the job in 1961," recalls Paul Pennell, who had just joined the athletic staff at the school as an assistant on both the basketball and baseball teams.

Bob Hart was notorious for possessing a calm demeanor in tight and edgy situations. He kept quiet when he didn't get the job. But following Whitaker's year as head basketball coach of East High, during which the team posted an 11–12 record—finishing a woeful fifth in City League competition—Whitaker abruptly left for Brookhaven High, a newly built school. He told acquaintances he was excited to be starting something at the new high school, and besides, he always loved coaching track and cross country more than basketball. "We were just like a misguided missile," recalls Bob Martin, who had played for Whitaker's 11–12 team. "I lost a lot of inspiration. We were losing games we should have won."

After Whitaker's departure, finally, in 1962, East High principal D. E. Wiley named Bob Hart head varsity basketball coach. Hart now had the job he had so badly wanted. And this was why he had chosen to live in the community, so he could get to know his players better, and get to know their parents as well. The coach did not want to feel like an interloper.

In Hart's first season as head coach of the East High Tigers, he welcomed six returning lettermen. Many of those players were still smarting from what they saw as Whitaker's inadequate coaching from the

Because Bob Hart emerged from World War II with a social conscience,
he ignored those who warned him against coaching at all-black East High School.

year before—and they hoped that Hart would institute new plays and schemes.

The ultimate goal of any good City League team is first to win the City League championship, then to progress to the state tournament, and, dream upon dream, to win a state title. East had won a coveted state championship back in the 1950–51 season, when many of the players trying out for Hart's varsity team at East High had been entering elementary school. Hart had a reason to be confident during team tryouts: He had coached almost all of these players on his reserve teams.

Hart ran his practices with a military-like fastidiousness. Certain drills were to be executed at particular times during practice. He kept a whistle around his neck, blowing it loudly when it was time to start another phase of practice. He had the kind of talented players who could adapt to his style, and he knew it. He settled quickly on a starting five: Mike Hammond at guard, Ed Waller at guard, Bob Calloway and Ken Fowlkes at forwards, and Avery Godfrey at center. "They knew his system," says Assistant Coach Pennell about those players who had already played under Hart.

There were those—like Coach Pennell—who thought the best player on the team was Bob Martin, a wiry forward entering his senior year.

Martin's family hailed from Reidsville, North Carolina. His father died shortly after he was born, and his mother, Jo, scrimped and saved to get the family out of the South and away from the job she loathed at the tobacco factory. When she finally had enough money and went to the train station, little Bob began crying without stop. The big locomotive, idling and hissing and belching steam, scared him something fierce. The boy refused to climb aboard. The family circled back to Reidsville. A short while later, his mom hired a friend to drive the family north to Ohio. Jo Martin got a job as a maid at a local college, St. Mary of the Springs (now Ohio Dominican University). As Bob grew up he fell in love with basketball. He starred at Champion Junior High for the great Negro coach Cy Butler. (Many in the black community believed that Butler, with his record of coaching winning teams over the years, was not considered for the head coaching job at East High School because of the color of his skin.)

Bob Martin was excited about his first season playing under Coach Hart. He streaked up and down the hallways of East High loose and happy. His sense of humor was unmistakable. He made others laugh; he was fond of pranks. In class one day, his teacher stepped out into the hallway for several minutes. While she was away, a student tiptoed up to her seat and placed a thumb tack, upright, on it. Every student was conspiratorially eyeballing her as she returned to the room, sat down on the tack, and squealed. There was much immediate laughter. She pointed to the person she thought was the culprit: Bob Martin. Neither Martin nor any other student ever confessed, but that was his first incident of school trouble. When he flunked a test in that same class, he was no longer eligible to play the first half of the basketball season. It was a discernible loss for the team and Hart knew it. (Two years earlier, as a precocious sophomore on the varsity team, Martin had scored 32 points against North High.)

No one was as eager for the 1962 season to get under way as Bob Hart. As the season opener neared, Hart scheduled several out-of-town scrimmages for his team. Beyond Columbus, in central and southern Ohio, sat many rural white communities, and Hart had to be smart and judicious about where he took his all-black team. This wasn't Mississippi or Alabama. He did not feel the kids would be physically attacked. The players themselves had already talked about what they would do in the event of finding themselves in confrontations: They were not going to back down. They figured they could take care of themselves. But Hart wanted them to be able to get their meals without any hassles. He did not want them exposed to verbal insults. "One of the things I remember," recalls the coach's daughter, Bobbi, "is Dad calling ahead to say to a restaurant owner, 'I have a team full of black basketball players. We want to stop for sandwiches. Is that going to be a problem?' "

Sometimes as the bus was slowly rolling into the parking lot of a restaurant the coach would hop out, motioning for everyone to remain on board. These were the restaurants he had not had a chance to phone in advance. He'd amble inside to take the measure of the place. If he saw a crowd he didn't particularly like, he'd return to the bus and march up and down the aisles taking individual orders. "I'd get off the bus and walk with Dad back inside," adds Bobbi, "and say, 'How come the players aren't coming inside with us?' " Her father would tell her it was easier for him to get everyone's food to go. And after waiting for their orders— burgers, hot dogs, fries, shakes, soft drinks—they'd bounce back onto the bus. The players, of course, were always fairly wise to what was going on.

Coach Hart's wife, Jane, was a stay-at-home mom. Her three daughters kept her quite busy. The coach was often absent with coaching duties. The challenge of raising her daughters without her husband was not the only thing that bothered Jane. She also began to chafe under his exacting household regimen. There was a ten-year age difference. "Mom was this little farm girl," says Bobbi. Jane was only in her late twenties; she wanted to get out of the house more often and have fun with friends her own age. The daughters could see their parents' marriage coming undone. Not long after, Bob Hart filed for divorce. Afterward, he went to family court and eventually won custody of his three daughters. He approached this new dimension of fatherhood the same way he approached everything else, with a clear focus and a particular fastidiousness. He took the girls grocery shopping. He bought cookbooks, though he never morphed into anyone's idea of a chef.

He'd load his three young daughters onto the team bus with the team. Lynne, the youngest, became the team mascot, her blond hair flowing, her cheeks glowing. "I remember people telling Dad, 'How can you let your daughter be on that big black boy's shoulder?'" Lynne's sister Bobbi would recall. Bob Hart would shake his head, sometimes let that little smile cross his wide face, and keep walking. The smile was just another weapon; Hart and his Tigers were on their way to whip the local boys. Bobbi felt mighty proud of her father at such moments.

They opened the season on November 29 against Chillicothe and beat them easily, 81–54. The next seven games were all victories. On a chilly Friday night they traveled to Cuyahoga Falls to play a team that had beat the Tigers a year earlier by 9 points. Three thousand fans squeezed into the gym to see the game. This time Bob Hart's Tigers had their revenge, winning by 9 points. Commentators were starting to refer to the team as quick, freewheeling, domineering. They whipped Columbus North, 68–44. Bob Hart took the victories in stride, careful not to show too much emotion. But secretly he mused about how good his team might become upon the return of Bob Martin, arguably the team's best player.

The Tigers traveled to Dayton for a game against Chaminade High— like East High also undefeated. Hart had warned his team about Chaminade. The school was competitive and had always fielded tough teams. East scurried to an 11-point lead during the first half. In the second half the score tightened considerably. East popped into the lead with thirty seconds to go, 49–48. Chaminade let the clock run down to fifteen seconds before Bob Hafer launched an eighteen-foot jump shot that went in. It was the Tigers' first loss of the season. Bob Martin watched the game from the stands. "If I'd been playing," he mused years later, "we would have blown them out."

East regrouped against archrival Linden-McKinley, beating them 59–42, and the Tigers found themselves ranked No. 4 in the state. In their matchup against local Central High, both teams found themselves with 5–0 league records. More than a thousand people had to be turned away at the door on game night. Even so, safety codes were violated as the school allowed eleven hundred fans through the doors. East dismantled Central, 75–54, leaving little doubt who was the best team in the city.

Heading deeper into the season, Hart's team got a holiday gift: Bob Martin was ruled eligible to return to play. There was already an established chemistry with the starting five, but Hart knew he would have to find time for Martin, so he decided to use him as the sixth man, the first player off the bench. (Martin had been dutiful about remaining in shape during his period of ineligibility. He had joined an amateur basketball team and traveled around the state playing games on weekends.)

East ripped off a string of victories to take the City League title. All five starters—Godfrey, Fowlkes, Calloway, Hammond, and Waller—made first team All-City, a feat the school promoted as unprecedented. Coach Hart was named UPI High School Coach of the Year.

East met Big Walnut at the beginning of the district tournament and cruised, 73–42. They then took apart Newark, 56–35, a notable win as Newark had been Central District champions the year before. East High players may not have been allowed into some of the restaurants in Upper Arlington, a white suburb of Columbus, but they set their own rules on the basketball court and ousted the suburban school 70–64 in tournament play. They next faced Watterson, where they notched their twentieth win, 63–52. Many were now wondering: Could Bob Hart's Tigers actually reach the state final game? To keep their streak going, they had to get by City League stalwart West High, which they did by shooting 47 percent from the floor. Their defense held West to 27.9 percent shooting, and the final score was 54–42. Lynne Hart, the youngest

Hart daughter, was hoisted up on the shoulders of the players, outfitted in a black sweater with a large "*E*" in the center.

Later in the week a nine a.m. pep rally was held at the school before the team departed for the Class AA regional tournament, where they would be pitted against Portsmouth. Portsmouth was dispatched in quick fashion, 71–52. Next up was a stiffer opponent, Canton McKinley, a team that always managed to make noise come tournament time. East would be playing inside always noisy Canton's Memorial Field House.

McKinley took a lead at halftime, 25–21. At the end of three quarters they were leading by 5 points. Hart glowered at his players, biting into the orange towel he always held in his hands. (East's school colors were orange and black.) Since his return to the East High team, Bob Martin had not had any explosive games. He was sent in as the first player coming off the bench, often to slow the opposition's highest scorer. But against McKinley, Martin shone: He gave East the lead by hitting a jump shot with 2:03 left, making the score 49–48. East then quickly found themselves down by one, 50–49. Martin then hit one of two free throws to send the game into overtime. The first overtime ended with the score tied, 54–54. McKinley couldn't contain East's Ed Waller, who scored 10 points during the two overtimes, leading East to a scintillating 60–58 victory. Waller had to share the spotlight for the victory with Bob Martin. It was to Martin that the press gave much of the credit for the victory. "He is the best sixth man around and could play for anybody," Coach Hart conceded afterward about Martin.

The victory put East High in the state tourney finals, where three other teams—Urbana, Marion Harding, and Cleveland East Tech (which, at 24–0 was the only undefeated team)—would be vying for the state title. East drew Cleveland East Tech as an opponent. The city of Columbus hadn't had a team in the state finals since 1958. Excitement throughout the state capital was high.

Bob Hart put his players through their last practice at East High on Thursday, the day before their tournament game. "You have devoted a lot of time to basketball here and you have worked hard," he told his gathered players. He was the kind of coach who commanded rapt attention. But he offered levity: "Now let's see you make one last layup." The players chuckled, loped off, and each flipped in a layup. "I would say we'll be ready," the coach allowed.

Tiger fans could be forgiven if they were more than a little worried about East Tech: This would be Tech's sixth straight jaunt to the state finals, an unprecedented feat. With that kind of record going into the finals, and after four years as head coach, Tech's head coach, Joe Howell, was a wily steward of his team. (Howell was the only black head coach in the state finals.)

When East Tech raced to a 6–0 lead, East's Bob Hart called a time-out. He glared at his players, told them to calm down, and quickly decided to draw up some defensive adjustments. They listened intently. Back on the court they dropped in 11 points. For the remainder of the first half and during the second half, Bob Hart's Tigers dismissed the East Tech pedigree: They outshot Tech 49 percent to 35 percent; they outrebounded them 36 to 22; and they outscored them. The final showing was 58–44. The rookie varsity coach was taking his team to the state championship game. They would be matched against the gritty Marion Harding team, which had whipped Urbana High 64–50 in the other semi-final contest.

Marion Harding had to sense trouble when East High took off with a 9–0 lead at Ohio State's St. John Arena in the state championship contest. Inside the third quarter, East High's tall trio of Godfrey, Fowlkes, and Waller intimidated the Marion Harding players so much that they managed only a single field goal. Figuring their best chance to win was to slow the game down, Marion Harding crept up the court, had the ball for long spells, all of which ignited the always fast-breaking Tigers to quicken the pace more than usual whenever they had the ball. At the end of three quarters the score was East 31, Marion Harding 19. And when the final horn of the low-scoring game sounded, East had outscored Harding 41–32 to claim the state trophy. Tiger fans swarmed the court. Hart's players lifted the getting-chubby coach skyward. Jimmy Hart, beaming, bounced from the stands toward his son and the team members. Then he found himself cackling with newsmen, saying his son had been crazy about basketball since he was a tot.

The day after the championship victory there was a parade to the statehouse—the caravan leaving from the school on East Broad Street, then making its way to High Street downtown. More than twenty-five hundred people showed up, among them Governor Jim Rhodes and Mayor W. Ralston Westlake.

A short while later a telegram landed on Hart's desk: ON BEHALF OF THE FIRST COLUMBUS EAST HIGH SCHOOL BASKETBALL TEAM TO THE FINE OHIO STATE CHAMPIONS OF EAST HIGH SCHOOL HEARTIEST CONGRATULATIONS—J Elwood Bulen 1899 class of East High School Basketball Team.

For Bob Hart, it was more than a state championship victory. He knew what was out there on the streets. Basketball, for the black kid, was something deeper than the game itself. It was a powerful step toward the road of freedom.

Jimmy and Mirza were so jubilant about the team's championship that they decided, in the days following the parade, to take the team out to dinner for a more intimate celebration. There was a nice dining spot the couple liked, Reeb's Restaurant, and Jimmy and Mirza decided that's where they'd all go. Jimmy phoned Freddie West, the restaurant manager, and asked to reserve the party room, a lovely and semi-private room in the back of the restaurant. West told him the room was available. Jimmy told the manager that he would be bringing the East High School basketball players. "I'm sorry, we can't do it," the manager said. He started up about the black boys, that their presence would be disruptive. The conversation became heated before ending abruptly. Jimmy was livid, and so was Mirza when he told her. Their friendship with the restaurant owners was damaged from that day onward. "It crushed my grandmother," recalls Bobbi, Bob Hart's daughter.

Jimmy Hart finally found an accommodating restaurant for his son's basketball team. They all went to Miller's Restaurant on Johnstown Road on the outskirts of town. Everyone had a fine time.

The East Side of Columbus could have been a stand-in for small-town black America. It was an urban setting, true enough, but was knitted by neighborhoods. Southern accents were not uncommon to hear. Neighbors celebrated community achievements. Cultural highlights came by way of movie openings and concerts. Those events were buffeted by accomplishments in the local sports scene. Most, however, simply saw sports and culture and politics blending together.

In the same winter week of 1963 that Bob Hart's Tigers were wending their way toward the end of the basketball season and on to the tournament, *To Kill a Mockingbird*, a movie based on the popular Harper Lee novel of the same name, opened in downtown Columbus at the Ohio Theater. For years Barbee Durham and Rev. Phale Hale, two local NAACP members, had lodged complaints about local theaters and their inhospitality toward blacks. There was no physical abuse of blacks who tried to see *To Kill a Mockingbird* at the Ohio Theater, but there was a feeling among blacks that they'd rather go to the theaters that catered to them on the East Side of town, which were the Pythian and Cameo theaters, the same theaters that the East High students frequented. The movie, which stars Gregory Peck, Mary Badham, William Windom, and Brock Peters, among others, tells the story of Atticus Finch, a lawyer who defends a black man accused of raping a white woman. The horrors of racial injustice in the movie are seen mostly through the eyes of the young Finch children, Scout and Jem, which layers the movie with a quiet—albeit still quite menacing—texture. The movie was widely hailed and went on to Oscar glory. "At the outset," Bosley Crowther wrote in his review of the film in the *New York Times*, "it plops us down serenely in the comfort of a grubby Southern town at the time of the Great Depression, before 'desegregation' was even a word."

In 1963, in Bob Hart's glory year at East High, "desegregation" was not yet a word in Columbus, Ohio, either.

The spiritual center for the East High athletes was inside Rev. Phale Hale's Union Grove Baptist Church, which sat mere blocks from the school. It is where the basketball team would go to hear church praise— along with the sermon of course—heaped upon them following their big victories. Reverend Hale was a pillar of the community, a potent voice against discrimination around town. The son of Mississippi sharecroppers, Hale had, as a young boy, turned to hoboing to get out of desperate straits in Mississippi. He was industrious and wound up gaining admission to Morehouse College. As a Morehouse graduate, he acquired an instant pedigree. ("You can tell a Morehouse man—but you can't tell them anything," went the quip.) Both Hale and his wife, Cleo, had known the family of Martin Luther King Jr. for years; Cleo and young Martin had been playmates in Atlanta. Reverend Hale brought King to Columbus in 1958 and chaperoned the young minister around town, the two of them bowing before the church ladies and cackling softly in the moonlight when discussing the less arduous facets of black life.

It was four months after the East High championship victory, which the family of Reverend Hale watched, with deep pride, when the TV news played footage of his friend Martin's speech at the National Mall in Washington. Roosevelt Carter, a local black photographer for TV station channel 10 and also an East High graduate and Hale acquaintance, wanted the station to send him to the much talked about event, but they would not, citing expenses. He found a local interfaith church that was organizing a caravan of buses that were departing from the East Side YMCA, and he went along. When he arrived in D.C. and saw the crowds, Carter had never experienced a gathering remotely like it. It seemed as if the whole of black America's aspirations, its heroes and heroines, singers and actors, had descended in the shadow of the Lincoln Memorial. Carter got some fine shots, a poignant one of baseball legend Jackie Robinson and his son.

King was the last to deliver a major address that day. His words were so hopeful, challenging, and powerful. "I say to you today, my friends, though, even though we face the difficulties of today and tomorrow, I still have a dream. It is a dream deeply rooted in the American dream. I have a dream that one day this nation will rise up, live out the true meaning of its creed: 'We hold these truths to be self-evident, that all men are created equal.' I have a dream that one day on the red hills of Georgia sons of former slaves and the sons of former slave-owners will be able to sit down together at the table of brotherhood . . . I have a dream that my four little children will one day live in a nation where they will not be judged by the color of their skin but by the content of their character." They were mighty words, poignant and powerful. An editorial, titled "Petition on a Bounced Check," appeared in *The Citizen-Journal,* the morning newspaper of Columbus, Ohio: "James Baldwin, the gifted Negro writer, dealt perceptively with the problem in a brief, off-the-cuff interview during yesterday's historic march on Washington. It is time, he said, for Americans to get over their terror of Negroes. If it is time, and we think it is, the march should have great impact." King's words and wisdom touched many. International wire services reprinted parts of his speech. Black teachers, custodians, mail carriers, and even high school athletes—who were unwelcome into even many northern restaurants— were surely lifted up.

King and the other speakers certainly felt America had bounced again and again on its promise of freedom and equality for blacks. It was as if the young minister from Georgia was holding a moral megaphone out over the entire United States of America, pricking the conscience of those who might deny citizens the right to vote.

Winning coaches have to keep on coaching, and planning, and looking ahead. Bob Hart didn't have to look far for budding basketball talent. Those three junior high schools, all predominantly black, that fed students into East High School—Franklin, Champion, and soon-to-open Monroe Junior High—had plenty of sports-loving students. Hart kept a close eye on those schools and their most gifted players. He kept old worn basketballs in the backseat of his car to hand out to especially promising young players who were bound for East High. He'd make them promise they'd practice hard before giving the ball to them. A good basketball was a precious commodity in a poor community. A kid would hide the thing under the bed, behind the furnace, behind boxes in the pantry room—anyplace where it wouldn't be taken by another sibling or relative and lost.

In the 1963–64 season, Hart had to make do without four starters from the previous year, significant among them Avery Godfrey, who was still in school but too old to play, and Bob Martin, the valuable sixth man from a year earlier. The team plowed its way to a City League championship but got beat in the district finals, a disappointing end to a season in which they fell short of making it to the regional tournament, let alone the state tournament to defend their crown.

It rankled Bob Hart that when the 1964–65 season got under way, city basketball prognosticators were talking up the likes of South High and Linden-McKinley High School. It was "a rebuilding year," Assistant Coach Paul Pennell had to confess. As the season neared an end, Hart had to realize that his team was not up to winning the state championship. They fell short of retaining their City League title, which was shared by three other schools: West, Linden-McKinley, and South High. South, with the stars Bill Bullock and Marion Iverson, tore through the district and regional tournaments, eventually winning the state title. South had been Bob Hart's high school, but at this point in time nostalgia held no appeal at all for him. The fans and followers of East High brooded and talked of next year.

When Hart began hearing of two young and precocious players who were still in junior high school, who were flat out frightening the rest of the junior high City League with their prowess, he made a note to himself that he would have to see them play. And when he finally saw Ed Ratleff, a ninth grader at Champion Junior High, and Nick Conner, a ninth grader at Mohawk Junior High, he raised his eyebrows. It wasn't mere promise that Hart saw in the two strapping ninth graders. It went beyond that. They both appeared to have a large amount of self-motivation. And while they had natural talent, and size, they also recognized and appreciated the technical aspects of the game of basketball. Hart realized they were already playing the game at a very mature level. These were the type of players a coach could build a program around. They were both already six foot four and obviously still growing. Hart decided he had to meet their families.

Of the two young phenoms, Ratleff drew the most curiosity. He seemed to be a naturally gifted athlete. He had already made up his mind which sport he wished to excel at, and it wasn't basketball; it was baseball. He could play most every position on the baseball diamond. He might have been the city's most feared young pitcher, who had been constantly praised by local sportswriters and opposing pitchers. But Larry Jones, a former East High basketball star who went on to star at the University of Toledo and play professionally, had seen something special in Ratleff on the playgrounds of Columbus. "Larry Jones set me straight on many things about basketball," Ratleff would recall. "He showed me how to stop on a dribble and shoot over a big man who can jump. And from him I learned how to protect the ball when I am dribbling."

Hart started the 1965–66 season with a touch more optimism than he had the season before. His juniors and seniors had a year's worth of experience to call upon. A nifty little guard, John Fraser, arrived from Chicago when his minister father was transferred to a Columbus church. The team was good and savvy enough to bring back the City League trophy. They then proceeded to win the district tournament but were ousted, 63–51, in the regional finals by the gritty Lancaster High team. It was deflating. A year earlier Hart had been beaten by his alma mater; now a suburban school had vanquished his Tigers.

Bob Hart was a keen observer of social and political forces, and he realized that a shift in college basketball was taking place. That spring of 1966, legendary coach Adolph Rupp's all-white University of Kentucky basketball team had been whipped in College Park, Maryland, by the all-black Texas Western team in the NCAA basketball championship game, 72–65. Bob Hart, and his players, saw it all as inevitable.

With another painful season behind him, Hart kept his eyes on the two ninth graders, Ed Ratleff and Nick Conner, who would be under his tutelage come the fall of 1966. Of the two players, Hart had gotten to know Ratleff rather well. During the 1965–66 basketball season at Champion Junior High, the gym had been closed because of renovations. It was proposed that the junior high basketball team play its home games that year at nearby Beatty Elementary School, one of the all-black elementary schools on the East Side. But Bob Hart, knowing his team's home games were held on Fridays—whereas Champion's games were held on Thursdays—suggested to Champion's school principal that the school play its home games at East High. When young Ed Ratleff was running up and down the East High court as a ninth grader, Bob Hart, eyeing him closely, must have thought that another Tiger would soon be loose at East High.

Because a good many of the East High families and students had roots in the Deep South, the news of what was going on during the summer of 1966 hardly eluded them. Either by print, radio, or TV, the uplift and despair of the civil rights movement reached the living rooms of their apartments and small homes on the city's East Side. But it hardly took news from Mississippi, Georgia, or Alabama to heighten their awareness of national events. A lot was happening close to home. On July 18, racial rioting erupted up in Cleveland and lasted for five days. More than 90 percent of Cleveland blacks lived in the Hough neighborhood; the uprising, which left four blacks dead and nearly three hundred people injured, later became known as the Hough Riots. Community leaders pointed to poverty and racism as the root causes of the uprising.

The median income for black households in Cleveland was 65 percent what it was for the whites. That summer the phrase "Black Power" entered the American vernacular, taken quite seriously when it was uttered and prophesied by Stokely Carmichael, the young leader of the Student Nonviolent Coordinating Committee (SNCC). Cleveland stood as the most black-populated city in the state. Its black citizenry stood ready to make an inroad into the city's white power structure. There were other race riots throughout the country, including in Chicago (Martin Luther King Jr. was pelted with stones while leading a march in the city); Omaha, Nebraska; and Lansing, Michigan.

They became an instant duo, Ed Ratleff and Nick Conner, tall and lithe bookend teammates. They were both forwards, and Hart knew they would create a nightmare for any opposing team trying to defend against them. During early season scrimmaging during the 1966–67 school year, he figured one of them might be stopped on any given night, but certainly not both of them. Everyone at East High was excited about that season of basketball. Coach Hart was downright giddy.

Hart settled on a starting five of Howard Harris, an overweight but wily point guard; Harry Hairston, who was quick and slippery; stalwart returning letterman Randy Bias; and Ratleff and Conner, the gifted sophomores. Hart could only marvel at how quickly this mix of new and veteran players jelled: They raced to a 5–0 record. They were soon 10–0, then 15–0.

When East made it to the regional tournament of the state finals, their foe was the pesky and gritty Linden-McKinley team, whom they had beaten during the regular season. Linden's backcourt combination of Jim Cleamons and Skip Young was dangerous. Young was actually thought by many to be one of the best guards not only in the state, but in the nation. And Cleamons was being recruited by Ohio State University, a school that had traditionally ignored local black basketball talent. "I was Robin and he was Batman," recalled Cleamons. Their coach, Vince Chickerella, had a game plan: to slow the ball down. It bewildered the Tigers, and they went down to defeat, 43–34. It was the Tigers' only loss of the season. Worse, it eliminated them from the regional tournament. Linden-McKinley went on to win the state tournament.

No matter how many balls the Tiger players bounced that summer, how many hours they worked at the game they dearly loved, trying to forget the frustrating end to their season, they couldn't ignore what was happening across the country. It was a summer of tricky and dangerous crosscurrents in the civil rights movement. Black activists Stokely Carmichael and H. Rap Brown were laying explosive challenges at the feet of moderate civil rights leaders, especially Martin Luther King Jr. The fiery Carmichael and Brown had amassed followers; many of them were high school and college students. "I had a big Angela Davis Afro," recalls East High cheerleader Sandra Montgomery. (Angela Davis was a young Black Panther who joined both the SNCC and the Communist Party in 1967.) Montgomery also says there was a particular book that had become very popular among East High School students at the time: *The Autobiography of Malcolm X*, published in 1965, just months after Malcolm was assassinated by fellow Muslims in Harlem. East High students proudly toted the book around and could be seen reading it in Franklin Park, across the street from the school, long the gathering place for black families and their weekend picnics. School administrators could feel the political reverberations. "Brothers and Sisters, a hell of a lot of us are gonna be shot and it ain't just gonna be in South Vietnam," Stokely Carmichael said in 1967 from the stage of a church in Harlem. "We've got to move to a position in this country where we're not afraid to say that any man who has been selling us rotten meat for high prices should have had his store bombed fifteen years ago. We have got to move to a position where we will control our own destiny. We have got to move to a position where we will have black people represent us to achieve our needs. This country don't run on love, Brothers, it's run on power and we ain't got none." His audience was clapping and saying amen as he went on: "Brothers and Sisters, don't let them separate you from other black people. Don't ever in your life apologize for your black brothers. Don't be ashamed of your culture because if you don't have culture, that means you don't exist and, Brothers and Sisters, we do exist. Don't ever, don't ever, don't ever be ashamed of being black because you . . . you are black, little girl with your nappy hair and your broad lips, and you are beautiful."

Going into fall 1967, however, the turbulence seemed to inspire the Tigers. They looked ferocious and almost feral on the court. They made their cuts quick and sharp, as if they were executing geometric plans in their heads. They passed the ball beautifully and crisply, the ball an extension of their ticking basketball mind-sets. They dunked with abandon, declaration-of-war dunks that stilled the opposition. They dunked and glared—scary—or they dunked and smiled—scarier. Any dunk seemed to be a simple warning that more such dunks were assuredly on the way. In their 1967–68 season, all this happened during warm-ups, all of it visible before any game, before the attendees had gotten to their seats, before the whispering and pointing; before the opposing coach got that Jesus Holy Christ look in his eyes; before the game's patrons had properly opened up their programs with their buttery popcorn–coated fingertips; before cool Mr. Chris Dixon, student gadabout, started leading the cheers and that thumping "I Went Down to the River" school fight song. Never mind any of that, though, because newsmakers from around the state were predicting that Dunbar High School in Dayton would be the team to go all the way and claim the state basketball crown.

Bob Hart's starting five for the 1967–68 Tigers consisted of Randy Bias and Howard Harris at guards, Randy Smith at center, and the rising duo Eddie Ratleff and Nick Conner, at the forward positions. Smith, at six foot six, was a towering presence and already being recruited by more than a hundred colleges. He had made All-State a season earlier. In the team's mind, the season before—with their single loss that had derailed their dream—had been a bust. They had lost to inner-city rival Linden-McKinley, which meant they had lost bragging rights for an entire summer, and it stung.

They opened the season with a 90–39 blasting of Northland. Then came Salem, Eastmoor, Marion-Franklin, a tough Newark team, Canton Lincoln—all of whom fell by double digits. Bob Hart marveled at his players, at their authority on the court. They went into battle undefeated against their nemesis, Linden-McKinley. East High fans grew nervous late in the second quarter when Linden went up, 32–25. But after halftime and going into the third quarter, East had regained momentum and the lead, 49–44. With 3:28 left on the clock, the score was tied up again. But the Tigers' Randy Smith was fierce and unstoppable. His two free throws—on his way to a 34-point night—clinched the East win, 72–70. The East High team tallied seven more victories before closing out the City League race with a 108–55 spanking of Brookhaven. They faced four teams in the district tournament. And like a baker dusting flour from his apron, they brushed them all away with double-digit victories. In late March after they comfortably dispatched Zanesville, 78–65, then Newark, 64–48, Bob Hart had his Tigers back in the state championship finals.

They would have to win two weekend games to claim the state trophy. First they were pitted against Euclid High.

East hopped out to a 9–2 lead, but Euclid eventually closed the gap, 24–21. That would be their opponent's last moment of euphoria. Euclid's big man, six-foot-eight Al Vilcheck, couldn't contain East's Randy Smith. Vilcheck averaged 25 points during the season; he fouled out with 4:35 to go in the contest, having scored only 10 points. East's Ed Ratleff was remarkable, going 12 for 22 from the floor; his teammate Nick Conner was just as potent, going 8 for 12 in field goals. The final score was 75–40, and only Hamilton Garfield now stood between the Tigers and a state championship trophy.

.   .   .

It was cold and icy outside St. John Arena on the campus of Ohio State University when the contest between East High and Hamilton Garfield got under way on March 23. Nevertheless, more than twelve thousand fans showed up for the game. Garfield proved a tough opponent. At the half Garfield trailed by only 4 points, 29–25. It remained a tight contest as the third quarter came to a close, East ahead, 42–38. Then East fell behind, 53–47, and Coach Hart could be seen biting harshly into that omnipresent orange towel. It would come down to East High asserting its will: With the score tied at 58–58, Ratleff nailed an eighteen-foot shot. Randy Smith then hit a mid-range jumper and the score was 62–58. Nick Conner tipped in a missed free throw with four seconds showing. When the clock sounded to end the game, it was East 64–60. It happened four years apart, but the Tigers had won another state championship under Bob Hart. There was pandemonium among the Tiger faithful.

More than two thousand attended the statehouse rally on March 24, among them Governor Rhodes, school superintendent Harold Eibling, and Rev. Phale Hale, the confidant of Martin Luther King Jr.

Nine days later, a racist, dope-smoking escaped Missouri convict by the name of James Earl Ray (using the alias John Willard) took a room at Bessie Brewer's Rooming House in Memphis, Tennessee. It was a funky little flophouse, eight bucks a week, described by one tenant as "a half-step up from homelessness." Ray was packing a Remington Game-master 760 slide action rifle, with a Redfield scope. The rifle was celebrated for its "knockdown power." Ray was in town intending to murder King, and he chose this particular rooming house because it faced the Lorraine Motel, where King and his aides were staying. King had come to town to aid protesting sanitation workers. A photo in the Memphis *Commercial Appeal* had showed King standing on the balcony in front of his second-floor motel room, number 306, so Ray knew King's exact location. On the evening of April 4, Ray spotted King on the balcony. Ray found a bathroom down the hall that had a good view of King's balcony, so he picked up his weapon and hustled down the hall. Once inside the bathroom, he locked the door, positioned his rifle through a small window, and peered through the scope. And there he was: Martin Luther King Jr., on the balcony of the Lorraine Motel, gabbing with some aides, smiling, the unquestioned moral leader of a nation torn asunder by race. Ray fired, the sound startling the rooming house guests, the bullet tearing into King's jaw and neck. The shooter wrapped his rifle up and scooted down the hallway, out the door, and to his car. A motel resident watched him race by. King was rushed to St. Joseph's Hospital. The doctors could see there was massive brain and spinal damage. Within the hour he was pronounced dead. Jesse Jackson, a young King aide who had been on the balcony, later spoke to reporters. Jackson had his detractors, allies of King's who thought he was spotlight hungry. But few could deny that Jackson could deliver eloquent speeches, seemingly off the cuff, in the midst of charged situations. "The black people's leader, our Moses, the once in a 400- or 500-year leader has been taken from us. . . . The pathology and the neurosis of Memphis, and of this racist society in which we live, is what pulled the trigger," he said. "To some extent Dr. King has been a buffer the last few years between the black community and the white community. The white people don't know it, but the white people's best friend is dead."

Across the country, the uprisings in black communities were swift. There were flames and deaths in Pittsburgh, Cincinnati, Chicago, Baltimore, Kansas City, Washington, D.C., Columbus, Ohio. The incidents of outbreaks kept climbing, more than a hundred cities being engulfed. "No man spoke harder against violence," the *Life* photographer Gordon Parks wrote of King following his assassination. "Yet few men suffered more from it than he. His worship of a higher law got him jailed, stoned and stabbed. He led us into fire hoses, police dogs and police clubs. His only armor was truth and love. Now that he lies dead from a lower law, we begin to wonder if love is enough."

Baseball legend Jackie Robinson was in New York when he got the news. "I'm shocked," he said. "Oh my God, I'm very frightened, very disturbed."

In Columbus, Rev. Phale Hale, King's friend, delivered his eulogy at the Fairgrounds Coliseum. More than eight thousand people attended. "A shot killed the dreamer," Hale said during the eulogy, going on to predict that the dream of racial conciliation would remain alive. A group of nine black businessmen from Columbus boarded a plane to Memphis following the assassination, in hopes of lending aid and some kind of comfort. Hale wasn't the only Columbus minister with connections to King. Rev. Ozark Range Sr. often regaled folks with his memories of King. Range hailed from the black Delta area of Mississippi. He had joined a ministerial alliance in Mississippi to fight for voting rights. He attended church conferences and gatherings with suit-wearing and straw-hatted black men plotting civil rights strategy. That was how Range came to know both King and fellow Mississippian Medgar Evers, one of the bravest men doing civil rights work in Mississippi. On the evening of June 12, 1963, Evers was returning to his home in Jackson, eager to see the wife and kids after a long day of work. He never saw the white supremacist crouched in the bushes, just a few yards from his driveway. As Evers stepped out of his car, a bullet tore into him, cracking the still night, leaving him dying in front of his wife and kids, who had rushed outside.

A day later, Rev. Ozark Range turned to his wife, Lydan, and said, "We have to leave Mississippi." Life had gotten too dangerous. He needed to find a church. He and his wife sent their two children, Ozark Jr. and Zita, out of town to stay with relatives while they scoured the country interviewing with various church officials in hopes of a job offering. Range was finally offered a pulpit at the Woodlawn Christian Church, two blocks from East High School in Columbus, Ohio. Upon arriving in Columbus, Reverend Range was delighted that he had landed in the center of the city's black community. He wasted little time in convincing other ministers that the city's rate of activism needed to be heightened.

College campuses proved ripe for protest, with the mix of youth and their literary provocateurs, the writers to whom they looked to for guidance: Franz Fanon, James Baldwin, and Malcolm X among them. On April 26, a group representing the Black Student Union at Ohio State University in Columbus took over the administration building, staging a "lock-in." The school had long had a deeply strained relationship with black students. Among student complaints were a lack of minority hiring and a paltry number of courses about black history. Sheriff's deputies swooped in and made arrests. Among those handcuffed were the student leader John Evans, who was seen weeping on the news as he was forcefully removed. The campus anger spread to the segregated East Side of the city, which meant Mount Vernon Avenue, the business hub three blocks from East High. Roosevelt Carter, the East High grad who became a photographer and had ventured to the March on Washington, feared that there might be serious property damage up and down Mount Vernon Avenue. He gathered some black civic leaders and went to see Columbus police chief Dwight Joseph. They told him about their rising concerns. Joseph was an unsmiling figure, law and order to the bone. "I will not send one of my white officers into that neighborhood," he coldly told the group, sprinkling his conversation with racial epithets. The National Guard had to be called out to take care of the rioting.

Teachers and administrators at East High were bedeviled by the grim sadness all around. The turmoil was both domestic and foreign. They winced again and again at news coming over the school loudspeaker about yet another former student killed in Vietnam. The April edition of *The X-Ray*, the student newspaper, offered a tribute to Pfc. Sydney Parks: "The X-Ray would like to express their condolences to the Parks family. Sydney has officially been discharged from the U.S. Marines, but he has just entered another army where he will be safe from harm; he is in God's Army."

Meanwhile, Martin Luther King's killer was now traveling as "Eric Galt," having fled from Memphis to Birmingham, then to Atlanta. In Atlanta he boarded a Greyhound bus and got off in Cincinnati. He rested, and soon hopped another bus, to Detroit. He arrived in Toronto by train. The entire apparatus of American law enforcement, from the FBI to local police departments, was on alert for the assassin of Reverend King, even if they had yet to positively identify him. In Toronto the assassin changed his name to "Ramon Sneyd." After several days, FBI agents unraveled all the aliases and determined the man they were looking for was escaped convict James Earl Ray. The FBI printed wanted

Martin Luther King Jr. arrived in Columbus for a visit in 1962.
His death in 1968 would hover over the 1968–69 school year at East High.

posters in both English and Spanish. There was a $100,000 reward for information leading to his capture.

Ray got aboard a flight out of Toronto and landed in Lisbon, Portugal. He found the city too exotic, the language barrier impossible to overcome. He decided to fly to London and make plans from there. In London, desperate for money, he plotted an eventual flight to white-ruled Rhodesia. He attempted to rob a jewelry store owned by a husband-and-wife team, but when he pulled his gun, they attacked him. He got off some blows of his own, then fled like a rabbit. He whiled away some time, then robbed a bank. He bought an airplane ticket to Belgium, and from there he planned to head to South Africa. At London's Heathrow Airport, he was stopped, questioned, relieved of his pistol, and finally, after sixty-five days of running, identified as James Earl Ray, wanted by American authorities for questioning in the murder of Martin Luther

King Jr. Ray would be convicted back in America and given a ninety-nine-year prison sentence.

Throughout the next school year at East High School, the assassination hovered—classroom to classroom, athlete to athlete—like a cloud over the students. Why did it happen? What did it mean? Would the nation give in to dark impulses, and even darker forces? Students craved a bright future, but they were being forced to acknowledge the dark past, which was evolving into an equally dark present. The times were bewildering and scary. "I guess I can understand why they killed Malcolm," Garnett Davis, one of the star athletes at the school at the time, remembers thinking about Malcolm X and the Nation of Islam infighting that surrounded him. "But King?"

All that summer, Bob Hart checked often on his basketball players. He did not want them getting into trouble during the long, tumultuous summer.

When the school doors to East High swung back open that fall of the 1968–69 school year, Jack Gibbs—who had become the school's first black principal in 1967—realized how much was at stake. He'd spot a student, make his quick inner calculation, and smile: Dave Reid, safe; Nick Conner, safe; Alice Flowers, safe; Linda Phillips, safe; Phil Ware, safe; Garnett Davis, safe. He seemed to know all of the students by name. It was an uncanny gift. And on and on he'd go, walking the hallways, making mental notes on who was back inside the building, the one place he could keep them safe from the smoke and fire.

The sweetness of Indian summer faded; the leaves started falling; the air grew crisp, then cold. Then the ho-hum football season came to a close. There was already talk of the upcoming basketball season. Chatter continued about the death of Martin Luther King Jr., and of Bobby Kennedy's death too. Bob Hart imagined it would be a challenging season ahead.

The principal kept patrolling the hallways: Eddie Rat, safe. Melvin Griffin, safe. Phillip Chavis, safe. Charlotte Thompson, safe. Kirk Bishop, safe. It broke Jack Gibbs's heart that King was gone, but he had to keep his kids safe.

Then came the sound of basketballs in the gymnasium. The basketball tryouts had begun. And Theresa Barnes, the cheerleader advisor, had assembled her cheerleaders. Bob Hart could hear their practices, their cheering, a sound that always delighted him. Hart was missing three gifted players from last year's team: Randy Bias, Howard Harris, and Randy Smith. (Smith took a scholarship to the College of William and Mary, becoming the first black basketball recruit at the Virginia school. He lasted one year in the land of Dixie before transferring. The academics, the racial epithets—it was all more than he had bargained for.) Hart knew those players would be hard to replace. He began confiding to boosters that South and West High were going to be difficult foes in the City League. He wouldn't dare mention anything beyond the City League tournament, because one's dream could die right there. No City League team had ever won back-to-back state titles anyway. And there was so much going on now out on the streets that it made everything unpredictable. A sports team was a fragile entity. Hart didn't know how his team would respond to the ills and dangers in the society around them.

But time and time again, the coach caught the rhythmic noise of the cheerleaders. Their cheering was so infectious:

> I went down to the river
> Oh yeah
> And I started to drown
> Oh yeah
> I started thinking about them Tigers
> Oh yeah
> And I came back around

It was actually rap before rap, a sing-along ode to the resilience of the school. The beat got his players juiced up. In the current climate, they couldn't help but feel as if they were starting over, as if the America that was out in front of them now had to re-create itself. President Kennedy's assassination had certainly touched everyone. But his assassination had not unleashed urban unrest. Martin Luther King Jr.'s assassination felt more dangerous and—throughout the black communities of America— far more intimate. Everyone—civic leaders, politicians, college administrators, and even coaches—had to acknowledge and adapt to the tenor of the times. It was not an exaggeration to imagine the survival of the nation was at stake.

Bob Hart blew his whistle and got the new season under way.

· 2 ·

Eddie Rat Meets
the Afro-Wearing Bo-Pete

What was happening around the country in the summer and fall
of 1968 sent shivers through the minds of athletic administrators who were responsible for black high school athletes in Columbus,
Ohio—and elsewhere. It was now—and suddenly—impossible to dis-
miss the dawning maturation of the black athlete. Reporters, for the first
time ever, were seeking out the political opinions of black athletes. It was
one of the more potent stories in the news media. *Newsweek* and *Look*
magazines, two of the most popular national publications, did big stories
on the political rise of the black athlete. At the center of attention were
black college basketball and track stars in sunny California.

Harry Edwards had earned a graduate degree at Cornell University in
1966, went west, and landed on the faculty as a visiting professor at San
Jose State University. (He had been a track star at San Jose State when
the civil rights movement was sweeping the nation.) Feeling that black
athletes were not being given access to the academic help and guidance
they needed, Edwards organized a series of protests. The upheaval, but-
tressed by the participation of a number of black athletes at San Jose
State, forced the school to do the unthinkable: It canceled the open-

ing football game in 1967 between San Jose State and the University of Texas–El Paso, lest there be the kind of negative publicity the school did not want. The school could not have known who it was getting in Harry Edwards, but Edwards—a black goatee-wearing hipster, fearless and erudite—aimed to make his time as visiting professor in the department of sociology count. He became fascinated with the intersection of the black athlete and social protest. "Athletes are on the field maybe four hours a day," Edwards had said in the summer of 1968. "The rest of the time, they're in the same garbage heap that most of the black people in this society live in. But they have access at a moment's notice to the mass media. Black athletes must take a stand."

With the 1968 Olympics looming in Mexico City, Edwards devised a strategy to bring attention to the plight of black Americans by engaging the black college athlete. He organized the Olympic Project for Human Rights. One of his first supporters was Lew Alcindor, and it was quite a coup getting him on board. Alcindor (later Kareem Abdul-Jabbar) was the best college basketball player in the country, having led UCLA to the NCAA basketball titles in 1967, 1968, and 1969. (His dominating presence was the reason the dunk was outlawed in high school and college basketball, and as a result, the East High Tigers were denied the pleasure of Eddie Ratleff's and Nick Conner's' acrobatic dunks.) Alcindor's coach, John Wooden, was made nervous by the activist rhetoric bleeding into the consciousness of black athletes. "I feel it's outside influences trying to use Negro athletes," he said. Wooden, a man who was both sedate and wily, figured he had gotten out in front of any possible tension by allowing his black players to wear Afros, a "natural" haircut seen as an expression of cultural pride. But then Alcindor announced he would boycott the 1968 Olympics. Some older black athletes, such as Jesse Owens and Willie Mays, thought Alcindor selfish and unpatriotic. They wished they could get the youngster alone in a corner; they'd surely give him a piece of their mind. When asked by members of the media why he had chosen to boycott the games, Alcindor pointed to racism. As other black college athletes headed off to Mexico City, with threats of some kind of protest humming in the air, Olympic officials were nervous. "It seems a little ungrateful to attempt to boycott something [that] has given them such great opportunity," Avery Brundage, president of the International Olympic Committee, said about the agitated black athletes. At the Olympic trials before the games, a young black man in the stands held a placard aloft: "Why Run in Mexico and Crawl at Home." Absent a question mark at the end of the placard, it was, wittingly or not, a profound statement.

But run they did. American sprinters John Carlos, who won a bronze medal, and Tommie Smith, who won a gold medal, whizzed around the track in the sweet October weather. They stepped up on the medal stand afterwards. Then, as "The Star-Spangled Banner" was playing—and with their heads rather serenely bowed—each raised a black-gloved fist in support of the civil rights movement in America. The fans knew immediately what they were witnessing: protest. A silent rebellion right in front of their eyes. The gesture elicited immediate outrage from Olympic officials, and from many people around the world. The two runners were quickly booted from the Olympic Village. The powerful moment, however, quickly entered the visual record of the American civil rights movement, like Rosa Parks sitting on that bus, the marchers defiantly walking across the Edmund Pettus Bridge in Selma, Alabama, and the photo of Amelia Boynton after she'd been tear-gassed and beaten unconscious by state troopers at the bridge in 1965. History captured by a camera lens, history that could not be erased. An Afro hairstyle, a black glove. These now were some of the ornaments of Black Pride. In time, snapshots of Carlos and Smith would appear on the bedroom walls of high school athletes across urban America.

Dwight "Bo-Pete" Lamar of Columbus, Ohio, was one of those young black athletes who allowed the sway and direction of the sixties to work its way inside of him.

In Columbus, in the middle part of the twentieth century, one could find the lower socioeconomic classes bunched predominantly in the vicinity of the city's factories. These locales were also where one could find low-

and modestly priced housing, as well as public housing that had been built by the federal government. Because there was no public transportation system, city leaders and factory owners knew they needed housing close to the factories, and that is how many black families came to be huddled there. The factories were big and noisy, with flinty names—the Malibu, D. L. Auld, Buckeye Steel Castings, Timken Roller Bearing, the Jeffrey Company. The work could be dangerous; the Malibu and Buckeye Steel were especially feared workplaces; countless workers had fingers, and fingertips, sliced off in accidents. But the work was steady, and it seemed the factories were always hiring.

It was the lure of the Malibu that convinced Lucy Lamar she should leave Sparta, Georgia, and relocate to Columbus. She had several relatives who had already left Georgia, landed in Columbus, and were drawing paychecks from the Malibu, a plant that made steel parts. The plants had really prospered during World War II, when there was a great need for their products such as ammunition and bomb-making equipment. There was something else that haunted Lucy Lamar: Her husband, James, whom she had met and married in Sparta, had been murdered. She was a single mother with four sons. Her second eldest was Dwight, whom everyone called Bo-Pete.

When she reached Columbus, Lucy Lamar settled on the North Side of town. The closest factory to her was not the Malibu, but Timken Roller Bearing. She did not have to step inside a factory to be convinced how harsh the work could be; she had relatives who passed along reports. She quickly determined she did not wish to work in a factory, so she settled on a job as a "day worker," a kind of lower-level maid for well-to-do white families in Upper Arlington and Bexley, two pricey white Columbus suburbs. "She had three or four houses she'd clean," recalls her son Bo-Pete. Sometimes the women who lived in those suburban neighborhoods would pick Lucy Lamar up in their cars and drive her back to their homes. The early sixties were roiling, and she wanted sometimes to start a conversation with her employers about the reasons she had left the South with her boys, but she mostly kept silent. "She had that southern mentality," Bo-Pete recalls, alluding to her constant deference to white people.

On the days when no one would come pick her up and she had to get to Bexley, Lucy would catch the bus from the side of town where she lived, ride downtown, then transfer to the East Broad Street bus, which took her down East Broad Street—past East High School—into the suburb. She suffered from terrible migraines but worked through them because her boys had to be fed. Bo-Pete started to enjoy the game of basketball when he was little. He'd dart out of the house around noontime, and Lucy wouldn't see him again until the skies darkened. As long as he wasn't getting in trouble, she didn't mind the endless hours he spent on the court. He was an extremely skinny boy. "Bo looked like Spiderman," remembers Jim Cleamons, who played with Bo-Pete in elementary school and would go on to basketball glory in the NBA. At Weinland Park playground, a few blocks from his home, Bo-Pete honed his game, dribbling the ball low so no one would swipe it in pickup games, perfecting the skills it took to shoot a long-range jump shot. "Bo understood the game," says Cleamons.

After a promising ninth-grade year at Indianola Junior High, Bo-Pete enrolled at North High School in the fall of 1966. There was no other option; those who lived in his neighborhood were assigned to North High. It was an overwhelmingly white school. Because of their visibility, the black athletes at the school assumed the role of black student leaders. The school had never had a black cheerleader, and the black athletes thought it was high time they did. "No one just ever thought to try out," says Roseanne Bell, who became the school's first black cheerleader in 1966. She could sense that other blacks at the school felt pride for her accomplishment. Also, she quietly accepted the intense stares she'd sometimes get from whites while she was attending away games. By his eleventh-grade year, Bo-Pete Lamar—still skinny, with long arms and a huge Afro that bobbed as he floated up and down the court—was leading the City League in scoring at 24 points per game. He shot from a variety of spots on the court, a lovely high arching shot that was lethal. "Bo had a free hand to shoot," says North teammate Curt Moody. "He had such range."

Simmering racial problems at the high school began to crest during the 1967 school year. Some white parents were aghast that their daughters were cavorting a little too closely with black male students, namely the athletes. As well, a good many black students began to voice displeasure about what they perceived as a lack of respect from faculty, especially concerning hair styles, specifically the Afro, which had become popular among black entertainers, activists, and high school students across the country. The Afro fad played out in national magazines. In an issue devoted to black culture, *Look* magazine highlighted a couple at the time: "American couple Win and Joyce Wilford are New York–propelled and Afro-oriented. Joyce, who wears a natural haircut and African jewelry, graduated in philosophy from Long Island University. She and Win are studying now with the Negro Ensemble Company and work as models through the Ford agency." One of the accessories the black high school student sporting an Afro had to have was the Afro pik, a plastic comb shaped like a pitch fork that pouffed the Afro. Bo-Pete was mighty proud of his Afro and the pik he sometimes twirled in his hand while in the hallways.

When North High reached the high school state basketball tournament, Head Coach Jim Kloman decided he had to have a talk with Bo-Pete Lamar, his star guard who had had a dazzling junior year. Since the team was in the tournament, and he was the team's heralded star, Lamar thought the coach wanted simply to talk to him about upcoming game strategy. But he did not. Kloman told his star player that he did not like his Afro, that some school boosters and fans—white boosters and fans—viewed it as an expression of militancy. Bo-Pete was taken aback. "I played the whole season with my Afro," he recalls. Lamar wanted to know which school administrators had complained, because he wanted to go talk to them. Perhaps he could reason with them about what the Afro hairstyle meant to black students. After all, they were in the state tournament. Their chances to advance would surely depend on having their best scorer on the court. The coach—young, white—grew more persistent, telling Lamar there was no option, that he had to get his Afro cut or he would be tossed off the team. Lamar, one of five blacks on the twelve-member team, was stunned. "We didn't know what Bo was going to do," recalls Curt Moody, Lamar's black teammate. "We're in the tournament. For him to be asked then to cut his Afro didn't make any sense." Donnie Penn, another black player on the team, who lived on the same street as Lamar, was livid. "Kloman didn't know how to deal with blacks," he says about the coach.

When he got home after his talk with his coach, Bo-Pete sat down and explained to his mother what had happened. Lucy Lamar reminded her son why she had left the South—for freedom, and not just freedom of expression. She had left the South in hopes that her children would be able to stand up to white authority when they felt they were being disrespected or misunderstood. Bo-Pete then immediately knew his mother would stand by him whatever decision he made about his Afro. The next day, Bo-Pete made his political statement: He quit the North High basketball team. His close friends on the team were stunned. They wondered if the coach would yield; Bo-Pete was their most gifted player. But the coach would not. Word about Bo-Pete quitting raced through the school and then the black community, through the homes of his classmates, in and out of Mr. Wallace's bootleg barbershop, which was just down the street from the Lamar home. "It was disappointing to the neighborhood," remembers teammate Donnie Penn. "All the blacks said, 'Why?'"

Without Bo-Pete, North was quickly eliminated from the state tournament, 81–70, at the hands of Gahanna High School. And as the school year neared a close, Bo-Pete was in limbo. Many black players in their junior year of high school had clashed with white coaches—the reason often cited as cultural misunderstanding—and would go on to forfeit their senior year of play out of pride and anger. But those often were not the marquee players on the team, and they could be dismissed as malcontents. They'd catch on with the local Boys Club and, in their minds, be none the poorer for it because at the Boys Club they could shine. But Bo-Pete was a star. And in 1968 America, his political move had the real potential to alter his life in a very negative way. Where would the family get the money for him to go to college if he did not get a basketball scholarship? The Lamar family did not know luxury. Not a single member of the family had ever flown on an airplane. It wasn't difficult for Bo-Pete to look around the neighborhood and spot older basketball players who had gone off to college, only to come back without a college degree. This was often the route that led to a job in one of the city's factories. There had been no black school officials at North High for Bo-Pete to confide in. But word reached Thomas "Doc" Simpson. Simpson knew the streets where all the good basketball players played in the summertime, and he even knew many of the stars from his own gallivanting about the city. He was only a few years older than many of the players. In the fall of 1968, he was going to begin his student teaching at East High. Thinking about Lamar's plight, he came up with an idea to get Lamar to come to East High. Simpson—having anointed himself a recruiter—planned to go visit Lamar. But he began to wonder if Lamar would seriously listen to him, inasmuch as he was merely a student-teacher-to-be. So Doc Simpson, a nervy sort, went and corralled Jack Gibbs, the East High School principal, and convinced him to come along on the visit to Lamar. Gibbs was sympathetic to stories about talented black kids mired in any kind of crisis situation in the city's segregated school system. So both men preached to Bo-Pete about their school—the kind of guidance he would get while planning for college—and about the basketball team, especially the basketball team. Bo-Pete listened intently and was moved that the two men would come to see him. He discussed the matter with his mother. In order to attend East, they would have to live in the vicinity of the high school. Lucy Lamar certainly didn't have to remind her son that they lived on her meager and inconsistent maid's paycheck. She could not just pick up and move with a snap of her fingers. Her son knew this, yet he also knew his mother was a prideful lady, and the powers that be at North High had mistreated her son, insulting her pride.

Nick Conner, thrilling ally alongside Eddie Rat, was not a rambunctious sort. He was, however, mature, and quite focused. He also had a fiendish affinity for winning. Bo-Pete Lamar was an All-City guard, set loose upon the city landscape, and now suddenly without a team.

It didn't really impress Eddie Rat that he got more publicity than Nick Conner. He was quick in heaping praise upon Conner. And he also realized that Conner had a genuine sense of what the concept of "team" meant. Conner was well aware that the upcoming basketball team would be without the potent backcourt firepower they had had last year. Little introduction is needed between gifted basketball players. Talent finds talent. That summer Nick Conner began hopping into his old Chevy and driving over to Bo-Pete's home. Together they'd ride around the city in search of pickup games. And during those rides Nick Conner also began making his pitch about East High and how wonderful it would be to have Lamar at the school if it was at all possible. "Man, we'd really like you to come," Conner told Lamar.

Lucy Lamar, mindful of her hopes for her children, started making some inquiries about moving to the East Side of town. She had relatives who already lived in Poindexter Village, the public housing complex near East High School. They told her she would like the neighborhood. Lucy, quiet, prim, and proud, went into deep thinking mode before making any moves in life. During the middle of the summer, she told her relatives in Poindexter Village to inquire about rental apartments there. She traveled across town to take a look. When she departed, she had a rental application in hand.

Poindexter Village had been named after Rev. James Poindexter, the father of black political coming-of-age in the city. Born in 1819 in Virginia, Poindexter had arrived in Columbus in 1837 with his wife, Adelia, intent on surviving as a barber—and abolitionist. He found hideaways in the city for escaped slaves trying to make it to Canada. He could be seen in the woods galloping on horseback, leading horses by their reins, bringing them to slaves who were in hiding. Poindexter became a minister and began conducting services at Second Baptist Church. It was a small congregation, and his parishioners grew extremely proud of him. But then something happened that he could not abide: A new parishioner, a black man and his family, arrivals also from Virginia, settled in among the congregation. All seemed fine until it was discovered that the black man had once been a slaveholder himself, a very rare but definite reality of the slave business. Poindexter abruptly left the church, taking some parishioners with him, and they formed the Anti-Slavery Baptist Church. He became a prominent abolitionist voice in the city. In 1858, his power now unquestioned—at least among blacks—he rejoined Sec-

*Dwight "Bo-Pete" Lamar, the dazzling transfer student, was lured to East High
with the promise he could keep his black-is-beautiful Afro hairstyle.*

ond Baptist Church as its head minister. He soon began a political career,
becoming the city's first black city councilman. It was a long and satisfy-
ing career, ending with his death in 1907. At his funeral, some spoke of
him with the same reverence they reserved for Booker T. Washington,
the great educator.

To build Poindexter Village, four hundred falling-down homes had to
be leveled in the section of the city once known as Blackberry Patch. By
the 1950s, the majority of Poindexter Village's residents were black, its
teenagers destined for East High School.

.   .   .

In the fall of 1968, the balled black fist seemed to be everywhere. The Afro—that ornament of cultural pride born of the black struggle—was peeking from storylines in mainstream magazines. Black actors on stage, TV shows, and in major motion pictures were sporting the Afro, and it signaled more than just a hairstyle. Most politicians grew wobbly, mentally snared in a cultural ravine, angry at the youth who were demanding honesty. President Lyndon Johnson—heroic in the cause of civil rights—grew disenchanted over the stalemate in Vietnam, which had been heightened by his own hubris. Black soldiers in Vietnam were constantly writing home telling family members and friends that they were following the press accounts of civil rights demonstrations and that the protests filled them with pride. White politicians had a hard time connecting the war in Vietnam with the war on American streets for racial justice. President Johnson finally announced a halt to the bombing. He also stunned the nation when he said he would not run for re-election. "There is division in the American house now," he said to the nation. "There is divisiveness among us all tonight. And holding the trust that is mine, as President of all the people, I cannot disregard the peril to the progress of the American people and the hope and the prospect of peace for all people." There was great weariness upon his face in his address to the nation at the end of March 1968. He went on: "With America's sons in the fields far away, with America's future under challenge right here at home, . . . I do not believe that I should devote an hour or a day of my time to any personal partisan causes . . . Accordingly, I shall not seek, and I will not accept, the nomination of my party for another term as your President."

The Democrats nominated Vice President Hubert Humphrey, and he faced off against the Alabama segregationist George Wallace, who was running as a third-party candidate and constantly nipping at Humphrey's heels. No one could forget what happened in Chicago during Humphrey's coronation when demonstrators were beaten bloody by Mayor Richard Daley's goon-like police squads. Did Americans want to usher another Democrat into the White House? Richard Nixon, defeated in 1960 by John F. Kennedy, rose up on a law-and-order platform. The social protest comedian Dick Gregory, mindful of racist police conduct, opined that "law and order" was just "a new way to say, 'Nigger.'"

In late September, a Gallup Poll delivered ominous news for Humphrey: He was 15 points behind Nixon. George Wallace faded when he picked his running mate, the World War II hero Curtis LeMay. (Wallace initially offered the running mate position to FBI director J. Edgar Hoover, an archconservative who privately loathed men of Wallace's ilk.) LeMay, born in Columbus and, like East High coach Bob Hart, a graduate of South High School, came under attack when he started talking about nuking perceived foreign enemies of the United States. People questioned his mental competence. LeMay's poor judgment, coupled with Wallace's racist language, proved a toxic combination. Humphrey belatedly began opposing the Vietnam War. Democrats finally began rallying to his side. The Mexico City Olympics—and the protests by black athletes—stole some political thunder, as did the soap opera–like news that Jacqueline Kennedy had jetted off to Greece to marry Aristotle Onassis, a shipping magnate. But Nixon kept making promises, an end to war, more law and order—especially more law and order. He had a modern political machine, with pollsters and advertising gurus; his running mate, Spiro Agnew, tapped into racial hostilities by dismissing minorities. "If you've seen one city slum," he said, "you've seen them all." On election day, Nixon got 43.4 percent of the vote, Humphrey, 42.7 percent. "Well, sir," Humphrey confided to one of his staffers, "the American people will find that they have just elected a papier-mache man." In time Humphrey's comment would prove to be an understatement.

In the late summer of 1968, just as East High School was starting to come to life—teachers were getting their classroom materials ready, school officials were finishing up necessary paperwork, janitors were waxing floors—a neatly dressed lady walked into the front door of the school, asked directions, then made her way to the principal's office. Paul Pennell, assistant basketball coach, had never met Lucy Lamar. He happened to be in an adjacent office, several feet away. "I'm Lucy Lamar," he heard her say. "We've moved into Poindexter Village. And I'm here to enroll my son Dwight Lamar." Pennell was astonished. He went to a phone elsewhere in the building and dialed up head basketball coach

Bob Hart. "I said, 'Are you sitting down?'" Pennell proceeded to tell Hart about the school's new enrollee. Hart was practically speechless. Coaches were not allowed to "tamper" with rival high school athletes. Pennell did not know about the secret mission undertaken by student teacher Doc Simpson and principal Jack Gibbs, or about Nick Conner's own personal overtures to Lamar.

When school began, it did not take long for word to get around that Bo-Pete, the dazzling basketball player from North High School, was now an East High School Tiger. Many people began looking beyond football season to the upcoming basketball season. And the school's grapevine grew hot with questions about Bo Lamar. "We were looking for him to fit in," says Karen Caliver, a school cheerleader at the time. "It was up to Bo to see if he could fit in." Kevin Smith, who was penciled in as a starting forward, began telling others that if Bo-Pete didn't play defense, he didn't see how he could benefit the team. Lamar ignored the concern.

But before basketball season could get under way, there was the Tiger football season. Many saw enduring the football season as an opportunity mostly to applaud the school's celebrated marching band. The football team opened their season by being blanked by Newark High, 34–0. Four games later Watterson High embarrassed them, 54–14. Their fierce rival, Linden-McKinley, got the best of them, 32–12. They tallied six losses and just three victories. Football season was often simply a letdown. But the Tiger faithful hardly complained, because of the marching band. It wasn't just any band; it was arguably the best band in the city. They were a high-kicking, horn-blowing musical combination of jazz, rhythm, and syncopated style. And because East High was the only high school in the city whose football field sat several blocks away from the school, band members had to strut those blocks to the field on game nights. And strut they did, lining up outside the school, horns honking at them, their instruments coming alive, before they began marching, drums thumping, down Parkwood Avenue. Local police would shut the streets off to traffic as they marched. At Greenway Street—the whole neighborhood seemingly on front porches in the autumn twilight, marveling—they'd turn right. Children would be shrieking, screen doors slapping open, the incessant beat of car horns melding into the band music. Entire families would be waving from porches. Four blocks down Greenway they'd reach Harley Field, home of the Tigers' football team, where the band's very presence softened the blow when the team was defeated.

> We are the Tigers, oh yeah, uh-hun, the mighty mighty Tigers, oh yeah, un-huh

Homecoming night represented the first celebration of any kind in the community since the death of Martin Luther King Jr. (Basketball players Eddie Ratleff and Grady Smith sat on the Homecoming Court, both looking dapper in tuxedos and ready for a night of dancing under the watchful eyes of teachers.) It rained that night—which came after the official indoor homecoming dance—the klieg lights slicing over and around Harley Field. Wanda Suber, Donna Bates, Sandra Montgomery, Linda Phillips, and Alice Flowers all competed for Homecoming Queen, smiling their black-is-beautiful smiles as they were paraded around the field in convertible automobiles. They had to open their umbrellas, but their smiles were undiminished. Alice Flowers was crowned queen. She looked incandescent in a checked outfit, white gloves, and a bow in her hair.

With the end of a dreary football season, the sound of basketballs inside the gymnasium was a sweet sound to Coach Bob Hart. The school was overcrowded, so it was not surprising that large numbers of boys showed up for tryouts. This had been a consistent occurrence in recent years, so much so that school athletic officials—in an effort to provide opportunities for the many boys sulking around the school after not making varsity—created a Hi-Y basketball team. It was like a third-tier varsity. The team members played in their own league throughout the city and suburbs. Jim McCann, the Hi-Y coach, was always around as Bob Hart made his first wave of cuts. He'd scoop up some of the players who didn't make the varsity team. He'd do the same with the final wave of cuts. The Hi-Y players had become stereotyped: Many believed that these players were difficult to coach, that they ignored academics, and that they didn't qualify to be on varsity—even if they were talented enough—because they exceeded the age deadline. There were kernels of truth in some of the insinuations, but Jim McCann believed they were good kids who just landed outside the numbers game, as Bob Hart kept only twelve players for his varsity team.

During varsity tryouts, a lot of eyes landed on Bo-Pete Lamar. Hart wasted little time in explaining to Bo-Pete how the team would be set up. "He told me, 'It's going to be Eddie's team,'" Lamar recalls, referring to Eddie Rat. "And he said, 'If you can't accept that, go back to North and average forty points.'"

Eddie Ratleff (though in the hallways at East the name had morphed into "Eddierat" or just "Rat") was born in Bellefontaine, Ohio, a small town in Logan County, to the west of Columbus. (Norman Vincent Peale, the widely praised minister, lecturer, and author who wrote *The Power of Positive Thinking*, had graduated from Bellefontaine High School. The book became a sensation, though some considered it full of baloney passing off as deep wisdom: "Find the upside of the problem"; "Focus on today.") The Ratleff family was one of the few black families who lived in the small, mostly white town. "Everybody knew everybody," Ratleff recalls. "No one had money," he adds of his own family and many others whom he knew. His uncles introduced him to sports at an early age. He fell in love with baseball first. Jackie Robinson was his hero. But when he began to sprout he was encouraged to play basketball, which he did, showing quite a smooth talent. He was not close to his birth father. His mother remarried and the family moved to Columbus, in time for Eddie to begin junior high school. His stepfather was a drunkard and a braggart, habits his stepson abhorred. At Champion Junior High, Eddie began to dominate in basketball. He started on varsity as a seventh grader. "He had natural ability," his junior high coach, Tom Brown, recalls of Ratleff. The coach also thought the kid—even-tempered, calm, and cool—had "a beautiful personality." Brown was somewhat astonished that a kid could have so much talent. So, because he often doubted his own coaching prowess, Brown adopted a different type of coaching philosophy: "I didn't coach basketball and baseball," he says, fifty years later while sitting in his basement office in Columbus, Ohio. "I coached life—and applied life to baseball and basketball." Translation: He coached on the fly; he mimicked other coaches. "Hell, if I saw a coach yelling, I'd yell."

In the summer of Ratleff's eighth-grade year, Bob Hart gave him a brand-new basketball and told him that when he returned it, he wanted it to be scuffed and well worn. In ninth grade, Ratleff led the City League in scoring. "He was the best basketball player I'd ever seen in my life," remembers Gene Caslin, a seventh grader at Champion Junior High when Ratleff was in his final year there. "Every time he took a shot, he would follow it up." (A player with quick instincts follows up any shot he attempts, giving himself an opportunity to retrieve a possible miss and either attempt another shot or start a play anew.)

Ratleff's reputation spread throughout the City League during his junior high years with a near spectral force. But not every player destined to play against him had seen him play, because other junior high players also had games on Wednesdays and Thursdays. Boys will be boys, competitive to a fault, and many players had no intention of expressing fear of Ratleff, even as his reputation grew. In anticipation of their upcoming game at Champion Junior High, the coach at Indianola Junior High warned his players about the prospect of facing Ratleff. "We all knew that we had never played anyone like him," recalls Curt Moody, who was on the Indianola Junior High team at the time. Moody remembers his coach creating a strategy of very aggressive play against Ratleff: "Our coach said, 'He can't be stopped by a normal defense. So we have to have a guy smack him around the face. And it can't be a starter.'" The Indianola coach quickly settled on a bench player by the name of Bodiddley Harris. Harris was a short, compact athlete, known in the neighborhood for having a quick temper. "All week in school," recalls Moody, "Bodiddley was talking about how he was gonna smack Ratleff." On the bus ride over to Champion Junior High, Bodiddley continued his bragging about his planned assault, much to the delight of his teammates, who hoped the tactic might unnerve Ratleff. The Indianola players alighted from the team bus and made their way inside the school, to the gymnasium and locker room. They were the first ones to take the court; Bodiddley was particularly happy and excited that he had been made an integral part of the game plan. There was a rumbling and clapping in the crowd as the Champion players trotted onto the floor in single file. The Indianola players couldn't help themselves; they slowed their pre-game shooting, swiveled, and watched. "Ratleff," remembers Moody, "was the last guy through their door. He looked like a giant. Bodiddley said, 'That's Ratleff? I ain't smacking that guy! No way! Are you crazy!'" Indianola, like every other team that faced Ratleff that year, became just another victim of Ratleff's junior high team.

Miller Barnes had considered Tom Brown a mentor. Barnes ended up being named basketball coach at Roosevelt Junior High, another mostly black school in the city. Miller Barnes had Tom Brown's number; his Roosevelt team was the only team that delivered a defeat to Eddie Ratleff during his junior high basketball playing days. One lesson that Brown took from the encounter was that he saw how a rival coach had plotted to stop his marquee player and he would be better prepared going forward in the season. The loss so bedeviled the players that they all quit, en masse. They were ashamed; they stalked off the court. "Eddie called a meeting," Brown recalls of his mature player. "And he told the team, 'Listen, we just don't need to lose any more games.'" So they regrouped and didn't lose any more games after the Roosevelt loss.

Bob Hart was always looking to the future. He was engaged in a constant youth movement. Any sophomore—a first-year student at the school—who had basketball prowess would draw his attention. Juniors on his basketball team had to worry over the summer about their senior year roles. If they were not bona fide stars, like Eddie Rat and Nick Conner, they risked being replaced by a sophomore or junior with greater potential. It was a brutal attrition scheme. When basketball practice began in the fall of 1968, Hart faced a conundrum: There was an abundance of seniors on the practice floor. Ratleff, Conner, Kevin Smith, and Bo Lamar were obvious locks. Beyond those players, however, Hart was unsympathetic and unemotional about winnowing the team down. Seniors not slated to start were vulnerable, and Roy Hickman was a senior. The previous year Hickman had been a backup forward, coming off the bench. Bob Hart had told him at the end of his junior year that he would not be guaranteed a spot on the following year's team.

Roy Hickman had a muscular build. Classmates called him "Handsome." He lived half a block off Mount Vernon Avenue, behind the Macon Bar, in a small home. In the 1950s and early 1960s, before integration, the St. Clair and the Macon were the two hotels that catered to a black clientele. The Macon became known for hosting touring black musical acts that came through town. By 1968, the hotel above the bar had closed and the bar had lost much of its luster. Roy owned a bicycle and he would ride it to play basketball all over the city. Leaving his home, he'd always have to be careful not to roll his tires over broken beer and wine bottles. He'd return late in the evenings and would be forced to dodge the drunks lolling behind the Macon Bar. Then he'd rise the next morning and take off again. "I had tunnel vision," he says. If it was raining, he'd wrap his sneakers in a bag, tie the bag over his handlebars, and start rolling. His father, who hailed from Tennessee, worked at the Timken factory; his mother, a Georgia native, had a civilian job with a government manufacturing plant. He adored his parents. They let him play basketball without making many demands on him, a luxury for a teenager. They'd been disappointed in their two daughters, who had gotten away from them, spent too much time on the streets, enjoying the fun and freedom of the sixties. "My mom," Roy recalls, "would say, 'I wanna see one of my kids do something.'"

She worried about him during the disturbances that followed the assassination of Martin Luther King Jr. Roy had no intention of getting into trouble, but still, he grieved over the King killing. "King was everybody's hero. And you could feel his death through the whole neighborhood. Some handled it well; others didn't," he says.

Hickman was only six feet tall—not ideal for a power forward—but played taller because he was blessed with a potent jumping ability. He knew to survive Coach Hart's penchant for cutting seniors he would have to make himself invaluable to the team. And that's what he set out to do in practices. He was quick and brutal beneath the rim, getting rebounds, intimidating other players with his strength. He also acted like a leader, barking out plays and showing great focus. And at the end of every practice, Hart found it impossible to cut him from the team. He decided he would have to keep Roy Hickman.

Nick Conner had always had to play in the shadow of Eddie Rat. But he didn't seem to mind; he knew what he could do, how much respect he had garnered from Ratleff. They were a duo now. Going into their senior year, both players were attracting nationwide attention and write-ups in boys' basketball magazines. It was common knowledge that Conner was the best jumper in the city. He had led every team he had been on in rebounding. Nick's mother worked in the cafeteria at Champion Junior High School. She was a tall, stout, single lady who beamed with pride when talking about her son. On East High game nights, she could be seen swooping through the neighborhood, picking up some of the "good boys" she just knew would want to go to the East High game. And off they'd all go in her beat-up automobile.

As Hart began filling his team out, he stuck to his belief about sentimentality and seniors: Any senior had to be an impressive contributor. Billy Nicholson, Ronnie Tucker, and Garnett Davis had played varsity basketball as juniors a year earlier. But now, as seniors—and as players who did not quite distinguish themselves in their junior years—they were vulnerable. Nicholson and Tucker were cut. Davis quit, partly in protest, believing his close friend Nicholson should not have been cut from the team. But Davis also convinced himself he should focus on the sport he loved the most, baseball. "Seniors tend to be disgruntled if they're not starting," says Assistant Coach Paul Pennell. "And Hart knew it." A year earlier, Hart had only three seniors on his 1967–68 team, and each had been a starter. For his 1969 team, Hart decided to keep six seniors—Lamar, Ratleff, Conner, Larry Walker, Grady Smith, and Hickman. He felt certain they would be his top players.

It fell to Larry Walker to keep this gifted contingent together on the court. He was only five eight, but he was the fastest player on the team, a thief in the open court when the other team had the ball. Walker was the team's point guard, charged with bringing the ball up the court and running the plays. A team's point guard is an extension of the coach on the floor, anticipating what plays the coach might want to call. A coach has to depend on his point guard, and Bob Hart depended on Larry Walker, because Eddie Rat depended on Larry Walker. The two had been teammates together at Champion Junior High and were close friends. They chased girls together and played pranks on each other. They had played so much basketball together through the years that they could communicate with one another by a head roll or eye contact. Larry Walker knew exactly when it was necessary to get the ball into the hands of Eddie Rat.

Ollie Mae Walker and her husband, Charles, arrived in Columbus in 1948. Like many others, they had had enough of the South. They came as yet one more black family clutching battered suitcases and boxes of clothes and moving to the Poindexter Village housing projects. Charles worked as a janitor. There were eight Walker children. One day Charles announced he was leaving, going back to Georgia. His wife and children assumed something was wrong on his side of the family, or there was some kind of family business he had to attend to. But he left and never returned. Ollie Mae had to raise the children all alone. She worked as a maid at the Jefferson Hotel downtown, and after her husband abandoned the family, she asked her supervisor if she could start doubling up on her shifts. He often would let her, so some days she worked sixteen hours. All she seemed to care about was keeping her family together, under one roof.

When he was in the ninth grade at Champion Junior High, Larry Walker turned an ankle on the basketball court. The team trainer taped it and he returned to the court. But over the next few days the pain wouldn't go away. At the hospital, X-rays were ordered, and they showed a tumor. "My mother worried it might be cancer. She didn't know if they were going to cut a part of my leg off or what," Walker recalls. He went into the hospital for surgery, a bone marrow graft. The tumor was non-malignant, but he lay in the hospital for a week. The welfare agency picked up the entire hospital bill. Every day his mother, Ollie Mae, would come gliding through the doorway of his hospital room, sometimes straight from a double shift.

Hart also prided himself on his bench talent, players whom he could use to spell the starters and insert into a game in strategic situations. He chose some savvy juniors who would accept their role playing. Kenny Mizelle—the oldest of nine children—was a gritty kid who lived in the Bolivar Arms housing project. He was a deft passer with Houdini-like hands, and nearly as fast as Larry Walker. Larry Mann, a junior forward, was smart and slithery around the basket and had a good basketball mind. Hal Thomas made the team as a sophomore.

Players who sat on Hart's bench were often asked why they didn't transfer to another school, with less fierce competition, where they might gain a starting position. And it came down to pride, to the old-fashioned joy—especially in the case of Robert Wright—of being on a team with a vaunted history, of playing and practicing alongside the likes of Nick Conner and Eddie Rat and now Bo-Pete Lamar. "We were precocious enough to understand who we were playing with," recalls Robert Wright. "We knew it would be an honor to practice with these cats every day."

Wright's mother, Erma, was a domestic worker in the white suburb of Bexley. Sometimes she found herself on the same bus gliding down East Broad Street as teammate Kenny Mizelle's mother, Mildred "Duckie" Mizelle, two black maids on their way to clean houses. Erma's husband, Daniel, was a criminal and had spent time in the notorious Ohio State Penitentiary. "He told me he once killed a man," Robert recalls. Daniel died when Robert was twelve years old. As a young boy, he figured he needed an extracurricular hobby to latch on to. He found it in basketball. When he reached East High, Bob Hart grew fond of Wright's work habits and dependability.

Still, when the school doors opened in the fall of 1968, Robert Wright, like many of the East High students, remained rattled over the King assassination. "We were, for the first time in our lives, frightened," he says of the entire East High student body. "We were used to white folks killing presidents. But Dr. King? We thought if they could kill King, they could kill any of us." Wright also felt the impact of the protests that had taken place at the Olympics in Mexico City. "We saw what was going on with John Carlos and Tommie Smith. We understood the only way to escape the neighborhood was to play basketball, and play it well." Wright also sensed a growing shift in sentiment among the student body: "We didn't look at King with the same reverence as with H. Rap Brown or Stokely Carmichael. You now had cheerleaders at East who wouldn't straighten their hair any longer," he says, referring to the growing numbers who preferred to wear Afros.

So the Afros grew thicker, as did the inquiries about freedom and equal rights everywhere. It could be felt in the classrooms. Seniors at East had to take a course titled "Problems of Democracy." (Everyone referred to it as POD.) The textbook was thick, its contents all about the challenges of government and governmental institutions. But many of the students now wanted to know exactly who was going to solve the ongoing problems of democracy right out there on the streets of Columbus, Ohio, and in Chicago, and in Indianapolis, and in Los Angeles—in all those places where riots and urban rebellion had taken place, and were still taking place. The students started insisting on conversations with their teachers about current events, about race and inequality. "I felt like I wanted to go out in the streets and throw rocks," recalls David Reid. Reid, however, thought better: He was manager of the boys varsity basketball team.

Sometimes Bob Hart wished he could whip that term paper out he had written back in college about the travails of black people, and the need for the nation to face its flaws and demons. But his power now lay in coaching a group of black kids in a tough neighborhood.

His team assembled, and with a couple weeks of practice behind them, Hart scheduled a scrimmage with the East High Hi-Y team, those basketball players who had been deemed not good enough to make varsity. Because many of those players still nursed grudges about having been cut, Hart always relished the opportunity to show them the beauty of playing under control, with a ref's whistle—the game skills he demanded of his varsity players.

Hart was playing coy with local reporters about announcing his starting lineup. His starting five would certainly come from among his top seven players. For the Hi-Y game he put a lineup of Conner, Hickman, Ratleff, Larry Walker, and newcomer Bo-Pete Lamar on the floor. The game was closed to the public. Some of the Hi-Y players were hyped up, figuring this would be a good time to show Hart he had made a mistake by cutting them. They were scrappy and fearless. As the game got under way, Hart could see it would take practice for Lamar to mesh with the rest of the players. There was the usual grunting and exhaustion, since the players from both teams were not yet in their best shape. But for all their prowess, Ratleff and Conner and Lamar and their teammates couldn't keep up with the Hi-Y team. The Hi-Y team was winning. Their players began wolf whistling, taunting the varsity players. Hart stopped the game and decided that at the end of every quarter the clock would be stopped. When each new quarter began, the game clock would start over, the score zero to zero. "The rules changed when we were losing," recalls varsity member Robert Wright.

"They beat us," remembers varsity member Kenny Mizelle.

"We were working on some things," Larry Walker says, going on to explain that correcting technique was more important to the team than a scrimmage that didn't count.

The varsity players indeed brushed it all off, telling classmates the next day it was just a scrimmage, that they were not about to overly exert themselves and get hurt, especially against the Hi-Y team. They promised all who kept asking that they would be ready when the season opened.

If there was a facet of the game in which Bob Hart wanted his current team to improve, it was long-range shooting. His teams had always been thought of as overdependent on inside caginess and muscle. At the beginning of the 1968 season, Hart brought Scott Guiler onto his staff as an unpaid volunteer coach. Guiler was in graduate school at Ohio State University, and he was a shooter. At Canal Winchester High School, an all-white school located east of Columbus in farm country, he had been one of the best high school shooters in the school's history. He possessed a picture-perfect jump shot. Were it not for a serious ankle injury in his senior year of high school, he would have gone on to play college basketball. Hart figured the jump shooters on his team—which mainly meant Bo-Pete Lamar—would benefit from just watching Guiler launch beautiful, high arching jump shots from all over the court. "Before practice," Guiler recalls, "I'd play three-on-three with the players—me, Nick, Rat, Hickman, Bo-Pete, Coach Pennell. I really enjoyed that." Bob Hart watched Guiler shoot and his Cheshire grin was hard to miss.

While he was sitting in a London prison awaiting extradition to America— and while the students of East High School in Columbus, Ohio, were demanding classroom time to discuss the King assassination—James Earl Ray was being hailed in some circles in America, namely by the Ku Klux Klan, and the Patriotic Legal Fund, the latter a crackpot mélange of undistinguished attorneys. Prison authorities at Wandsworth prison worried about Ray's mental state and were on guard for suicide attempts. None occurred. "He just hated black people," a prison guard who had befriended Ray would recall. "He said so on many occasions. He called them 'niggers.' In fact, he said he was going to Africa to shoot some more." Alexander Eist, the prison guard, concluded that Ray might be insane. "I can raise a lot of money, write books, go on television," Ray told him. "In parts of America, I'm a national hero."

Back on American soil and in a heavily guarded cell in downtown Memphis, James Earl Ray confronted the overwhelming evidence against him. There was a good chance of a first-degree murder conviction, for which he might be executed in the electric chair. So Ray pleaded guilty in lieu of a jury trial and received a ninety-nine-year prison sentence. He soon told a feverish and fanciful story about the King killing to journalist William Bradford Huie, claiming that he had been a pawn in a conspiracy, that he personally didn't pull the trigger. Huie was the perfect vehicle for such a tale. In his reporting career, Huie had seesawed between itinerant magazine reporting and giving lectures. He was a hustler of words and stories and storytelling. In 1955 he had covered the trial of the white men in Mississippi who had murdered fifteen-year-old Emmett Till for whistling at a white woman. The all-white Mississippi jury quickly acquitted the men. Huie then paid them $4,000 to tell him of their guilt. The men, realizing they could not be charged twice, took the money, told Huie of their murderous deed, and Huie wrote his story, forever becoming identified with "checkbook journalism." Huie didn't seem to mind the stigma. He certainly knew how to track and follow a good, dramatic story. Huie had covered the trial concerning the murders of James Chaney, Andrew Goodman, and Michael Schwerner, civil rights workers who were cut down by police officers and rogue associates on the night of June 21, 1964, in rural Mississippi. The local court acquitted the men, but they were eventually sentenced to prison on federal charges. Huie wrote the story in *Three Lives for Mississippi*, a book about the murders. While covering the civil rights movement, Huie had met Martin Luther King Jr. He was able to engage King to write an introduction to an edition of *Three Lives for Mississippi*. King was enamored of Huie's interest in telling civil rights stories. Not long after that book's publication, Huie was interviewing King's assassin and writing a book about the murder. The King and James Earl Ray assassination story, in all its permutations, would appear in newspapers and magazines throughout the 1968–69 Tigers basketball team's season.

The first game of the East High season was scheduled against Mohawk High School. The public clamor for tickets to the Saturday night contest was so intense that city athletic officials moved the game to the Fairgrounds Coliseum. Mohawk High was located near downtown Columbus and had been built in an effort to ease some of the overcrowding at East High School. Basketball fans were eager to know which five players would start for Bob Hart's Tigers. Hart coolly planned it this way: The public would know at the point the players were introduced inside the Coliseum. One thing was for sure: Bo-Pete would have plenty of followers at the game. The Coliseum sat on Eleventh Avenue, just a few blocks from his former home on the city's North Side.

The public announcer made a big deal of introducing the starting East High lineup. On the East High sideline—after the players in their white cotton warm-ups had trotted from the bowels of the stadium onto the Coliseum floor, greeted with thunderous applause—the bench players stood, shielding the starting five from the crowd. One of the things rival teams always gushed about were the East High warm-up uniforms, the outerwear players wore over their game uniforms. The Tigers' were white cotton, pants and a jacket—the cotton as soft as the cotton that some of their parents used to pick in the South. "You dreamed of wearing that uniform," remembers Gene Caslin, Ratleff's former junior high school teammate. Bob Hart had long sensed there was something important about appearance on the basketball court. "Basketball color is an intangible quality that can be identified with morale," he once wrote. "This can be incorporated in your equipment, uniforms, or style of play. Clean, well-fitting uniforms will dress up your boys and make them look like champions, whatever else they may be."

As the announcer's voice boomed, the standing players parted and, one by one, a player would rise from the bench and trot to the middle of the floor. There came Ratleff, the standing players parting—like an accordion—then closing again once Ratleff was out on the floor. There came Nick Conner. (He and Ratleff were team captains.) There came Roy Hickman, the players continuing to close after each starter had slipped out onto the floor. There came Larry Walker. There was one more player to be introduced. And when the standing players parted one last time, there he sat—Bo-Pete Lamar, the gunslinging rebel from the neighborhood, the player who came of age on the courts just down the street from the Coliseum. The crowd exploded. Bo-Pete, a wide grin flowing across his face, rose and coolly trotted to center court.

The Mohawk fans made their own noise as their starters were introduced. Mohawk's premier players were Al Harris, a gritty-playing forward who would have attended East were it not for overcrowding; Fred Saunders, a six-foot-six forward with a steely determination; Bruce Nelson, sporting the biggest and wildest Afro on the team; Keith Young, a player who depended on finesse; and Louis Hale, their point guard who was a dangerous streak shooter. *The Columbus Citizen-Journal*, the morning newspaper, had predicted that Mohawk would be one of the top teams in the City League. Coach Hart echoed a similar sentiment: "Mohawk will be a serious threat for the league title," he said, "and a very formidable foe for an opener."

As gifted as Mohawk was, from the outset of the game they seemed bewildered by the array of East High's offensive weapons. Both Ratleff and Conner began by scoring at a wicked clip. Hart unleashed his vaunted 2-2-1 defense, the opposing team staring at twin giants Conner and Ratleff as they simply tried to get the ball inbounds. "It was designed for you to throw the ball away," Mohawk player Al Harris remembers of the East defense. During a Mohawk timeout, Harris was furious, questioning his teammates' drive and nerve. Players were talking over one another. "I'm like, shut up and play," remembers Harris. It appeared fruitless. By halftime Ratleff had scored a whopping 32 points. By game's end, Bob Hart's Tigers seemed to be sending a warning: They would be worthy foes for any team. The score: East, 95, Mohawk, 63. Bo-Pete scored 17 points in his debut for the Tigers. Mohawk's Harris, who had a nifty 22-point game, mused that East had got the better of Mohawk because it was the first game of the season, and three of their stars—Harris himself, Fred Saunders, and Louis Hale—had been on the school's football team and were still rusty from the season. It was the type of reasoning that elicited little pity.

Back at school on Monday morning, up and down the East High hallways, the Hi-Y basketball players who had whipped the varsity team in the earlier scrimmage had to wonder: Had the varsity boys been playing possum with them?

East High's next foe was Dayton Dunbar, a game that was quickly moved to the Fairgrounds Coliseum as well because of ticket demand. Coach Hart had always held the Dayton high school teams in high regard, so he cautioned his players. But Hart's running and gunning Tigers showed little concern on the court. By the end of the third quarter, they were up by 20 points, 70–50. Conner and Ratleff each poured in 27 points; Conner went a cool 10 for 20 from the field. Bo-Pete chipped in with 17 points again, and Roy Hickman finished with 13. The final score felt like déjà vu: The Tigers beat Dunbar, 92–69.

When high school students look outward, across neighborhoods, they often reduce those alien neighborhoods along socioeconomic and class lines. Which houses look better? Which neighborhood has the sleekest cars in the driveway? The two largest public housing complexes in Columbus—Poindexter Village and Bolivar Arms—were both on the city's East Side, which meant East High educated the students who came from those housing projects. And while not all East High students lived in abject poverty, enough did that the school was sometimes maligned and stereotyped. The racial angst left the student body alternately with a chip on its shoulder and with a determination to cultivate its own pride.

Eastmoor High School was the East High Tigers' next opponent. Eastmoor sat northeast of East High, and East High students knew that the kids at Eastmoor were, for the most part, better off economically than they were. The school was located in the Berwick neighborhood of Columbus where many of the black middle class—lawyers, teachers, doctors—resided. The high school students who lived in Berwick wore their stature with a certain panache. Gene Caslin, who had played with Ratleff in junior high, was now a varsity player for Eastmoor. Only a sophomore, he did not expect a lot of playing time and sat listening to his teammates boast that they would upset the Tigers. Eastmoor had two stars in Harold Sullinger and Ron Lech, and their coach hoped their talent would offset some of the Tiger firepower.

At the end of the first quarter, Eastmoor had taken a 21–16 lead, which did much to boost their confidence, but with Ratleff and Lamar firing at will, East snatched the lead by halftime, 42–35. After halftime, Lamar reminded the throng of onlookers why he had led the city in scoring the previous year: He netted 13 points in the third quarter alone. After that, the Tigers began to pull away. The East High margin of victory against Eastmoor was 27 points, the final score 85–58.

The team's next foe was Marion-Franklin, on Friday, December 13, on Marion-Franklin's home court. At halftime the score was East 68, Marion-Franklin 34. By the third quarter, Marion-Franklin's bad luck had worsened: the Tigers held a 40-point lead. In the fourth quarter, Bob Hart, realizing it was the charitable thing to do, took his starters out of the game. Tom Kahler, the Marion-Franklin coach, didn't appreciate the gesture and left his starters in. The tactic annoyed Hart, who summoned his starters back into the game. "I put 'em back in because the guy at the other end wouldn't take his regulars out," Hart snapped later. "Our first string made the gap and he leaves his boys in after we took ours out." Ed Ratleff scored 45 points, tying a City League one-game scoring record going back to 1959. East High logged a 109–76 victory.

It might have been thought Bo-Pete was overly eager to face the next opponent, North High, his former team. But the team's approach was calm and even-keeled, as if they were above plotting petty revenge against the school that had given up on Bo-Pete. East scouted opposing teams and wrote scouting reports, which they distributed among team members. But they didn't bother to scout North High. The team had lost not only Lamar, but also its other leading scorer, Donnie Penn, who had transferred to Linden-McKinley, his own personal rebuke to North High for what they had done to his friend Bo-Pete. East High had another victory by another wide and embarrassing margin: East 63, North 36. Coach Hart did not stop Bo-Pete from lingering after the buzzer sounded, chatting with former North High teammates. He had a huge smile on his Afro-framed face as he embraced old friends from the neighborhood.

There was still a long way to go in the season, but it was becoming difficult to hide the optimism that this 5–0 East High team was already generating. Ratleff and Conner seemed as unstoppable as ever. Bo-Pete had started jelling with the starting five, even if he had yet to have the kind of explosive game he routinely showcased at his former school. There was enough trickiness in his repertoire that the Tiger faithful—whose hands cupped their mouths when they witnessed a long jump shot or a dazzling spin move—knew it was only a matter of time. And the bruising forward Roy Hickman was playing as if he had something to prove every game. He remained annoyed that the coach had wondered about cutting him this very season.

The Tigers' next opponent was Linden-McKinley, its longtime foe and the only school to beat East High in the past two basketball seasons. The game was played at the Fairgrounds Coliseum as part of a much-hyped doubleheader, the other game pitting undefeated South High against Central High School. There were more than a few titillating attractions in the East-Linden matchup. Linden's backcourt, featuring Donnie Penn—Bo-Pete's former teammate at North High—and Calvin Wade, an electrifying guard, was being talked up by many as the best backcourt in the city. Linden's forwards, Cliff Sawyer and Willie Williams, were both drawing the attention of college scouts. And Linden's first-year varsity coach, George Mills, had become the first black head basketball coach in the city. There was also the issue of student politics. Because of white flight on the city's North Side, the number of white students at Linden-McKinley had been rapidly declining. By 1968, the school had the second largest concentration of black students, just behind East High. So inner-city bragging rights were at stake.

At the top of the East High scouting report on the Linden-McKinley Panthers, Coach Hart had inserted a little piece of Norman Vincent Peale–like advice: "If you have something to do that is worthwhile doing, don't talk about it. Just do it. After you have done it, your friends and enemies will talk about it."

The game went back and forth, with flashes of athletic brilliance from players on both teams. At the end of the first half, East held a fifteen-point lead, 49–34. But the Panthers were dangerous, and no lead was quite comfortable enough. In the third period, East misfired shot after shot, hitting a miserable 4 of 16 attempts. Hart was furious. It certainly did not help that East High's Eddie Ratleff was in foul trouble and sat out a large portion of the third period. With Ratleff on the bench, Linden's Willie Williams went to work, scoring nine points in the period. The Coliseum grew raucous, each school's large fan contingents trying vainly to out yell the other. On three occasions in the fourth quarter, Linden inched to within two points. But then the Tigers found their shooting touch, hitting their next seven of ten shots from the field. They went to the free throw line five times, hitting all five shots. Linden, on this afternoon, did not disrupt the Tigers' winning streak; the East team triumphed, 77–69. Ratleff finished with 30 points, while Bo-Pete Lamar slipped in 20, and Roy Hickman 16. The Tigers' most reviled foe had been vanquished again.

On the East Side of the city—where the sorrow over King's death lingered the deepest—the influx of jobs to the area was undeniable. Many actually traced the development to King's activism. In his 1964 State of the Union speech, President Johnson vowed "an unconditional war on poverty." Nearly a fifth of the American population of 192 million at the time made less than $3,000 a year. Hungry babies were clawing paint off of walls in ghetto apartments and eating it, becoming sick. "It will not be a short or easy struggle," Johnson said of his War on Poverty. "No single weapon or strategy will suffice. But we shall not rest until that war is won." In LBJ's mind, the assault on poverty would be similar to Franklin D. Roosevelt's ambitious New Deal. The LBJ program flowed from his Economic Opportunity Act, which funded community-based programs to "give every American community the opportunity to develop a comprehensive plan to fight its own poverty—and help them to carry out their plans." Suddenly a gigantic machinery was created to combat poverty and provide opportunity. Among the various agencies were the Neighborhood Youth Corps, Legal Services Program, and Head Start; the impact of all of these programs was felt in Columbus.

On the East Side of Columbus, the biggest War on Poverty programs were headquartered at 700 East Broad Street, several blocks west of East High School. People from the impoverished East Side went there to seek training and jobs, made possible by the Comprehensive Employment and Training Act (CETA). These were the first jobs that were created to lift blacks in the community away from oppressive and dangerous factory jobs. (There was a satellite office on Mount Vernon Avenue, just around the corner from where East High player Roy Hickman lived.) Many of the East High athletes found summer jobs during 1968 through one of the War on Poverty programs.

As the 1968 basketball season had gotten under way at East High, the presidential campaign was also in motion. Yard signs supporting one or the other candidates could be seen up and down East Broad Street. Five years of war, ongoing civil unrest, and their bloody and chaotic convention in Chicago did not bode well for the Democratic ticket of Humphrey and Edmund Muskie. Civil rights advocates were leery of both Nixon and Agnew. Alabama governor George Wallace, a segregationist and a frightening figure to blacks, didn't stand a chance of winning, but he was making noise throughout the South, heightening racial tensions throughout the country. Nixon's "law and order" approach to civil protest caught on with the so-called silent majority, whites living in the suburbs across the nation. When, after the election, Nixon failed to name a black to his cabinet—or to any high-level position—many in the minority community who distrusted him felt they had even more reason to do so. The Nixon administration tried to curb efforts to implement school integration plans, leaving all-black schools, such as East High, in limbo in the decades-long fight for educational equality.

If an outsider was looking for a school that was ripe for civil protest beginning in the fall of 1968 in Columbus, Ohio, they would have quickly learned about East High School. The school sat on the city's activist East Side. The school had an all-black student body, and one-fifth of its teachers were black, far more than at any other high school in the city. The students were full of cultural pride. Every day they walked by those Black Power posters that peeked from the storefronts on nearby Mount Vernon Avenue and East Long Street. The students were also blessed with a beloved figure in Jack Gibbs, the city's only black high school principal.

Inside the story of Jack Gilbert Gibbs lay plenty of complexity and mystery. At East High, as every student—and gaudily dressed pimp who tried to recruit the comely young ladies at the school during lunch period would tell you—Jack Gibbs may well have been loved. But he was also feared.

The House That Jack Built

She had to escape.

Her name was Mamie Bell, and she was poor, she was black, and she lived in the tiny town of Washington, Georgia. Like many places in the South, the town had its own dash of recorded history: In Washington, Jefferson Davis, leader of the Confederacy, had settled down for a night in 1865 while Union soldiers were galloping around in search of him. After a night in a soft bed, Davis fled again into the woods. He was finally caught in Irwinville, Georgia, in May of 1865. Confederate General Robert E. Lee had surrendered a month earlier, but Davis had his own maniacal hopes about toppling the United States government.

The Civil War was long over by 1938, but the powerful residue of that conflict was still deeply felt throughout the southern states. That was the year Mamie Bell found herself in a desperate situation. She was carrying on a secret affair with a local white sheriff. The sheriff's power overwhelmed her common sense, for at times during the illicit affair she thought something good might come of the relationship: Perhaps the sheriff would leave his job and family and they would all flee up north. When she became pregnant, the seriousness of her situation was impossible to ignore. Mamie gave birth to twin girls, Agnes and Edna, who looked white. Mamie was the target of nasty and hurtful gossip. The truth about the father remained hush-hush in the white community, but there were blacks who knew more than they were supposed to know. One day the family of the white sheriff showed up and told Mamie they wished to take her twin infant girls. They told her it was simply an act of charity, that the sheriff's family would find someone prosperous to take the girls in and raise them. The affront only reminded Mamie of her impoverished state and also of her relative helplessness, and left her deeply rattled. Mamie Bell had no power against such people, and she knew it. But she had no intention of giving up her girls. She huddled with family members. Against the unimaginable thought of having her children snatched from her, she cried. And then she plotted. There were family acquaintances in Cincinnati. One night, with the help of other family members, Mamie fled the town with Agnes and Edna in her arms. She hopped a train to Cincinnati. All during the trip, she couldn't help but fear strangers and any lingering stares. After she finally reached Cincinnati, she quickly realized she had no way to properly care for her twins. Soon enough, she heard of a job working for a white family in Harlan, Kentucky, where her family friends in Cincinnati also knew people. She needed to find work and save money. She found a Catholic orphanage in Cincinnati and pleaded with them to take her girls, promising she'd return in a short period of time to get them. In the backbreaking year of 1938, in a nation still reeling from the hard woes of the Depression, the orphanage had heard many such stories. Sometimes parents simply never returned. They took in Agnes and Edna.

In Harlan, Mamie Bell worked as a domestic for the Scott family. The hours were long, but she was treated decently by the family. She saved her money, and after a few months she returned to the Cincinnati orphanage for her daughters. The family returned to Harlan, and for the first time in a long time Mamie experienced unalloyed joy.

Harlan was a tough and dangerous town. The battles between coal miners, strikers, and strikebreakers were legion. Moonshine running led to clashes between law enforcement and the locals. The town was known as "Bloody Harlan." Shootings took place in broad daylight. Ethnic factions formed; fistfights were common. The small black community, residing in an area known as Clovertown, was closely knit, aware that their position on the socioeconomic ladder was always perilous. Mamie Bell's twins, Agnes and Edna, grew up, and their mother was proud to see them in the kind of nice clothes she could not have afforded for herself back in Georgia. By the time they reached their teen years, the twins began to date.

Clarence Gibbs was a porter at the Lewallen Hotel in Harlan, one of the nicest and largest hotels in the town. It was a far safer job than working in the coal mines. His salary plus the tips he earned—he had a warm smile that drew pleasantries from the hotel customers—made him an attractive suitor. He fell in love with Mamie Bell's daughter Edna, and they married. They began to have children. Three boys came first—Clarence, Robert, then Jack. The couple's first daughter, Edna Pearl, came next. As expected, she was doted on. Neighbors came by to get glimpses of the infant. When she was nearly six months old, Edna Pearl began to cough. Home remedies did not quiet her coughing. The bouts worsened, and sometimes she turned red, squirming in obvious distress in her mother's arms. The hard wheezing sound coming from her throat was whooping cough, a dangerous affliction for any infant at the time. Edna Pearl, only six months old, died June 4, 1938. Her parents and brothers were stricken with grief. They buried her in nearby Baxter, at the Negro cemetery, her gravesite wedged up and onto the side of a mountain. The sight of little Edna Pearl's coffin elicited wailing sobs that echoed along the mountainside. Edna Gibbs's sons had never seen their mother so distraught, so helpless and weakened. Mamie made weekly pilgrimages to the gravesite to visit her daughter. Passersby would spot Edna, prostrate at the site of the grave, talking to herself, mumbling. Often her son Jack, quite a sensitive child, would accompany her.

If it were not for two visionaries who cared about black children like him, little Jack Gibbs might not have received the jolt early in life that stamped the importance of education into him.

.   .   .

Julius Rosenwald and Booker T. Washington were both born in America. Washington, a black man, was born a slave, his life valued in dollars and cents. Rosenwald, white, was born into a family with means, his father a successful businessman; he did not know suffering growing up.

When he was a child, Booker T. Washington's worth was put at $400. He and his family were freed by President Lincoln's Emancipation Proclamation. Young Booker was nine years old at the time. When he was old enough, he went to work in a West Virginia coal mine. As a free man who had received an education at Hampton Institute, his achievements were profound; he took on the causes of black mobility and progress. He began to lecture and write. His popular book, *Up from Slavery*, caught the attention of Julius Rosenwald. Washington founded a college, the Tuskegee Institute, in Alabama. President Theodore Roosevelt invited him to the White House for a private chat and dinner. White southerners howled in protest that a black man had been invited to dine at the White House.

Julius Rosenwald would often state that his Jewish heritage gave him a sympathetic understanding of the need to aid blacks. With the financial input of two other businessmen, Rosenwald became a principal in Sears, Roebuck & Company. It was primarily a mail-order clothing business, and the company's fortunes soared. Rosenwald became rich. From his Chicago base, he turned to notable acts of charity and philanthropy. There were many things holding black advancement back, and Rosenwald concluded that a lack of school facilities was high on that list. Booker T. Washington was the best known black educator in America. Emissaries of Washington and Rosenwald arranged a meeting on May 18, 1911, at Chicago's brand-new Blackstone Hotel, where Rosenwald hosted a luncheon for Washington. The black man was the hotel's first black guest. "Whether it is because I belong to a people who have known centuries of persecution," Rosenwald said to the gathering as he began to introduce Washington, "or whether it is because naturally I am inclined to sympathize with the oppressed, I have always felt keenly for the colored race."

In time, realizing Rosenwald's fervent desire to help southern blacks get a better education, Washington proposed a plan, telling Rosenwald that if he gave adequate funds, black communities could match those funds with labor and begin to build schools throughout the South. It was just the kind of proactive thinking that Rosenwald liked. The schoolhouses began to rise—in Alabama, Georgia, Mississippi, South Carolina, Kentucky. "You do not know what joy and encouragement the building of these schoolhouses has brought to the people of both races in the communities where they are being erected," Washington wrote early during the construction of the Rosenwald schools.

Jack Gibbs began his formal education at the Rosenwald School in Harlan, Kentucky. He was a happy-go-lucky child who took eagerly to learning. He became passionate about books. He borrowed books from the library for leisure reading, and when he returned them, he borrowed more. He sidled up to teachers after classes, asking questions about events around the world. The codes of discipline may have bothered other children, but not Jack Gibbs. He obeyed instruction and seemed to be more focused than many other children his age.

Edna Gibbs gave birth to two more children, both daughters. And every child of hers was constantly reminded of their deceased sister. They'd be brought to the gravesite. They'd watch their mother cry when it was time to leave, as dark came quickly to the mountains. Edna's husband, Clarence, began to drink heavily. Edna would make excuses for him, telling others the death of their daughter had sent him into a depressive state. Edna could tell her children were unnerved by their father's change in behavior. She couldn't help but think of the future of her children. She did not wish for her sons to spend their lives in the coal mines. Everywhere she looked in Harlan—from sidewalks to inside the shack-like homes of other blacks, up to the cemetery on that mountain—she could sense pain. She demanded of her husband that they all move to Columbus, Ohio, where she had an aunt, Mary Ellis, who would help them get settled.

So, just as her own mother had done, Edna Gibbs escaped.

Weakened by alcohol, Clarence had no stamina to argue with his wife. It was not difficult for either parent to imagine a better future for all their children in Ohio.

·   ·   ·

The Gibbs family settled on the West Side of Columbus. One would have been hard-pressed to find a young boy in the Midwest who took such exuberant advantage of the times as did Jack Gibbs. As a mature thirteen-year-old in a new city, he quickly ingratiated himself with playmates, neighbors, and schoolteachers. His mind seemed to whir. He took to the sunshine and ran and played, putting on muscle as he grew, becoming more and more interested in sports. While his father continued drinking shamelessly, young Jack leaned into his books and sports. He excelled at boxing, in time competing in the Golden Gloves tournament, getting his picture in the local newspaper. By the time he reached West High, he had grown to six foot two inches, and he weighed a solid 180 pounds. He had a cinnamon-colored complexion. The girls thought him quite handsome.

Jack Gibbs only dreamed of playing football at West High. He could clearly see how much his mother was scuffling, trying to feed five children and deal with an alcoholic husband. So he never played high school football, or any other sport at school. Instead, after school he raced to his job in an aircraft plant. His earnings greatly helped out at home. He assumed the role of man of the house after his mother and father divorced. On weekends he listened to the radio and the popular Ohio State Buckeyes football team. He thought that maybe someday he'd get to go to college. A Gibbs had never gone to college.

Now and then, the Catholic church Jack attended would host dances for teens. He liked getting dressed up. His job had given him the luxury of buying nice clothes. At one dance—with the music playing sweet and bouncy, and the church chaperones eyeing everyone fiercely—he spotted a beautiful young lady named Ruth. "I knew he liked me," she recalls many years later. "He would ask me to dance." Ruth thought that Jack might ask her father for her hand after high school. He was smart and industrious enough to graduate early. But instead of asking for Ruth's hand, he took off, without a car, and hitchhiked all the way to California.

He was out in the world now, a boy quickly becoming a man in wild

California. His wit, independence, and sturdiness of body and mind saved him from ruffians. But far away from Columbus, he realized something: He missed Ruth, who was still his girlfriend. "That's when he wrote me a love letter and said he had been many places," she says, "and that he realized I was the one he loved and I had the qualities he wanted in a wife."

Once back in Columbus, Jack Gibbs told Ruth he had two immediate goals in mind: He wanted to marry her, and he wanted to get enrolled at Ohio State University. She said yes. And he got himself admitted to Ohio State in 1951. He enjoyed classes, enjoyed roaming around the big campus, eating at the cheap campus dining spots along North High Street. Before the start of his sophomore year, Jack announced to Ruth—and anyone else who would listen—that he was going to go out for the Ohio State football team. It sounded like some kind of a crazy pipe dream. Jack Gibbs had not played one down of football at West High School. He had only been a sandlot player! But there he was, one early fall afternoon after classes, hustling over to the football stadium, nervously approaching Coach Woody Hayes, and telling him he wanted to try out for the team. Hayes was accustomed to hearing similar pitches from young men. They wanted to "walk on" to the team, to try out. And although some had played high school football, this was hard-hitting Big Ten football. This was a game where single-strapped helmets flew off and where bones were broken in the snow on Saturday afternoons. The coaches let Gibbs try out. They had nothing to lose, and besides, they knew players like him were just dreamers. Just like that onetime OSU student James Thurber—who attended East High when the school was all white—and who went on to write for the *New Yorker* magazine and created a big-time dreamer by the name of Walter Mitty. Mitty, who became an outlandishly popular figure in fiction, imagined himself in all kinds of fanciful situations. Jack Gibbs was no Walter Mitty. He was just Jack Gibbs, who had never earned a high school varsity letter. The OSU coaches took note of Gibbs's endurance. He had natural on-the-field gifts. He announced that he was a fullback. Coaches squinted at the way he moved. He seemed fearless. And, against all odds, he made the Buckeye football team. Even Ruth was surprised. And there was something

*Jack Gibbs's moment of glory on the Ohio State football team filled the
black community with pride. Later, with community passion behind him,
he battled his way to become the first black principal at East High.*

else Jack Gibbs intended to do: He was going to keep his job—the shift
from midnight to eight a.m. at the North American Rockwell plant.
Ruth knew he could never keep up such a schedule. But he told her he
had to take care of not only her, but his two younger sisters and mother
since his father barely contributed anything to the family. Ruth rolled
her eyes. He was obstinate. She packed his middle-of-the-night snack
before he trudged off to work.

To his coaches, Jack Gibbs was dependable on the practice field, just
as he was dependable at the factory. (That dependability at practice
rarely was rewarded with actual playing time during games.) He slept
during the five hours between dinner and reporting to the plant for his
midnight shift. Teammates knew of his grueling routine and were in
awe of him. The football team finished the 1953–54 season with a 6–3
record. The three losses, against Illinois, Michigan State, and Michigan,
were extremely painful given the intense rivalry between those schools.
The Michigan contest had long taken on a venomous edge, something

akin to an annual border war. The two schools first played each other in 1897. The ensuing games through the years were followed by the national media with hyped-up eagerness and curiosity. Politicians made good-natured wagers. In 1950 Michigan defeated Ohio State, 9–3; Ohio State coach Wes Felser, so distraught and maligned, resigned after the loss. The school then hired Woody Hayes. Hayes was a World War II Navy veteran who had coached at two Ohio schools, Denison University and Miami University in Oxford, Ohio. He didn't have to tell anyone that he also considered Michigan a mortal enemy. But Woody Hayes did something other Big Ten coaches did not: He wasn't going to shy away from putting black players on the field.

No one would have minded if Jack Gibbs had decided to forgo football his senior year, which would begin in the fall of 1954, because he had a wife and was still working his full-time job. Besides, the season before he hadn't even made the traveling squad. The Buckeye coaches were so sure that he wouldn't come out for the team again that they didn't even put him on the pre-season roster. But once a player had donned the scarlet-and-gray uniform of the Buckeyes and stepped into that stadium, which sat on the banks of the Olentangy River, and heard the symphonic roar of 80,000-plus fans, it was a dream that was hard to step out of—unless the coaches themselves ended it. And Jack had built up more than enough goodwill to remain on Woody Hayes's team. So Jack "Walter Mitty" Gibbs reported for practice for the 1954 season and again made the team. He was assigned fullback duties, albeit third string, which was about as far down the chart as one could get.

Midway through the season, the Buckeyes stood at a surprising 4–0 after defeating thirteenth-ranked Iowa, 20–14. Four games later they stood at 8–0, with an upcoming standoff against the team's bitter foe, Michigan. The Michigan contest suddenly took on epic importance. The game was in Columbus, inside the horseshoe-shaped OSU stadium. Game tickets were looked upon like rare pearls. Not only would Ohio State be playing for the Big Ten championship, but a national championship now appeared within the team's reach.

After the game's opening kickoff, Michigan marched right down the field into Ohio State territory. Their halfback, Dan Cline, bolted into the end zone from seven yards out. Michigan, quickly up by 7, played well, dominating the first half, silencing the 82,000-plus hometown Ohio State crowd. As play went on, the Buckeyes began to be hobbled by the hard hits from Michigan players. Several injured OSU players had to be helped to the sidelines. In the second quarter, in need of replacements, Coach Woody Hayes scanned his sideline. Surprisingly, he motioned for Jack Gibbs—who had played only fifteen forgettable minutes the entire season—and sent him into the game. Normally a fullback, Gibbs was called upon to play defense, at linebacker. Michigan coaches took note of the substitution and aimed to exploit it. Jim Maddock, the Michigan quarterback, immediately threw a pass to his receiver, who happened to be in Gibbs's territory. The throw had no zip on it. Gibbs leapt toward the ball and snatched it. The crowd sprang up and roared. Ruth Gibbs's eyes nearly popped out of her head. Jack Gibbs dashed toward the Buckeye end zone. He gained twenty yards, then thirty, then forty, as the decibel level rose. He was finally brought down only ten yards from the end zone, a forty-seven-yard interception return. The noise inside the stadium was deafening. Even the taciturn Hayes felt his chest jump. Moments later, Fred Kriss, an Ohio State split end, caught a touchdown pass, tying the score. Kriss was jubilant, but not as jubilant as Jack Gibbs, who was on the sideline still accepting hearty slaps for his interception. When the fourth and final quarter got under way, the score still remained tied, 7–7. Then Hopalong Cassady, the Ohio State All-American, went to work, mauling up yardage, leading to another scoring strike from Ohio State's quarterback to Dick Brubaker: Buckeyes 14, Michigan, 7. Late in the fourth quarter, Cassady dashed any hopes of a Michigan comeback when he scored again, making the score 21–7, which is how the game ended with tens of thousands rushing the field. The Michigan players and fans were crushed. Ohio State had won the Big Ten title. A Rose Bowl berth was now assured, the outcome of which would decide a national championship.

As well as Hopalong Cassady had played in the game, the newspaper reporters only wanted to talk about no. 35, Jack Gibbs, and his intercep-tion, which had changed the game's momentum. "That play turned the game around," Ruth Gibbs, who was in the cold stands, remembers. Jack was mobbed inside the Buckeye locker room. The player who had very rarely played had done something with storybook implications. "Gibbs a Hero," proclaimed the photo caption in the Sunday *Columbus Dispatch* newspaper. The sports writer thought the Gibbs play was important enough to diagram it in the next day's edition. There was a picture of Gibbs racing downfield: "This was the second period play that cracked the pall of gloom over Ohio stadium and lit the Buckeye scoring fuse," the reporter wrote. "Gibbs made himself a hero by catching the ball on the Michigan 43 and returning it to the 10." In a city that—unlike Cleveland or Cincinnati—had no major professional sports franchises, the exploits of Ohio State's athletic teams were always magnified. The stars of the Buckeye teams were widely heralded throughout the city; through the years, the football players who helped visit defeat upon the Michigan Wolverines became near folk heroes in their own times. At the Buckeyes' football banquet—scheduled in the days following the Michigan game, which was always the last game of the regular season—Gibbs was cited by Governor Frank Lausche and received a standing ovation.

Ohio State went on to defeat the University of Southern California, 20–7, in the Rose Bowl on New Year's Day 1955, capturing the school's second national championship. Jack Gibbs had his two front teeth knocked out during practice in Pasadena. He still played in the game, only adding to his stature and the admiration coaches and players heaped upon him. (The Buckeyes, however, had to share the national championship with UCLA, also unbeaten.)

It had not been lost on Jack Gibbs, or any of the few black players on the OSU football team in 1954, that they would not have been welcomed as students on any college campus in the American South. As fate would have it, the 1954 collegiate football season followed, by mere months, the great NAACP lawyer Thurgood Marshall's successful and epic *Brown v. Board of Education* desegregation lawsuit won before the United States Supreme Court. Marshall had made several visits to Columbus before 1954 to lecture about the evils of segregation. Chief Justice Earl Warren wrote for the court in its unanimous ruling:

Segregation of white and colored children in public schools has a detrimental effect upon the colored children. The impact is greater when it has the sanction of the law, for the policy of separating the races is usually interpreted as denoting the inferiority of the negro group. A sense of inferiority affects the motivation of a child to learn. Segregation with the sanction of law, therefore, has a tendency to [retard] the educational and mental development of negro children and to deprive them of some of the benefits they would receive in a racial[ly] integrated school system.

The most renowned black athlete in Ohio State's history had been track star Jesse Owens. Although he broke several Ohio State track records, the school still would not give Owens a scholarship; he had to put himself through school. He garnered national acclaim at the 1936 Berlin Olympics, when he won four gold medals and shamed both Adolf Hitler and the German sense of Aryan invincibility. It was common for Olympic victors to be invited to the White House for a meeting with the president, but Owens received no invitation. In the years after Ohio State, he was so strapped for money that once he was talked into racing on a track—against horses. Horse racing fans snickered and howled.

The few black players who had played football at Ohio State in the Jim Crow era realized their opportunities beyond the football field would be different from the futures of gifted white players. That is, unless you were a Bill Willis. Willis was an outstanding lineman, and an all-American, on the 1942 Ohio State national football championship team. After he graduated, he worked in recreation, then took a coaching job at Kentucky State College, a black school. When he heard that Paul Brown, his former Ohio State coach, had taken a job as the first coach of the Cleveland Browns, he angled a tryout. Brown signed Willis, who broke the color barrier in professional football two years before Jackie Robinson broke it in baseball. (There had been black players in the National Football League before 1946, but when George Preston Marshall, who owned the Washington Redskins, came into the league, he started influencing other owners to adopt an unwritten rule: ignore black players. While a few black players would make it onto rosters, Marshall himself did not sign a black player, Bobby Mitchell, until 1962. Marshall held a decades-long lease on the D.C. stadium where his team played. Robert F. Kennedy, attorney general at the time, warned Marshall that if he didn't integrate his team, the lease, on federal property, would be revoked.)

Bill Willis was a graduate of East High School in Columbus.

In the 1954 Ohio State football season, Coach Woody Hayes fielded ten black players, more than had ever donned uniforms on an OSU team in the past. The white citizenry of Columbus—and of the nation—paid no attention to the story. But the Negro press in Columbus did; they gathered the black players one evening over at the student union for a celebration and photograph.

Like Willis had done before him, Jack Gibbs, upon graduation—because he was hardly dreaming of the pros—went to work for the Columbus recreation department. Recreation was one of the few good jobs—the other being teaching—that were available for onetime black athletes from OSU with college degrees. Gibbs realized, more than most, how fleeting life could be. So while he was working recreation, he coached young boxers, Little League football, and a semi-pro football team. He even found time to manage the swimming pool in the summer at Maryland Park, the East Side public pool where blacks swam. At the Maryland Park pool his reputation as a disciplinarian and a brawler got its start. Young black kids, teenage toughs, harassed other kids there. They whispered vulgarities at the girls. At closing time they lingered outside the gates of the pool ready to start fights. Gibbs went after them. He berated them, pushed them along, dared them to fight him. When it was necessary to detain someone until the police arrived, he would, using his muscled football body to great effect. Miscreants and rabble-rousing teens infuriated Jack Gibbs. He wrote letters to the editor of the local newspapers talking about the problem. He visited the households of teens he knew to be troublemakers, and he harangued their parents.

In 1956 Jack Gibbs was hired as a teacher at Central High School, where he also became an assistant football coach. There were no black head coaches at any high school in the city, or even assistant coaches, and Gibbs's fortune in getting his position could be traced to two connections: Hopalong Cassady and Woody Hayes. They both put in a good word for him. Eventually, Gibbs decided he wanted to get into school administration. The two black junior high schools in the city at the time were Franklin and Champion. Monroe wouldn't open until the mid-1960s. In 1961, Gibbs was named assistant vice principal at Franklin Junior High. Two years later, in the fall of 1963, Columbus school board officials thought it wise to have a black vice principal at East High School, and Gibbs was their choice. One can only wonder how much Dr. King's galvanizing speech that year had on their decision. He and Ruth celebrated. When the news of his administrative job reached them, the folks back in Harlan were quite proud. There were those who imagined that if Gibbs did well, and a vacancy occurred at any high school in the city—though especially at East High—he would be seriously considered for a principal's position. The city, which was quite conservative on racial issues, had never had a black high school principal. There were principal openings at other high schools over the next two years, but Jack Gibbs did not receive a job offer at any of those schools. Then Don Wiley, the white principal at East High, announced he was resigning.

At times during the sixties, Wiley had seemed bewildered by what was taking place out on the streets of Columbus and beyond. He was a formal, by-the-books administrator, and the times had changed. Protests and protesters were everywhere. Wiley planned to move to Florida, far away from the brutal Ohio winters. Many quickly assumed Gibbs would be offered Wiley's job. After all, the second half of the sixties was supposed to be about upward racial mobility. Municipalities, goaded by new integration laws, were compelled to open more doors to minorities. The local school board, however, decided to mull over Wiley's replacement.

Parents who backed Gibbs suddenly became nervous. It is true that vice principals rarely have a chance to shine. It is an administrative job, and one not easily judged by anyone beyond the vice principal's immediate boss, the school principal. There were school board members who were unsure if Jack had the mettle to lead an urban high school. And in the end, the sentiment of those school board members won out. Duane Reed, an outsider, a white educator, was brought in and named principal of East High. Gibbs was crushed. Black parents felt an injustice had been done but had no clout downtown. There was nothing they could do. "The world of high school principals then was all little white men who had been around a long time," says Paul Pennell, the assistant basketball and head baseball coach at the time. "It's a good question as to why he didn't get it," adds Pennell. "But those were the times. Should he have gotten the job? Absolutely. Did we think he would get the job? Absolutely." There were times Gibbs pondered leaving. He had always been an industrious sort. But he also had an inner vision for the school. He thought of what might happen to the students if he left. And he wanted his own children, Jack Jr. and Cheryl, who were in junior high, to attend East High while he was there. Additionally, he and Ruth had just purchased a home, northeast of the city, in a little subdivision filled with black families. The land, just off Sunbury Road, had been sold to black families by a white landowner in the city who sympathized with their hardships in trying to buy property in the city. So Gibbs stayed at East High. "His whole life," recalls Paul Pennell, "was those kids at East High School."

Then, after just one year, Duane Reed surprised everyone when he abruptly left East High for another school in the city. Now surely the job would go to Gibbs. But again, there was a delay on the part of the school board. That sentiment did not sit well with the OSU football coach Woody Hayes. When word reached Hayes that the board might pass on his former player yet again, he went into action. He contacted the school board and told them in no uncertain terms that they should hire Jack Gibbs, that he was the best man for the job. In a city where Hayes was already a legend—in addition to the 1955 national title, his OSU team also took national titles in 1957 and 1961—his word was sacrosanct.

In 1967—with the streets of America on fire and the black community of Columbus on edge, and the black parents of East High ready to plot some kind of civic revolt—Jack Gibbs was appointed principal of East High School, the first black high school principal in the history of the city.

He took his mother to visit his sister at the segregated cemetery in Harlan, Kentucky.

He told his wife he'd be working very long hours.

And then Jack Gibbs set about making everyone pay attention to an all-black school on the mean side of a city that had paid no attention to the 1954 United States Supreme Court school desegregation ruling.

He went out into the community to recruit black teachers who had once been students at East High, imploring them to come back to teach at the school, which did not have enough black teachers. He told them the kids needed role models. "He wanted East High to be the best," recalls Mike Gordon, who joined the faculty under Gibbs. But just because Gibbs recruited a person to come teach at the school did not mean he intended to turn them into a teacher's pet. Once he had charmed a teacher into coming to work at the school, he laid down his rules as soon as they were on the premises: He did not want teachers fraternizing with students outside of school. He did not want teachers hanging out at any of the speakeasies and dives around Mount Vernon Avenue and East Long Street. Other schools might allow teachers to wear jeans and fashions conceived during the relaxed hippie craze, but that would not happen at East High under Jack Gibbs. He expected suits, ties, skirts of an appropriate length. "This," recalls Mike Gordon, "is what he said to me: 'We've got to set an environment so students can achieve what they want to achieve.'"

The school did not have adjacent open fields where students could play during gym class, so students had to follow their gym teacher down the hall and out the door, across East Broad Street, to Franklin Park, the city park that had been the setting for black families' summer picnics since the 1940s. Now it was an impromptu playground for East High students. One afternoon Scott Guiler, the assistant volunteer basketball coach, was leading his gym class through the hallways. They were making noise, and to Principal Jack Gibbs, the noise sounded like rowdiness. The next day Gibbs cornered Guiler and told him from then on he was to take his gym class outside the building and have them walk *around* the school to the park. Guiler could feel Gibbs's intensity. "He ran a tight ship," Guiler remembers years later.

When black parents complained about inadequate resources for East High, Gibbs told them to stop complaining. He told them to join his effort by volunteering their nonworking hours to help with school benefits and functions, and that would make up for the resources they lacked.

He increased membership in the East High Booster Club, telling new boosters their participation was vital to the school's success. Pop James became a booster. James's family had been among the first black families who moved into the Poindexter Village housing projects in 1940, fresh off the tobacco roads of Virginia. James had graduated from East High in 1948. (That was when the school was mostly all white.) During the years that James worked with the Booster Club, the phone would ring: it was East High principal Jack Gibbs, rattling off a list of things he needed James to do for the school—for the kids, is actually how Gibbs always put it. James found himself helping to clean the school after events. He'd help drive athletic teams to games. "Jack would call me and ask me to do this, to do that," he says.

To the black students, Gibbs represented change, and a huge source of pride: The first black principal in the city was now at East High, their school. "He understood the black psyche," basketball player Robert Wright says of Gibbs. Gibbs knew cultural concessions had to be made. A cake cutter was normally used for culinary purposes, but it was also good for combing out Afros. He allowed the students to carry them. Yet if students thought the color of Gibbs's skin granted them reprieves when it came to discipline, they sorely misjudged Jack Gibbs. He went after those boys who played craps, tossing dice from their palms like the gamblers did in all those movies set in Las Vegas. At East High, seven or eight boys would often hunch in a circle in the bathroom and play craps for money. Sometimes they would have a lookout, sometimes not. One morning Gibbs quietly ambled into the boys' bathroom, shocking the boys. They bounded up, trying to conceal the dice. Gibbs looked around and calmly told them to resume playing. He was grinning. The boys could not measure his grin; perhaps he merely wanted a tutorial, so he could better understand the attraction of the activity? They allowed his grin to convince them they were not in trouble, and they did as instructed, resuming the game. But when the dice rolled, Gibbs told the gathered boys that whatever number came up, that would be the number of hits he would deliver with his paddle down at his office. And after the dice landed, the parade began down to his office, where he pulled out his paddle and commenced the whacking. Afterward, those brave enough to continue playing crap games moved their activity away from school grounds and the sleuthing of their principal. Gibbs could be spotted driving his vehicle down alleyways near the school in search of miscreants, as alleyways were popular spots for small-time gambling.

It was the high school girls at East High who really worried Jack Gibbs. Roger Dumaree, East's vice principal, knew that Gibbs wasn't going to sit idly by while would-be Lotharios cruised up and down the side streets by the school. "After school," recalls Dumaree, "[the young men would] come to pick the girls up. Me and Jack would be watching. If a girl went over and started talking to the guy, Jack would walk up to her and say, 'Give me your books, honey. You're suspended for a day.' And she'd say, 'Why?' Jack would say, 'You know why. No contact with nonstudents.'"

Pregnancy among high-school-age girls had become such a problem that the city created a night school at Central High School. (The school's mascot was the Pirates, but because its student body came from another low-income area of the city, and the school sat on the banks of the Scioto River, many other students derisively called the students there the River Rats.) The Night School was set up for students who had aged out of the public school system, but mostly to accommodate the high school girls who had had a baby while attending another school. In the school system at the time, if you gave birth, you wore a kind of scarlet letter: You were not allowed to return to day school, ever again. School officials feared a young female student with a baby might have an unsavory effect on other girls, so they banished her. The young mother had a baby to care for during the day, and an enormous hurdle to overcome to complete her education. It took pluck and moxie to be a parent all day and then, at dusk, get downtown to Central Night School to attend classes from six to ten p.m. Many young parents did just that, intent on getting their high school diploma. The teachers at the night school adopted a rather sensitive approach because they realized the challenges the young girls faced. There was even a rather progressive approach to selecting the class valedictorian. Being given the title wasn't always based on grade point average, but rather on individual presentations given on a stage. Students were asked to talk about something important and memorable in their lives. The teachers were looking for a story, a narrative, a personal experience of the journey to this particular point. There were plenty of gut-wrenching stories among the night school student body.

Rather than talk to small groups of students about life's many challenges at East, Jack Gibbs would call an assembly, the announcement coming over the school's loudspeaker: "Everyone is to report to the auditorium at ten this morning for an assembly." Some students groaned; others were happy to have the morning interrupted. The topics discussed at the assemblies varied. They might talk about the Vietnam War, about the deaths of Martin Luther King Jr. and Robert F. Kennedy. "Gibbs held 'women assemblies,'" recalls Zita Range Moses, a student at the time. "He was disturbed by the high pregnancy rates at some of the other schools." So the girls—young women—would troop into the assembly and be met by nurses and health officials who would talk to them about sex education. "The assembly hall is the principal's classroom," Gibbs once told a group of educators. "And to those of you in schools [that are] predominantly white who tell me that you can't work on racism in your schools, I say you can. I have had to work on black racism in mine, and black racism is just as bad and evil as white racism. Both are wrong. The principal has to have the courage to speak out."

Jack Gibbs was at a school athletic event at East High in the aftermath of the 1968 Tommie Smith and John Carlos protest at the Mexico City Olympics when he spotted one of his students, Joe, doing the same thing: standing as still as a museum piece with fist raised. Monday morning at school Gibbs did what he was wont to do when he wanted to make a point: He called an assembly. He explained to the student body that he supported the black athletes at the Olympics because they had achieved so much in working with their communities away from the track. But he questioned whether Joe had ever done anything for the community that gave him the right to stage such a protest. Two days later Gibbs personally summoned Joe to his office. "Have you ever worked on community problems, Joe?" he asked the student. "No," Joe replied. "Have you ever been to a city council meeting?" Gibbs asked. Again, Joe replied no. Then came the point Jack Gibbs wished to make to Joe: "You can go to college and have great input on the campus. You can come back as a

leader in the community and help us to change things, or you can stand
around some place in a corner holding your hand up."

Gibbs was also worried about crime. The East Side had the city's
highest crime rate, so to keep the minds of students away from mis-
chief, Gibbs made sure teachers kept the students constantly busy. East
High became part progressive laboratory, part military school, a place
that had high expectations for student achievement. He began a cultural exchange program, bringing in students from an all-white school to
interact with East High students in daylong activities and conversation.
Many of the white students freely admitted they had no black friends,
had never had black friends, and knew little of black culture besides
stereotypes they gleaned from the media. Administrators of the white
school then returned the invitation and hosted the black students of
East High at their school, which actually had been a condition outlined
by Gibbs when he first proposed the idea. "What made East different,"
says Zita Range Moses, "is that it was ahead of its time. Jack Gibbs was
a networker. He brought in different people to talk to the students. East
High was a career center before the city had a career center."

Gibbs wanted each student to feel important. If you were just returning to school from a hospital stay, it would be announced on the school
loudspeaker. The same would happen if it happened to be your birthday.
"You can't imagine," Gibbs said, "what it means to a student to have
people wishing him 'happy birthday' all day."

Appearing before audiences outside of Columbus, Gibbs felt comfortable talking about the unfair perceptions of his school. Giving a lecture on the campus of Central State University in Wilberforce, Ohio,
he admitted he received a lot of phone calls from people asking about
the pregnancy issue. "I tell them it's just the same as at any other school.
The difference is that our students go to the general hospital and become
statistics, while in the suburban schools, the girls are sent away somewhere and the whole thing is hushed up." He then talked about Upper
Arlington, the kind of place you read about in a John Cheever story—
and the hometown of golf great Jack Nicklaus: "The same thing goes
for the police reports. In Upper Arlington the kids get in just as much

trouble, but it's handled in the back room of the police station because the parents have influence."

With all of the daily challenges of running an inner-city school, Jack Gibbs seemed to thrive on the pressure. If he failed, he told himself time and time again, it might be a mighty long time before another black became a high school principal in the city.

There was a rule: Radios could not be played in the school. But it was nearly impossible to enforce. Pocket-sized radios were stashed in hallway lockers, in purses; black America thrived on music. Gibbs finally gave in because he realized the powerful influence music had always had on blacks, its contributions to the strength and daily survival of black America. Gospel hymn singing had kept people's spirits strong on southern plantations. Street corner musicians in cities became popular in the 1940s and 1950s. And doo-wop caught on just as jazz had done. During the 1968–69 school year, Gibbs decided to go look for Mel Griffin, one of the many seniors he had come to trust. Griffin had been making some on-air public service announcements for radio station WVKO, getting an introduction to radio. Gibbs thought Griffin had been handling his radio work quite nicely. Gibbs asked Griffin to set up a makeshift radio studio inside the school and to play music for the lunch crowds. Suddenly, for two hours every day, the Tiger lunchroom was full of sweet soul music. It wasn't very loud, lest nearby classrooms be disturbed, but it was loud enough to get the students swaying and tapping their feet. Griffin had a robust collection of 45s, the small records that contained a song on each side and were popular at the time. The main record stores in the city that sold black music were the Miami Record Shop, on Miami Avenue, and Early's Record Shop, on Mount Vernon Avenue, both within walking distance of East High. (One could also hustle downtown, where Kresge's Department Store—bowing to the times—had set up a little record section that specialized in soul music.) Griffin recruited Chris

The 1969 East High Rainbow Ball was seen as an antidote to the misery of the King assassination and racial unrest in the city.

Dixon, a fellow senior, to join him. Betty Cupoli, a faculty member, was assigned to oversee the in-house radio operation. It was doubtful that an all-white administration would have allowed music to be piped into the cafeteria, but this was Jack Gibbs's school, and he believed—as his students did—that the music of Marvin Gaye, Nina Simone, Sly and the Family Stone, and others had a powerful relevancy to what was going on in America. "We played music by the Friends of Distinction, the Temptations, the Supremes, the Chi-Lites, the Delfonics," Griffin recalls. "I was the first one at East High to play 'Oh Happy Day' by the Edwin Hawkins Singers. It was a gospel tune that Hawkins brought into the mainstream of contemporary music, making it a genuine crossover hit."

The radio room was just around the corner from the cafeteria. It was a swaying scene, knots of students with their Afros pouffed skyward, boys in leather jackets and turtlenecks and bell bottoms, girls in skirts and tight blouses. Whenever one of the popular basketball or football players walked into the cafeteria, conversations shifted and necks craned. Their popularity never diminished. But the nearly anonymous varsity baseball players were mostly ignored.

.   .   .

There was an annual cotillion in the Columbus black community, an event during which the daughters of the black upper-middle class were feted. It was a night of glittering gowns and white gloves. The young black teens who were invited did not attend a gritty school like East High. They came from Bishop Hartley and Eastmoor. To combat any feelings of inadequacy the young girls at his school might have because they couldn't attend a cotillion, Jack Gibbs organized what he called East High's Rainbow Ball. It was a formal affair also. He had a runway built and a platform. The community made a big deal about the event. As teacher Phillip Pool recalls, "Jack said, 'Hey, it's not only the wealthy families that can have a ball. We can do it too!' And at the ball, every young lady who was graduating would be introduced to society. Jack would read off where they were going to college. Dads would dance with their daughters." Amos Lynch, editor over at the *Call and Post*, the weekly black newspaper, would send Mirt Wood, his photographer, over to the ball to get plenty of photos. Then those photos would be splashed across several pages of the newspaper. (The flagship edition of the *Call and Post* was located in Cleveland. The Columbus edition had quite a healthy readership.) "That was his way of giving something to the girls who couldn't afford cotillion," student Zita Moses says of Gibbs and his Rainbow Ball.

There might not have been a PTA member at the school who was more excited about the annual Rainbow Ball than Mrs. Wynn, a school volunteer. She was always at the school. "We called her 'Ms. East'" says Pool. Mrs. Wynn seemed to be living for the day when her daughter, Dottie, would be a senior and could go to the ball. But when Dottie's senior year rolled around, she announced she wasn't going. She was very self-conscious about being overweight. Dottie's Tiger friends tried to get her to change her mind, but she would not. "We went to Dottie," remembers Pool, "and said, 'You are breaking your mom's heart.'" It was early afternoon on the day of the ball when Dottie finally said she would go. "We had to run around and get her a dress! We got her there that night," says Pool, "and she was presented. Oh, it was really something else."

There was little that seemed to slow the tide of young men in their twenties who gathered around the school during recess looking for young female students. In Gibbs's mind, he had done all he could by hosting the Rainbow Ball as a way of elevating the sense of pride he wished the community to have in the female students. He did not want these black girls to become casualties of teenage pregnancies. He did not want them devoured by street life. But these young men cavorting around the school were fast talkers, hustlers, pimps. They sat on the hoods of their cars, legs crossed, a cocked hat on their heads—in good weather there would be soul music blaring from the car radio—inviting East High coeds to go with them for a ride. Sandy's, a hamburger joint on nearby Mount Vernon Avenue, was a popular destination. So was Spencer's, which specialized in Coney Dogs, with their "secret recipe" chili sauce. The vice squad at the downtown police department showed little inclination to aggressively pursue small-town local pimps. But the presence of those pimps, mostly based on the East Side of the city, did not go unnoticed by parents, and especially by Jack Gibbs.

Coast-to-coast street literature of the 1960s boosted the notoriety of the Columbus, Ohio, pimps. They borrowed the prestige of such characters and swaggered about, living off it like currency.

In 1967, Robert Beck, a former Chicago convict, published the book *Pimp: The Story of My Life*. It was a blunt treatise about the pliable women who came under his spell and fell into a dark side of life involving prostitution and drugs. He'd beat the women on a whim, then whisper to them about love and devotion. Many of the girls came from broken homes, and many had children in their early teen years. The Beck memoir, a hot seller, was less an allegory and more a braggart's tale of ruining lives. Damn the literary reviews—which were few, anyway, even as some urban dwellers deemed the book a "classic"—*Pimp* caught on as a primer on how to live a certain kind of life. Just as in the Beck book, the more colorful the street moniker, the better known the pimp seemed to become. Beck's nom de plume was "Iceberg Slim," a name he had earned because in confrontational situations, with police or fellow criminals who were about to strike him, he remained preternaturally cool. In Columbus, everyone seemed to know of Precious Herb and Sweet Jesus. But the best known pimp in the city needed no embellishment. He was Calvin Ferguson—handsome, well built, and with the gift of gab. He had learned how to mix cocktails in his early teens. He had also been one of the more promising student-athletes in the mid-1950s at East High School. The local police had a file on him.

During his youth in Columbus, Calvin Ferguson sat at the feet of his father, a bartender who hailed from North Carolina and who now worked at the Yacht Club, on Mount Vernon Avenue. (There wasn't a yacht in sight, nor a man who owned a yacht. It was an inside joke.) Inside the Yacht Club, aside from the pretty women, there was doo-wop, bourbon, and young Calvin Ferguson, a kid entranced by the tall tales he heard. Calvin listened to the men talk about women, scrapes with the law, and making money. It was the dawn of the 1950s, and he was old enough to smile and nod at the dark tales, but not wise enough to ignore the cockamamie monologues. There was simply too much laughter and raucous good times. At East High School, Calvin made the varsity football team in 1954 as a sophomore. He was a gifted halfback, and he started on the team again during his junior year, racing off tackle as teammate Jim Marshall brutishly cleared the way for him. (Marshall later had a celebrated career with the Minnesota Vikings in the NFL.) Before his senior football season got under way, Calvin took part in a prank: Someone had stolen a varsity letter—an *E*—out of a locker. It landed in Calvin's hands. He sold it to another student for $20. "I bought me a pair of pants with the money," he recalls years later. "I went to Spencer's to eat. It was $20 and I had a good time." But the theft was uncovered. The prankish deed cost him his spot on the football team his senior year.

The onetime football star was somewhat aimless after high school. There were no college scholarship offers because he hadn't played his final year of school. He helped form the Esquire Club, a mélange of neighborhood boys who liked nice clothes and girls and having a good time. They hosted dances, spinning records by Ray Charles, the Platters, Chubby Checker. They met in private homes, where their mothers complimented them on their manners and good taste. They thought they were world-beaters with their cocky strutting and silky clothes. But there were times Calvin Ferguson still itched to play football.

One day Ferguson heard about a local semi-pro football team, Garland's Equipment. He arranged a meeting with the coach, who had played for the national championship OSU Buckeyes: The coach was Jack Gibbs himself! Calvin Ferguson tried out, made the team, and was happy. "Oh man, we had beautiful uniforms. The owner treated us nice," Ferguson remembers. They played a lot of prison teams, going behind high barbed-wire fencing to face inmates who played with extra aggression because of their circumstances; they'd joke and dream about running right out the front gate, then chuckle it all off because of the armed guards. After three years, the semi-pro team folded. That's when Calvin Ferguson turned his attention full-time to girls, coercing them to work for him selling their bodies. He became a pimp. "I did what I had to do to survive," the onetime pimp says. He hung around East High for a simple reason: "East had beautiful girls," he says.

Jack Gibbs loathed Calvin Ferguson. Sometimes he'd spot Ferguson on Parkwood Avenue, on the east side of the school. He'd charge out the door and demand that he leave. Ferguson would do as ordered. Other days Gibbs would spot him on Taylor Avenue, on the west side of the school, and out the side door Gibbs would march again. It became a familiar routine played out between the pimp and the principal. The students skipped back and forth from window to window, watching Gibbs jawbone with Ferguson and other pimps. "Pimps just hung around the school," says Cynthia Chapman Kasey, a cheerleader at the time. "Gibbs put a stop to that."

There were students who were impressed by Calvin Ferguson. He had become a local celebrity in a city without celebrities. The coeds who wanted to be near Ferguson—without agitating Gibbs—would meet him away from East Broad Street. Some days Gibbs would get in his car and go looking for female students he thought were keeping company with Ferguson. He'd get riled up, his still fit and thick body tensing up as the car turned the corner from East Broad Street onto East Long Street, then looping over to Mount Vernon Avenue. Gibbs was so perturbed by

Ferguson's presence—sometimes Gibbs would spot the bold Ferguson sitting in his Cadillac right next to school grounds!—that he called an assembly. "He was condemning Calvin Ferguson," former student Skip Anderson says about that particular assembly. "He talked about Calvin having had this great football career at East, and then he turned to a life of crime. The speech was not that well received because there were kids who thought pimping was cool."

In 1968 Calvin Ferguson—cruising around town in a Cadillac Eldorado—heard that Bo-Pete Lamar was on the East High basketball team. He befriended Bo-Pete and would buy him a suit or shirts, because Bo-Pete liked nice clothes. "Bo listened to me. I didn't want him going down the wrong path," Ferguson says. In 1969 the pimp was run out of Columbus. "A friend of mine told me the police were going to put me in jail," he ruefully recalls. He landed in New York City, a desperate place in 1969, but a fine city for a pimp who had been run out of the Midwest.

So Calvin Ferguson and any other pimps who swirled about the school had to go, and the rascals who haunted the school had to go, and the girls who got pregnant had to go (city policy), and the disgruntled teachers complaining about Gibbs's disciplinary ways had to go. Jack Gibbs even kicked Sandra Montgomery off the cheerleading team because her Afro was too big. Gibbs didn't mind his students wearing Afros, but if a student was representing the school in some activity, and the hair became too big—wild and billowing like activist Angela Davis's Afro—then the principal would approach the student and tell them to trim it a bit. Sandra Montgomery wasn't going to trim her Afro, so she was off the team. The man who escaped poverty in Kentucky, who had talked and worked his way onto a winning college football team year after year, who had gotten his master's degree, who had kept his children in the house for five straight days after the murder of Martin Luther King Jr. because he convinced them that was the way to show respect, was going to do everything he could to make his high school mean something to the white citizenry and power structure of the city, and also to make it a matter of pride for the residents of the East Side of Columbus.

If Jack Gibbs was seen marching a student to his office for discipline, or shaming an alcoholic parent about their lack of focus on their child's education, or telling a black female teacher her skirt was just a little too short, or returning to the school in the evenings to check how the janitors had done their job, it was all because he was doing all he could to make the high school a source of true pride for the community. But there was another side to Jack Gibbs. He was so bighearted, so warm and generous, that it was little wonder his students, teachers, and the community at large came to, well, love him. Ruth, his wife, accepted his feverish commitment to the school, sometimes shaking her head, some-times with a smile. "One of the secretaries came to work one day," she recalls, "and my husband said, 'No, no. It's too cold.' She couldn't afford a good coat. My husband took her to get a coat." He knew the kids who had threadbare wardrobes, and he wanted to take them shopping also. He had seen crushing poverty growing up in Harlan, Kentucky. "Whatever those kids needed," Ruth Gibbs says, "he dug in his pocket and got them what they needed. He wanted all of them to know they were somebody."

Nothing excited Gibbs as much as when one of his seniors got a col-lege acceptance letter. More than a few of his seniors were bound for all-black Central State University, a two-hour drive from Columbus. If there wasn't a car in the student's family—and often there wasn't—Jack Gibbs would tell the student he was coming over on the weekend, that they were going to visit the school, but before leaving he would ride around the neighborhood and pick up the few other students who had been accepted into the school. His car would be full, and they would be rolling down the highway and singing East High School fight songs.

He had no hobbies, save for the students and the school. Some of the students called him an "Uncle Tom," an extremely derisive term when heaped upon any black person by another black. An insecure teacher or administrator might become extremely agitated at hearing such an accu-sation. Because Gibbs was full of confidence in himself and his mission, the slur simply sailed by his ears. He was beyond slurs and name-calling, as if he could instantly forgive any perpetrator because he had more important work to do.

On weekends he often cornered businessmen in the city and pleaded with them to sponsor yet another event for the kids. He bragged as much about the school's sports teams as he did about their participation in the *In the Know* quiz program, which pitted four students from one school against a team from another school on local TV. Phil Miller, Sue Williamson, Richard Smith, and Lisa Reed made up the Tigers' *In the Know* team. Sue Williamson might have been the brightest of the group. She organized evening study sessions in her home, setting out cookies and punch when other *In the Know* students trooped over. When the black kids from East High whipped the white kids from a suburban school, it was as if you could hear the whoops and hollering throughout the homes and housing projects on the East Side. East didn't win the *In the Know* crown that year, but when they were down 100 points to the well-heeled students of St. Francis DeSales High School and came storming back to win the contest, that might as well have been a championship.

When East High student Vonzell Johnson first began fighting in the Golden Gloves boxing tournaments in 1968 over at the state fairgrounds, Gibbs had no idea. He found out about it and summoned Johnson to his office. "Why didn't you tell me?" the former Golden Gloves boxer asked Johnson, who wondered if Gibbs was going to disapprove of his boxing. "We have to announce the results of your fights. I want the school to know about this." Johnson won the national amateur title in 1974. In his first twenty-three pro fights, he was 22–1. He was a feared light heavyweight. In the ring, before the starter's bell, he'd often be singing a little ditty from the Bolivar Arms housing projects, where he had lived while attending East High: "Our neighborhood is classy; we have rats as big as Lassie." In 1981 he fought in Atlantic City for the world light heavyweight title and lost a close, bruising battle to Matthew Saad Muhammad.

When yet another former East High student was killed in Vietnam and Gibbs sensed how forlorn the student body was, he'd surprise everyone by getting on the school loudspeaker and announcing there'd be a dance the following night at the Valley Dale Ballroom. Gibbs would thumb through his Rolodex once again and finally find some community do-gooder willing to foot most of the bill for the dance. You could hear the happy howls in the school. (Frank Sinatra and Bing Crosby had crooned at the Valley Dale back in the 1940s. It had been, and remained, a lovely old vintage ballroom out on Sunbury Road.) Jack Gibbs would stand and watch over his students, his kids, as they sashayed and danced. He was truly happy. His kids knew how to look out for one another. And they did so many things when he wasn't looking that made him so proud. There were memories of East High student Henrietta Norman, born with a birth defect; she was confined to a wheelchair. Her smile was beyond tender. Every day at East High, students would debate about who was going to lift Henrietta, in her wheelchair, up and down the steps. They sometimes argued for the honor, lifting Henrietta with nary a complaint. It was a point of pride to get Henrietta to her next class on time. Any large football or basketball player coming down the hallway, spotting students around Henrietta, bulled them out of the way, lifted Henrietta in her wheelchair, and whoosh, they were gone, up, up, up. Henrietta died March 4, 1966, at eighteen years old. The student body set up a memorial scholarship in her name.

By the beginning of the 1968 school year, Jack Gibbs had the kind of school he wanted: tough, disciplined, respectful, and resilient. It was as if he had created his own version of a modern-day Rosenwald School.

So when student Chris Dixon started hollering one day in the basketball gym when another game was on the line and students and guests were all crowded inside, among them some board of education officials who had come to see the hot team at East High, everyone nervously looked when Principal Jack Gibbs rose from his seat. Was he going to tell Dixon to tamp the noise down? Kick him out of the game? All eyes remained glued on Gibbs as he made his way back toward Dixon. Then, in mid-stride, he reached down, took a bullhorn from one of the cheerleaders, and continued walking over to Dixon. He handed Dixon the bullhorn. And Chris Dixon knew exactly what to do with it. He raised the bullhorn to his mouth and started one of the best known school cheers:

> I went down to the river
> Oh yeah
> And I started to drown
> Oh yeah

I started thinking about them Tigers
Oh yeah
And I came back around

"We pulled him out of that back row and got him a cheerleading uniform," Gibbs later said about Chris Dixon, "and he was the best one we ever had." Everyone that day could see Jack Gibbs swaying, and singing, and hollering, and pumping his fists along with the entire gym. The whole collection of students and parents were up, out of their seats. "They loved him," says Louise Williams, Jack Gibbs's sister. "That's why they called East High 'the House That Jack Built.'"

· 4 ·

Momentum

By the time a high school athletic team gets beyond the first quarter of its season, a team identity has been established. Not only do the coaches better understand their players, but the players better understand one another and feel more secure in their collective roles. With the East High Tigers now angling toward the middle part of their 1968–69 season with a 6–0 record, team sensibilities were jelling. Roy Hickman knew that when Nick Conner went up for a rebound and yelled, "Go," it meant he should start streaking down court because Conner was going to let loose with a long pass. Larry Walker knew that when Ratleff and Conner crouched to initiate the full-court press on the opposing team, he should lurk nearby—like a getaway driver—because the ball would often be deflected by Ratleff or Conner right into his hands.

Bob Hart knew that when the Tigers dominated that tough team from Dayton early in the season, it was a good omen. His Tigers had defeated Dayton Dunbar in their second game of the season. Now, in their seventh outing, they had to travel seventy miles west of Columbus to face another Dayton team—Dayton Chaminade. Chaminade had been state champion three years earlier, a victory that was recent enough

Bob Hart preached unselfishness. The Tigers, left to right: Nick Conner, Dwight "Bo-Pete" Lamar, Larry Walker, Roy "Handsome" Hickman, Eddie "Rat" Ratleff.

that the team still walked in the glow of that accomplishment. Even from the confines of the locker room before the game, the East High varsity players could hear the roar of the Dayton crowd: The Chaminade reserve team had defeated the East High reserve team, 60–58, an hour before the varsity teams took to the floor. The Tiger varsity players were intent on seeking atonement and revenge for their underlings.

By the end of the first quarter, East High held a 30–13 advantage. Neither team made a first-quarter substitution. East kept up the intensity, and by halftime their lead was an impressive 48–27. The lack of substitutions by the Dayton coach sent a signal to the Chaminade fans that either he hoped to prevent a drubbing at all costs—and he was willing to exhaust his starters in the process— or he imagined that those starters would mount a successful comeback. Bob Hart matched the strategy quarter by quarter, also not making any player substitutions, keeping his starting five on the floor throughout. Hart's strategy prevailed; by the end of the third quarter his Tigers led, 67–47. The Dayton starters played hard into the fourth quarter, tightening the gap between the two teams, but it was hardly enough; the final score was 78–65. Eddie

Rat, a nemesis of every Dayton team since his sophomore season, scored 25 points. Bo-Pete Lamar, no stranger to Daytonians either, walked off the floor having chipped in 21 points. His ten field goals left many in the crowd in awe; a lot of his shots were launched from a bombs-away distance.

In the days ahead, Ohio reporters were rubbing their hands together in anticipation of the looming matchup between Columbus East and Cleveland East Tech. Traffic on Interstate 71 heading south, from Cleveland to Columbus, was always heavy when Cleveland East Tech came to the state capital. Both teams had formidable reputations and a large fan base. On game day, their respective followers packed the Columbus Fairgrounds Coliseum. The reporters who arrived early began setting up their typewriters and checking the teletype machines. Following their morning trip to Columbus, the Cleveland players glided from the parking lot into the tunnel of the arena, many sporting the be-bop and Apple and stingy brim hats that had become so sartorially cool because of a series of blaxploitation movies popular in urban theaters—*The Split, Putney Swope, Black Jesus*. The two teams bumped into each other while walking around the Coliseum. "I remember we were standing around before the game," says Larry Walker of East High. "They were wearing these Apple hats. They were saying they were going to kick our butts." Nick Conner and Eddie Rat were undemonstrative figures away from the court. They could be as quiet as museum guards. They certainly heard the bragging from the East Tech players, but they refused to engage their cocky rivals. Their disposition only added to their mystique. Roy Hickman, however, glowered. He did not like the pre-game bragging by the East Tech players. The players from both teams strutted to their respective locker rooms like agitated peacocks. In the huddle before tipoff—the Coliseum boisterous with more than three thousand spectators—Larry Walker looked at Roy Hickman, who looked at Eddie Rat, who looked at Bo-Pete, who looked at Nick Conner, who looked back at point guard Larry Walker, who said to everyone: "We're gonna kick their asses."

And it was East High's Hickman who did a lot of the ass kicking. He hit three baskets in the second quarter, thrilling the crowd and giving East a 29–17 lead. East would hit on 48 percent of its field goal attempts; by the middle of the fourth quarter, they had put the game out of reach. Cleveland fans were stunned. The stylish be-bop hats on some of the men in the Coliseum seats were pulled off and on and even yanked clean off their heads in frustration. Hart cleared his bench with five minutes left, the time-honored gesture of many winning coaches to the vanquished team at the other end of the court. Hickman finished with 19, Ratleff with 22. The game ended as an ignominious defeat for the Cleveland team, 85–59.

As one of the schools constructed in Columbus in 1963 to contend with white flight—in this instance from the Linden-McKinley area—Brookhaven High sat in the northern reaches of the city. By the time the 1968 athletic season rolled around, it had only been fielding teams for five years. It was not idle chatter to say that East High's athletes often played sports—basketball, baseball, football—as if their lives depended on it, because often they did: Scholarships and futures were genuinely at stake. At Brookhaven High, the athletes were not playing for such high stakes. Sports were extracurricular entertainment, especially in those early years before the school had a chance to fashion an athletic identity. Losses could be yawned away. Life in the suburbs with Mom and Dad was comfortable and quite nice. There were no civil rights movement clashes or fallout in the neighborhoods surrounding Brookhaven High. So when East High embarrassed Brookhaven, 89–35, to climb to 9–0 for the season, no one at Brookhaven fell apart. Who cared if some black kids from the East Side rode roughshod over our boys? The nights were velvet, even in wintertime. On television that year Andy Griffith was protecting the all-white town of Mayberry. Fred MacMurray was the dad in the all-white world showcased on *My Three Sons*. But the inner city was finally creeping into TV: there was also the police drama *The Mod Squad* and its character, Link, played by Clarence Williams III, who had the biggest and most stylish Afro in all of television land.

In time, the college recruiters began following the East High Tigers everywhere. Coaches from the West Coast who had games in New York City swooped down on Columbus to catch a look at Eddie Rat and

Nick Conner, but Bo-Pete Lamar wasn't on anyone's big-time recruiting radar just yet. Even though there were still several superb and undefeated teams in the city, East High had climbed to the top of the state rankings. It was a heady feeling to be wooed by colleges. These were looming opportunities the players' parents had never experienced. "We really wanted Ratleff and Conner. Then we all started paying attention to Bo Lamar because he could really shoot," recalls Joe Roberts, an assistant coach at Western Michigan at the time and one of the very few black assistant basketball coaches in Division 1, the largest division in college athletics. Roberts had his eye on what was going on at East because he had graduated from the school in 1957 and had a brief pro career before going into coaching.

The seniors on the East High basketball team had pretty much made a collective decision: They were not going to go to college anywhere below the Mason-Dixon Line. Their mothers had warned them not to entertain such offers, and the saga of Randy Smith at William and Mary—the racial taunts he had suffered, his leaving the school after just one season—had affected them all. Eleven of the twelve players on the East High team had southern roots. The murder of fourteen-year-old Emmett Till in 1955 in rural Mississippi had made headlines and radio broadcasts thirteen years earlier, but the heart-thumping fear planted in the hearts of black mothers of young boys was still very much alive. "My mother was afraid of any of her thirteen kids going down south, for reasons like Till," remembers East High student Vonzell Johnson.

Moses Wright had, at great risk, identified in court the white men who had murdered Till. Wright had to bolt Mississippi immediately after the murder happened. One of his destinations was Columbus, Ohio. He was coming to tell what happened in those dark woods to the black teenager who was his great-nephew.

AN INTERLUDE

What the Mothers Feared Most

It happened before Rosa Parks sat on that bus, before Martin Luther King Jr. set foot in Columbus in 1956, when he preached just blocks from East High. It happened before four little girls were blown up in a Birmingham church, and it happened before voting rights activist Medgar Evers was gunned down in his Mississippi driveway. And because Emmett Till was "just a child"—as the black church women lamented in their pews for months after it happened—it was thought to be the tragedy that ignited the galvanizing, soul-stirring, and nation-shaking civil rights movement. In the late summer of 1955, here is what a determined black Chicago woman had made up her mind she was going to do: She was going to get her slain son back to Chicago, and she was going to invite the nation—the world even—to see what those racist murderers had done to her Emmett down in Mississippi. She had made up her mind that his casket would be open. It was as if she had convinced herself that she had no other recourse but to force humanity to look at the gruesomely disfigured face and body of her son. The nation—especially black folk—were aghast, sure enough. More than fifty-thousand mourners would eventually view the battered body. *Jet* magazine, based in Chicago, published photographs of young Emmett. It wasn't long after that the thunder of the civil rights movement was in full motion. Emmett Till was both dead and alive. But in looking at the Till family, one could actually feel the gyrations—and possible psychological depth—of black America and its torment even beyond American shores. It helps to peer into World War II and the life of a soldier named Louis Till, the father of Emmett Till.

In many cases the life of an orphan can be sad, disrupted, and unpredictable. Louis Till had two strikes against him: He was black, and when he was born in 1922 he was sent to an orphanage in segregated Missouri. He came of age honing devious habits. As he grew up, he leaned into life with a nasty disposition hidden by a charming smile. He'd get liquored up and become violent. He slapped and beat Mamie, the woman he married when they were both teenagers. They had one child, Emmett. She feared her son would be subjected to violence, so she eventually filed charges against her husband. More domestic violence followed. A judge told twenty-year-old Louis Till he had two options: a jail sentence, or World War II military service. The wife beater shipped off to Uncle Sam's segregated army. Soon enough he found himself in the European theater. In Italy he worked on a transportation detail. On the night of June 27, 1944, near the small town of Civitavecchia in Italy, three local women were brutally assaulted: Two were raped, and a third woman was shot and killed. The surviving women stated that they had been attacked by four men. An investigation led the army to arrest three black soldiers and a white British soldier. One of the black men admitted that all four had taken part in the crimes. He also admitted that Till—possibly a sociopath—was the one who had initiated the crime spree and had done the shooting. Till remained silent during his arrest and court-martial. On July 2, Till and Fred McMurray—the black soldier who confessed— were hanged in Italy.

It wasn't just the guilt of Louis Till and the others that would be debated in the years to come. It was also the starkly different judicial treatment meted out to blacks and whites during World War II. Between the years 1943 and 1946 in Europe, seventy American GIs were sentenced to judicial executions. Although blacks made up only 8.5 percent of the military, they comprised 80 percent of those who were hanged. This was the type of inequality that Army Lt. Col. Bob Hart covered in his senior thesis at Ohio Wesleyan University. And this was why the boys on the basketball team at East High School meant so much to him. Beyond the bouncing of the basketballs, he was aware, more than most, of American history and the rickety ladder blacks had to grasp and climb to success.

Mamie Till (née Bradley) did not have many lovely stories to tell her only son about his father, and Chicago was a difficult place to be without a father. In the summer of 1955, Mamie sent Emmett to spend time with relatives in Mississippi. A little country living, she thought, would certainly do him good. And she wanted him to spend time with male relatives. "Avoid trouble," she instructed her only child.

A fourteen-year-old Chicago youngster who had to grow up too fast without a father thoroughly convinced himself he possessed big-city smarts. He wouldn't have been much intimidated by the customs of segregation. So when Emmett Till arrived in Mississippi that summer to spend time with relatives, among them his great-uncle Moses Wright, he had no experience of living the way his black relatives down south lived—being careful to hold their tongue and not whistling in the company of white women. Matter of fact, he bragged about white girls he had dated back in Chicago. His cousins listened with rapt awe. Like many enduring those humid summer days in the Delta, Emmett couldn't resist an opportunity to take a trip to the local country store on that narrow road in Money, Mississippi. The place had shelves of candy and potato chips and cigarettes and cool soft drinks and other items. Emmett had seen big, fancy stores of all kinds up in Chicago, and he was also happy to regale relatives about visits to those places. Once inside Bryant's Grocery and Meat Market, he began looking around. And that's where he first laid eyes on Carolyn Bryant. She was twenty years old and owned the store with her husband, Roy. Roy was a military veteran, an unrepentant racist, and he happened to be away on a fishing trip the Wednesday evening that Emmett strolled in. What Emmett Till did in that store might have seemed harmless and a little flirty and utterly forgettable if he had been visiting one of those white ethnic grocery stores up in Chicago. But in Mississippi, in 1955, he crossed a line: He either whistled—the most common version of the story that swept the world—or winked, or tried to caress her hand, or smiled too suggestively at Carolyn Bryant. Whatever he did, it unnerved her, and she mentioned this young unknown, fresh "nigger" to her husband as soon as he arrived back in town. Roy went into a rage.

It didn't take a lot of wits to play country detective, and Roy Bryant quickly found out that Emmett Till was the great-nephew of Moses Wright, a local cotton farmer. Bryant rustled up his brother-in-law, J. W.

Milam, in the middle of the night and rode out to Wright's little shack of a home. Carolyn Bryant was in the car. Bryant and Milam banged on Wright's door. Wright was a bony stick of a figure with very dark skin. Mississippi, and all she stood for, had crushed so much out of Moses Wright through the years. He opened the door. An unarmed black man now faced two armed white men in the middle of the night. Bloodshed was a mere whistle away. The two men demanded to see Emmett, who was in the back of the house asleep. Wright didn't want any trouble; he imagined some kind of misunderstanding, and surely it could be worked out. He took the men to where Till was sleeping. They pulled the youth outside, to the car; all the while Wright was stepping to keep up, his heart pumping fast, wondering about the evil intentions of these two white men. They showed Emmett to Carolyn Bryant and asked if this was the boy who had come into the store. She said yes. They then forced a terrified Till into the car and drove away. Moses Wright called the police and reported that Emmett had been kidnapped. The policemen were intent on apprehending the men who Wright told them had taken Emmett. Wright then called Till's mother in Chicago to tell her that her son had been kidnapped by white men. She knew Mississippi, and she feared the worst.

Emmett may have been just a child, a stout kid really, about to enter high school. But none of that made any difference to his abductors. He was taken to a shed miles from Moses Wright's place and was beaten mercilessly. Then he was shot in the back of his skull. Using a rope, his killers then tied him to a big fan and dumped his body into the Talla-hatchie River. Another kid later discovered the body and ran to get the sheriff. Moses Wright identified the body; Emmett was wearing a signet ring that had "LT" on it, the initials of his father, Louis Till. Milam and Bryant were arrested and charged.

White America had to see this. President Eisenhower had to know about this. Which is why Mamie Bradley insisted that her son's body be brought back to Chicago. It arrived at the Illinois Central Railroad sta-tion. Bradley saw her son's face was torn and smashed, completely unrec-ognizable. After studying his body, Mamie Bradley, seemingly beyond rage now and feeling for vulnerable young black boys everywhere, told the funeral home she wanted an open casket. They cautioned her that she might wish to rethink her decision given the condition of the body. The dead boy's eye sockets bulged out like huge rocks. His jaws were grotesquely swollen. She still adamantly insisted on an open casket and public viewing "so everyone can see what they did to my boy." The public viewing stretched across two days—people fainted, ministers railed, and the story remained front-page news around the country for an entire week. International news outlets carried coverage about the crime. *Jet* magazine published the stark photos of Till's mangled face. Emmett Till's ghastly murder became a signature moment in the nascent civil rights movement. And it was a deep stain on the American justice system, because the U.S. Department of Justice in Washington steered clear of the case. Roy Wilkins, the highest-ranking official in the NAACP, said, "It would appear from this lynching that the state of Mississippi has decided to maintain white supremacy by murdering children."

Considerably more had been opened up than just the lid of a casket. The whole way of life in small-town Mississippi—with its fear and tyranny—had been exposed as never before.

Moses Wright had to get out of Mississippi. He had been an eyewitness to the kidnapping. In the immediate aftermath of the incident, he had sometimes taken to sleeping in the woods with a rifle for his own safety. The NAACP realized as much and quickly got him to Chicago, where he was able to commiserate with his niece, Mamie Bradley. He was soon off to New York City, because the NAACP hierarchy wanted him and Mamie Bradley to go on a nationwide speaking tour to help raise awareness of southern brutality and injustice. The two decided to go to separate cities to reach a wider number of audiences. The tour had a long and blunt title: "The National Prayer Mobilization Against Racial Tyranny and Intolerance in Mississippi and Elsewhere." "Mississippi hasn't got any law," Moses Wright said before one gathering. Mamie Bradley was scheduled to appear in, among other cities, Dayton, Cleveland, and Columbus, Ohio. But there were late disruptions in her schedule, and she asked her uncle, Moses Wright, to visit those cities and speak on her behalf. Speaking to a full house at the Tabernacle Baptist Church in Dayton, Moses Wright felt compelled to answer a question he had been asked while out on the road: How come he didn't intervene and fight off the two men who kidnapped Emmett right in front of him? "It didn't make no sense to fight when a man has a .45 in his hand," he explained.

In Columbus, William Durham of the NAACP—a constant presence on the city's East Side fighting for equal rights—played host to Wright. Durham was one of the NAACP's most respected representatives in the region and handled Wright's financial compensation for both the Dayton and Columbus visits. Durham informed Wright he'd receive $100 for his Dayton appearance, and another $100 for his Columbus appearance. "Can't you make it $150 plus expenses?" a relative of Wright's asked Durham. "Uncle doesn't have a suit of clothes. He had to leave everything he had down there, crops and all." Durham agreed to the fee increase. Durham didn't plan on taking any chances with Wright's safety in Columbus, so he arranged a police escort. "It will add to the drama of our meeting" he said, aware that this would be good for marketing and publicity. At the gathering in Columbus, Wright looked exhausted and a little bewildered from all the traveling. He told the people the same thing he had told the other assembled groups: Mississippi was lawless and evil. He told them how much he worried about the upcoming trial. He told them blacks in Mississippi lived in daily fear.

Those who had seen Moses Wright in Columbus, would not easily forget his appearance.

Meanwhile, back in Mississippi, a Tallahatchie County grand jury indicted Bryan and Milam for Till's kidnapping and murder. On September 20, a Mississippi prosecutor presented overwhelming evidence, including solid testimony from some surprise witnesses who also had been in hiding, that Roy Bryant and J. W. Milam had kidnapped Till. Moses Wright told the courtroom that Bryant and Milam had kidnapped his nephew. Wright was a smallish man; J. W. Milam was hulking. To Murray Kempton, a New York reporter inside the courtroom, Wright was "a black pygmy standing up to a white ox."

The defense's argument was that the body of Till was so mangled that there was no way to definitively establish that it was Till. They opined that Till might have fled the state and might be hiding anywhere up north. During the trial, local whites first heard the story of Louis Till having been hanged in Europe by military authorities in 1945 after he was found guilty on charges of rape and murder. An all-white jury—its own native prejudices further poisoned by Louis Till's military record—acquitted both Bryant and Milam of murder in just sixty-seven minutes. Whites inside the courtroom nodded their approval and slapped backs. There was sweaty laughter. In response, former first lady Eleanor Roosevelt wrote, "It is true that there can still be a trial for kidnapping, and I hope there will be. I hope the effort will be made to get at the truth. I hope we are beginning to discard the old habit, as practiced in part of our country, of making it very difficult to convict a white man of a crime against a colored man or woman." Her hopes were dashed. Another grand jury acquitted the men of the kidnapping charge. Protected by double jeopardy, the accused men later admitted they had killed Till. This was the story they told to the ethically unbalanced journalist William Huie, who paid the men to talk.

Of course, it wasn't just Mississippi. It was the entire American South that could elicit fear. A year after Emmett Till's death, Joe Roberts, who had been a senior at East High School in Columbus in 1956 and was a star on the school's basketball team that year, begged his parents to allow him to return to Alabama to visit friends. School was out and it was summertime. The Roberts family hailed from Lanette, Alabama, and had moved to Columbus in the late 1940s. Roberts's parents were against the trip, but he kept pleading. The students and families he wished to visit were people he had known from his Alabama childhood. Finally, the family relented when an uncle told them he'd allow Joe to drive his new Pontiac, relieving them of their worry that he might experience mechanical problems on the long drive. Joe loaded up the car and took off from Columbus. A couple days later, he crossed the state line into Alabama. "I rode into this gas station," he would recall years later. "I was driving my uncle's brand-new Pontiac. This white guy came over and started calling me names. I knew I had to get out of there. From 1956 to 1985, I never went back to Alabama."

In 2007, the United States Senate passed the Emmett Till Unsolved

Civil Rights Crime Act. The bill was designed to provide funds and resources to investigate civil rights murders between the years 1955 and 1969. The organizers of the bill realized just how real civil rights killings remained throughout the South up through 1969 and that justice needed to be found for the victims.

Not long after the Till Unsolved Crime Act was passed, Carolyn Bryant—now Carolyn Bryant Donham—confessed to author Timothy Tyson that she had lied about Emmett Till. He had never touched her, she told the author, who in 2017 published a book about her confession and the case. It was all a damnable lie, a lie that ran deeper than the Mississippi River, a lie and a horror that weighed on black America for generations, a lie that propelled black mothers out of the South.

When the 1968 calendar flipped over to 1969, the nation was still contending daily with reverberations from the King assassination. High school superintendents and teachers across the country were reporting more student activism. Black students in particular were threatening school walkouts at an alarming rate. Their complaints revolved around school reading lists, the racial makeup of cheerleading squads, the right to protest perceived injustices. Jack Gibbs held gatherings inside East High to talk about the teachings of Dr. King. The simmering tensions made him nervous, as he explained to a group of educators: "We've got 18 groups in our community, anywhere from the Urban League at one extreme to Black Panther type groups at the other extreme, but we have all these groups doing something constructive for our school. People can do two things with a brick: They can throw it at you or they can carry it for you, and I want those people carrying bricks for East High School."

At the beginning of the year, stories showed up daily in the Columbus newspapers and elsewhere about the aftermath of the King assassination. Many blacks were calling for a governmental probe. James Earl Ray was saying he was looking for a new set of lawyers. The word "conspiracy" took on new weight. The white school officials in Columbus spent a lot of time worrying about the student political leaders inside Linden-McKinley, West, and East high schools. Winter in the Midwest seemed somewhat to slow high school talk of rebellion. And at East High, Jack Gibbs figured if he could keep the students busy—academics, sports, music—he would have a good chance of keeping the school under control. And while he contentedly welcomed discussions about King's life among faculty and students, he continued to monitor carefully any signs of agitation or threatened rebellion. It helped that the basketball team was winning and remained a powerful marquee attraction.

The only students allowed to run up, down, and along the labyrinth hallways of East High were athletes, and that was only after the final bell of the school day had rung. (Pity the male student wearing hard-soled Stetson shoes caught running down the gleaming hallways of Jack Gibbs's school and leaving scuff marks. There would be after-school detentions.) As school commenced after the holiday break, a new group of athletes could be seen and heard running East High's steps and hallways. It was the baseball team, engaging in their own version of spring training. Hardly anyone paid attention to the baseball team. During the previous season, attendance at some of the home games had been in the single digits, a laughable fan base. But Assistant Basketball Coach Paul Pennell, also the head baseball coach, was happy to see his baseball players stretching, running, engaging in voluntary workouts. So Garnett Davis, Roger Neighbors, Robert Kuthrell, Richard Twitty, Phil Mackey, and other team members ran the hallways getting in shape. When he caught a glimpse of them, basketball star Eddie Rat realized how much he himself couldn't wait for baseball season. He was the team's star pitcher.

Fresh into the new year, Bob Hart had to prepare right away to face two teams—South High and West High—that could not be taken lightly. South was second in the City League standings, impressive enough to be ranked fourth in the state, and, like East, undefeated. West High had a gritty team, featuring Mike Stumph, one of the top centers in the state and the second highest scorer in the city behind Ed Ratleff. Athletic officials wished they could have scheduled the South High game at the fairgrounds, but the Coliseum had already booked another event for that week. The matchup was going to be a huge draw wherever the teams played. The game got shifted to South High School—Bob Hart's alma mater.

There were four high schools in the city whose basketball courts were built on a raised stage: Central, South, East and West. It was a stylistic feature of these older schools, and it gave the games played upon those stages an extra bit of theatrical drama. For players who were not used to playing in such a confined space, the court could create problems, a sudden feeling of vertigo inside the fast-moving action when one realized there was a drop-off into an offstage pit. But East High's cagers knew the dimensions of the floor very well and had adjusted their game to it.

Tickets for the South vs. East matchup sold out within an hour. "It was the hottest thing going," remembers South High guard Terry Holliman. "At school, everybody was hyped up." Dick Ricketts, the South High coach, told his players that they could beat East. "Everything would have to go right," he told Holliman and his teammates. During pre-game warm-ups for the Friday night game, school janitors at South High had to scramble and bring in extra chairs. The crowd kept swelling until a school official announced no more people would be let in. At the end of the first quarter, East was up by only two, 13–11. The foot stomping upon bleachers sounded like the hooves of horses breaking from a barn. The noise inside the South High gym was so loud both coaches had to scream instructions to their players while cocooned inside the huddle. In the second quarter, South High's sweet shooting guard Brad Hoffman had time and space in the corner to launch another jump shot. Like a giraffe rising up above a tree line, East's Nick Conner stretched in the direction of Hoffman and forcefully slapped the ball out of bounds. The Tiger fans roared. South's players seemed to come unglued. It was as if Conner had given the entire South High team a stern warning: that even on their home court, they were not safe. East scored 28 points in the second period while South only scored 14. At halftime the score was East 41, South 25.

In the second half, Bo-Pete Lamar, with prodding from Coach Hart, went to work. He began firing from long range, some of the shots from beyond twenty-five feet. South fans followed the arc of each shot when it left his hands, then blinked in disgust when it swished through the net. Of the seven shots he took, he misfired on only one. The South High Bulldogs also had a wicked time contending with East High's full-court press. They committed 21 turnovers, giving the ball away like cheap raffle tickets. With two minutes to go, the Tigers were leading 71–55, and Bob Hart decided to remove his starters from the game. He quickly regretted it. South clawed back as East turned the ball over several times. "If you had one turnover," recalls East High's Larry Walker, "you were going to be sitting." The action was fast, and Hart had to reinsert his starters. South didn't have enough time and the horn blew to end the game, with a final score of 71–66. Hart exhaled, happy to have escaped. He half grinned and half scowled. He was beginning to realize that Bo-Pete Lamar, with his shooting prowess, was a godsend. The game against the Bulldogs was Bo-Pete's breakout game as a Tiger: The senior guard scored 25 points. Lamar's fellow guard, Larry Walker, thought that Lamar was providing a secret and dangerous ingredient to the team: "Coming into our senior season, we had no good outside shooters. I knew with Bo, we could always be in the hunt," Walker says.

Less than twenty-four hours later, the East High basketball team was back in uniform for another engagement, this one at West High. It was one of the schools in the city where many whites rebelled against black political aggressiveness, and the friction was felt almost daily. "There was racial tension in the school," concedes Mike Stumpf, the six-foot-six star of the West High team. "But not on the basketball court." Fred Heischman was coach of the West High Cowboys. He was an older coach, a retiring gentleman, and one who rarely raised his voice. East led at halftime, 37–28. A 9-point deficit was nothing for the Cowboys to be ashamed of; the West players imagined they were still very much in the game. Perhaps Coach Heischman would come up with a new defensive game plan to stop Bo-Pete Lamar, who was scoring from deep corners on the court. But he did not. Heischman remained unemotional, like a man whistling his way toward retirement. "I remember at halftime all he said was, 'Boy, they can surely shoot free throws,'" recalls Stumpf. Lamar was like a one-man campfire. He remained hot from having tamed South High, and he torched West High with jump shot after jump shot. By the end of the third quarter, East held a more comfortable double-digit lead, 64–43. "We had a full-court press," remembers East's Larry Walker. "No one from West could get the ball up court on us. Rat and Nick would be up front on the press. Someone would try to throw the ball over the top of them and that's when I could steal it." East held West's big man, Stumpf, to 18 points and won by a score of 71–58. Lamar tallied 25 points, the same number he had scored a day earlier. He was becoming more dangerous as the season went on.

There were those who would look at Bob Hart's players and wonder just how much coaching he actually had to do. The grumbling sometimes annoyed him, but he paid it little mind. They were mostly armchair analysts, jawboning from the comfort of Coliseum seats. Down on the court, with Ratleff slicing behind Conner for a perfectly thrown pass from Bo-Pete Lamar, or Roy Hickman suddenly appearing from ten feet out to accept a crisp pass from Kevin Smith, one could sense drawn-up plays, specific designs. Hart's full-court press looked like some kind of algorithm, with players subtracting and adding their presence depending on the amount of pressure needed. His Tigers had the ability to execute both classic basketball—clinical, methodical, fundamentally sound— and jazzy basketball, a spirited, stylish, free-form, and improvisational way of playing. "They were structured," says the West High player Mike Stumpf. "They were not only talented but disciplined. In order to have discipline, you have to have structure."

The young black boys of the East Side of the city—elementary and junior high kids—were already among East High's most fervent followers. (At the time, the local high schools didn't field girls' basketball teams.) But then the fever began to spread to the white sections of the city.

Dave Hanners was one of the young white kids in Columbus who became enamored of the 1968–69 East High basketball team. He played basketball for Johnson Park Junior High. He'd beg his folks to let him go to the Fairgrounds Coliseum to see East High play. He'd cadge a ride with Chuck Fowler, his junior high coach who happened to also be the announcer for the high school games at the Coliseum. Some still referred to the Coliseum as a cow palace because of the rodeos that took place there. Fowler loved the place; even the smell of manure didn't bother him. Fowler had gotten his first job working at the Coliseum back in the 1950s, when the locker rooms had potbellied stoves filled with coal to warm the players. He'd pile the coal in while the players were out on the arena floor. By the time the 1968–69 basketball season rolled around, Fowler was convinced he was looking at pure dynamism. "That's the reason he took me down there with him," Hanners recalls of Fowler and his desire to watch East High play. "He told me it was the greatest high school team, talent wise, he had ever seen," Hanners says. Hanners peppered the coach with questions during the ride to the Coliseum, wondering how the East High players learned to jump so high, to shoot with such lethal accuracy, to play with such controlled flair. Young Dave Hanners might as well have been stepping into some version of Xanadu. "They'd win by fifty," he says of the Tigers. "But they were gracious. They were running up the score and couldn't help it." If he wanted to get good, Hanners figured he had to go find where the East High players played during the summer. There was a funky playground on the East Side, at the corner of Main and Eighteenth, but the rims were sturdy and had nets, and the competition was always fierce. So he'd bum a ride to the playground and join in the pickup games. "I wanted to find the best caliber basketball players," he says. "It just so happened in Columbus the best players were black." The black players called him Youngblood. Sitting inside the Fairgrounds Coliseum, he'd get lost in his concentrated focus on the style and play of the East High team. "There was no one within five states like the three of them," he says of Ratleff, Conner, and Lamar.

Hanners himself played guard, so he paid particular attention to Bo-Pete Lamar: "He never got tired. He was fast. He could jump. He could dunk; he was only six foot two, and nobody did that. He was also a tremendous jump shooter. He took shots nobody else would take." The player in the professional basketball ranks who reminded Hanners of Lamar was Earl "The Pearl" Monroe, who was the National Basketball Association's 1968 NBA Rookie of the Year. Monroe had also been an All-American at Winston-Salem State College, which he had entered in 1963. A lot of the local kids couldn't stop talking about the night the Pearl came to the Fairgrounds Coliseum to play against the Cincinnati Royals, led by Oscar Robertson. It was only an NBA exhibition game since Columbus didn't have a professional team. But for every kid in the city who could get Mom and Dad or Aunt or Uncle to take them to the game, it was simply divine. There was Earl "The Pearl" in living color. "Bo-Pete was a better shooter than Monroe," Hanners believes.

Following their victories against South High and West High, East High prepared to face Walnut Ridge. The game would have a sentimental res-onance for both coaches: Jack Moore coached the Walnut Ridge team, the same Jack Moore who had been at East High years earlier and who had encouraged Bob Hart to come to the school. The two schools were genuine proof of a tale of two cities: Walnut Ridge boasted a student body of twelve hundred. They had one black student. "It was still quite a segregated mess," says Ed Stahl, a member of the Walnut Ridge bas-ketball team.

The game between the all-white school and all-black East High was played on Walnut Ridge's home court. Jack Moore's team had some tal-ented young players, among them Stahl, a six-foot-ten sophomore who had earlier in the season scored 27 points in a City League game. But every Walnut Ridge player realized the strength of the East High team. "We had such great respect for those guys," recalls Stahl. "They were the standard of excellence. Not only in the state, but in the country."

Greg Olson, a player on the Walnut Ridge team, was another white kid who dared to venture into black Columbus to play pickup games against the best players. "This was during the late 1960s during racially charged times," Olson recalls. "But we wanted to be like them," he says of the East High players. Everyone feared Ratleff and Conner, but East

High's Bo-Pete Lamar really worried Olson. "He was probably the most prolific scorer and creator I'd ever seen. He was rail thin and could really jump. He was cocksure of himself, to the point of borderline arrogance."

There were more than a few times when teams stayed close to East High for the first quarter of action. At the end of their first quarter, Walnut Ridge could be proud they trailed by only 4 points. But it was a cruel mirage. By halftime, Bob Hart's Tigers had exploded for a 20-point lead, the score 43–23. "I remember being in the three-second lane," recalls Olson. "I gotta do something. I ball fake. Nick Conner doesn't go for it. I shoot the ball. He knocks it fifteen rows up into the stands." By the end of the third quarter, the Tigers were up 31 points, 64–33. Eddie Rat had 34 points already. That was enough; Bob Hart sat him on the bench for the entire final period. The final score was 77–51. Equally impressive was that East High turned the ball over only eleven times, playing the role of Scrooge beyond the holiday season. Both Stahl and Olson of Walnut Ridge went on to fine college careers, but they never forgot their matchup against East High. "If you looked at them," Stahl recalls of the Tigers, "it was like a show. Some teams play with an aura. They earned it. They kind of moved like a marching band." Greg Olson was perhaps the most socially conscious player on his Walnut Ridge team. He had sat down that year and explained to his parents that the 1968 Fair Housing Act was going to be a good thing. Even in a large school with just a single black student, change was coming.

On the East Side of Columbus—and in the much smaller black pockets of the city—those visual displays were now becoming more noticeable than ever: There were portraits of the slain Martin Luther King Jr. displayed in retail shop windows, in barbershops and hair salons, on telephone poles, in community meeting halls, on the dashboards of the taxis operated by the all-black East Side Taxi Company. In emblem and portraiture, it was as if Martin Luther King Jr. were rising from the grave. Blocks from East High, over at Union Grove Baptist Church, King's longtime friend, Rev. Phale Hale, was already constructing a room devoted to his friendship with King and King's visits to the church.

Before Martin Luther King Jr. there had been no singular black figure who claimed, from church pulpit to street corner, the breadth and reach of his message across racial divisions.

There were only three games left before the start of district tournament play for the Tigers; they were within shouting distance of the City League title. But with their unblemished record, they were now most certainly thinking of bigger goals. In setting up his team's schedule at the beginning of the season, just as he had done in years past, Bob Hart was aggressive in arranging out-of-town matchups in the season's schedule. The strategy was twofold: His team just might meet one of those out-of-town squads in the state tournament, and already having played them would be of benefit. Secondly, the later games kept his team sharp and gave them a sense that if their coach feared no opponent, neither should they. So Cincinnati's Purcell Marian High School confidently entered the Fairgrounds Coliseum with an impressive 10–2 record, and featuring one of the state's best players in Derrek Dickey, the leading high school scorer in Cincinnati. True to form, the Tigers—like hungry animals lying in the shade until ready to sate their appetites—showed tricky benevolence toward Purcell, allowing the team from Cincinnati to race out to a 10–5 start. Then it happened: Ratleff scored, Conner scored, and Bo-Pete Lamar scored. East led by 7 points by the end of the first quarter. Their lead was even wider by the end of the first half, 51–26. East went on to whip Purcell, 83–65. Bo-Pete Lamar and Roy Hickman led the Tigers with 24 and 20 points respectively. Eddie Rat scored 15 points, well below his average. Some afternoons Bob Hart, because his team had such a scoring lead, had the comfort to sit Eddie Rat on the bench. A little rest for the golden boy. And Eddie Rat would sit there with the serenity of an old man on a park bench whiling away a weekend afternoon.

East High had two remaining games—Whetstone and Northland—on its City League schedule. Both schools played a role in the city's desire to retain a certain social order: Whetstone opened in 1961 and Northland in 1965, both to accommodate white flight from the inner city of Columbus. Neither school possessed the pedigree or talent to contend with the Tigers. The Whetstone matchup was first. The Whetstone reserve team whipped the East High reserve team, 51–44, and the Whetstone varsity players slapped the palms of their reserve players by way of congratulations. It would be their last moment of giddy joy for the evening. At halftime of the varsity game, East had doubled their lead, 35–17. By the end of the third quarter, it was 49–26. When Bob Hart relieved his starters in the fourth quarter, it meant the Tigers had secured the City League championship. The final score was 70–37. Whetstone's nervousness had showed in its anemic shooting percentage. They made just 16 of 62 field goal attempts, and committed 27 turnovers—the equivalent of giving money away at the bank teller's window. East High's starting five distributed the ball with an egalitarian flair: Ratleff and Walker had 12 points (nearly 20 below Ratleff's average), Conner 11, and Lamar 14. "It didn't matter who scored," Ratleff said years later. "We just wanted to win." Hart congratulated his players in the locker room for securing another City League title. But because they had bigger dreams so vividly in mind, they were rather calm. They showered and dressed like young men at the end of a business workday.

Northland was next, the final game for the Tigers before the start of district tournament play. It would have been hard to convince the Northland players of Ratleff's expressed sentiment that it did not matter who scored. In fact, he reminded Northland of his All-American stature by hitting for 33 points, while Bo-Pete Lamar tossed in 20. In a season already chock-full of scintillating moments, Bob Hart stared at the stat sheet in wide-eyed wonder after the game. His Tigers had hit 15 of 20 shots in the third quarter alone. They bested Northland by 40 points, the final score 100–60. The regular season was at a close.

Hart and Paul Pennell, the Tiger coaches, were convinced they had done as much as they could to make their team ready for the district, regional, and—should they get that far—the final games of the state tournament.

It had become evident deep into the season that the Tigers were doing things on the basketball court beyond the teachings of their coaches. They were doing things instinctually, carving up designed plays and improvising at the last minute, causing fans to rise from their seats as if they were at some kind of revival. Individually, they were all gifted players. But collectively, they were better than even the sum of their individual parts, a formula that seemed to naturally jell because Bob Hart refused to "over"-coach his team. He allowed them to impose their will on the opponent. And their cohesion had resulted, thus far, in an undefeated record.

Hart and other coaches from the Ohio High School Athletic Association met in February at the Willard Restaurant in Columbus to find out which tournament brackets they would be playing in. Every Class AA team would be invited to play in the tournament. Hart often found it difficult to look beyond the very next game. "He was always aware of playing one game at a time," Assistant Coach Pennell says.

When the tournament matchups were finally announced, East High drew an intriguing first-round game. They would be playing an assortment of young juvenile delinquents from the Boys Industrial School in Lancaster, Ohio. The young men were serving time for a variety of crimes, among them assault, robbery, breaking and entering. The inmates had their own high school on the grounds, Lancaster Reemelin. The East High coaches were a bit challenged trying to attain dependable scouting reports. "Their enrollment was fluid, month to month," recalls Pennell. "A player might be on their team one month, then his sentence is up and he suddenly gets released."

One of Reemelin's most famous alums was comedian Bob Hope, sent there May 18, 1918, from his home in Cleveland, charged with juvenile delinquency. Before the end of 1918, Hope was paroled, but back for a parole violation in March of 1919. He found the place grim and unfunny, so he escaped. The school authorities never heard from him again until he became rich and famous and started donating money.

Lancaster Reemelin was the kind of school that pained East High principal Jack Gibbs. The students were the dead-end kids, and he wondered how many boys were just being warehoused there without sufficient efforts at rehabilitation. He knew many came from broken homes. Still, when boys from the Boys Industrial School were released and came back to the East Side of Columbus, to East High, Jack Gibbs had a stern lecture ready for them: They would be given a solid second chance, but they would have to join the janitorial corps at the school. They would have to work themselves back into Gibbs's good graces. They would have to rake leaves, shovel snow, and mop. If they screwed up on work assignments, they would be booted from the school for good. In the mind of Jack Gibbs, they had paid their debt to society; now they had a debt to pay to East High School.

As the game against Lancaster Reemelin got under way, some of the East High fans found themselves having empathy for the opposition. "We knew they were jailbirds," East player Larry Walker says. "We thought we'd give them something to remember when they got old." The Reemelin fans in the Coliseum were a touching sight. They consisted of school staff, parents who had made their way to the game, and former involuntary residents of the school. Instead of wanting to remember, the Reemelin players might well have wanted to banish the game's final outcome from their memories: East, 101, Reemelin, 33. The margin of victory was one of the largest in tournament history. After the game, the East High ballplayers—after bestowing courtesies to the Reemelin players—boarded their team bus for the ride back home. The Reemelin players—with a law enforcement officer accompanying them—returned to their place of incarceration.

Westerville High faced East High in the next round. Westerville came to the Coliseum with a decent 15–6 record, but by halftime they were down 44–20; by the end of the third quarter they were losing by 31 points, 69–38. Westerville, like nearly all of the suburban Columbus schools, featured a predominantly white student body. The Fairgrounds Coliseum had become the main setting in the city for the largest comingling of blacks and whites. The Coliseum seating was segregated by choice and based on school pride. Still, it was a stark spectacle: East's black following on this side of the Coliseum, Westerville's white following on the other side. Both school principals had preached against foolishness, and everyone was kind to one another. When the final seconds ticked off the clock, the foot-stomping and well-mannered East High

Tiger fan base was treated to another invigorating victory, 93–55. Eddie Rat had poured in 32 points.

There were beautiful rural settings beyond the city limits of Columbus, wide fields dotting quaint little towns like Chillicothe, Zanesville, London, Urbana. They were farm towns populated by whites, where cows grazed and the corn grew high in season. Because the towns' schools were small, their basketball teams often had to be cobbled together. Coaches in those settings figured the mechanics of the game of basketball had to be taught with a vigilance; stylish individualism, which rarely erupted anyway, was almost frowned upon—save for the eye-popping jump shooter who sometimes emerged from behind the doorways of a farmhouse. Jerry West was one such player. His family lived in a tiny West Virginia community, down in a hollow. His picture-perfect jump shot got him the hell out of there and into West Virginia University, where he had a great career. By 1968 he had been in the NBA for several years, punishing opposing teams with his shooting. He was revered by high school basketball players everywhere, including those at East High.

More often than not, most white players were not playing as if their lives depended upon the sport—as Bob Hart had once said his players were. A white rural coach might get lucky and come across a Jerry West. But the city game of the black player seemed to mature beyond X's and O's; the late-night hours of practice—if a player was coachable—added a certain type of rich seasoning to a player's game. There was also the added depth of history: The white players, more often than not, had a community lineage. Their families had been in London, Chillicothe, Zanesville, and other places for years. So many black players in Columbus, Ohio, had been products of a family migration from the South. They were not rooted. There was no family farm or lineage to fall back upon. Success in a sport could make a family's surname respected. A better future could be envisioned. This was opportunity. The awful things that had gone wrong in their families could be righted, fixed, altered with a basketball, a football, a baseball. By the time Bo-Pete Lamar arrived at East High, he had already advanced beyond anything Bob Hart could teach him. His family had nothing. But now they had his basketball prowess. It was for Lamar as it was for Ratleff, Walker, Hickman, and

Smith: Beyond the death of Martin Luther King Jr., they were cracking a world open.

More than seven thousand fans arrived at the Fairgrounds Coliseum on a Tuesday night to eye East High take on their next opponent, the London High Red Raiders. Ray Chadwell was their well-respected coach. His team had won their conference title and came bouncing into the Coliseum with a formidable 19–1 record. School kids had lined the corridors of the old, creaky Coliseum, hungry to see the high school players from both teams, but especially Ratleff, Lamar, and Conner. To the entire black community, the East High Tigers had become the city's marquee team. Ten months after King's death, East High had given the black community a reason to hope again, even to strut a little.

Once again East High fell behind its opponent shortly after the outset of the game, 8–4. And once again, they shifted into gear and became unstoppable. They went on a 15-point scoring binge in that first quarter, dizzying the opposition. Eddie Rat scored 10 points. There were two more runs of 10 and 11 points, with Bo-Pete Lamar showing some lovely passing, smooth as a butler handing off a cup of tea: This pass is for you, Mr. Ratleff. London was being blitzed; the halftime score was 56–24. Having been beaten only once that season, Ray Chadwell's team was not accustomed to this kind of manhandling. By the end of the third quarter, East still had a significant lead, 74–37. Hart began pulling his starters in the final quarter. Eddie Rat left the game with 28 points, Conner with 13 points and 12 rebounds. Both had seen only twenty-five minutes of action. The final: East, 94–51.

The beauty of the admission price at the Coliseum during tournament play was that a single ticket gave you the opportunity to stay the entire afternoon and into the evening to watch all the games you desired. There could be as many as four games in a single day. It was heaven for basketball junkies, as well as the grown-ups working the concession stands. Not many East High partisans decided to leave the Coliseum after their team's victory against London. They wanted to see who won the following game; the victor would be the Tigers' next opponent in the upper bracket of the tournament. It turned out that opponent would be Linden-McKinley, East High's hated rival.

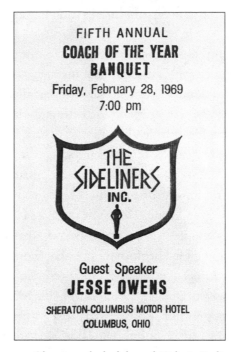

FIFTH ANNUAL
COACH OF THE YEAR
BANQUET
Friday, February 28, 1969
7:00 pm

THE
SIDELINERS
INC.

Guest Speaker
JESSE OWENS
SHERATON-COLUMBUS MOTOR HOTEL
COLUMBUS, OHIO

*Jesse Owens, the great Olympian who had shamed Hitler in Berlin, addressed a group
of Columbus athletes and coaches on the eve of the state basketball tournament that year.*

Bob Hart and Paul Pennell also stayed around to watch the contest
between Eastmoor and Linden-McKinley. If there was one team in the
City League of Columbus that made them nervous during tournament
time, it was Linden-McKinley. The Tigers had beaten them by a mere
8 points during the regular season. Linden-McKinley's players were
already champing at the bit to take on East High again. They wanted
to advance, and they wanted revenge. That evening, fans were already
rushing to the ticket counter at the Coliseum to buy a seat for the looming matchup between the two teams. Bob Hart's team had three days to
prepare for a game that would either lengthen their season—or bring it
to an abrupt end.

On February 28, the Sideliners Club of Columbus hosted their annual
awards banquet at the Sheraton-Columbus Motor Hotel. The group

consisted of black former OSU athletes, most of whom had played for football coach Woody Hayes. Since they had been so often blocked from participating in mainstream awards banquets, in 1964 they simply formed their own club. An array of sports figures—professional, college, high school—were honored. Jack Gibbs was mighty proud that his basketball coach, Bob Hart; one of Hart's players, Nick Conner; and his baseball coach and basketball assistant coach Paul Pennell were among the honorees. But the star of the show, the guest speaker, was Jesse Owens, the onetime track star who, more than three decades earlier, had revealed to the world quite a bit about the grace of a championship athlete, about world politics, about swift black beauty. When Owens walked to the microphone, the applause was loud. "That was a real coup," Paul Pennell remembers. "He was star power. He was very commanding. His delivery and presence stood out."

Jesse Owens was still a handsome man; he still walked with the grace of a sprinter. But his emotions were sometimes conflicted. Yes, Owens was among his fellow Ohio State alumni, and yes, he had brought glory to the school. But the school had also refused to give him a scholarship, forcing him to work as a night elevator operator to pay his way through college. And the school had not allowed him to live on campus with the white athletes. Further, his life after the 1936 Berlin Olympics was peripatetic and challenging. He joined up with a jazz band. In 1942, he took a personnel job with the Ford Motor Company, given supervision over only black workers. After four years he quit to join the West Coast Baseball Association, an offshoot of the Negro baseball league. The nascent franchise folded in eight weeks, and the great sprinter was reduced to racing those horses on racetracks to earn money. He told those who thought such activity beneath him that he couldn't eat gold medals. Whites were perplexed by the comment; blacks understood it from all angles. At one point the great Jesse Owens found employment working at a gas station, pumping gas for customers, some of whom drove up to the station just to see if it really was him.

By the time Owens walked into the Sideliners banquet and looked out over the East High athletes and coaches and others seated at the tables, his fortunes had been on an upswing. Three years earlier, in 1966, the

United States government had named him a goodwill ambassador. There were speaking engagements overseas, then more engagements when he was back on American soil. "Time has stood still for me," he said about his Olympics fame. "That golden moment dies hard." His talks were about patriotism, honesty, and living a good, clean life. William Oscar Johnson, in *Sports Illustrated*, summarized Owens's speechifying as "a kind of all-round super combination of 19th century spellbinder and 20th century plastic p.r. man, full-time banquet guest, eternal glad-hander, evangelistic small-talker." When Owens finished his speech, Bob Hart, Paul Pennell, and Nick Conner stood in awe. Hart choked up; he had fought in the European theater to defeat Hitler, and in 1936 Hitler had sent his German Olympians out to defeat Jesse Owens, and, by extension, black America. Owens was not just a special human being to Hart. He was a symbol of what had been overcome, what could be overcome, and what still needed to be overcome.

· 5 ·

Keeping Food in the Pantry

There never seemed to be enough food at home. No one was starving, but there simply wasn't enough of a comfort zone; a second or third helping was never a guarantee. On out-of-town games, the coaching staff would marvel at how much food the players ate.

The mothers, mindful of the appetites of their athletic sons, would set aside supper for when they arrived home from practice. But the sons, coming through the door and seeing their younger siblings, some of them still with hungry looks on their faces, would start sharing the meal they had grabbed from the stovetop. Scenes like this were emblematic of the poverty of black Americans. These households were suffering various kinds of hurts—overdue rent, not enough food in the pantry, an ex-husband missing yet another child support payment. The East High coaches had visited some of the homes of their players. They had seen the gnawing poverty up close.

In 1967, Senator Bobby Kennedy had traveled to the Mississippi Delta to investigate hunger. The pictures appearing in national magazines and newspapers showing black children with the distended bellies of the malnourished were heartbreaking, a stain on rich and powerful

America. Bo-Pete's mother, Lucy Lamar, shook her head when she saw the photos of Kennedy's trip on TV: If only people knew of the struggles single mothers like her were having outside Mississippi, in a place like Columbus, Ohio, at the Poindexter Village housing projects! Barbara Crump, Eddie Rat's mother, and Beatrice Conner, mother of Nick Conner, also harrumphed when they saw those pictures from the Mississippi Delta. There were plenty of mornings Lucy Lamar woke up and wondered what she'd be able to scrounge together to put on top of the stove come dinnertime when her three sons were expecting to eat.

Some of the basketball players' families had to scrape by on Aid to Families with Dependent Children, otherwise known as welfare. Lucy Lamar couldn't depend on regular maid work, and her migraines were always an issue. Moving from the North Side of town to the East Side so her son could play basketball—and keep his Afro—had not depleted her savings, because she had no earthly savings. She lived week to week. She was in a constant state of worry. During summers, the families could depend on the players working jobs, bringing in a little extra income to help out, but not during the winter, during basketball season. The one good thing about subsidized public housing—and several of the basketball players lived in public housing—was that the heat never got turned off because it was regulated by the on-site housing office.

Young athletes, everyone knew, needed plenty of food, and mothers worried about getting it. So, in 1969 on the East Side of Columbus, everyone fairly celebrated when Carl Brown opened his grocery store—an expanded one from his earlier mom-and-pop operations on Mount Vernon Avenue, just a few blocks from East High. The trek there from the high school was even shorter if you cut through the Poindexter Village housing projects. Before Carl Brown's store, mothers had to hop a bus or get a jitney taxi to take them over to East Main Street or North High Street where they could shop at a large, traditional grocery store. In the wintertime it was an arduous trip. Waiting at a bus stop with bags of groceries could be wearisome. Not to mention the fact that the cost of transportation cut into the food-buying budget.

Carl Brown was one of the few blacks of his generation in Columbus who was not born in the American South. He was born in 1917 in Westerville, Ohio, a rural community twenty miles outside of Columbus. At Westerville High School, he felt quite lonely. There was not another black in his senior class. His family badly wanted him to graduate, so he withstood the racial slurs and survived the fisticuffs. Following high school, there were odd jobs, but nothing he thought would lead anywhere. So he hatched his own business plan: he would start a one-man farm stand, using his entire savings of $84. He went around to car dealerships, trying to talk them down to the lowest price for a dependable car. He finally came to an agreement and purchased a Model T. He got permission to set up a little fruit and vegetable stand on Mount Vernon Avenue. He'd go around to farms in rural Ohio and load up with fresh fruits and a variety of produce. Fridays and Saturdays were popular days on the avenue because women began shopping for Sunday dinner. Carl Brown's outdoor market became a mainstay on the avenue for years. To improve his profit margin and bypass wholesalers, he began traveling to southern states—Georgia, Tennessee, the Carolinas—to get the kinds of items his customers wanted: collard greens, okra, watermelons, peaches, corn. He'd embark on his journeys on weeknights, be gone for a few days, then get back to Columbus, his borrowed truck quite full. He didn't want to risk the wear and tear on the Model T. In time he had small storefront booths, but nothing to brag about.

People kept telling Brown he should open a big store of his own. It sounded like wishful thinking. How was he going to get the kind of money it would take to open a grocery store, with a roof, aisles, shelves of food, and his own staff?

If Carl Brown were a white man, he could have marched downtown to one of the big banks in Columbus, applied for a loan, and most likely gotten it. But black men in Columbus were not routinely getting loans to start businesses in the 1940s and 1950s. Then Carl Brown met Don Tishman.

Don Tishman had grown up in the tough Brownsville section of Brooklyn, New York. His parents, Jewish immigrants, worked in and around the garment industry. Emmanuel Tishman, Don's father, did

some organizing work for Emma Goldman, the renowned labor orga-
nizer, and suffered his share of run-ins with the police. Young Don saw
how the garment workers were mistreated. He had grown up hearing
stories about the ghastly Triangle Shirtwaist Factory fire in Greenwich
Village. On March 25, 1911, fire erupted from within the building and
quickly spread. The workers, mostly Jewish and Italian, started to flee,
but chaos ensued as they realized many of the doors were locked. The
owners later claimed they had had to lock the doors to keep workers
from taking unscheduled breaks and from stealing. Many of the workers
eventually made their way to the roof, from which they jumped to their
deaths to escape the flames. The death toll was 146; many others were
injured. The owners of the factory were tried on various charges and were
shamefully acquitted. Each family received a paltry $75 for their loss.

Don Tishman was twelve years old when his family relocated to Ohio,
first Youngstown, then Columbus. He served in the Navy on a subma-
rine during World War II, survived the war, and later attended Ohio
State University Law School. The life he had seen on the mean streets of
New York City as a child had bred in Tishman a strong social conscience.
He felt strongly about fair housing, the rights of blacks, and unions.

The Republican Party ruled Columbus in the 1940s and 1950s, and
Tishman didn't like that at all. A fearless Democrat, he thought Republicans were holding back social progress. The Wolfe family, who owned
the local newspaper and wielded a lot of influence, came to consider
Don Tishman a damn nuisance. He wrote letters to the editor, gave fiery
talks, sometimes to anyone who was within earshot. In 1960, Tishman
chaired John Kennedy's Ohio presidential campaign. Ohioans' support
of Nixon proved he had a solid grip on Ohio, but Kennedy won in a
squeaker nationwide. Tishman celebrated.

A go-for-broke liberal in a conservative city, and one of the big Democratic supporters in Mayor Jack Sensenbrenner's rise, Tishman started
filing lawsuits on behalf of blacks who couldn't get decent housing. He
regularly dragged his little daughter, Tracy, to church basements full of
black people; he wrote down their complaints, vowing to do something
about them. "He was so determined about helping people," Tracy Brown
recalls. Once, while Tishman was engaged in a housing lawsuit brought

against the rural town of Centerville, Ohio, a Centerville official cornered him in a parking lot and called him a "nigger lover." It was a bad move: Tishman cold-cocked the man, flattening him, then he got in his car and drove off. The punch didn't make the papers. "What was the guy gonna say—that my dad knocked him out?" says Dan Tishman, Don's son.

Don Tishman became a familiar face on the black East Side of the city. It was hard to miss a tall white man loping about with an easy manner. He could backslap and cuss with the best of the residents of the area. One day Carl Brown, who had been making a living working out of the Eastern Market, an indoor farmers market, mentioned to Tishman that he wanted to open a major grocery store on Mount Vernon Avenue. Tishman—who seemed to know every enterprising black in the community—wanted to know why Brown didn't go ahead and do it. Brown explained that he couldn't get a bank loan, and he figured it was because of his skin color. Tishman grew furious and decided to take action. He took Carl Brown downtown, to the headquarters of the Huntington National Bank, into the office of Franz Huntington—one of the family's banking heirs and a Tishman acquaintance—and insisted that Huntington give Brown a loan. And that is how, in that tumultuous year of 1969, the big Carl Brown IGA store opened on Mount Vernon Avenue. It was the first full-fledged stand-alone grocery store on the avenue, and a black man operated it. Tishman lived in the white enclave of Bexley, but he got a kick out of coming over to Carl's store to shop. He'd jawbone with customers, get agitated when he heard more of their woes, and slap a business card into their hand.

Lucy Lamar, Mildred Mizelle, Beatrice Conner, Ollie Mae Walker—and all the other mothers of the East High basketball players—finally had a place to get fresh groceries that could compete with some of the big grocery stores on Main Street and High Street. And when they were short on money, Carl Brown told them they could open an account, allowing them to shop and pay their grocery bills in two- or three-week intervals.

·   ·   ·

But if the mothers were helped in their efforts to keep food in the pantry at home, there always seemed to be other challenges blowing in like fierce winds.

Eddie Rat's stepfather, John Crump, was an alcoholic. Eddie's mother, Beatrice, had moved away from Bellefontaine, Ohio, to get away from one no-good husband, only to end up saddled with another. Beatrice knew she could not make a living doing maid work—day work—by herself while she raised her children. She felt she needed a husband. But now she was mired in a bad second marriage. John Crump began to show up at East High basketball practices, trying to tell Bob Hart how to coach his stepson. He'd wobble about, slurring his words, plowing his way into the locker room after games and practices. It was embarrassing, but Eddie Rat had to endure it. He knew that living "in a tough area" was hard on his mother, and he simply did not wish to bring any acrimony into the home. It didn't take a family therapist to realize that John Crump was jealous of his renowned stepson.

Meanwhile, over in the household of Bo-Pete Lamar, Lucy Lamar worried about the pull of the streets on Bo-Pete and that he might give in to the allure of street life. Denizens of the city's nightlife were attracted to Bo-Pete because of his marquee magnetism. Pimps and hustlers wanted to give him rides to school. They wanted to give him gifts. Both Lucy Lamar and Jack Gibbs were vigilant about the questionable characters gravitating toward the star basketball guard. Many nights Lucy could not fall asleep until Bo-Pete had returned to the apartment.

Ollie Mae Walker, mother of basketball player Larry Walker, didn't much worry about him, but she did worry about her other son, Charles, who was living on the wrong side of the law, hustling and pimping. She worried about the police knocking at the door looking for Charles.

Nick Conner liked to walk. Sometimes he'd just leave the house and start walking, and that made his mother, Beatrice, nervous. Police brutality was a constant concern of the local NAACP. She'd often tell Nick that Dr. King didn't give up his life so her son could go out into the night and get into some kind of scuffle with the police, or, worse, lose his life in a confrontation with them. She knew that he had occasionally been stopped because he looked older than most seventeen-year-olds. Nick withstood the questioning because he was mild-mannered, but it still bothered him.

Mildred Mizelle, mother of the basketball player Kenny Mizelle, was pregnant again. She was already raising six kids in the Bolivar Arms housing projects. She was a stern, loving mother, but soon there would be another mouth to feed.

In 1969, blacks accounted for approximately 12 percent of the American population. Yet in government statistics that measured poverty—households bringing in less than $3,000 a year—blacks made up 31 percent of poor families. Impoverished black families headed by women dropped even further down the ladder of poverty than those headed by a black male. More than half of the Tiger basketball players lived in households headed by impoverished black women. The lives of these young men could sometimes seem cobbled together by government assistance, the will of their high school principal, charity from local black churches, and their own basketball talent.

Not a single basketball player owned a car. During the summers, Nick Conner would at least get to borrow his mom's car and would invite other players to go with him to scout playgrounds for games. But during the school year, the players were like nomads, cutting through backyards and alleys, wrapping their leather coats tight around them against the cold winds, pulling down their be-bop and stingy brim hats. And as lunchtime neared inside East High, they were counting the precious nickels and dimes in their pockets as they made their way toward the cafeteria. When they could get away with it, the student cafeteria workers would heap a little extra food on the athletes' plates. Yes, the team members got little advantages inside the world of poverty that they lived in.

Carl Brown, a longtime Tiger booster, was always proud to see the players drop by his store. Jack Gibbs—who always appreciated Brown's paid ads in the student yearbooks—made sure that the business teachers at the school used the example of Brown to inspire the students. Gibbs saw Brown's ascendancy as a moment of genuine hope in the community. Less than a year earlier, buildings on Mount Vernon Avenue had been torched during the urban rebellion in America. Now a building had risen. And a few more jobs (after-school employment for East High students) were available in the community. On a big corkboard in the store, Brown would tack up pictures of East High students who had distinguished themselves in some recent event at the school—a music recital, a scholarship winner, someone who had shone in an *In the Know* academic contest. And you certainly couldn't miss the pictures of the Tiger basketball players in action.

Brown loved hearing commercials for his store on WVKO radio. The store meant so much to the ladies of the Poindexter Village housing projects. Lucy Lamar and Ollie Mae Walker could now step out their back doors and walk to Carl Brown's store and pick up their ham hocks. The hell with trekking on the bus all the way over to High Street. (A ham hock is a piece of flavorful pork used to season southern dishes such as collard greens, pinto beans, black-eyed peas, or lima beans.) Thanks to Carl Brown, there were many afternoons when apartment living rooms inside the Poindexter Village housing projects smelled of sweet smoky ham hocks cooking inside huge boiling pots.

· 6 ·

So Many Dreams
in the Segregated City

Public education in America has always been fraught with battle and strife. In theory, communities want their children to be educated, but the issue of money is often at odds with the need for learning. In the early decades of the nation, children were very much needed for labor, and families rebelled against high taxes needed to fund schools. The English High School of Boston was founded in 1821 as the first high school in America. It took support from a state charitable organization to bring it into existence. Little attention was paid to educating blacks, and what their legitimacy meant to the nation. Though it was hoped the presence of Homer Plessy would have the opposite effect throughout the nation, his life only deepened the grief of the black community in its quest for equality.

In the summer of 1892, Plessy, a Louisiana Creole considered black under Louisiana law, boarded a train in New Orleans. He took a seat in the "white carriage," was summarily arrested (in keeping with Louisiana's Separate Car Act), and eventually was brought before a judge. His attorneys argued that the Fourteenth Amendment protected him from such segregationist practices. Judge John H. Ferguson ruled against Plessy and his legal team. The next step was an appeal to the Louisiana Supreme Court, which allowed Plessy to take his case to the United States Supreme Court.

The Plessy decision was finally issued in 1896. Associate Justice Henry Billings Brown wrote the court's decision, which proved fateful to a large segment of the population. A part of Brown's court ruling read: "The most common instance of this [state-sanctioned separation of the races] is connected with the establishment of separate schools for white and colored children, which has been held to be a valid exercise of the legislative power even by courts of States where the political rights of the colored race have been longest and most earnestly enforced." The decision was rife with doom for black constitutional rights, not to mention a complete ignoring of the Fourteenth Amendment. Now a policy of racial segregation had been constitutionally pounded into the law. From city to rural hamlet, the nation had now been presented a green light to discriminate against its black citizens. No facet of black life was immune to the capricious ruling. Associate Justice Brown had twisted the meaning of "equality." He went on: "We consider the underlying fallacy of the plaintiff's argument to consist in the assumption that the enforced separation of the two races stamps the colored race with a badge of inferiority. If this be so, it is not by reason of anything found in the act, but solely because the colored race chooses to put that construction upon it."

Given a metaphorical inch, the court took a mile with its gaze onto black life and rights. The justices all but blamed millions of blacks for their second-class citizenship. The ruling was startling for its mendacity. But there was a dissent, and it was powerful. It was written by Justice John Marshall Harlan, a native of Kentucky who had once owned slaves. During the post–Civil War era he had seen the viciousness meted out to blacks, and it had turned both his mind and heart. In his dissent he predicted that the *Plessy* ruling would unleash terrifying waves of discrimination in the nation: "If laws of like character should be enacted in the several States of the Union, the effect would be in the highest degree mischievous. Slavery, as an institution tolerated by law would, it is true, have disappeared from our country, but there would remain a power in the States, by sinister legislation, to interfere with the full enjoyment of the blessings of freedom to regulate civil rights, common to all citizens, upon the basis of race, and to place in a condition of legal inferiority a large body of American citizens."

After the *Plessy* decision the ladder that could lead to freedom for blacks grew painfully crooked and minus the kind of steps that could lead to progress. Without freedom of movement and protection by the judiciary, it was certainly more difficult for blacks to reach the desired plateaus of education. But even deeper than education—the be-all and end-all for black advancement—the *Plessy* decision psychologically touched American life on a day-to-day basis. Blacks must drink here, not there; must live here, not there; must go to the side window of that restaurant, not the front door.

Ohio may not have seen the gothic and bloody racial dramas that long took place in the American South, but the state had its own warped racial construct. In 1804 the state of Ohio took away most of the rights of blacks. The state implemented a decree that blacks had to cough up a $500 bond just to enter the state to reside. The sum was out of the question for nearly all black people. Runaway slaves fleeing the Kentucky border area of Cincinnati, however, found a haven farther north in Columbus, where there was an active Underground Railroad operation. When black voting rights finally arrived in 1870, joy was palpable in the black community. The city's ward-based political machinery meant that the East Side would have black political representation. This voting movement gave rise to the brief political career of Rev. James Poindexter, who knew the sacred importance of education to blacks. "No people ever attached greater value to education than do the colored people," he wrote. "They are more worried about their ignorance than about their poverty. They feel slavery, in depriving them of the means of education, inflicted upon them greater wrong than it did in working 200 years without pay."

But then things happened that further deepened the misery of blacks and their quest for equal education in the city. The first involved William Oxley Thompson, president of Ohio State University, the most powerful institution in the city. The school was growing at a rapid pace, and the words and pronouncements spoken by its president were given much attention and respect. Thompson was not only president of the university; he was also a member of the Columbus school board. No one on the board wished to go against the university president when he declared, "It is in the best interests of both [races] that they be educated in separate schools."

Those words were all it took to begin the political revamping of the city's school system, separating blacks from the white schools they had been attending without much debate or white backlash. School districts began to be gerrymandered to create all-black schools. Blacks didn't swallow the upheaval quietly. They gathered in a skating rink on Mount Vernon Avenue to criticize the Ohio State University president and his position. Black parents clearly saw the oncoming creation of all-black schools and lamented their powerlessness to stop it from happening. "Such separation of the races, even if the laws of the State did not forbid it," they wrote in a resolution, "always results ultimately in inferior school equipment for colored children, and, moreover, tends to set the races farther and farther apart, and so to hinder that mutual sympathy and understanding which close personal contact in the plastic years of childhood helps to cultivate." The resolution fell on deaf ears.

President Thompson's decision on separate schools was made manifest as the city opened Champion Junior High School in 1909, where Eddie Ratleff, Larry Walker, and several other East High players on the 1968–69 team would come to attend many years later. It was the initial salvo that opened the door to a segregated school system. By 1922 the city added more grades to Champion, enlarging the school to accommodate more black students. The momentum kept up. By 1943 the city had five schools earmarked for blacks—Pilgrim, Felton, Garfield, Mount Vernon, and Champion. Black high-school-age students were sent to East High; some ended up downtown at Central High, located in a notoriously impoverished area. (It hardly went unnoticed that in 1912 the city had moved to at-large elections, also dooming black political clout for the next fifty years. In an at-large election, the outcome favors the majority white population even as blacks are robustly represented in a segregated part of a city. "The Negroes," a local chronicler would observe shortly after the turn of the century, "are almost completely out-side the pale of the white people's sympathy.") Ironically, shortly before Champion opened, the very first junior high school in the nation had also opened in 1909 in Columbus. It was Indianola Junior High School, the junior high that Bo-Pete Lamar later attended.

The city of Columbus suffered mightily in forging its identity. It was a landlocked city; unlike Cleveland or Cincinnati, there were no waterways that served as shipping ports to allow for the exporting and importing of goods. The city did not grow like other industrial cities such as Detroit and Pittsburgh. Real estate and banking became the main engines of the Columbus economy. Absent the tide of immigrants that had peopled the Rust Belt cities, Columbus had to concern itself with the largest group of minorities in the city, and they were black. There were no profes-sional sports teams—football, basketball, baseball—in the city, and that is exactly the way the conservative power brokers in the city liked it. In their limited imaginations, they had convinced themselves pro sports might bring vice. Their athletic appetites were filled by the activities at Ohio State University. Some professors quipped that the school spent more for manure (for its agricultural programs) than it did for literature.

Despite its provincialism, a media empire grew in the city. It was cre-ated by the Wolfe family, who brooked no opposition to their arch-conservatism. Harry and Robert Wolfe started the Wolfe Brothers Shoe Company in the 1890s. As the family's profits grew, so did their empire. They later owned TV stations and the city's dominant newspaper, *The Columbus Dispatch,* which became their flagship possession. Its report-ers were white, often homegrown, and usually plucked from Ohio State University. No politician could rise in the city without the editorial backing of the *Dispatch.* "Directly and indirectly," a chronicler of the family's dealings would write, "the Wolfes exerted unchallenged, if not unquestioned, authority over civic affairs in Columbus from the turn of the century to the onset of World War II, acting primarily on the premise that what was good for Columbus was good for the family and vice versa."

.   .   .

In 1952, a series of school desegregation cases brought by Thurgood Marshall, the chief legal counsel for the NAACP Legal Defense Fund, based in New York City, started to wend its way to the United States Supreme Court. The plaintiffs hailed from Delaware, Kansas, South Carolina, Virginia, and Washington, D.C. Marshall and his team of lawyers were attempting nothing less than to bring about the collapse of the *Plessy* court decision issued decades earlier that had disenfranchised blacks nationwide. The distinguished white lawyers representing the southern states told the court that upending segregation would destabilize a way of life, possibly putting America's long-term stability at risk. Thurgood Marshall, who had made half a dozen trips to Columbus, Ohio, before his arguments in front of the high court, got to the point quickly during his *Brown* desegregation presentation, telling the court that children who played on the streets together—and did not do so in one another's company—certainly would not wither in one another's presence inside a school building. He leaned further into that position by mentioning the same results would likely occur were they to be sitting beside one another in college or university classrooms.

Following the *Brown* argument, Justice Felix Frankfurter, an impish and brilliant Supreme Court justice, wrote a memo to himself—a form of thinking aloud on paper, which he often did. This memo bit into America's racial history with insight: "The outcome of the Civil War, as reflected in the Civil War Amendments, is that there is a single American society. Our colored citizens, like the other components which make up the American nation, are not to be denied the right to enjoy the distinctive qualities of their cultural past. But neither are they to be denied the right to grow up with other Americans as part of our national life. And experience happily shows that contacts tend to mitigate antagonisms and engender mutual respect."

In the immediate aftermath of the NAACP arguments, Chief Justice Fred Vinson died of a heart attack. President Eisenhower appointed former California governor Earl Warren as chief justice. Whereas Vinson had been skittish about taking on racially charged cases, Warren

looked forward to it. On May 17, 1954, the high court issued its decision, striking down *Plessy* and sending a titanic ruling out across the
nation. "We conclude unanimously," Chief Justice Warren said, "that,
in the field of public education, the doctrine of 'separate but equal' has
no place. Separate educational facilities are inherently unequal." (Warren
personally inserted the word "unanimously" to emphasize the strength of
the decision.) Black communities rejoiced, even as southern politicians
excoriated the ruling. The foundation of legal discrimination—on paper
at least—had been cracked open and proven illegal. The news reached
foreign shores and their publications. The psychological and legal impact
of the ruling was one thing; the implementation of it was quite another.
Warren knew as much, and foresaw that the implementation would be
incremental. His ruling took into account that there would be attorneys
general in the states who would need to appear before the court and
iron out how the ruling pertained to their jurisdiction. Some school
districts fitfully adapted, but most did not. Virginia shut down many of
its schools. Some schools needed the intervention of federal troops. For
years, the American educational system remained in flux, bedeviled by
the issue of race.

There were precious few blacks who rose in city governments throughout America during the days of lawful segregation. During the 1940s
and 1950s, there were no black mayors or police chiefs in any major
American city; the mere idea would have been unthinkable. Segregation
had rooted itself deeply in the grain of America. There were, however,
small cracks beginning in the early 1960s. Here and there could be seen a
black assistant city attorney, a black assistant prosecutor, a black municipal juvenile court judge. These individuals often hailed from esteemed
colleges and universities. They were not radical in any sense of the word
and had mostly kept a distance from those so-called radical blacks who
were demanding rights by sitting in at lunch counters. They were also,
more often than not, light of skin. The skin issue was a peculiar but
noticeable dynamic: White America seemed to feel more comfortable
around lighter-skinned blacks than darker-skinned blacks. The roots of

this psychological reality could be traced to the days of slavery, when the "field slaves" were often darker-skinned and the so-called "house Negros"—who got easier work—were often light-skinned. The Negro press wrote about the conundrum, but with a light and almost nervous touch.

In Columbus, Ohio, in the 1950s, a young black man began to rise into the upper echelons of the most coveted jobs in the city. Whites embraced him; he was well-educated with his law degree—and he was also quite light of skin. He was a Republican, which also fit in with the city's white power structure. His name was Robert Duncan. Why, many whites would excitedly say at certain gatherings, here comes Bobby Duncan! He had been accepted.

There would come a day when Bobby Duncan would teach this city a cold and hard lesson about segregation.

The city of Columbus, to stanch overcrowding, built new schools all right, but they were in white areas. In the 1950s, enrollment in the Columbus school system exploded by 87 percent. But black school construction nearly halted, and black schools became overcrowded while remaining underfunded. The Vanguard League, which had been counted upon to bring the grievances of blacks to City Hall, disbanded. There were whispers—never proven—of Communist influence. Anna Mae Durham, a Columbus activist in the 1950s, was disheartened by the white school board's inaction on behalf of black students. "There wasn't any effort by the school board to follow Brown," she said of the Supreme Court ruling.

Since public schools, especially segregated black schools, had to scuffle for both money and respect, it fell to the local black community to support their own schools. "There were 'black schools' and 'Columbus schools,'" said Ted Turner, an administrator within the black school system who attended downtown Columbus school board meetings and was peeved at the disinterest shown on behalf of black schools. The widest and deepest areas of the city's black population took in East Long Street, went up and down Mount Vernon Avenue, and included several blocks of East Broad Street. East High School was the nexus of it all, and many were willing, across the years, to wage battles on behalf of the school. To fortify themselves, the black community created its own world around the schools. The black nightclubs and theaters were on Mount Vernon Avenue. More clubs and haberdasheries were located on Long Street, parallel to Mount Vernon Avenue.

In 1948, Dr. Watson Walker arrived in Columbus from Georgia. Like many others, he came north looking for opportunity. Not a single white hospital in Columbus would hire him. He finally found employment putting his medical skills to use, but it was downtown at the Ohio State Penitentiary, a notorious place of confinement that had once housed Civil War prisoners. (In later years members of bank robber John Dillinger's gang were imprisoned there.) Beans and fatback bacon were staples of the prisoners' diet.

Dr. Walker ingratiated himself with the local black community over the years. In 1961, he got himself elected to the school board. The story of his election was noteworthy enough to wind up in the pages of *Jet* magazine, the widely read, pocket-sized national magazine that had highlighted Emmett Till's Chicago funeral. As soon as he made it onto the board, Walker made it his main mission to look out for the needs of East High School. And one of the things that had been upsetting the black parents of East High students for years was the fact that the football field did not have night lights—when all the other schools in the city did. "I knew this was one of the things the black community was incensed about," Walker would recall. "They had been working on it for years and had been rebuffed at every turn. The only reason [white board members] didn't want lights for East was the white schools would prefer to play East at daytime because they figured if they came out in the east end at nighttime they were going to get beat up. These were prevalent racial attitudes that had to be erased." School board members intimated that lights were a luxury at any high school, choosing to drop the matter. Walker decided to launch an investigation. He got sleuths to help him out. At a subsequent board meeting, he produced his findings. "How many schools with football fields do you have that are not lighted?" he asked board members. They grew agitated by his line of inquiry. But it was a board meeting and someone was compelled to answer. "One," a white member finally answered, confessing that the school was East High. The public revelation finally forced the school system to install lights on the football field at East High School.

By the time of East High's 1968–69 athletic season, a few black newspapers in the community had folded. The surviving newspaper was the Columbus *Call and Post*. It was located in a three-story Victorian home set off East Broad Street, on Hamilton Avenue. Amos Lynch, the editor of the paper, had grown up around newspapering. Lynch's mother, Beadie, was a self-taught journalist for the *Columbus Advocate*, a local black newspaper published in the years before World War II. Beadie preferred taking phone calls about story tips and ideas; she considered the grunge work of newspapering out on the streets beneath her. So she'd send her young son, Amos, out to do the shoe-leather work, interviewing people and getting the color for her story. He'd bring the quotes back to his mom, and she'd shape and write the story.

Young Amos enrolled at Ohio State University, intent on becoming a journalist. But World War II interrupted his education in his freshman year. He became a Navy corpsman, fortunate in that he never got close to battle, spending his military service between New York and Illinois, tending to injured soldiers. Back home in 1946—more mature, energetic as ever, and still a fool for journalism—he resumed his education at Ohio State. But he found himself awash in freelance newspaper work, which made him an inattentive student. He left school for good and went to work for the *Ohio Sentinel*, focusing on the rise of the black community, its population constantly growing after World War II. More than a few black servicemen who had exhibited special flying skills during World War II settled on the city's East Side after the war. Their renown as Tuskegee Airmen was still decades away from being celebrated.

While covering a football game at all-black Wilberforce University in 1947 (the great W. E. B. DuBois had once been on the faculty) for his newspaper, Lynch met a young lady, Geraldine, and began courting her. She loved his intensity and how he always seemed to have his ear to the drumbeat of the black community. They soon married. A few years later he went on to help start the *Ohio State News*, yet another black newspaper. It had nothing to do with Ohio State University; the use of the school's name was seen as a marketing edge. The university didn't seem to mind.

Amos Lynch was often heard before he was seen: His voice was gravelly and had a bark to it. His skin was cinnamon-colored, and his mouth was constantly moving because of the chewing gum he was always smacking on. Like many black newspaper editors of the time, Lynch was shameless in advocating for his community. This was life-and-death journalism—at least that was how Amos Lynch approached the job. It was community survival. In 1955, when the idea was hatched to create the Mount Vernon Avenue District Improvement Association, Lynch quickly jumped in. He knew just who would make a great publicity director: He would! The business owners accepted his suggestion. There was a formal ceremony, and a city official administered the oath of office to members of the group—three men and a woman at the time—as they all raised their right hands and posed for a photograph.

There were certain names from the civil rights movement in the South that were starting to reach the ears of the black populace of Columbus. On December 1, 1955—not long after Thurgood Marshall's NAACP school desegregation victory—Rosa Parks refused to abandon her seat in the white section of that Montgomery, Alabama, bus. Her arrest set off a year-long and steadfast bus boycott that ignited other marches and protest movements. The civil rights genie was permanently out of the bottle. Rev. Phale Hale had started inviting the young Martin Luther King Jr. to Columbus. Ann Walker, who got her start writing under Amos Lynch for another publication, was asked by a local TV station to interview King in 1956. The station had no blacks on its reporting staff. Walker knew the King family and jumped at the opportunity. "His wife was a friend of my husband," she says of Coretta Scott King, who accompanied her minister husband to the city. "He wasn't as well known at the time," Walker says of King. "I asked him questions about the Montgomery bus boycott, and about his general plans for blacks across the country."

In 1962, his squabbling with superiors and his aggressive nature eventually got Lynch fired from the *Ohio State News*, but he wasn't idle for too long. Lynch was asked to open a local edition of the Cleveland *Call and Post*, one of the largest black weeklies in the nation. It was making money, so their owners decided to open the Columbus *Call and Post*. By the time Amos Lynch took that paper's helm, he had contacts throughout the city and had attained a reputation of respect across the color line. Among the main issues he aimed to focus on were the school integration effort, the battle for fair housing, and the goings-on over at East High School. He had a small staff—three reporters and a managing editor—and worked them to the bone. The hours were long and the idea of overtime pay for the reporters was laughable. Stories about local black crime—murderous affairs and the like—drew wide readership. There were times Lynch was criticized for getting mighty close to a form of tabloid journalism. But he knew the salacious stories would pull readers in, and then they'd notice the serious stories! There were also stories about Hollywood celebrities and singers—Lou Rawls, Dinah Washington, Big Mama Thornton, Nancy Wilson—who passed through town to perform. If Harry Belafonte or Sammy Davis Jr. or Eartha Kitt appeared on some TV variety show or television movie, there'd be a big splashy spread about them inside the pages of the *Call and Post*.

Few things, however, made Lynch as proud as uplifting stories about East High School. While he himself had attended South High, he realized the following East High had in the city. Issues of the newspaper sold speedily when there were stories about the school: stories about football, basketball, baseball games; stories about those East High state championship seasons; stories about the vaunted marching band that was getting invitations to march on college campuses; stories about his good friend Mayme Moore, the local businesswoman who had been invited in 1963 by Dr. Martin Luther King Jr. to Washington to join him on the dais where he made his unforgettable speech; stories about Jack Gibbs being named the first black principal of East High School. Amos Lynch turned himself into a big man around town. And like so many others, he became an East High Tiger booster. The school *was* the community.

It was the community where Harvey Alston Sr. lived. Alston graduated from East High in 1925. In 1937, he joined the Columbus police force. Black patrolmen found it almost impossible to climb the ranks. In 1943, black officer Leslie Shaw filed a lawsuit, won, and got promoted. And when Harvey Alston got promoted to police captain in 1952, the Negro press around the country made sure to cover the story.

Amos Lynch told groups his newspaper could not survive were it not for the keen minds and savvy business skills of merchants up and down Mount Vernon Avenue. The reason was simple: They placed ads in his newspaper, and ads were revenue! There were certainly bigger and fancier stores on North High Street in downtown Columbus, but they didn't cater to the black community. Their items were often more expensive, although often of higher quality. Although Columbus had relaxed its policies about blacks trying on clothes and hat wear before the cities in the American South had done so, blacks in town still felt many of those downtown stores were off-putting and snooty.

To walk from one end of Mount Vernon Avenue to the other was to get a sense of a whole other thriving business district, separate from the main downtown shopping district in the city. Ernest Mackey worked as a salesman at Spicer's Furniture Store on Mount Vernon Avenue. There was a big awning above the store, which protruded out over the avenue. Charles Spicer was owner of the store, but it was Mackey whom many customers revered, so much so that they treated him as if he were the owner. And that was because Mr. Mackey—as he was always called— would take care of you: He'd put something in layaway—keeping it for you longer than initially agreed upon if he had to—and let you keep paying on it until you could complete the purchase. He'd mark an item lower on the spot if he saw you were short the advertised price; he'd even find a couple of handymen to transport that couch—for free—to your home or apartment.

Not far from Spicer's was Edna Bryce's Floral Shop. Bryce was a native of Alabama, a fine-boned thin woman who had a sense of churchy grace. She held teas and taught etiquette classes out of her home. Her floral business grew steadily in the 1950s. She supplied flowers for funerals, weddings, union hall events. She became so highly respected she rose, in time, to become president of the Mount Vernon Avenue District Improvement Association. Jack Gibbs of East High adored her. Those corsages for the girls attending the Rainbow Ball at East High? They came from Mrs. Bryce's Floral Shop. Amos Lynch also depended on Edna Bryce to keep his newspaper informed about society news—which local black son or daughter had spent a holiday in California, which local family member was striking out for the wicked world of entertainment in New York City. She was nosy, but not gossipy; proud, but not arrogant.

Every community needs a go-to lawyer. On Mount Vernon Avenue it was William A. Toler. (The "A" stood for Adolph, a quite uncommon name, middle or otherwise, for a black child.) A product of the West Virginia coal mines, he wanted to become a lawyer. The state of West Virginia thought it was a noble idea, as long as he didn't wish to go to law school in West Virginia. As was the custom of many southern states and their segregated law schools, West Virginia paid for blacks in their state to go to law school elsewhere. Toler graduated from Ohio State University and, afterwards, decided to remain in the city. There was service in World War II; he came home with medals. Within minutes in his company, it was hard to forget him and the sidelong stares began: He stood five-foot-five, had both a temper and a Napoleonic complex, and dazzled people with his IQ of 141. His small law practice, which he started in the late 1940s, was quite active. As with many personal attorneys, some of his clients were of questionable morals. He handled the cases of pimps, thieves, and prostitutes. Because of his size, his clients thought they could take advantage of him. But he often shocked them by throwing the first punch, rearing back again for the follow-up punch, following that with wild-eyed glaring and cursing. His wife, Toni, had had him admitted to mental hospitals more than once. Walking from mental hospital to car, he'd tell his wife that he was fine, that his brief stay had actually calmed him down. Toni got used to it. When he had to, Jack Gibbs would hit William Toler up for free legal advice.

There was only one photographer like Gordon Parks, the famous *Life* magazine staffer who had become the most celebrated black photographer in America in the 1950s. George Pierce was the Gordon Parks of the East Side of Columbus. A native of Alabama, he had long fancied becoming a photographer. When he founded his own studio on Mount

Vernon Avenue in the 1950s, his dream came true. People would see him hustling out of the studio to his car, his cameras swinging from around his neck. He photographed the NAACP marches—there was a huge one on the statehouse lawn in 1959—and he photographed celebratory parades, crime scenes, events at East High School, and Martin Luther King Jr. when he came to town. When President Lyndon Johnson came to Columbus after having signed one of his landmark civil rights bills, Pierce hustled out to the airport. He had to be a little aggressive with the media horde because he had to get into a good position and get his doggone pictures; he would tell anyone who would listen that LBJ had freed the black race. And when he got his pictures, he nearly wept. He revered LBJ.

These were among some of the men and women who had carte blanche to come visit Amos Lynch, the *Call and Post* editor. Any one of them could climb the stairs to the second floor of the converted house, where the tiny newsroom sat, and be invited to pull out a chair and unload their concerns and sentiments about the community. The dining-room-cum-newsroom could instantly take on a salon atmosphere. (When Martin Luther King Jr. was assassinated, it was as if the creaky front door of the house never stopped swinging open and shut.) If Hiram Tanner or John Combs, the reporters, weren't on deadline—it was a weekly, the deadlines were every five days—the gabfests could go on for hours. Tanner covered sports. A native of Arkansas, he was a large man and shambled as he walked. He was old enough to have remembered, in detail, the odyssey of Jackie Robinson as he broke the color barrier in professional baseball, as well as the best fights of Joe Louis and Jersey Joe Walcott, some of which he covered for other Negro publications. Ohio State coach Woody Hayes would always try to make time for him, knowing that Tanner had different deadlines and different story angles for his readers. Sometimes Amos Lynch, whose office was on the first floor of the converted living room, would climb the stairs and interrupt Tanner in the middle of one of his long monologues, and Tanner would roll his eyes, two gruff men in the middle of the make-do newsroom staring like bulls until Tanner finally turned in the direction of the manual Smith-Corona typewriter on his desk. Amos Lynch had a newspaper to get out, and the printing press folks up in Cleveland, where the paper was actually printed, would start riding him as deadlines approached.

As the 1968–69 basketball season at East High had gotten under way, Hiram Tanner was calling friends around the country, telling them that he had never seen a trio like Eddie Ratleff, Nick Conner, and Bo-Pete Lamar at the high school level. On game days he'd shamble around the Fairgrounds Coliseum during East High's games, an old black reporter who couldn't break the color barrier in newspapers like Jackie Robinson had done in baseball. He wore thick glasses and couldn't always make out the people who called his name out—"Hey Tanner!"—so he'd just wave his forearm. Hiram Tanner was quite happy in this black world within Columbus.

Whereas Tanner was voluble, another *Call and Post* writer, the pipe-smoking John Combs, was pensive and rather quiet. His pipe smoke filled the office with a sweet aroma, and pipe ash covered his desk and flecked his clothing as if dusty snow had fallen. His reporting skills were admired when he was writing about the minutiae of municipal government. But what truly excited him was writing about crimes of passion and the horrors of sex crimes. In 1952, when he was writing for the *Ohio State News*, Combs got hold of what he felt was his most gripping and sensational story yet.

Betty Butler, petite and beautiful, a resident of Cleveland, Ohio, had married young and given birth to two children. But the marriage crumbled and she left Cleveland, settling in Cincinnati. She met a local woman, Evelyn Clark, who showed more than a casual interest in getting to know the young divorcée. Clark was a lesbian. Butler was out of money and in the city all alone. She felt vulnerable. Clark offered to help her financially, provided the two could become lovers. It was a brief and tumultuous affair; there were arguments, a lot of drinking and partying. On September 6, 1952, while the two were out in a rowboat at Sharon Woods, not far from Cincinnati, an argument erupted. Deezie Ivory, a third member of the boating party—and the one who had been rowing—quickly brought the boat back to shore, the voices of the two women ringing in his ears. Once on shore, an enraged Butler grabbed a handkerchief and began to strangle Clark, who lapsed into unconsciousness. Ivory stood motionless, shocked, his eyes darting about, up and down the shoreline. Butler dragged Clark to the water's edge and proceeded to drown her. Some nearby fishermen watched the whole thing unfold, too far away to render immediate help. Park rangers were alerted and arrested Butler.

The murder trial was swift: a black woman, a lesbian affair, the year 1952 when such a thing was genuinely taboo. Butler was sentenced to death and was sent to the Marysville Women's Penitentiary. There were three appeals, all for naught. Her execution was finally set for June 11, 1954, to take place in Columbus, at the Ohio State Penitentiary, which housed the electric chair. She was a quiet prisoner. She learned to sketch drawings while awaiting her fate, lamenting that she hadn't had enough focus in life to become an artist. Her last meal was simple: eggs with cheese, apricots on the side. John Combs, the *Call and Post* reporter, got into the penitentiary on the execution date. He couldn't get over how beautiful Betty Butler was. On her date with the electric chair, she was dressed in a pink-and-black dress and wore Oxford shoes. She had a rosary in her hand, having converted to Catholicism while in prison. As she began her walk to the electric chair, two female guards took her by the arm, fearing she might faint. Butler snatched her arms away. She seemed fearless, and her courage made Combs shudder with awe. Outside the walls of the penitentiary, after it was all over, making his way to his office, Combs couldn't shake the image of a stoic—and still beautiful—Betty Butler slowly walking to the chair. In his story Combs pulled a line from the poet William Cullen Bryant to describe Butler's final steps—"the majesty of her death." He was mighty proud of that literary touch. On that day in 1954 when Combs's story on the death of Betty Butler was published in the *Ohio State News*, the vendors on Mount Vernon Avenue sold the paper at a rapid clip.

So this was the street in Middle America that the black citizenry of Columbus called "Our Town." It was on Mount Vernon Avenue where Bo-Pete Lamar's mother shopped, and where Larry Walker's mother shopped with her maid's earnings; and where Robert Wright's mother purchased her sweet potatoes from Carl Brown's grocery after her back-bending maid's work; and where Kenny Mizelle's mother bought her children's school clothes from her government check or her intermittent maid's work as well. And it was off to Mount Vernon Avenue where Jack Gibbs went when he needed money for new athletic equipment for his segregated school, or money for an important college trip for his students, or money for one of those esteem-building Rainbow Balls he was holding at the school. It was on Mount Vernon Avenue where pictures of the 1968–69 East High Tigers basketball team adorned so many store-fronts, taking window space alongside the portraits of the slain Martin Luther King Jr.

INTERLUDE

Other Voices from Farther Up East Broad Street

The news that coursed through black America onto the pages of the black press in the 1960s—stories of faith and triumph, but also of mar-tyred deaths—was reaching beyond the black community of Columbus. Some whites in the city began to recognize the massive and deep dishon-esty of segregation, and to realize that the city was being harmed by it. Nancy Jeffrey was the wife of Tad Jeffrey, whose great-grandfather had founded the Jeffrey Company, one of the coal manufacturing plants that served as a magnet for blacks to leave the South and go to Columbus. Nancy Jeffrey spoke her mind when it came to civil rights. "People have always said to me, 'Why do you have strong feelings about race?' We had two black women who ran our house. I was the youngest of five. They formed my character. I adored them like family. I've always thought black women salvaged the character of people—and got no adulation for it." She grew up around wealth in Irvington-on-Hudson in Westchester

County, New York. "I had a different outlook on the world than most [white people] who grew up here," she says of Columbus.

She and her husband arrived in Columbus in 1956 and moved into the white enclave of Bexley—on East Broad Street, the same street as East High, but also a world away. "The discrimination was accepted in Columbus," she says of the times. "It was the accepted rule in the homes of the white leaders. And people didn't want to be seen running concurrent to that. But I came from the East Coast." She became part of the United Community Council, a social service organization in the city that battled discrimination. They wrote a memorandum about needed health services that could be provided by the five settlement houses in the city. One of the authors was Bernie Wohl—Jewish, liberal, brave. Born in New York City, Wohl came to Columbus in 1961 to become director of one of those settlement houses. Four years later he joined the faculty at Ohio State University, teaching social work. On a campus with very few progressive voices, he stood out. "The rumor was that Wohl had a printing press that printed Communist materials," says Jeffrey of unproven gossip that tarnished Wohl's reputation among the conservative crowd in the city. (By 1972 Wohl had had enough of Columbus and returned to his native New York City, where he became the highly respected director of the Goddard Riverside Community Center.) Nevertheless, Jeffrey took the United Community Council's memorandum about needed health services to *The Columbus Dispatch* newspaper, hoping they would run a story. The *Dispatch* did not. "They wouldn't have any part of printing our social agenda," says Jeffrey. "J. Walter Wolfe [a family heir] didn't want anyone messing with his sleepy town. And Ohio State University wasn't rocking any boats. It was the women these businessmen brought to Columbus with them that loosened the ice" among whites, Jeffrey says.

Mary Lazarus was yet another of those white women. She came to Columbus in 1953 with her family from Connecticut. Before coming to Columbus she had worked in New York City for the National Scholarship Service and Fund for Negro Students. The fund identified gifted high school students in the South and found scholarship money for them to attend northern schools. Her husband, Robert Lazarus, hailed from the family that had founded Lazarus, the big downtown Columbus department store. "The city was pretty segregated," she remembers of Columbus at the time. "It was stagnant."

The Lazarus family also lived in Bexley, right off East Broad. "East Broad Street was the dividing line," she says about the city's racial dynamic. She also sat proudly on the board of the United Community Council. "I thought it was kind of our way of addressing the issues of race and the community's well-being." When National Urban League president Whitney Young came to Columbus, Mary and Robert hosted a dinner for him at their home. But there were simply too few like-minded whites to make effective change. The powerful Wolfe media empire held a grip on the city's politics that was proving impossible to loosen: "The Wolfes were terribly conservative and reactionary. That was the tone of the newspaper. We were very disgusted with the *Dispatch*'s editorials," she says. "They were very influential."

Bert Kram, a young lawyer who arrived in Columbus in 1966 from Chicago, was no stranger to urban education. But he was surprised at how segregated the Columbus school system was. Kram worked at the Bricker & Bricker law firm, one of the oldest firms in the city. He took his lunch at the downtown Athletic Club, like other successful white men in the city. When he and others wanted to have John Bowen, a black state representative in the Ohio legislature, join them for lunch, they were rebuffed. "The Athletic Club was not accepting blacks," he says. So the members who sided with Bowen began taking their lunch at the nearby Neil House Hotel. In 1968, following the death of Martin Luther King Jr., a group of attorneys, Kram and attorney Fred Isaac among them, went to the Columbus Symphony with an idea: They wanted the symphony to host a series of free concerts around the city—"tensions were very high in the city," he says—and make their concern known to the black East Side of town. "It had never been done before," Kram says of the proposal. The symphony officials liked the idea. They went to see East High principal Jack Gibbs. And Gibbs, being Gibbs, suggested they rehearse at East High, which they did. The concert was held in Franklin Park, just across the street from Gibbs's school. There was talk among concertgoers of King's life and the direction of the nation now. Symphonic music swept across the park. There was the mingling of black and white. For many whites in the city, it was the first racial mix they had witnessed aside from sports events that took place at neutral sites. Franklin Park was decidedly on the black side of town. The two worlds of East Broad Street, if only for a moment, came together.

But Ohio State University and the city's black East Side had a difficult time in coming together. The few notable blacks on the campus through the years had been athletes, and of that paltry number most had come from East High. It was as if the university were saying to the city's black East Side: Send us the best of the best of your athletes, but not your scholars and students seeking higher education. It wasn't until the tumult of 1968–69 that the university hired its first black administrator. His name was Madison Scott, and he was soon heading up their Office of Minority Affairs. He got more than he imagined upon taking the job; he was under constant siege by the round-the-clock protests about the widespread racial insensitivity throughout the campus. When a group of students was charged with felonies for taking over the administration building as part of their protest, the rancor only increased. Eventually, most of the charges were dropped, but the Ohio State administration seemed not to realize the depth of the spreading anger. They expected praise for bringing Earl Scarborough—the artist given modern credit for coining the "black is beautiful" phrase—to campus. But the protesting students were interested in political undertakings, not bestowing hosannas upon Earl Scarborough and his artistic coinage.

If Columbus was so conservative, how did it, in 1954, come to elect a Democratic mayor, M. E. (Jack) Sensenbrenner, and keep electing him all through the 1960s? (The city before then hadn't elected a Democratic mayor since the Great Depression.) And how come this Democratic mayor never was able to alter the political cast of the city? Why did he allow its segregationist mind-set to prevail for so long? The reasons for Sensenbrenner's rise varied, but it could be traced to his nonthreatening demeanor and the power of the banking and real estate barons who actually ran the small city. Sensenbrenner turned his leadership on racial matters into a kind of vaudeville shtick—understandable, as he had once tried to make a go of it in Hollywood. "It's a bad town for a football coach," the *Saturday Evening Post* would opine about the city in 1952, "but a good place for a politician." In that article, there was not one reference made to the black populace of Columbus, or the strains of segregation.

Jack Sensenbrenner was born in 1902 in a little farm town, Circleville, thirty miles outside of Columbus. In secondary school he was a cutup; teachers had to grab him by the ears plenty of times. It was a dream of his to make the Circleville High football team, something on offense, maybe split end. He ended up becoming the water boy. When the family made its way to Columbus after his high school years, they settled on the city's West Side. In those days, only the moneyed class were able to send their kids to college, and the Sensenbrenner family did not come from money, so Jack hit the open road, all the way to sunny California. He took some Bible college courses, thinking he might become a minister, but never completed the course load. He was skinny, had big dark eyebrows, and was quick to smile. California was mesmerizing, and it seemed wide open. He worked in oil fields, then sold ads for the *Los Angeles Times*. He reconnected with Mildred Sexhauer—he had fun pronouncing her last name—who had been his high school sweetheart. At heart he was a rube, and not at all ashamed of it. Mildred actually liked that trait about him. He went job to job, even laughed his way around the outskirts of Hollywood when he got work as an extra in movies. But in time they both decided to return to Columbus.

There were low-end civil service jobs, but they didn't really hold Jack Sensenbrenner's interest. He started to make a name for himself when he opened a store on the city's West Side, where he sold Bibles and religious knickknacks—a grinning Bible salesman. Knocking about the community in a straw skimmer hat, he handed out miniature American flags to children and strangers. The patriotic fervor from World War II still hung heavily in the air. The Kiwanis Club leadership, sensing his conviviality and fondness for interacting with the public, invited him to join, and he did. When he announced he was running for mayor in 1954, people laughed, including members of his own family. The GOP faction in the city was bickering internally that year, and while they were, Sensenbrenner went on TV, a novel move, and people recognized him as the guy always handing out flags around town, always stopping people in parks and chatting them up. His margin of victory was a mere four hundred votes, but he was on his way to City Hall. During his term in office, he made people laugh; he socialized on Mount Vernon Avenue, made friends with blacks. Some of the hard-core businesspeople wondered if he was a bit "touched" in the head. He lost his re-election bid in 1959; many felt he had bungled the city's reaction to a local flood. But he won election again in 1964. The white men who ran the city did not pay much attention to Jack Sensenbrenner because he was a kind of mascot, a harmless and grinning cheerleader for the city. "My mother called him 'Mayor Senseless-brenner,'" says basketball star Bo-Pete Lamar.

The flag-bearing mayor was in cahoots with the real estate barons in the city because he backed the annexing of suburban land, and so they supported him. It was a land tactic that kept the segregated neighborhoods segregated. When Sensenbrenner first entered City Hall, the city totaled forty-one square miles. During his years in office he tripled the city's square miles. So the power brokers kept patting Jack Sensenbrenner on the back. He was making the city money! In 1958, Columbus received an "All-America City Award" from the National League of Cities. But Sensenbrenner wasn't doing anything to shake up the social order. He never tried to deal with the city's segregation, or confront the issue of police brutality in the black community. The local black citizenry felt no reason to celebrate the city receiving any kind of award.

But there was something else that certain denizens of the black community celebrated: the numbers-running business. Numbers running was an illegal gambling enterprise that grew out of the Great Depression. In Columbus, the mafia-linked business was run by Frank Baldassaro and Marie Baldassaro, his sister. Jack Gibbs loathed the Baldassaro clan and their kind, but he couldn't stop their infiltration into the community. Law enforcement officials admitted the Baldassaros had control of more than 80 percent of the community's betting activities, drawing around $250,000 a week. In 1963, someone placed a bomb in a flower bed outside of Frank Baldassaro's home. The five family members at home at the time were lucky to escape injury. In 1969—during the East High basketball season—Frank Baldassaro was arrested and charged with having eight Columbus police officers on his payroll. Some of the blowback pointed at Mayor Sensenbrenner, who lacked tight control over his police department. The Baldassaro arrest was a juicy crime story, made all the more dramatic when Baldassaro hired F. Lee Bailey, one of the country's top criminal defense attorneys, to fight the charges. Bailey won an acquittal for Baldassaro and his co-defendants.

Despite not having a civil rights agenda, Mayor Sensenbrenner received a pass from the black community. The biggest reason was because he championed East High School. He attended its games, bopped into the school when he was in the neighborhood, laughed alongside the students—while handing out those flags—as if the best thing in the world would have been for someone to snap their fingers and transport him back into a high school. He wore his orange Tiger sweater to East High games.

So just like all the East High Tiger fans across the city in February of 1969, Mayor Sensenbrenner was extremely excited about the forthcoming East High–Linden-McKinley tournament matchup scheduled to take place at the Fairgrounds Coliseum.

Jack Sensenbrenner may not have done things in the city to advance the cause of civil rights, but, in their own way, the East High Tigers basketball team did: They were the boys whose pictures appeared on the front page of *The Columbus Dispatch* in previous years when the basketball team had won state championships. The photos on page one of the newspaper represented the largest number of black faces that had ever appeared on the newspaper's front page. The photos—above the fold—stunned many readers. But those pictures hadn't been of black-white racial unrest. They were of glory. And now the Tigers of Bob Hart were trying to repeat that glory.

· **7** ·

Panthers and Tigers, Oh My

Aside from their fierce rivalry and dominant black student populations, both the Linden-McKinley and East High School communities had one other defining thing in common during the 1968–69 school year: They were both contending with the forces of modernization, which were sapping the viability of businesses in their respective neighborhoods.

The Linden area had been an enclave for Italian families before and following World War II. The neighborhood was six miles from East High, on the city's North Side. Its business hub on Cleveland Avenue began to suffer in the 1950s, with the growth of the American suburb. Residents flocked to the nearby and newly built Northern Lights Shopping Center. White flight soon followed. Black families, eager to move into neighborhoods that offered minimal resistance to them, eagerly filled the gap, generating additional white flight. The effects could be seen in the hallways at Linden-McKinley High. "When I started," says Larry Mays, a senior on the 1968–69 Linden basketball team, "the school was 60 percent white, 40 percent black. By the time I graduated, it was 80 percent black and 20 percent white."

The East High dynamic, of course, was somewhat different: Its engineering into a segregated area had been designated by powerful city forces beginning in the early 1900s. Just as a new highway helped transport the Linden residents to their shopping center in the 1950s, the construction of Interstate 71 later in the 1950s deepened the East Side's isolation, further cutting off the business district of Mount Vernon Avenue from downtown. The highway only abetted a psychic isolation already in place. Both communities were looking for ways to survive the 1960s.

When it came to school bragging rights, the supporters of both teams were fiercely invested in winning. Both schools had bulging athletic trophy cases and could claim state championship basketball titles. East had been the first high school in the city to have a black principal, and the Tigers took every opportunity to remind any Linden High Panther of that. But when George Mills was named head basketball coach at the end of the previous season, Linden-McKinley became the first high school in the city to have a black head varsity basketball coach. And the Linden faithful took every chance they could to remind the Tigers of that fact.

George Mills was a native of Thorpe, West Virginia, a small coal-mining town. He was born in 1932, during the Depression, and he had a hard childhood. Following high school, he took one of the quickest routes to earning a paycheck (aside from working in the coal mines) when he joined Uncle Sam's army. He had been a good high school basketball player, and the military put those skills to use, placing him with a touring army basketball team. The team traveled to various bases, playing games and entertaining troops. When his military service ended, Mills returned to West Virginia and attended all-black West Virginia State College, where he eventually became captain of the basketball team. (One of Mills's closest basketball friends was Earl Loyd, who also played at West Virginia State College. On October 31, 1950, Loyd officially became the first black to play in an NBA game. Two other black players were selected days later for other teams that season. In 1968, following an illustrious NBA playing career, Loyd became the first black named an NBA assistant coach in the league with the Detroit Pistons.) Not long after graduating from college, George Mills made his way to Columbus, where he began his teaching and coaching career. In addition to the pressure of being the first black varsity basketball coach in the city, Mills also faced constant reminders of his predecessor, Vince Chickerella, who was revered for leading Linden to its 1967 state title. When Chickerella took the head coaching job at Capital University in the city, Mills had stepped into the shoes of a legend. To gain similar respect, he had to do one thing: win.

There was one area in which East High one-upped Linden-McKinley and that was on the radio airwaves. Blacks in the city faithfully listened to WVKO, the white-owned and black-produced radio station that played the kind of music—soul, the blues—that was heard in black America at the time. Kirk Bishop, an East High student, was one of its disc jockeys. His Tigers could do no wrong, and on radio he cackled as he made little effort to conceal his favoritism for the Tigers.

In case there was anyone in the city who had been hiding beneath rocks—or not listening to radio station WVKO—there was an ad in *The Spectator* newspaper two days before the March 8 game: "Two Old Cage Rivals—East and Linden—Clash in 'AA' District Tourney Finals Saturday.'"

Bob Hart had prepared as fastidiously as ever for the game. On Friday following the team's practice session at school, he handed out a printed twenty-four-hour schedule labeled a "Tournament Bulletin." Highlighted on the top of the bulletin and in capital letters was yet another pearl of wisdom Hart had rummaged up from someplace: THE WORST THING ABOUT CROSSING A BRIDGE BEFORE YOU GET TO IT, IS THAT IT ALWAYS LEAVES YOU ON THIS SIDE OF THE RIVER. Billy Williams, the team's student manager, who had polio—"he worked so hard," remembers Bo-Pete Lamar—always got a chuckle out of Hart's little ditties.

The players were going to be sequestered the night before the game at a local motel. That evening after practice they had to get home, have supper, and wait for the assigned coach to pick them up for the trip to the motel. Hart's itinerary was minutely detailed with player pickups: "Mike Owens (8:30); Roy Hickman (8:37); Kenny Mizelle (8:40); Robert Wright (8:45)." The strict timeline reflected his military training. And shame on the player who was even a minute late when the coach tooted the car horn. (Everyone on the team remembered the time star player Eddie Rat was late to meet the team bus and had to get to the game on his own.) Assistant Coach Pennell picked up a group of four players, and Pete Basich—an assistant football coach who happily volunteered for driving duties—picked up the remaining players. Once the players settled in at the motel, Hart huddled with his assistant coaches to go over the game plan. He was concerned with the speed of Linden's backcourt, Calvin Wade and Donnie Penn, as well as the skill of Willie Williams, the team's gifted senior center. All had double-digit scoring averages.

Scott Guiler, the Tigers' volunteer coach who compiled all of the team statistics, had been watching East's center, Nick Conner, closely all season long. He was just as amazed at Conner's leaping ability as anyone else. Every Tigers fan would howl—*whooooo!*—when Conner menacingly blocked an opposing player's shot. "He'd knock it into the stands," Guiler recalls. "They [the opposing team] would get the ball back. So I started saying to Nick, 'Don't slap the ball into the stands; slap it to one of your teammates.'" It was a little thing, yet not so little. Conner played much of his game on instinct. Coaches and players had always marveled at his jumping ability. A swatted ball into the stands sent a clear message. But a ball that was swatted to one's own teammate increased the chances of a Tiger breakaway fast break and possible points. And that is what Nick Conner vowed to do going forward in the tournament: block shots toward one of his teammates, not away from them into the stands.

The East High Tigers departed their motel at exactly 12:45 p.m. Saturday, March 8, for the fifteen-minute ride to the Fairgrounds Coliseum. Because high schools had to pay a rental fee to use the Coliseum, most teams didn't play games there except during tournament time, when the school system helped out with fees. But Jack Gibbs knew that East High represented more than just the school itself; it was a vibrant part of the black community at large. So for the past few years, in order to build up a little financial nest egg for the fees it cost to play at the Coliseum, which East did more than any other school, he went to his alma mater, Ohio State University, and asked them if East High could set up a concession booth at OSU football games to raise money for the school. The university obliged, so when the 1968–69 basketball season rolled around, East High had enough money on hand to host practically all of its games at the Coliseum. It gave them an edge come tournament time. Yet again, it was just Jack Gibbs being Jack Gibbs.

When the East High team pulled up to the Coliseum grounds, they could see the waving gold-and-white pom-poms of the Linden fans as they sashayed between cars in the parking lot. They could also see the orange-and-black pom-poms clutched tightly in the hands of the Tiger faithful scooting into the Coliseum. There was also a lot of chatter between opposing fan bases. Recent matchups between the two teams had resulted in close scores—60–56, 77–73, 72–70, 77–69—and everyone expected another tight battle. While East had a psychological lift—they were riding a No. 1 ranking in the state polls—Linden had its own adrenaline kick: they were the last team to defeat the Ratleff-Conner duo back when the two seniors were sophomores.

Mills, the Linden coach, was in his locker room with his players, huddling over team strategy. Before the season began, he had told his Panthers they could defeat the Tigers if they managed to contain Ratleff and Conner. Mills believed the Tigers were a one-dimensional team. The addition of the thoroughbred Bo-Pete Lamar certainly upset that assessment.

Still, the Linden coach had devised a strategy: "It was going to be speed versus a tall rebounding team," recalls Larry Mays, one of the Panthers' starting forwards. "They had an inside—and with Lamar—now an outside threat. We had all-around speed. The strategy for us was—start to finish—a full-court press. And when the ball went inside, we were to collapse. Their only outside threat was Lamar."

Hart was constantly asked about the two teams during the season. "It's always been a game where we have the size and they have the speed," he had remarked. "They have that quickness and the shooting ability out front that we have to stop." Hart was not shy about praising his two dynamic forwards when talking to reporters. "I don't believe there is a team in the country that has two players the caliber of these boys," he opined about Ratleff and Conner. But he had also begun talking up the gifts that Lamar and Hickman had brought to the team. Hickman had turned into one of the team's wiliest and most versatile players. "I didn't even figure on him as a squad member before the season," Hart confessed about Hickman during the tournament. Hickman's average of 11 points per game had become a welcome scoring gift. But what Hart really liked about Hickman was his improved ball-handling skills. When teams were overpowering Larry Walker, the diminutive East guard, Hickman could help out with his deft ball handling.

On the day of the East–Linden-McKinley matchup, Mount Vernon Avenue was mighty quiet. Everyone was at the game.

More than seven thousand people had taken their seats for the tip-off. Among them were Bob Hart's parents, who deemed the game important enough to fly in from their summer home in West Palm Beach, Florida. Jack Gibbs strolled into the East locker room before the game. It was a familiar ritual, a moment to wish the team well, to talk about sportsmanship and shake the players' hands. But as he scanned their faces, Jack Gibbs saw something he did not like. Nick Conner hadn't shaved; he had too much facial hair for Gibbs's liking. Gibbs expressed his displeasure. Suddenly the players' attention was yanked away from Coach Hart, who was ready to discuss game strategy. "Gibbs said, 'Somebody get an electric razor,'" Tiger player Kevin Smith recalls. Conner was soon handed a razor and everyone stood around as he shaved. Even away from East High and inside a Coliseum locker room, his students were still part of the house that Jack built.

By the end of the first quarter, with a raucous crowd bouncing up and down in their seats, East had raced to a 5-point lead, 24–19. Because Mays had muscle and used it well beneath the boards, Linden's coach had assigned him to guard Eddie Rat. Mays knew the Ratleff mystique quite well. "He was not overrated," he recalls years later. "He could do what people said he could do." At one stanza the Tigers had a 15-point lead. The Panthers were simply unable to contain the Tiger frontcourt. By halftime Linden had narrowed the East lead to 9 points. The faces of the Panther faithful were marked by distress.

Mills, a tall and elegant man who dressed in sharp suits, told his team during halftime that not only could they get back in the game, but they could win it, provided they stuck to their game plan—the full-court press and getting up and down the court as quickly as they could. "And we played them end to end," Linden's Mays recalls. Once the game resumed, East continually broke the Linden full-court press by simply positioning either Ratleff or Conner on the wings; they were tall enough to jump and get a pass from Walker or Lamar and pass it on downcourt. Linden's balanced scoring, however, was a problem: Donnie Penn—Lamar's former teammate—was dazzling the crowd en route to an 11–17 shooting night. Linden's Willie Williams, on his way to converting 8 of 13 field goals, seemed intent throughout to prove he would not be intimidated by Conner or Ratleff. As the minutes wound down in the third quarter, the Panthers, on a basket by Cliff Sawyer, drew even with the Tigers at 53–53, and the Linden crowd erupted in bedlam. The Tigers answered with a scoring spurt of their own, but it subdued the enthusiasm of the Panther partisans, who were still thumping when their team was down by just 4 points at the end of the third. Panther momentum was undeniably building. Early into the fourth quarter, East found itself unable to extend their lead; with 6:22 left on the clock, they led by just 2 points, 61–59. But it was in that fourth quarter that the Tigers of Bob Hart, as if it were all but inevitable, began to truly impose their will and dominate. Eddie Rat slithered, snakelike, dropping in shots from a variety of angles, using finesse to counter the muscle of Larry Mays. Linden was whistled for more than a dozen fouls on Eddie Rat; he converted 9 of 14 free throw attempts. He made an astounding 13 of 17 field goals on his way to a blistering 35-point night. Bo-Pete Lamar chipped in 19 points as East High brought Linden's season-long dream to a close, defeating them 79–71.

Once again, a victory against Linden-McKinley felt like some kind of hard-earned escape. Jack Gibbs began making his way to the locker room to join the players. The Tiger fans were already chanting the familiar fight song:

> I went down to the river
> Oh yeah
> And I started to drown
> Oh yeah

I started thinking about them Tigers
Oh yeah
And I came back around

After being shoved fully clothed into the locker room shower by his players, Bob Hart stood around grinning. His daughters and parents surrounded him, planting kisses. The Panthers had been the elephant on the Tigers' back. Now the Panthers—and the elephant—were gone.

The East High faithful began hoping, and praying, that their Tigers would keep this dream alive.

· **8** ·

The Church Where
Martin Luther King Jr. Preached

Rev. Phale Hale and his wife, Cleo, wasted little time in congratulating the East High Tigers on their recent basketball tournament victory. Mrs. Hale got a kick out of the boys and their good manners when they visited the church. At the church's Youth Days, when kids would come in from all over the city to dine and have intellectual debates about the important issues of the day, it always seemed that an East High student walked home with one of the Youth of the Year awards. The intellectual debates weren't the only draw: "There were a lot of pretty girls at Reverend Hale's church!" remembers East basketball player Kevin Smith.

One of those pretty girls was Marna Hale, a classmate of Eddie Rat who would also be graduating with the Class of 1969. Her sister, Janice, was a 1966 graduate of East High. (She was away at Spelman College.) The Hale girls were known to be proper, poised, and quite conscious of the weight the family name carried throughout the community.

Cleo Hale noted that her husband seemed fond of the basketball players. He respected that they had not participated in any kind of disturbances after the death of King. The Hales thought quite highly of Jack Gibbs and were quick to give him credit for turning the school

Martin Luther King Jr. in Columbus in 1956 to talk about racial tragedies sweeping the South. He preached at Union Grove Baptist Church.

around academically. They could also see the influence East High's basketball team had on their own small son, Hilton, who had already begun playing basketball. (He'd star at East High in later years.) Following the team's big victories, Mrs. Hale and the impressive cooks in the Union Grove congregation always tried to fulfill the boys' requests for sweet potato pie. It was a common dessert among southern families; household recipes had been brought north during the Great Migration. "I remember those pies," says Bob Whitman, a reporter for *The Spectator* newspaper who covered the 1968–69 team. "The coach liked them too."

.   .   .

The black church has always been a bulwark for black communities throughout the country. Ministers of large congregations were not just ministers; they were so often conduits to the white community and downtown politicians. They often turned their churches into job counseling and social service centers. They allowed their churches to serve as community gathering places in the aftermath of racial tragedies. They could be seen marching into the offices of newspaper editors demanding fairer coverage. And many of these ministers, during the fire of the 1960s, stood at great risk as they led economic boycotts against businesses that practiced discrimination. Over the decades the black church had morphed into an intense religious and social service organization. Black ministers were often wary of bringing politics into the pulpit, that is until they were no longer able to avoid doing so. As the civil rights movement dawned, they couldn't help but write sermons that reflected the realities on the streets. While Union Grove Baptist wasn't the only notable black church in Columbus, it was one of the most prominent— political and outspoken. Reverend Hale had entered the backbiting world of politics himself in 1966, becoming a state representative, all with the blessings of his congregation.

Although many churches were founded because of dissension in other parishes, Union Grove grew from the seeds of a Sunday-school class and the progressive thinking of a white missionary.

Cordelia Thompson looked around the city in the years following slavery's demise and could see the desperate conditions of blacks and how they hungered for places of worship. Traversing the city's East Side, she came upon not a rock, but a large oak tree on Champion Avenue. She thought it was a good place to summon Negro families to worship. The gatherings from that first Sunday grew, with girls and boys parading down Mount Vernon Avenue wearing their dresses and bonnets and knickers, holding their parents' hands. Everyone sat outside on simple chairs in the open air of this makeshift church. As interest continued to grow, the idea of a structure—a roof over everyone's head—was talked about, especially as the weather began to change. A fund-raising effort was begun, with pennies, nickels, quarters collected, whatever congregants could contribute from their own humble earnings. When there were ample funds, construction began, and by the early spring of 1888, a log cabin rose on the site. Members kept joining, and quickly the cabin was no longer big enough to hold the swelling congregation. A new, more solid structure was completed in 1889.

As with churches throughout time, there were changes in the pulpit at Union Grove, and wrenching concerns about finances. Some ministers were sent packing because they were unable to galvanize the congregation, or add to its membership. The separations were not always quiet; some former ministers publicly grumbled about being owed back pay. In 1911, Rev. R. Doyle Phillips took over the pastorate of the church and added stability. On one fine day in April of 1913, he guided sixty-one souls over to Alum Creek—just yards beyond East Broad Street—and dipped their heads in the chilly water, baptizing them to rapt applause. Phillips was also responsible for building the church—impressive looking with its rising steps going upward from ground level—that still sits on North Champion Avenue today. Following Reverend Phillips's tenure, the church summoned Rev. Morris Allison Trier. His was a successful pastorate; he paid off the church's debt on its building, a point of pride for church members. The church also managed to purchase a parsonage—a church home for minister and wife—under Trier's leadership. After twenty-two years in the pulpit, Trier stepped aside, receiving a bounty of gifts. Word raced about the Negro Baptist church grapevine that Union Grove was in need of a new pastor. They found him in Fort Wayne, Indiana.

As a young minister, Phale Hale realized that in his occupation he might be setting off on an itinerant journey and lifestyle. When young Hale was at Morehouse in 1938, he met Joel King Sr., Martin Luther King's brother. Joel King already had his own church but had come to Morehouse because he thought a pastor should buttress his oratory with intellectual study. Joel King's approach had a great effect on student Phale Hale, who sought King out as a mentor, a role the minister eagerly accepted. In a short time, Joel King took Hale over to meet the King family, and the Kings brought him into the family fold. There was an uncanny physical resemblance between Martin Luther King Jr. and Phale Hale; everyone teased the two about that. (Years later, in 1952, when the great Vernon Johns was preparing to leave Atlanta's Dexter Avenue Baptist Church, the deacons considered a host of possible young ministers as his replacement, among them Martin Luther King Jr.—and Phale Hale. "My father instead took a job in Fort Wayne," says Janice Hale. "My father and Reverend King always talked about how history could have been quite different.")

Phale Hale started out at a small church in La Grange, Georgia. But he was often back and forth to Atlanta, where he had met Cleo Ingram. The Ingrams were a middle-class Negro family who resided in the same neighborhood as the King family. Cleo Ingram's father was a chauffeur in Atlanta for a well-to-do white family. The family had the resources to send Cleo off to Spelman College, where she was studying when she met Hale. The two were married in 1943, her junior year. They lived apart for a year as Hale took over the church in La Grange, a small rural community. He undertook investigations into the lynching of blacks, telling his wife he was not going to shy away from a bold ministry. Soon another church opportunity presented itself.

In Fort Wayne, Indiana, at Union Baptist Church, Hale and his wife established themselves as progressives. They were staunch members of the NAACP; Hale once led a successful sit-in to desegregate a lunch counter in the city. The whites in Indiana had long had a reputation for being hostile toward blacks. The state was seen as safe territory for the Ku Klux Klan and their wicked deeds. In 1930, three young black men who had been accused of murder and rape were rousted from their jail cells in Marion, Indiana, fifty miles from Fort Wayne, and taken to the town square. The evidence on the murder charge was strong; the alleged rape victim later denied she had been raped. But it wasn't a case that would ever reach a courtroom. Two of the accused, Thomas Shipp and Abram Smith, were lynched a day after their arrests. They hung from a tree for hours while whites sneered and laughed and posed for Lawrence Bietler, the photographer, whose photos of the lynching became quite famous. The third accused, sixteen-year-old James Cameron, was spared because someone spoke up at the last minute and said he hadn't participated in the crime. He was rushed out of town, though he ended up serving four years as an accessory to the murder. Local blacks were able to engage the Quaker community to help in their cause to improve the charged racial environment in 1940s Indiana.

When the Hales arrived in Columbus to take over at Union Grove Baptist, they were intent on putting their potent connections to good use. Traveling to Baptist conventions over the years, Reverend Hale had gotten to know many of the great black preachers of the day, among them Gardner Taylor, from Brooklyn; Adam Clayton Powell Jr. from Harlem; and, of course, Martin Luther King Jr., who, before he could claim a national following, had ministered at churches in both Alabama and Georgia. The Hales began inviting the Kings to Columbus in the late 1950s, and the Kings made several visits to the city and the Hale home over the years.

Coretta Scott King, a native of Alabama, had attended Antioch College, in Yellow Springs, Ohio, and then Boston's New England Conservatory of Music. She met Martin Luther King Jr. in Boston, where he was attending Boston University, studying for his doctorate in theology. He wooed her with poetry, asides about civil rights in America, and stories about Mahatma Gandhi's protests in India. At first she found his powerful sense of self off-putting, but as time went on she found his self-possession impressive and ultimately endearing. They were married on June 18, 1953, in Alabama. They drove around after the reception, hunting for an attractive place to spend their wedding night. No white-owned resorts or hotels would serve them because of segregation laws, so they knew to bypass them. They became exhausted from looking. Through family connections, Coretta knew of a roomy residence, but it happened to be a place where the dead went: It was a well-appointed Negro funeral parlor. They chuckled about it, but they were husband and wife, and very happy.

When Martin Luther King Jr. fully got going in his ministry and activism, the country realized it had never seen anyone like him. There had certainly been Negro figures on the national stage, but they had often been looked upon with a jaundiced eye by mainstream white America. W. E. B. DuBois, the Harvard-trained scholar, was brilliant but was considered aloof and cranky, and besides, the world of academia was flagrantly segregated. The majority of whites simply ignored DuBois— both his scholarship and prophecies, profound as they might have been. Daddy Grace and Father Divine, ministerial figures who claimed newspaper headlines along with large black followings, had a whiff of eyebrow-raising strangeness about them: Women were their main acolytes, and both ministers talked about reincarnation while they celebrated opulence. Paul Robeson, the aggrieved athlete and actor, had a towering visage that did not exactly lend itself to balancing the stereotyped images many whites already held of any oversized black man. He acted onstage alongside white women. He visited Russia, where he was seen in the company of more white women. As well, he had been wounded by aligning himself with Communist sympathizers, which doomed any chance of his gaining widespread appeal. The young Martin Luther King Jr. was a different story altogether.

King had burnished his ministerial ambitions with a sterling mainstream education, first Morehouse College, then Boston University, where he earned a legitimate PhD. (The "Dr." affixed to the name of many Baptist ministers during King's era was often a decoration.) From King's first sermon at Dexter Avenue Baptist Church in Montgomery, Alabama, on September 5, 1954, he let the congregation know he was going to be an activist minister. "Every member of Dexter must be a registered voter," he would later tell his flock. Then came the bus boycotts, spurred by seamstress Rosa Parks. Financial contributions poured into Montgomery to support the boycott; money was sent from church groups all over the nation, including Union Grove Baptist in Columbus. There were marches and protests all across the South. Then came those visits to the White House to see President Eisenhower. King visited pulpits across America, from Milwaukee to Chicago to Columbus, Ohio, and points in between. Then came the March on Washington, followed by a meeting at the White House with President Kennedy. Then came Selma. On March 7th—without King—a group of demonstrators gathered at the foot of the Edmund Pettus Bridge in the small Alabama town. An all-white police contingent, some on horseback, viciously attacked them. The bloody scene was horrifying. Many of the peaceful demonstrators would later need medical attention. Two days later, King led another march across the bridge. It was an epic scene, and the racially mixed gathering and march touched many across the world. On October 14, 1964, in Oslo, Norway, King was awarded the Nobel Peace Prize and gained international acclaim. Then came more arrests and more marches. It all ended on April 4, 1968, during the trip to Memphis when the escaped convict, crouching at a window, fired.

Phale and Cleo Hale had found much to like and emulate in the lives of Martin Luther King Jr. and Coretta. When they journeyed to Baptist conventions and ran into the Kings, there was so much to catch up on besides church matters; there was also their children and relatives and mutual friends to talk about.

On Saturday, April 14, 1956, King was in Columbus to address a statewide NAACP meeting. That evening he gave a rousing NAACP address at the Veterans Memorial in downtown Columbus to raise money for the boycotters in Montgomery. The Hales proudly played hosts. The Kings were back again in 1960. King always preached from the Union Grove pulpit when he was in Columbus. "It was like double Easter," recalls Janice Hale. "There were chairs in the aisle. There were people in the basement. People were standing outside. I had never seen anything like it."

After his sermon that morning, Rev. Phale Hale escorted King to the basement of the church where he signed copies of his recent book, *Stride Toward Freedom.* There was extra security at the church book signing because of a gruesome incident that had happened when King was autographing copies of his book on September 20, 1958, at Blumstein's Department Store in Harlem. A black woman, dressed rather elegantly, approached his table. "Is this Martin Luther King Jr.?" she asked King upon reaching him. In a flash, she pulled a letter opener from beneath her coat and thrust it into King's chest. King saw the blade coming but couldn't stop it. There was immediate pandemonium. The assailant, whose name was Izola Curry, cried out, "I've been after him for six years! I'm glad I done it!" King was rushed to the hospital, the blade still poking from his chest. At the hospital, the doctors saw how delicate their procedure to remove the blade would have to be. The blade was lodged between King's heart and lung. In order to extract it, doctors had to crack and remove two of King's ribs and a portion of his breastbone. A doctor told King something that made Negro America, and many other Americans, shiver: If King had sneezed with the blade inside him, that close to his heart, he would not have lived. Curry, the would-be murderer of King, was committed to the Matteawan State Hospital for the Criminally Insane.

"I remember in 1960 when King was staying at our house," says Janice Hale, "and he was taking a bath. He called my father into the bathroom and showed him the scar from where he had been stabbed. He told my father he could have died." The Hale parents did not believe in banishing their children to other parts of the house while grown-ups were having dinner. The children sitting at the dinner table were expected to engage in the conversation. "To sit and listen to my father discuss the civil rights movement was just amazing," says Janice Hale, who was a twelve-year-old in 1960.

The preachers with whom Rev. Phale Hale most aligned himself philosophically had certainly turned their churches into hubs of activism. So it was not surprising that he decreed that a part of Union Baptist's budget would go to the NAACP and the Southern Christian Leadership Conference (SCLC), two leading organizations in the fight for equality. His successes in the area of civil rights in Columbus could not be disputed, and it is little wonder he faced no blowback when he decided to enter politics. As a state representative, he forced the city to hire the first black bank teller, and then he forced the state to hire the first black state highway patrolman. His protests forced Ohio State University to hire its first black professor. A bill he promoted desegregated local cemeteries. He met the famous men and women of his times and personally welcomed many of them to Columbus: Joe Louis, Eleanor Roosevelt, Jackie Robinson, Robert F. Kennedy. He stood on Mount Vernon Avenue alongside President Jimmy Carter, who came to the city to celebrate the opening of a shopping plaza built in an effort to save the street from further blight.

But 1968 was a painful time for Phale and Cleo Hale. Their friend Martin was gone. The riots across the country from the summer left them both bewildered. Cleo checked in as often as she could on Coretta Scott King, who was in deep pain. Spirits slowly lifted for the Hales as the months rolled along. The victories piling up by the East High basketball team gave them reasons to smile. Reverend Hale couldn't help calling out team members when they were at the church for Sunday services, asking them to stand up. At home, he'd flip open the newspaper and smile as he read the story about the Tigers and their 1969 tournament climb. Then, as so often that season, there would be another story in the same edition reminding him of what had happened in Memphis.

On March 17, 1969, *The Columbus Dispatch* had a story about Eddie Rat being named UPI AA player of the year. In that same edition—right on the flip page of the Eddie Rat story—was a story about the King assassination with the headline "Ray's Judge Admits Case Baffles." The piece focused on Judge W. Preston Battle of Memphis, who had heard Ray's guilty plea, given in lieu of a trial. Battle revealed he had plenty of questions surrounding the case. "I would truly like to know how Ray actually found the spot from which to fire. How did Ray know where Rev. King would be? How did he determine the type of weapon to be used? What are the details of the actual purchases and selection of the weapon? Was he alone in surveillance of the Lorraine Motel? Most puzzling of all is his escape from Memphis. To me, it seems miraculous that he was able to flee to Atlanta despite the all-points bulletins without his white Mustang being spotted on a highway."

Since the death of King, the Hales, like so many, had been pondering many of those same questions. They had been mulling them over from the moment news of King's death reached them in the humble and elegant parsonage where they lived, where they had sat regaling King about the schools in the city, about the burgeoning protests in Columbus, about the inroads they had been making in civil rights.

9

St. John Arena

Following their defeat of Linden-McKinley, East High's reward was a Thursday night Central Region semi-final match at the Fairgrounds Coliseum against the Zanesville High School Blue Devils. Before the regional finals games took place, reps from all four teams—East, Newark, Zanesville, and Portsmouth—gathered at the Fort Hayes Hotel in downtown Columbus to discuss the tournament.

Both Newark and Zanesville, co-winners of the Central Ohio League, had traditionally fielded good, solid basketball teams. They were the only high schools in their immediate rural surroundings, and, therefore, they were large schools with a wide swath of students. Each school automatically drew the best athletes from their area. A section of Franklin County—where the Columbus schools were located—might have three high schools in one section of the city. The good players were dispersed among them. To play against Zanesville or Newark High was like playing against an all-star team from each of those respective districts.

Zanesville had beaten Bellaire St. John, 72–52, to get this far. Bellaire had one of the most prolific scorers in the state, Allan Hornyak, who averaged 38 points per game, and Zanesville held him to just 14 points by playing stellar defense. "Zanesville does a lot of things well," Bob Hart noted. "They're methodical and very well disciplined." As had long been his habit, Hart sought out gritty teams to scrimmage with before the start of each season. Before the current season had gotten under way, he had taken his team to Newark. "And we were pretty even," he remembered.

By this time, East had played more than enough games during its undefeated season for any team to get a good scouting report outlining their strengths and weaknesses. The Zanesville coaches were well aware that Linden-McKinley had often collapsed on the inside against the Tigers when Ratleff or Conner had the ball, believing the duo had only one outlet if they didn't shoot and that was to kick the ball back out to Bo-Pete Lamar. The implication was that the Tigers didn't have a player who could destroy an opponent from long range aside from Lamar.

Grady Smith (no relation to the team's Kevin Smith) had not seen a lot of action during the season. He was an able player and possessed a very sweet outside jump shot. There were those among the student body who imagined his basketball fortunes had been stymied by Lamar's transfer to the school. The feeling was that if Lamar hadn't joined the East team, Grady Smith would have started alongside Larry Walker. Grady Smith was a senior experiencing his last hurrah on the high school court. Bob Hart had a motto—and accompanying thoughts—that he had shared with his team and coaches: "Good team spirit and morale, one for all, all for one, is the most important asset of a winning team. So I believe the solution to the problem of morale is very simple—all you have to do is win and your squad morale will be good." The Tigers were winning; Grady Smith didn't whine about his lack of playing time. And now, thick in the tournament, Bob Hart, knowing his team had been scouted in depth, just might need Grady Smith's outside shooting at some point.

High school gyms tended to be small and rather intimate, so the canyon-like space of the Coliseum was a bewildering environment that most teams had to get used to. But to East High, the Coliseum was as comfortable as a home court; they had played eleven games there thus far in their season. Don Stahl, the Zanesville coach, complained to the Ohio High School Athletic Association that East High had an

advantage because it had played so many games there. Coliseum officials huddled and decided to give Stahl's team extra practice time on the
Coliseum floor. When Stahl's team arrived for practice, they shivered in
the locker room. It was chilly. Perhaps the custodians hadn't turned on
the heat for the locker rooms just yet? Surely the court would be much
warmer. It wasn't. The Coliseum was always a drafty place, the tempera-
ture sometimes hovering around 40 degrees. Players were blowing their
warm breaths into their hands. Stahl cut the practice short after just
fifteen minutes. Hart challenged the grumbling from coaches about his
team having an advantage at the Coliseum. In his mind, the fact that a
brand-new floor had been installed at the beginning of the season neutralized any advantage his team might have had. "That new floor is a big
difference now," he opined in early February, trying to quiet the complaints. "It's completely neutral to any team in the tournament, and that
includes East." The coach was being a bit disingenuous. The Tigers did
indeed have an advantage at the arena.

At East, a day before the game, Hart put his Tigers through a ninety-
minute workout. Mostly it consisted of shooting drills. He didn't want
to hear any Tiger player talking about the last time they had played
Zanesville, in a regional tournament matchup a year earlier that East
won, 83–51. The Zanesville team this year was vastly superior to the
squad from a year ago. They had proven they had better balance and
more outside shooting power.

Bob Hart sat and watched as the Blue Devils of Zanesville High raced
up and down the court with genuine confidence at the game's outset. It
was a savvy and all-senior starting lineup. They hit their first two shots,
then hit three more. That sent a buzz through the crowd, and the buzz
kept up as Zanesville, astonishingly, fired in three more consecutive
shots. Eight for eight. Hart didn't panic but his eyes widened. There was
a reason Zanesville was currently ranked No. 4 in the state. Hart called
a timeout. He saw that Zanesville was completely ignoring his point
guard, Larry Walker—who had an anemic outside shot—and crowding
their defense down low against Ratleff and Conner. Play resumed, and
minutes later the buzzer sounded, bringing the first quarter to a close.
The Tiger faithful saw something they were absolutely unaccustomed to

seeing on the scoreboard: An opponent was leading their Tigers, 19–14. The Zanesville High followers, crowded onto their side of the Coliseum, were ecstatic. Hart looked over at Grady Smith and motioned for him to check in to the game at the start of the second quarter. Then he drew up plans for either Eddie Rat or Roy Hickman to handle the ball and scoop it over to Smith when he rounded the perimeter. "East knew it was in for a tough night" is how local reporter Lou Berliner put it.

Seizing on his moment, as if sent straight from central casting, Grady Smith started shooting, and scoring. His first jump shot went in, as did his second. He was feeling it. So he shot again, and it went in. Yet another shot. And it also went in. The East crowd rose up out of their seats. As the half drew to a close, East had reclaimed the lead, 37–33, the last points the result of a lovely lob pass from Conner to Eddie Rat, who scored. It was not a comfortable lead, but it gave the tired Tiger players a burst of needed confidence as they made their way to the locker room. The Zanesville coaches were fairly content. Their 2-1-2 zone, principally designed to stifle outside shooting by the opponent, had been working perfectly, and their senior leadership was beyond being rattled against a tough opponent.

Midway through the third quarter, Zanesville was up again, 43–41. Conner quickly tied the score with a basket. (Conner scored only 3 points in the first half; he'd produce 14 points in the second half.) By the end of the quarter, East had a 56–49 lead that seemed more fragile than a 7-point spread should have been. In the fourth quarter, Hart called for a semi-stall, slowing the momentum of the game with his team holding on to the ball as long as possible before taking a shot. They cut two minutes off the clock on a couple of possessions, frustrating Zanesville. With six minutes left, the East High lead was 60–52. With 3:55 left, Eddie Rat broke loose for a score, then Conner did the same thing. East was now leading 66–54. The East bench players, leaning onto the court and displaying wild exuberance, got called for a technical foul. It mattered little as Zanesville couldn't catch the Tigers now. The game ended—and none too soon for Bob Hart—with a score of 72–65. Ratleff had 16 points, Conner 17 points, and Lamar 23 points. And East outrebounded Zanesville, 35–26. But it was the unsung Grady Smith—who had come off the bench and deposited 12 points at a crucial time in the game that most impressed Hart. "You've got to throw all kinds of bouquets in Grady Smith's direction," Hart allowed after the game. "We worked all week with Hickman out on the point to set up Grady."

With all of the City League teams from Columbus eliminated from the tournament save East High, the city, and especially the inner-city denizens, began turning its attention and support toward the Tigers. Fans who had railed against the East High juggernaut during the season when the fate of their own teams was at stake were now coming out to root for the Tigers. It was city pride. The outpouring of black Tiger fan support quadrupled. Given the continuing turmoil over the King assassination, law enforcement in the city sensed a potential for urban mayhem at the Coliseum, a feared clash between white and black. It meant extra pressure on Jack Gibbs: If any unrest was ignited, he knew East High would bear the brunt of the blame. He had told his students as much. Whether it was the presence of extra security, or Gibbs's warnings about unrest, there had been nary a problem thus far. The unique ball skills of East High's team had tamped down all those murmurings of disorder. Jack Gibbs swelled with pride. Local whites began rooting for the Tigers.

After the victory against Zanesville High, the small restaurants and burger joints up and down Mount Vernon Avenue filled up with East High fans. They bounded into the Chesapeake Bar and Grill to order the pork chop sandwiches. They sidled up to the counter at Sandy's, the hamburger joint on the avenue, and ordered fries and burgers and milkshakes. The coolest of the cool stood around on the corner in front of neon-lit Sandy's in their leather jackets wolfing their burgers down, talking about what Eddie Rat, Bo-Pete, and Grady Smith ("Gradeee!") had just done against Zanesville. In the cold and winning night, everyone was happy.

With their defeat of Zanesville, East High had won one of the two regional final games. Next they needed to get into the final of the state tournament. But first they had to face Newark High, which also had a mighty basketball pedigree. Those who wanted to be nostalgic might mention that the school had won three state basketball titles, one in 1936, another in 1938, and a final one in 1943. Many years separated the present team from such glory. The team, however, was talented, physical, and, because of their state title drought, hungry.

Despite some nifty defensive efforts against them by double teaming Ratleff so often, it would have done opposing coaches well to remember that East High's current team was averaging a school record 84 points a game. They were capable of exploding at any moment in a game. Earlier in the season, Fred Heischman, the West High coach, had said that East could certainly be beaten, but everything would have to be "on your side," meaning the team that would beat the Tigers would have to have some luck.

Of all the teams he had faced thus far in the tournament, Bob Hart admitted that Newark gave him the most concern. They were a physical team with enviable height and crafty veterans. "Newark could have the strength to challenge the Tigers inside, along with a size advantage at three of five positions," noted *The Columbus Dispatch* sportswriter Dick Otte. Newark's front line—the players who would be grappling with East's Conner and Ratleff—consisted of six-foot-five Dennis Odle; six-foot-four Gary Carter; and six-foot-three Bruce Kibler. Otte wrote that that trio possessed an "ability to get out and move on offense, or block shots defensively while retaining the muscle to contend for rebounds at either end of the court." John Daniels, at six foot four, was an aggressive guard known for his shot-blocking abilities. (He also had been one of the state's finest quarterbacks.) Newark's other guard was five-foot-ten John Snow.

Newark coach Dick Schenk's plan to beat East was to slow the ball down. He and his assistant coaches figured the best chance for their team to win was to play a very methodical game. And that is exactly what Newark did in front of the noisy crowd during the first quarter. East's scoring was anemic; Nick Conner didn't score a single point the entire first quarter. When the buzzer sounded, Newark led, 14–8. Eight points represented East's lowest first-quarter scoring all season. It became evident in the second quarter that East was having a hard time containing the Newark trio of Snow, Odle, and Carter, all of whom were on their way to double-digit scoring nights. At one point during the second period, Newark jumped out to a 12-point lead, large enough to be alarming to the East partisans. Even the Tiger cheerleaders looked worried. On defense, Newark employed their stingy 2-3 zone, the players' claw-like hands smothering East's outside shooters during the limited occasions when they were touching the ball. When the buzzer sounded for halftime, Newark was leading, 25–19. East had managed to cut Newark's 12-point lead in half. Perhaps just as significantly, Newark's Dennis Odle committed his fourth foul, this one involving Roy Hickman; he had one foul left before fouling out of the game. Walking to the locker room, Bob Hart was already strategizing about the second half. He realized he would have to make some quick changes to upset Newark's potent scheme.

The shifty Wildcats of Newark had a unique ability to adapt to any team they were playing, a tactic that had bewildered their opponents. When they had played rival Zanesville earlier in the season, Newark got stomped, 74–43. The rematch was a different story: Newark took Zanesville into double overtime and won the game, 44–42, using, once again, their slow-down game plan. In the current East game, East, which prided itself on its rebound prowess, had already been outrebounded, 23–18.

When Hart and his Tigers emerged from the locker room after the first half, they had a new game plan in place. Hickman, the more physical player, replaced Larry Walker at the point guard position running the Tiger offense. Kevin Smith, the six-foot-five forward, started in place of Hickman. The chess moves by Hart were to counter Newark's height and physical play. Both Ratleff and Conner were having an off night offensively, constantly pestered by the tall Newark players. That problem showed again early in the second half when Conner got into a scuffle with a couple of Newark players. The refs jumped in quickly as crowds from both sides of the Coliseum started grumbling. The Tigers were in need of a scoring lift. It was time for Bo-Pete Lamar to start shooting—and he did. He hit two well-timed, long-range jump shots. East finally took a 1-point lead as the third quarter came to a close. Newark's Odle had returned in the third, but East's taller lineup had neutralized him. In the final five minutes of the fourth quarter, the game remained tight, and the lead change was seesawing back and forth. Fans on both sides were wild with emotion. When the clock got down to thirty seconds, East had the ball. It was in the hands of Lamar, who did what he was accustomed to doing: He shot it. When he missed, the ball bounced right back to him, and he shot again, missing. Hart grimaced on the bench as Newark raced up the court. Newark took one shot close to the basket—with the crowd on its feet—then another, and a third, all close in, missing all three. East got the ball back, and Newark, now desperate, fouled Eddie Rat. He connected on both free throws, making the score 55–50. The seconds ticked away, dooming Newark until the clock ran out of time, sending East High's sweating Tigers off the court with a nerve-racking victory. They were drowned in wild applause. Their coaches were grinning; Jack Gibbs was looking for someone to bear-hug. The Tigers were bound for the four-team state tournament. "It was a great game," conceded Newark coach Dick Schenk. "And it should have been the state finals." Eddie Rat, who was once again headed to the state finals, had been held to 9 points, his lowest total all season. He was sanguine about it. "They wouldn't go in, but we won. That's more important," he said. Bob Hart singled out Kevin Smith, and Bo Lamar—who finished with 20 points—for special praise.

It was a testament to the preparedness of Jack Gibbs that he was ready to answer any and all questions about tickets for the next game. He had mimeographed the guidelines on a piece of paper and distributed them to reporters. "Tell the folks that the East High students and the faculty will be given first crack at our tickets," he said, amid the hullabaloo. "Students can buy their tickets Monday and Tuesday in their classrooms."

The stage was now set. Four teams had punched their way to the state championship finals. They were Toledo Libbey, Canton McKinley, Dayton Chaminade, and East High. The games would be played at St. John Arena, the venerable arena that sat on the edge of the Ohio State campus.

The Tigers of East High were defending state champions. They would be going against the tide of history as no Columbus team had ever won back-to-back state basketball titles.

.   .   .

*Coaches Bob Hart and Paul Pennell with three Tigers who played
on both the basketball and baseball teams during that historic season.
The players, left to right: Kenny Mizelle, Eddie Ratleff, and Larry Mann.*

When it came to basketball, Ohio carved up its statewide AA teams—
the largest schools in the state—into four regions. The Columbus
coaches—with their eye on making it to the regional competition—were
long accustomed to facing unforgiving competition within their own
City League: Three Columbus schools (South, Linden-McKinley, and
East) had taken state championships between the years 1965 and 1968.
The toughest teams in the state's history seemed to emerge from the

schools of Columbus, Cleveland, and Toledo and their immediate areas. Cleveland East Tech won back-to-back state championships in 1958 and 1959. Middletown High School, ninety miles from Columbus, won back-to-back titles in 1956 and 1957 when they were led by future Hall of Famer Jerry Lucas. During the 1968–69 season, it was easy to spotlight the very good schools away from Columbus—Cleveland East Tech, Canton McKinley, Toledo Libbey—because they were all in the state finals alongside East. If there was one team that was haunted by its past and seeking redemption in the 1969 tournament, it was Toledo Libbey, East's upcoming foe.

Burt Spice, the Libbey coach, had grown up dying to play organized basketball. He practiced every chance he got. In high school he got cut from the team the first two years he went out for it. But his senior year, 1950, when he had sprouted to six foot three, he finally convinced the coach he had something to offer. His grit and spirit were rewarded with playing time. He ended up scoring double figures often, and his DeVilbiss High School team won the city title. He became a confident basketball player. In 1954, he was on a University of Toledo team that won the conference title. That was the year of the Supreme Court's *Brown v. Board of Education* case. Spice found the decision long overdue and told himself if ever the moment came, he intended to land on the right side of civil rights.

After college, Spice played a little professional basketball for the Toledo Mercurys, one of those midwestern teams that served as a comical foil for the touring Harlem Globetrotters. It was slapstick, but he was still in the game that he loved. Eventually, he made his way into teaching. In 1961, Toledo Libbey had a head coaching vacancy, and Spice got the job. He was a quiet-voiced man who showed concern for his players and their lives off the court as well as on. When he told the team that year that the best five players would comprise the starting five, he meant it. Well, the best five, anyone could see in practice, were black. So when the season started, five black players were introduced to the community as Libbey's starters. Blacks in Toledo were proud; many whites were disappointed. A short while later, Spice was summoned before a group of school officials who oversaw athletic programs. They criticized Spice about his all-black starting lineup. Racial slurs were bandied about in the room and Spice recoiled, expressing his displeasure at hearing such language. The council members would not tolerate hearing such dissension, so they fired him, on the spot. Spice drove home, furious, and told his family all about it. Everyone was shocked and saddened. But as soon as Philo Dunsmore, the public schools superintendent, heard about the firing, he reinstalled Spice as head coach. Spice had stood his ground, and members of the black community were proud of him.

In 1966, Spice and his Libbey team found themselves in the state's AA title basketball game, pitted against Dayton Chaminade. In the third quarter, Libbey had a 15-point lead and seemed on their way to the school's first ever basketball title. But Chaminade kept scoring, cutting into the Libbey lead. Many thought Spice would call a timeout, if only to slow Chaminade down, but he did not. He imagined his senior lineup would stop Chaminade, but the Dayton team's comeback was unstoppable. He explained his decision not to call a timeout by saying, "I didn't want to split up my senior group because they had really good chemistry." Chaminade ended up defeating Toledo by 6 points, denying Libbey a first ever state basketball crown; the defeat haunted Burt Spice. But in 1969 he was back. And he had two senior players, guard Ed Trail and second team All-State guard-forward Abe Steward, who were two of the most gifted players he'd ever had. Spice believed Steward was "the best basketball player in the state of Ohio." He added: "What do you have to do to convince people?" It was all a rebuke of Eddie Rat's fame. Spice thought Steward could stop Eddie Rat, or at least stop him from having a wildly productive night.

Joe Ungvary, coach of Cleveland John Adams, had faced off against Spice's Libbey team earlier in the same tournament. His team took a 72–51 thrashing. Ungvary was going around telling folks he thought Libbey had a real good chance to beat Bob Hart's Tigers. Spice himself issued a warning: East High, he wanted folks to know, had never faced a defense the likes of which his Libbey team was about to show them. Hart had a scouting report on Libbey. "They're real physical," he said. "One of their biggest items is going to the boards so well and taking the ball from the opponent."

*Mayor Jack Sensenbrenner was a big East High booster. But neighborhood
and school segregation worsened during his years in City Hall.*

The night before the game, the East High Tigers were encamped at a
hotel near the OSU campus. Jack Gibbs took the team and coaches out
to a buffet dinner. When they returned to the hotel, Pop James knew
exactly what Nick Conner wanted—he had made a request out of the
earshot of Gibbs and the coaches: "He said, 'Hey Mr. James, bring us
that record player!'" So Pop scooted out to his car and quietly retrieved
it. And after the coaches went to their rooms, the players crowded into
Nick Conner's hotel room to listen to soul music on the little turntable.
Pop James thought the players were relaxed, and that made him feel
good.

On game day at St. John Arena, the two marquee games that would lead
to the state title game—heralding the end of a long season—once again
brought the politicos out. Gov. James Rhodes entered with his security
staff. Mayor Sensenbrenner, grinning like a game show host, showed up
wearing his orange-and-black East High sweatshirt and waving pom-

poms. The East and Libbey players, gliding about the arena with all their fierce high school pride, had a chance to watch a bit of the first game, in which Canton McKinley spanked Dayton Chaminade, 78–46. So the winner of the East-Libbey matchup would face Canton McKinley in the state final. Canton McKinley player Nick Weatherspoon (bound for the University of Illinois on a scholarship) had gotten nearly as much newspaper coverage as Eddie Rat throughout the season. He flummoxed Dayton Chaminade with a cool 28 points. More worrisome for Canton McKinley's upcoming opponent was the fact that the players had made more than 50 percent (.525) of their field goal attempts. Canton McKinley boasted sharpshooters.

Inside the arena that Friday night, March 21, more than fourteen thousand spectators were in attendance. East and Libbey took the floor shortly after 9 p.m. The respective cheerleading contingents danced and shimmied about. Thirty minutes later the refs blew the whistle and the starting lineups were announced. For Libbey, it was Abe Steward, Ed Trail—each trotting out to center court followed by cascading Toledo applause—John Houston, Carl Ham, and Dexter Holloway. Burt Spice had already announced he was leaving the school after the season in hopes of landing a college coaching position. His Libbey players—the team had one white player on its roster, and he was not among the starters—had a fierce determination both to whip the East High Tigers and to give their coach a fitting farewell.

Because the game was being played in their hometown, the East High fans were raucous and loose, heightening the noise and wild waving. The starting Tiger lineup was introduced: Ed Ratleff, Nick Conner, Roy Hickman, Larry Walker, and Bo-Pete Lamar. Hart, looking stoical on the bench in his thick spectacles, with the countenance of a small-town pharmacist, had refused to tell the press that Conner had come down with strep throat, requiring two shots of penicillin the night before. With the impenetrable ardor of youth on his side—and his having slept with sweet soul music humming in his ears—Conner was above complaining about anything as it related to the game.

By the end of the fast-moving first quarter, East held a 6-point lead, 21–15. Unlike with Newark, there would be no slowing down of anything in this game. At the end of the first half, it was East, 35, Libbey, 30. But there was something about Libbey that caught the eyes of the reporters: They appeared quite poised; they did not seem at all rattled. Libbey had not made a single substitution during the first half of play, displaying an iron-like stamina. "Libbey looked every bit a 23–1 team, if not better," one reporter on the scene said. In the third quarter, Libbey's star player, Abe Steward (on his way to 25 points), was having his way with the Tigers, scoring inside and out. As the third quarter drew to a close, the East fans grew restless; Libbey was furiously nipping at the small Tiger lead. With five minutes left in the quarter, the game was tied, 40–40. When the buzzer sounded, the Libbey fans sprang up from their seats in jubilation: Their team had overtaken East High with a 48–46 lead. In the huddle, Spice, the Libbey coach, asked if any of his players needed a rest. Not a single one said they did. That was what he wanted to hear. They were all seniors, players he had known and coached for a long time. He was going to let them stay on the court until they ran East High into the ground, or off the court, whichever came first. He had gotten oh-so-close to a championship title back in 1966; he damn sure didn't want this game to get away from his team.

In the fourth quarter, the lead seesawed. East High's Hickman went up for a shot, was fouled, and his shot went in. Sent to the free throw line, Hickman made the shot, and the score was now East 61, Libbey 57. Mayor Sensenbrenner was beside himself, whooping and hollering amid the Tiger fans. He had enough sense to know what everyone seemed to know: This game was going down to the wire. Ed Trail, the Libbey guard, got fouled. He slipped in a free throw. Then two Libbey players, Steward and Houston, scored two points apiece, and Libbey was suddenly back in the lead, 62–61. East's Bo-Pete Lamar told himself he had to do something; as soon as he got the ball again and saw an opening, he was going to shoot. He did. And missed. Libbey grabbed the rebound. The Libby coach immediately yelled for a timeout. With 1:40 left in the game and Libbey up by a single point, Tiger fans could barely breathe. As play resumed, many imagined Libbey would try to get the ball to Abe Steward, its star, which was exactly the plan their coach had outlined during the timeout. But East's dangerously quick Larry Walker stole the inbound pass. He caught sight of Bo-Pete Lamar and scooped the ball over to him. Lamar bolted for the basket, lofted a shot, scored—and was fouled. Tiger fans and their cheerleaders erupted. Lamar stepped to the free throw line and calmly sank the shot. The score was 64–62, East. Libbey got the ball but was called for traveling, so the ball was turned over to the Tigers. Hart called a timeout. There was 1:11 on the clock. In the huddle, Eddie Rat asked the coach if they should shoot the ball or simply hold on to it. Hart told him to shoot. But as soon as play resumed, East was called for a dribbling violation, which returned the ball to Libbey. Steward, of Libbey, badly wanted the ball and screamed to a teammate to pass it to him. When he got it, he shot, missed, but was fouled. Tiger groans cascaded. Steward—one of the greatest players in the history of Libbey basketball—stepped to the free throw line. There were 49 seconds left. He could tie the score by making his two free throws. He missed the first one, made the second. East, 64, Libby, 63. East got the ball. The final seconds ticked off the clock. Eddie Rat went into the lane and tossed up a soft hook; he missed. The ball, suddenly and surprisingly, was back in Toledo Libbey's hands. The East players paid particular attention to Steward and Trail, believing one of them had to take the final shot.

Instead, guard Carl Ham drove down the middle into the forest of East High players.

The forest got the best of him; his shot was deflected.

Steward got the ball—with 9 seconds on the clock—and shot for the victory.

His shot went up. And the Libbey star missed. The ball caromed along the left baseline, the noise palpable as a buffalo herd. Libbey's Dexter Holloway sprung and grabbed it.

With only 3 seconds left, Holloway threw up a shot. It was soft. It rolled around the rim, as if preparing to make up its own mind.

Some fans covered their eyes; most did not.

Bob Hart was in a sudden nightmare. "That one will haunt me for a while," he later recalled of Holloway's shot.

The ball toyed along the inside-outside edges of the rim, twisting the hearts of both sets of fans by the millisecond. Finally, the ball rolled off.

No basket. Eddie Rat reached for it like a fireman for a baby tossed from a high window. The clock showed one second. Then none. It was all over. But there was silence among the East High followers in the stands, as if they were suspending their belief until they were absolutely sure. Their eyes raced to the clock. Then the scoreboard. They had their proof: Columbus East, 64, Toledo Libbey, 63. Still alive by virtue of a single point. There was pandemonium. The Tiger bench players erupted. They rushed onto the court. The Afro-wearing Bo-Pete Lamar grinned wildly and was embraced by his teammates.

A heartbreak averted.

The Tigers were going to the state championship game.

The Libbey coaches and players were crushed. Spice was furious. "Why didn't they call a foul when Carl Ham took that hook shot?" he asked. "He got hit on the arm. You could hear the slap."

Hart had very little time to be haunted by Libbey's last shot. "I can still see it sitting on the rim," he was confessing after the game. But he knew he had another game to prepare for. "We did a good job of forcing them into the shots that they didn't want to take," Hart allowed. "We denied Abe Steward and Ed Trail."

It would be different for Spice, the Libbey coach: "Two inches," he would repeat over and over, "that's the margin Holloway missed the last shot."

Next up: Canton McKinley High.

All those around the state who had been hoping for the dream matchup between the two most decorated players in Ohio—Canton's Nick Weatherspoon and East's Ed Ratleff—had their wish. Jim Turvene, the Dayton Chaminade coach whose team had just been whipped by Weatherspoon and Canton McKinley, certainly sounded as if he were siding with Canton McKinley in the matchup: "The way [the Canton McKinley team members are] playing now, they're going to be a tough team to beat in the finals." Spice, the Libbey coach, announced his own feelings about the potency of the Canton McKinley team and the upcoming game. "It'll probably go right down to the wire, much like this one did.

East has a great basketball team," he offered, "but McKinley has an excellent team, too."

And so it would be that eleven months after the murder of Martin Luther King Jr., the black kids from East High would be going to the state championship game. It gave King's old friend Rev. Phale Hale a reason to smile. The team gave East High principal Jack Gibbs a reason to smile. As he left the arena, Gibbs thought to himself how beautiful it would be if all the mothers of the East High players could come to the state championship game the next night. These were the mothers who had feared so much for these boys. These were the mothers who couldn't get to the games because they were working on their hands and knees. They were fixing meals and ironing clothes for white kids. They were emptying trash cans for white families. They were the mothers who had left thank-you notes for the white families they worked for when they were given hand-me-down clothes for their own children to wear. They hadn't gotten to many of the games because they didn't have cars. Jack Gibbs knew some of the mothers worked on weekends out in Bexley and Upper Arlington. He couldn't stop thinking about Lucy Lamar, how she had uprooted herself just so her son could keep his Afro, his pride, and play basketball.

Jack Gibbs went home that night and told his wife, Ruth, that he was going to start making phone calls right away. He was going to get the mothers of the boys to the state championship game.

For the teams that were advancing in the state finals, the back-to-back tournament games were grueling. Just twenty-four hours to regroup, twenty-four hours to plot how to keep another team from shattering East High's dream. The Tigers were back at the arena a day later to face Bob Rupert's Canton McKinley team. Like the East High team, the Bulldogs of Canton had a pristine record and some awe-inspiring, intimidating scores. They had whipped Columbus North by 41, Kent Roosevelt by 35, and Cleveland John F. Kennedy by 40. They didn't let up when it came tournament time, destroying West Branch by 35, Massillon Washington by 38, and Cleveland St. Joseph by 45. Their only loss—the third game of their season—was to Farrell High School, a powerful Pennsylvania team that was the eventual winner of their own state basketball tournament. So the McKinley partisans could brag that their team was—just like East High—undefeated inside the borders of Ohio. On Fridays and Saturdays during basketball season in Canton, the McKinley games would habitually be sold out. "We had five thousand people at every game," recalls Stan Rubin, McKinley's starting guard that season.

For away games, McKinley's fans hit the road, chartered buses, and traveled in caravans of cars rolling across snow-swept Ohio. "Our fans traveled everywhere," says Rubin.

They came in slowly, dressed beautifully, and some of them seemed in awe of the huge surroundings and the attendant pageantry. Not all of them had been sure they were going to make it, and they were fussing with nervousness up to the last minute. It was a combination of things that had gotten the mothers of the Tiger players to the Coliseum: The game fell on a Saturday, and those who worked domestic jobs—as most did—often had Saturdays off. Jack Gibbs had made absolutely sure they'd have transportation to the game if they needed it. They could be forgiven if they were dressed as if they were going to church on Easter Sunday. They wore hats and silks and tweeds and precious jewelry. They had hard lives, living from paycheck to paycheck. Time and time again, America had baffled them. They had been grieving about the loss of Dr. King for months now. They needed something wonderful to grasp on to. They were so very proud of what their sons had already accomplished. Inside St. John Arena, they took their seats, all but anonymous except for a few Tiger fans who knew them from their neighborhood.

Bob Hart had made plans to deploy his players so that they would meet the challenge of such a strong opponent. He assigned Eddie Rat to guard Nick Weatherspoon, the great McKinley player. If one wanted to see how the sorrows of black impoverished family life so often traveled

across America, one need only look at Ruby Weatherspoon and her son
Nick, the McKinley star. Ruby hailed from Emmett Till–haunted Mississippi. She had left Greenwood for Canton, Ohio, to make a better life
for herself and her family. She worked just as hard as the mothers of the
East High players did; Ruby Weatherspoon, on hands and knees, bent
over a washing machine, sunup to sundown, also worked as a maid.
At McKinley High, after the assassination of Martin Luther King Jr.,
a group of black students—they were outnumbered by whites in the
school—staged a walkout in protest. Their parents supported them.

In addition to the fourteen thousand people who flocked to St. John
Arena for Saturday's game, there were TV cameras because the game was
going to be televised statewide.

The McKinley coaching staff knew what to expect from Ratleff
and Conner. There was one player who really worried them, however.
"We were concerned about Bo-Pete Lamar," recalls Rubin, who had
played against Lamar a year earlier when McKinley had hosted Columbus North High School, Lamar's former school. "Lamar had thirty
against us."

The East-McKinley matchup was the game many imagined the basketball gods had ordained. East High was ranked No. 1 in the state
by the AP poll, and McKinley No. 1 by UPI. On five previous occasions, McKinley had reached the state final championship game, coming
away runner-up each time. Now boasting a twenty-three-game winning
streak, they felt they had undeniable momentum. East High's Eddie
Rat, though, was undaunted, telling teammates that McKinley was a
one-man team. Hart's directive to Ratleff about guarding Weatherspoon
was simple and direct—"keep a hand in his face and keep him off the
boards."

Bob Hart kept remarking to his assistant, Paul Pennell, that he felt
good about Nick Conner because he had devoured such a good, hearty
breakfast that morning.

As the game got under way, Hart could sense the confidence of the McKinley team. The first quarter was extremely physical. Midway through the

quarter, Hart thought a McKinley player was a little too physical and the coach complained loudly to the refs. Pennell cautioned him about being so vocal. Hart ignored him, kept complaining, and got whistled for a technical foul. The Tiger fans' boos swelled inside St. John Arena. McKinley made the free throw, got the ball back, and scored again. They were up, 18–12. At the end of the quarter, McKinley still held the lead, 21–17. The Bulldogs averaged 80 points per game during the season; a 21-point first quarter score was on par with that average. They had confidence. Weatherspoon connected on several smooth jump shots. Bo-Pete kept missing. Hart wondered if the exhausting Libbey matchup the night before had taxed him. When the buzzer sounded ending the first half, East High held a 1-point edge, 34–33. It was enough to get Mayor Sensenbrenner up out of his seat and dancing his patented "Tiger Rag," something between a vaudeville shuffle and a goofy two-step.

Neither coach had a sense of comfort back in the locker rooms. McKinley's players reminded themselves they had scrimmaged with East High before the season got under way, and they left the court sensing they had just as much talent as the Tigers did. (In Cleveland, the bookies who were taking bets on the East-McKinley matchup liked McKinley to win by 9 points.)

In the East High locker room, Lamar showed frustration about his missed shots, and his coach could sense it. "We told him he just had to keep putting it up there," Hart recalled.

In the second half, Nick Conner—quiet thus far in the contest—came alive. He started blocking shots. He seemed to put extra viciousness into blocking Weatherspoon. The Tigers were also getting more shots at the basket than McKinley was—"two shots to our one," McKinley's coach Rupert realized. Midway through the third quarter and at a 42–42 tie, the Tigers exploded: They connected for 8 points, a blur of action involving Ratleff, Conner, Lamar, and Kevin Smith. A cascade of foot stomping seemed to envelope a large part of the stands. When the third period ended, the Tigers were ahead, 52–44.

The foot stomping—many fans now standing—didn't let up until the fourth quarter got under way. And as soon as the last quarter began, Lamar fired from long range connecting on a dagger-like shot. The score was now 54–44, and McKinley looked confused. During a pause in the action, Eddie Rat went up to each of his teammates and hit him on the rump. "We gotta win," he said. "We're ten points up and we gotta win." Conner heard his teammate's admonition loud and clear and began snatching McKinley's missed shots off the rim with the impatience of a man needing to escape the arena and catch a plane. If McKinley had a chance, they realized they now had to stop Eddie Rat. They couldn't.

The thousands and thousands of Tiger fans began leaning forward in their seats, then rising up, as if they were ready to bolt onto the floor, past the state troopers who were the last line of defense between the fans and the court. Eddie Rat's teammates had tired of hearing Nick Weatherspoon being trumpeted as the best player in the state. So they started passing Eddie Rat the ball as often as they could, imploring him to score, and he did—lovely jump shots, the ball dropping into the net like an olive being dropped into a martini. The East High lead grew to 11 points. The clock was ticking now toward game's end. Here's to you, Mr. Weatherspoon. The lead grew to 13 points. Hart started clearing his bench players, allowing his stars to exit to standing ovations. Hart's daughters began making their way toward their dad down on the floor. Mayor Sensenbrenner was doing his awkward Tiger Rag jig again in the stands, drawing guffaws from all around. Jack Gibbs, a man both tough and emotional, was smiling. Down on the court, the McKinley players looked dejected. On the Tiger bench, Eddie Rat was trying to say something to Nick Conner, and Roy Hickman was trying to say something to Larry Walker. Everyone's words were getting drowned out by the noise. Then there were 20 seconds left, and when those seconds vanished from the clock, Bob Hart and his band of Tigers had achieved something historic, something no other Columbus high school had ever done: They had won back-to-back state basketball titles. The score, 71–56. But this one was different, and everyone knew it. This one had come in the aftermath of Dr. King's assassination. This one had come with the school feeling its very soul was on the line. This one had come amid so much pain.

The players from both teams walked toward one another for the traditional handshakes. The Tiger cheerleaders were sashaying and teary-eyed. Athletic officials made their way to the center of the court to present the championship trophy. Mayor Sensenbrenner was excitedly looking for the City Hall photographer to make sure he got lots and lots of pictures! Flashbulbs were popping. Bo-Pete Lamar—the rebel, the transfer student—had stood his ground in honor of his beloved Afro, and now he was on a state championship team. His mother, Lucy, up in the stands, had forgotten all about her pounding migraines. Eddie Rat—the golden boy of the golden moment—had dropped in 31 points against McKinley. He was clipping down the nets and raising them above his head for everyone to see.

The Tiger players began circling their trophy to get a better look.

Bob Rupert, the McKinley coach, had his own opinion about what Bob Hart's Tigers had just accomplished inside St. John Arena: "This team is of a different era," he said.

When the big gleaming trophy was finally handed over to the Tiger players, another round of roaring erupted inside the arena.

Someone handed Eddie Rat the microphone. He talked about sportsmanship and thanked the McKinley players for theirs. He thanked the fans of East High. Then he instructed his teammates to go find their mothers in the stands and escort them onto the court. And a short while later the Tiger mothers were there: Mildred Mizelle, escorted by her son Kenny; Erma Wright, escorted by her son, Robert; Barbara Crump, escorted by her son Eddie Rat; Lucy Lamar—in a beautifully printed hat—escorted by her son Bo-Pete; Beatrice Conner, escorted by her son, Nick; Barbara Sawyer, escorted by her son Kevin Smith; and on and on they came, until all the players and their mothers were at center court. And there they stood, the kleig lights upon them, sons and proud mothers for all the world to see.

Anticipating victory, Jack Gibbs had hatched a plan requiring the help of Kirk Bishop, the East High student who was the youngest deejay in the city. James Brown, the messianic soul singer, was appearing in Columbus at the Veterans Memorial Auditorium that same night. Brown had been riding a crest of favorable publicity for months because of his actions in Boston the day after the King assassination. He did not cancel a planned Boston Garden concert in the city; he told city officials he certainly believed—as they imagined—that his charisma and stage

presence could help the city stay calm. (Brown's song, "Say It Loud—
I'm Black and I'm Proud," had been released just as the school doors
were about to open at East High in the fall of 1968, and it had resonated as a kind of black anthem throughout the country.) Brown spoke
from the stage in Boston that night in tones both defiant and soothing.
Even when some aggrieved youths tried to storm the stage to disrupt the
concert, he kept them back, sounding like a cross between a storefront
preacher and a high school principal. Boston was one of the few big
American cities that didn't explode after King was murdered, and Brown
received much of the credit.

As soon as the game ended Gibbs and his student co-conspirator, Kirk
Bishop, hurriedly made phone calls from inside the arena to Brown's
downtown venue. They sent word for the players to shower quickly and
hustle along. The players and cheerleaders couldn't believe it. They were
going to a James Brown concert! Upon arriving at the Veterans Memorial
Auditorium they were escorted in through a side door. Brown had just
finished his concert—though not the encore. The singer had a notorious
reputation for being moody and unpredictable. But when an aide told
him that local East High had just won the state basketball championship
game less than ninety minutes ago and wanted to meet him, Brown nodded his approval. In his juvenile delinquent days, Brown had been crazy
about sports. He had even dreamed about playing professional baseball.
In his presence, the Tigers all but stood agog. "James had on a blanket,"
remembers basketball player Kevin Smith. "He was soaking wet. Our
mouths were wide open." There was something that really impressed
basketball player Larry Walker: "I finally met someone shorter than me."
Cynthia Chapman, the cheerleader, looked down at Brown's footwear.
"He was wearing lifts in his shoes," she says.

Kirk Bishop rushed out to the stage area and got permission to bring
the victorious team onstage and introduce them. Brown had congratulated the team and was going to leave, but when he started hearing
Bishop's commentary—about the long, hard year and how the school
had stuck together—he couldn't resist. He walked back out onstage; the
audience erupted. He took the microphone. "Look at them," he said, his
voice gravelly and sweet with respect. "They champions."

Shiny convertibles rolled down East Broad Street in the basketball parade.

·   ·   ·

On the morning of March 23, a phalanx of convertibles lined up on East Broad Street in front of East High School, ready to take the Tigers slowly rolling along the street where they would be saluted by the community. The usual cast of city officials and politicians was on hand amid the throng of seven thousand mostly black residents of the city. "You brought a great honor to the city of Columbus and to the state of Ohio with your behavior," Gov. Jim Rhodes said. The next morning's headline in *The Columbus Dispatch* read: "Rhodes Salutes Ohio's Champions." Above it stretched a much more somber headline: "Battles Rage Across S. Vietnam—Allies Lose Six, 225 Reds Killed."

Five days later, Governor Rhodes summoned the cheerleaders and players—and also the players' girlfriends—to the parlor room of the Governor's Mansion. The governor identified with the team because he had attended Ohio State University with the hope of playing basketball. He

*Jack Gibbs, in the auto on the left, leads the celebration
with the school's soul-strutting marching band.*

wasn't, however, one for keeping his head in the books. He dropped out before the end of his first year. He went into business and opened Jim's Place, a convenience store near the campus, where he sold a hodgepodge of items. Among his inventory were stag (porn) films, a fact he'd chuckle away whenever it was brought up during campaigns. Rhodes presented the Tigers with specially designed mugs and cuff links. The girlfriends received corsages, which the players delicately pinned on them. After the governor had presented the players and girlfriends with their gifts, he looked around the parlor. His mind whirred to his own joyful high school days. He motioned for Eddie Rat, Nick Conner, and some other players to come closer to him. He asked them to help him move some of the furniture into an adjacent room. Of course his aides rushed to help. And when the furniture was moved out of the way, the governor told the players and their girlfriends it was a good time to have a dance! An aide ran off and returned with a stereo player. And just like that, the dancing began.

"Say it loud—I'm black and I'm proud!"

Their fathers were mostly absent. Many of their mothers worked as maids. But no one could deny their ability to emerge as basketball champions.

. . .

In the days immediately after the East High basketball championship victory, students strolling by the gymnasium could hear, then see, two boys inside. One was tall and rangy. He was throwing fast pitches to another player about ninety feet away. That player was crouched, catching the balls being thrown to him. The balls were coming at a blazing speed. The pitcher was Eddie Rat. The catcher was Garnett Barney Davis. They were getting ready for baseball season.

The East High students never really paid much attention to their baseball team. Students told themselves they had plenty of other things to do during springtime besides trouping over to the old, ill-attended Harley baseball diamond located blocks from the school.

Still, Eddie Rat had always told everyone his favorite sport was baseball. No one believed him.

PART II

10

The Ballad of Jackie Robinson

Before he was a bellwether for race in America, before he was an icon who claimed national and international headlines, before he sent angry whites—popcorn kernels and spittle flying from their mouths—into spasms inside all those lovely old ballparks around the country, before he snatched the throne as the most inspiring black athlete of his era by integrating professional baseball, before all the magazine articles and essays and books were written about him, Jackie Robinson was just a black kid with a glove, a bat, and a mom who worked as a maid.

The East High baseball players got earfuls about Jackie Robinson from Hiram Tanner, the reporter who followed the team for the community-published *Call and Post* newspaper. In his younger days, Tanner had a brief stint playing for the St. Louis Stars of the Negro Baseball Leagues. He'd regale the East High players with stories about Robinson, Cool Papa Bell, Satchel Paige, and other great Negro leaguers. Eddie Rat, East High's star pitcher, was just one of the players on the team who was enamored of Robinson's legacy. "You learned to respect players like Robinson," he says. "Jackie Robinson was my hero." Ratleff would have asked for Robinson's no. 42 if it had been available, but the team numbers didn't go higher than number 24. And the school simply couldn't afford new uniforms. "Once East High became a black school," says Jim Henderson, the school's assistant baseball coach in 1969, "there never was enough money for athletics and uniforms." That was true especially for the baseball team.

At East High, basketball was king. Football was not far behind, a beloved prince. Baseball at East High was looked down on as the court jester. There were students who never even thought of attending a baseball game. April 4, 1969, was the one-year anniversary of Martin Luther King's murder, and Jackie Robinson was still periodically popping up in the news because commentators were tracking him down for quotes regarding the deaths of King and Bobby Kennedy, asking him to share his feelings about America and the state of politics and baseball. Although he was only fifty years old in 1969, Jackie Robinson would live only three more years.

The story of the Negro player who wore number 42 for the Brooklyn Dodgers is a story so galvanizing, so triumphant and gut-wrenching, that it remains timeless. More than any other sport, baseball was America's favorite pastime, and the fallout after black players crossed the color barrier showed the country's deep-seated racial ideology. And in 1969, Jackie Robinson remained the touchstone for any black kid alighting from a front porch or stoop with a bat and glove in hand.

Jackie Robinson was born in the American South on January 31, 1919, the last of Mallie Robinson's five children. She named him Jack Roosevelt Robinson. (His middle name was given in honor of former president Theodore Roosevelt because the Robinson family believed he had been a good president for blacks.) Jackie was born in a time of racial fire: 1919 was known as Red Summer in America because of the racial riots that erupted in the South and Midwest, triggered when blacks and whites battled over jobs and some blacks, desperate for work, crossed the strike lines. In Arkansas more than a hundred blacks were killed.

Mallie Robinson was suffering through a bad marriage with a philandering husband. She desperately wanted to get out of rural Georgia, where the family lived on a plantation and worked as tenant farmers. She loathed the environment and made her opinion clear to the overseer, who knew her temperament well. "You're about the sassiest nigger woman ever on this place," the overseer told her one day. If she wanted a better life for her children, she knew she had to get away. She had family contacts in Pasadena, California, and she had been told she could get maid's work there. A year after Jackie's birth, her mind firmly made up, she loaded up her family, scooted to the train station, leaving her husband behind, and took off for Pasadena. She was nervous about the unknown, but held a firm belief that more pain would come to her family if she didn't leave the South. Mallie Robinson, too, had to escape.

The city of Pasadena is just a dozen miles outside of Los Angeles. It was a world away from the rural woods and the daily racial fears of blacks living in Cairo, Georgia. The Robinson children—four boys and a girl—liked the weather in Pasadena, especially the ocean breezes. True to the promise made to her, Mallie Robinson found maid's work with a local white family. She was happy to have a job, and the family she worked for treated her well. The Robinsons eventually moved into a house at 121 Pepper Street. Jackie Robinson later remembered the struggles the family endured: "Sometimes there were only two meals a day, and some days we wouldn't have eaten at all if it hadn't been for the leftovers my mother was able to bring home from her job."

Sixteen-year-old Jackie sold hot dogs and hawked papers at the recently built Rose Bowl stadium in Pasadena. He excelled at all sports: football, basketball, track, tennis, baseball. His varsity letters and trophies began to accumulate. His brother Mack was also an accomplished athlete. Mack Robinson, nearly five years older than Jackie, broke track records at Pasadena Junior College. He went to the 1936 Berlin Olympics and placed second to Jesse Owens in the 200-yard dash, bringing home a silver medal. After her older son's accomplishments at the Olympics, Mallie Robinson was thoroughly convinced that God had led the family out of Georgia for brighter days.

At John Muir Technical High School in Pasadena, Jackie dazzled coaches and fans. He suffered injuries, doubtless because of the grueling overlapping schedules of the many sports he played. Jackie broke some of the very records his brother Mack had set in track and field. Mallie Robinson found it hard to get away from her maid's job to see her son perform, but Jackie delighted in telling her about what his team had accomplished. The *Pasadena Star-News* noted that for two years, Jackie Robinson "had been the outstanding athlete at Muir, starring in football, basketball, track, baseball, and tennis."

If Jackie Robinson had stayed and been raised in Georgia, he might have acquired habits and tendencies that would have kept him from getting involved in edgy confrontations with whites. He might have become deferential and intimidated. While Pasadena was hardly a racial oasis—even after his Olympics glory, the only job Mack Robinson was offered in the city was as a street sweeper—the Robinsons' experiences there were a far cry from the racial brutalities blacks experienced in many southern cities. And because the schools Jackie attended in Pasadena were overwhelmingly white, he was accustomed to a certain kind of integration. Jackie Robinson grew up with a sturdy sense of self. He knew how to throw a punch; he fought back against racial insults, and there were insults from the football field to the baseball diamond. (There were also white friends who aligned themselves with him.) Although he once got hauled before a juvenile judge for fighting—his sports acclaim got him off—he wouldn't let anything vanquish his cultural pride.

The youthful Jackie Robinson was perhaps the sassiest negro Pasadena had ever seen.

Deciding to stay close to home, Robinson enrolled—as his brother Mack had done—at Pasadena Junior College. It was 1937 and the country was still in the grip of the Great Depression. College was a luxury for anyone, especially Negroes. The Robinson boys were attracted to Pasadena Junior College as the University of California system provided free tuition for California residents at the time. Also, they could reside at home. Still, there were challenges: getting to and from school, purchasing books, the constant need to convince their mother that school was more important than getting a job and adding to the family income.

There were upwards of sixty blacks in the student body of about four thousand at the junior college. John Thurman, the baseball coach, was quite familiar with Jackie Robinson, whom he had tutored at a baseball camp the previous summer. Thurman had no doubt about who would be playing shortstop on the Pasadena Junior College baseball team. In those early games on the baseball diamond, Robinson's talents were indisputable. Against the ranked Modesto Junior College team, he stole second base, third base, and—why not?—home plate as well. The *Pasadena Post* judged that he had "created a sensation" with his athletic gifts. The 1938 team had a fourteen-game winning streak in which Robinson played a crucial role. By season's end, he was the best player on the squad. The *Pasadena Post* concluded the team had "one of the most successful baseball seasons in the history of Pasadena Junior College."

Robinson's second season on the baseball team eclipsed the first: His batting average was an astonishing .417; he stole more than two dozen bases; he was named an All-Star. The college newspaper proclaimed him to be "the greatest base runner ever to play on a junior college team." That year, Robinson played in an exhibition game against members of the Chicago White Sox, who had been in Pasadena for spring training. Against the American League team, Robinson stole a base, smacked two hits, and engineered a double play. "Geez," uttered Jimmy Dykes, the White Sox manager, "if that kid was white I'd sign him right now."

There was a lot of gossip around Pasadena about which college Robinson would attend. The Jim Crow segregated schools, as expected, completely ignored him. The University of Oregon, which his brother Mack attended, offered a scholarship, as did other more enlightened schools. But in 1939, Robinson chose UCLA, buoyed by the fact that Babe Horrell had just been named its football coach. Horrell had attended the same Pasadena high school as Robinson. The new coach was aware of Jackie Robinson's achievements, and UCLA had been recruiting black athletes, drawing praise from the black community of Los Angeles.

Robinson's first notoriety at UCLA came while he was playing on the football team. Woody Strode—later a Hollywood actor—and Kenny Washington were two of the other black stars on the team. The UCLA Bruins won their first two football games against Texas Christian University, 6–2 (a baseball-like score), and the University of Washington, 14–7. Against the University of Washington, Robinson streaked up the field on a 65-yard punt return. The team finished undefeated with two ties. That first year, Jackie played basketball, football, baseball, and ran track. He lettered in four sports, the first UCLA athlete to do so. He was an honorable mention All-American in his second football season. But by spring, Robinson announced he was withdrawing from the school. He needed to make money; he could no longer bear to see his mother working as a maid.

Upon leaving UCLA, Robinson had been such a versatile athlete that he had yet to become singularly identified with any one particular sport. Sensing that his sports opportunities were limited—the mainstream white sports in America remained rigidly segregated—he took a job with the National Youth Administration, working at one of its California camps, counseling kids. He also managed to hitch on with a semi-professional football team in Honolulu but left after a few months because he was unhappy with playing conditions. The next decision was beyond his control: The Japanese attacked Pearl Harbor and he was drafted into the army.

It was a Jim Crow segregated army, even if the military had begun desegregating its military bases and accepting blacks for limited fighting and flying duties. For blacks, as always, military duty meant a way for them to illustrate their patriotism and perhaps convince the country that segregation was stifling national unity. In January 1943, Robinson was commissioned an army officer, a second lieutenant. (It had taken the intervention of boxer Joe Louis—who was also serving in the army—for Robinson to get his officer's stripes. The stripes, however, had limited impact.)

Robinson was assigned to the 761st Tank Battalion at Fort Hood in Texas—an all-black unit—and had the authority to issue orders to Negro troops only. One early evening he walked onto a military bus and spotted the wife of a friend seated in the middle of the bus. He took a seat beside her. The white bus driver, eyeing where Robinson was sitting and becoming upset that Robinson had not proceeded to the back of the bus, rudely confronted Robinson, ordering him to the back. Robinson refused. The military police were summoned. Robinson was ushered before military superiors and subjected to a series of questions. It was trouble and he knew it. Soon it was announced that 2nd Lt.

Jackie Robinson would be court-martialed—for refusing to move to the back of the bus. The Negro press got hold of the story and the NAACP got involved. During the court-martial, Robinson's defense argued that he hadn't violated any Articles of War, that the bus driver had uttered racial epithets and was the aggressor. Robinson was acquitted. The army then concluded it did not wish to have a so-called belligerent Mr. Jackie Robinson as a soldier. He was honorably discharged in late 1944. The 761st Tank Battalion, known as the Black Panthers, landed at Normandy without Robinson, but with General Patton's forces. They would go on to distinguish themselves in battle, capturing more than thirty towns across the European theater and receiving more than three hundred Purple Hearts.

Once the war was at an end, what was a multitalented twenty-five-year-old athlete to do in a sports-mad nation where he could not join a professional team because of his skin color?

In addition to sports, Jackie Robinson had love on his mind. He had met a nursing student named Rachel Isum in Pasadena. She'd already broken off one engagement with him, but they still were deeply interested in each other. He wrote her love letters when he was in the army; he was no poet, but she got the message, and after the war, they began dating again.

Robinson took a job as athletic director of Sam Houston State College in Huntsville, Texas. It was an all-black school with not much money in its athletic budget. He brought along some of his college awards and trophies and put them in a trophy case. He was never a braggart, but he wanted to inspire the athletes. At the end of his first year on campus, Robinson agreed to "try out" for a position with the Kansas City Monarchs of the Negro Baseball League. He liked basketball and football well enough, but he knew, deep down, he possessed a special gift for baseball. The Negro Baseball League—an amalgamation of various leagues that started, stopped, and started again over the years—was formed as a solution to the decree, in the late nineteenth century, disallowing blacks from further participation in Major League Baseball. By 1944, the Kansas City Monarchs were considered the class of the league.

Baseball was the first Negro team sport in America that black boys rushed toward. Boxing was too individualistic; basketball had yet to become widely popular. But baseball was everywhere in the minds of black kids. When Jackie Robinson joined the Negro Baseball League in 1945, it boasted some of the best baseball players—white or black—in America, among them Satchel Paige, Josh Gibson, Larry Doby, Monte Irvin, and Buck Leonard. Some of these players were destined to become Hall of Famers. There were many others like them, earning a living as Negro league players and barred from showcasing their talents for the whole of the nation. "Do we, by any chance," wondered a sympathetic Dave Egan of the *Boston Record* newspaper, "feel disgust at the thought that the Negro athletes, solely because of their color, are barred from playing baseball?"

The somewhat vaudevillian and helter-skelter mannerisms of the Kansas City Monarchs did not always sit well with Robinson. The management of the league was sometimes shoddy. Players had understandable complaints: The teams had to travel great distances by bus; the decent white hotels would not put them up; black dining places were often inferior. "I didn't like the bouncing buses, the cheap hotels, and the constant night games," Robinson said. He had played "white" baseball in college, where there was genuine structure and impressive organizational rules to follow. Nevertheless, in the forty-seven games he played with the Monarchs, Robinson batted .387, which was good enough to land him a spot on the All-Star team. And it was also good enough to garner the attention of Branch Rickey, of the all-white Brooklyn Dodgers.

In 1904, Branch Rickey had coached the Ohio Wesleyan University baseball team, which had a black player, Charles Thomas, on its roster, an extremely unusual feature at the time. The indignities Thomas had to endure made a profound impact on Rickey, a devoutly religious man. In later years, Rickey entered professional baseball, managed the St. Louis Cardinals, and became general manager of the Dodgers in 1943. It was in the back of his mind that he would find a way to break the onerous color line in professional baseball. Rickey wanted a talented player to meet the challenge, of course, but he also wanted one who could with-stand the inevitable cruelties that were sure to come.

In America, World War II had given blacks more reason to protest the laws of segregation. But also in America, sports was seen as a connective tissue bringing communities together. Football stadiums, baseball fields, and basketball arenas were places to meet and greet neighbors. And since most communities were segregated, the average white sports fan did not expect to see blacks on any of those playing fields. To the mainstream white population, its sports heroes were—just as they were—white. And lurking deep in the recesses of many white minds was the deep fear that white women might start to salute black sports stars if they gained wide entry into pro sports. In the minds of those blacks who had joined or been drafted into the military, segregation in sports was a constant reminder of the ills across the nation. Blacks had fought Hitler; now they demanded that America ensure their rights as outlined in the U.S. Con-stitution. Branch Rickey aimed to come at segregation using the popu-larity and sway of baseball. His family and many others tried talking him out of it, predicting lost revenues and uprisings among those whites who believed the game should remain segregated. Rickey was steadfast.

Rickey sent a trio of scouts out across the country. They came back with names of talented Negro players. Jackie Robinson's name kept ris-ing to the top of the list. In time, Rickey was convinced that Robinson might be his man, provided he had the temperament for the task. Clyde Sukeforth, one of Rickey's scouts, tracked Robinson down in Chicago. Somehow he had to get Robinson to agree to go to Brooklyn to meet with Rickey without telling him the real purpose of the meeting for fear word might leak to the press. So he told Robinson that Rickey was interested in starting another Negro league team and that he wanted Robinson to join the team.

On August 28, 1945, Jackie Robinson made his way to the fourth floor of 215 Montague Street in Brooklyn, where Branch Rickey sat awaiting him, smoking a cigar. There was some small talk, then Rickey finally told Robinson he wanted him to break baseball's color line. Rob-inson could hardly believe what he was hearing. He swallowed hard. "I was thrilled, scared, and excited," he later remembered. "I was incredulous. Most of all, I was speechless." Rickey explained to Robinson he'd have to have both smarts and guts, that there would be pushback, and that there would be racial epithets aplenty. The college-educated and court-martialed Jackie Robinson assured Rickey he had both smarts and guts and knew how to handle himself, but Rickey cut him off: "I'm looking for a ballplayer with guts enough *not* "to fight back." The two men talked for the next two hours, and Robinson agreed to a $600-a-month contract and a $3,500 signing bonus, provided he proved his abilities with the team's minor league club, the Montreal Royals.

Robinson realized his mission would be fraught, but the stakes were extraordinarily high and the long-term benefits unprecedented. He'd certainly be screamed and howled at; some fool might try to stab or shoot him. "I had to do it for several reasons," Robinson later admitted. "For black youth, for my mother, for Rae [Rachel], for myself. I had already begun to feel I had to do it for Branch Rickey."

Baseball was apple-pie America. It was America singing and whistling to itself on weekend afternoons at the ballpark. It was a sacred sport where a white wife and white husband could take their white children to a game and enjoy themselves without having even to imagine the superiority of a black athlete on a baseball diamond—or anywhere else for that matter.

Jackie Robinson was being sent to the Brooklyn Dodgers minor league farm team, the Montreal Royals in Canada. W. G. Bramham, the commissioner of the minor leagues, minced no words in voicing opposition to Robinson, saying that Rickey was "of the carpetbagger stripe of the white race who, under the guise of helping, is in truth using the Negro for their own self-interest, to retard the race." Another potential Robinson foe was Clay Hopper, the manager of the Montreal Royals, who was a genuine bigot. When he was in his native Mississippi, Hopper operated a plantation with a harsh hand. "Mr. Rickey," Hopper once asked the Dodgers president, "do you really think a nigger's a human being?"

Excitement and emotion about Robinson swept the country. Negro publications were ecstatic. At a later press conference in Brooklyn, Robinson expressed his gratefulness at the historical importance of his signing. "Of course I can't begin to tell you how happy I am that I am the first member of my race in organized baseball," he told the gathering. "I realize how much it means to me, my race, and to baseball. I can only say I'll do my very best to come through in every manner."

Robinson married Rachel Isum, his California sweetheart, and then the couple went to Florida for spring training. The whole of black America—from Detroit to Dallas, from Tulsa to Columbus, Ohio—seemed either to be listening via radio or reading the Negro newspapers to keep up with Jackie Robinson's brave foray into Major League Baseball.

Just after Robinson's arrival, the Montreal players could see that Jackie could play baseball and play it quite skillfully. John Wright, another black player, was on the roster, ostensibly so Robinson wouldn't feel so isolated. The problems began almost immediately. During the exhibition season, opposing teams canceled games because they refused to take the field with a black player. A police chief in Florida threatened to have Robinson arrested if he took to the field. The Montreal Royals manager was forced to yank Robinson from the lineup.

At Branch Rickey's invitation, Wendell Smith, a highly respected black reporter for *The Pittsburgh Courier,* began traveling with the Montreal Royals. Smith had been instrumental in his writings in pushing the cause of integration in baseball. Raised in Detroit, he had been a gifted pitcher for American Legion teams while in high school. He once threw a shutout for his team at West Virginia State College, from which he graduated in 1937. He drew the attention of a major league scout, who told him he was disappointed he couldn't sign him because of the color barrier. Smith became a newspaperman with a cause. His columns on breaking the color barrier were erudite and poignant, and they caught the attention of Branch Rickey.

It was April 1946 when the Montreal Royals arrived in Jersey City to play the local minor league team, the Jersey City Giants, for their first game in the North. There were 25,000 fans inside Roosevelt Stadium. Everyone wanted to see Jackie Robinson. In his first at bat, Robinson weakly grounded out. It was his second at bat that caused the hullabaloo: With two teammates on base, Robinson sent a ball soaring toward the left field fence. The entire stadium rose from their seats as the ball disappeared into the stands for a home run.

The legend had begun.

Wendell Smith was covering the game in Jersey City for his newspaper: "And high up in the press box, Joe Bostic of the *Amsterdam News* and I looked at each other knowingly, and we two laughed and smiled . . . Our hearts beat just a bit faster, and the thrill ran through us like champagne bubbles . . . It was a great day in Jersey . . . It was a great day in baseball!" The final score was Montreal, 14, Jersey City, 1. Robinson had three more hits in addition to his homer. He seemed fearless, a natural leader on the field. Fans—kids especially—mobbed him at the end of the game. Someone quickly got word to Branch Rickey up in Brooklyn about Robinson's exploits during the game. "Make no mistake," wrote the *Montreal Gazette* of Robinson, "the man can play ball." The *New York Times* reported that Robinson had "converted his opportunity into a brilliant personal triumph." The Negro press—particularly Wendell Smith—could rightfully pat itself on the back, for it had been writing about baseball and the need to integrate the sport for years. Some of the black reporters had been writing about Jackie Robinson with such intensity that the white press was compelled to take on the story with greater urgency. Never before had the white mainstream press covered a black story with the consistency with which they began to cover the rise of Jackie Robinson. As the black newspaper the *Amsterdam News* would put it: "Thus the most significant sports story of the century was written into the record books as baseball took up the cudgel for democracy and an unassuming but superlative Negro boy ascended the heights of excellence to prove the rightness of the experiment. And prove it in the only correct crucible for such an experiment—the crucible of white hot competition."

The rough and harsh treatment certainly came, and not always in southern cities. In Syracuse, New York, one of the opposing minor league players tossed a black cat onto the field. "Hey, Jackie," came a voice, "there's your cousin." Robinson's demeanor—stoical, disciplined—was amazing, just as Rickey had warned him it must be. He knew he was playing for more than just himself. He was proving something to the American public on behalf of a race of oppressed people.

By the end of the season, his .349 hitting average was enough to earn him the minor league batting crown. His Montreal Royals won the pennant, and then a set of play-off contests, which qualified them for the so-called Little World Series. The team, certainly owing to Robinson's presence, also broke their attendance record by a large margin. Robinson was honored with the league's Most Valuable Player award.

The team traveled to Louisville to play the opening three games of the Little World Series against the Louisville Colonels. The racist epithets hurled at Robinson continued nonstop. Louisville city officials allowed only a limited number of blacks inside the stadium. Trailing two games to one, Montreal had to return to their home city, and Robinson and his teammates got their revenge. The final run in the final game was scored by Jackie Robinson, who hit a blistering .400 for the series.

After that championship clinching game, Robinson emerged from the clubhouse. Fans were everywhere, awaiting him. It was quite a scene. A *Pittsburgh Courier* writer witnessed the scene and reported: "It was probably the only day in history that a black man ran from a white mob with love instead of lynching on its mind."

In early 1947, Robinson was still playing for the Royals. On April 10— while in New York for a game between the major league Dodgers and their farm team—Robinson was summoned to a meeting with Branch Rickey, who told Robinson that the Brooklyn Dodgers had purchased his contract. Jackie Robinson was being called up to the big leagues. One of Rickey's assistants prepared a news release. "The Brooklyn Dodgers today purchased the contract of Jackie Roosevelt Robinson," the release began. "He will report immediately."

Even if it was news that many had begun to anticipate, given Robinson's explosive minor league season, it still carried quite a wallop.

.   .   .

In the beginning of his stint with the Dodgers, Robinson was mired in a hitting slump. His swing was off. He had been placed at first base and felt awkward at the position. There was a stretch where he went hitless on twenty trips to the plate. Arthur Daley, writing in *The New York Times,* opined that "the Negro first baseman hasn't been any ball of fire." During his first days on the team, Robinson realized that some of his teammates were hoping he'd fail—and that this realization threw off his game. He also came to understand early on that home field advantage was not always home field advantage for him. The Philadelphia Phillies came to Ebbets Field, and along with them came a horde of fans who hurled epithets at Robinson, the words so loud it was as if they were coming from a microphone. "Hey, snowflake, which one of those white boys' wives are you dating tonight?" (The language was actually more vile than what the press reported it to be. They were, after all, writing for "family" newspapers.) Robinson had to steel himself. "They're waiting for you in the jungles, black boy." He entertained vengeful thoughts: "I could throw down my bat, stride over to that Phillies dugout, grab one of those white sons of bitches and smash his teeth in with my despised black fist." But Jackie Robinson knew that doing so would derail his momentous opportunity.

When the month of May came to a close, Robinson's stats had improved. He was hitting .283. The Dodgers were just two games out of first place. Players and fans began to sense that Robinson was coming into his own. In June, he hit .381. That captured the attention of everyone around the league. On June 24, playing the Pittsburgh Pirates, he stole home, a daring feat that highlighted Robinson's speed and grit. By the end of June he had a sixteen-game hitting streak. Many were awed by Robinson's talent. Branch Rickey cautioned them: The best was yet to come. "You'll see something," Rickey said of Robinson, "when he gets to bunting and running as freely as he should."

That summer the Cleveland Indians signed Larry Doby, snatching him from the Newark Eagles of the Negro leagues. His signing made Robinson happy. And Robinson, even if his playing elicited anger in various major league baseball ballparks, seemed to make many baseball fans happy. His 28 stolen bases were tops in the league. He and Pee Wee

Reese led the Dodgers with 12 home runs apiece. His batting average was an admirable .297. He was named Rookie of the Year.

The World Series was a fan's dream: the Dodgers versus the Yankees, Joltin' Joe DiMaggio's Yankees. The Yankees went up, two games to none. The Dodgers won the next game at Ebbets Field. Robinson had two singles and a run scored, and he started two double plays. The fourth game was tense and hard fought going into the ninth. Cookie Lavagetto came in for the Dodgers as a pinch hitter. His picturesque 2-run double off the wall in the ninth game gave the Dodgers their victory and fans a nighttime's worth of narrative to relive on the subway rides home. Now each team had won two games apiece. The Yanks won the fifth game; DiMaggio smacked a home run and looked beautiful, as ever, doing so. It was three games to two. The resilient Dodgers tied the series up. In the deciding seventh game, the Yankees prevailed, 5–2. "I've played a lot of ball," Robinson later remembered of the series, "but I've never seen the likes of that."

Many things happened in America in 1947—explosions, natural disasters, race riots—that merited front-page newspaper coverage. But if you were black and living anywhere on the East Coast, or on one of those undulating and sweaty plantations in the South, or scraping a living out on the flat plains of a dust bowl state, or living in an urban neighborhood in the Midwest—especially if you were a black kid playing baseball over at some segregated park in America or a coach for a group of those black kids—the story of Jackie Robinson's first year in the major leagues resonated in an epic manner. It was bigger than the story of Joe Louis. It was bigger than the story of Jesse Owens. More boys—white and black—wanted to play baseball at that time than wanted to box or run track. The feats of Owens and Louis were achieved in individual sports; Robinson had integrated both a team and a sport, and that sport was the national pastime of America. He had blasted through a tunnel and lifted up millions, and he had shamed the warped minds of millions of others. He was twenty-eight years old; he had lost precious time barnstorming and playing in the Negro leagues. But at long last, his time had come. *Time* magazine was not accustomed to putting blacks on its cover. But Jackie Robinson landed there.

.   .   .

His 1948 season was decent enough; he led the team in hits, batting average (.295), runs scored, doubles and triples. But the Dodgers didn't win
the pennant; they finished in third place. Critics complained that Robinson had played much of the season above his normal playing weight.
It was true; he was accustomed to the rich calories of the southern diet—
collard greens, chicken smothered in gravy, okra, peach cobbler. On the
baseball integration front, there were still only seven blacks in major
league baseball. A barrier had been broken, but in a stubbornly segregated nation it was difficult to open the gate wide.

Robinson was eager to begin the 1949 season. On opening day, April
19, playing the Giants, he smacked a homer and singled twice. As May
closed, his batting average rested at .311. The average increased to .344
in the first part of June. Another player from the Negro leagues, pitcher
Don Newcombe, had joined the Dodgers. He was a terror. "He can win
the pennant for us," Robinson said of Newcombe. Come July, Robinson's average had spiked again, up to .361. When the All-Star votes were
counted, Robinson came in second after the great Ted Williams.

Jackie Robinson certainly realized his baseball career was intertwined
with his symbolism as a racial figure. Politics for the nation's most
renowned black baseball player could be downright tricky. Robinson
was summoned before the House Un-American Activities Committee
to talk about his thoughts on Paul Robeson, the mercurial former college football All-American, singer, and actor who had become a political activist. Robeson had aligned himself with communism and urged
blacks not to fight for America if war with Russia erupted. Robinson
told the committee he didn't agree with Robeson's pronouncements, but
the ballplayer didn't shy away from expressing his feelings about blacks
in America and the hardships they faced daily. He said that they could
be counted on to be patriotic: "They'd do their best to help their country
stay out of war; if unsuccessful, they'd do their best to help their country
win the war—against Russia or any other enemy that threatened us." He
went on: "Every single Negro who is worth his salt is going to resent any
kind of slurs and discrimination because of his race, and he's going to use

every bit of intelligence, such as he has, to stop it. This has got absolutely nothing to do with what Communists may or may not be trying to do." There was no doubt Robinson would have been badly hurt if he had expressed any support of communism.

Meanwhile, back on the diamond, Jackie Robinson was having an astonishing year. "You must admit," the *New York Post*'s Jimmy Cannon wrote of Robinson, "this is the Most Valuable Player in the National League." Toward season's end, *Look* magazine anointed Robinson as "the Ball Player of the Year." Hitting .342, Robinson beat out Stan Musial for the batting title. Throughout the league, no one had more stolen bases than Jackie Robinson. When he was named the National League's MVP for the 1949 baseball season, it seemed as if there wasn't a juke joint on the black side of any city or town where someone wasn't raising a toast to Jackie Robinson. Even though the Yankees beat the Dodgers, 4–1, in the World Series, the luster of Robinson's season—and unfolding career—couldn't be dimmed.

No one was under the illusion that Jackie Robinson's bat could lift Negroes en masse up higher on the socioeconomic ladder. The picture for the American Negro remained desperate and gloomy. In 1949, in Jackie Robinson's MVP year, seventeen states—as well as Washington, D.C.—adopted laws that deepened racial segregation in school systems. It was a brutal blow to black parents everywhere. That same summer, James Baldwin, a young novelist, wrote an essay in the *Partisan Review* critiquing Harriet Beecher Stowe's *Uncle Tom's Cabin* and—though less harshly—Richard Wright's *Native Son* and its protagonist, Bigger Thomas. "For Bigger's tragedy is not that he is cold or black or hungry," Baldwin wrote, "not even that he is American, black; but that he has accepted a theology that denies him life, that he admits the possibility of his being sub-human and feels constrained, therefore, to battle for his humanity according to those brutal criteria bequeathed him at his birth."

Baldwin, only twenty-five years old, was brilliant in his insights into America's racial quagmire, but Baldwin wrote his essay from Paris.

By 1949 he had given up on America, believing the nation would be doomed by its inability to treat its black citizens fairly.

If Baldwin relished playing the outsider, Robinson was proud to play the American insider. His nation's social policies were never far from his mind. "I simply don't want all-black classrooms and all-black schools in a system where the best teachers and the best equipment and the best administration go to the white school and the worst to the black," he said. "I see more value in making a ghetto school great enough to induce parents of all races to send their children to it."

Jackie Robinson looked forward to the 1950 season for several reasons, not just for the joy of playing baseball. As summer began to deepen in 1950—and the cracks of bats were heard echoing inside baseball fields—the Brooklyn Dodgers were sitting pretty; they were atop the National League standings. In the last game of the season, the Dodgers played host to the Philadelphia Phillies at Ebbets Field; the winner would claim the pennant. The hearts of Dodger fans broke in the ninth when the Phillies' Dick Sisler hit a home run, giving his team the win. Robinson would not win a second consecutive MVP award, but he did finish the season with a .328 batting average.

At the beginning of his major league career, Jackie Robinson agreed with Branch Rickey's desire that, for the time being, he should refrain from making comments about the racial politics of baseball. As difficult as it was for Robinson to hold his feelings in check, he kept his promise. But a few years into Robinson's career, that ban was lifted, and Rickey told him he was free to speak his mind. Robinson let people know he was aware of the dynamics of the playing field as it related to his race. He had to deal constantly with the boos from certain quarters. Boos, of course, were a part of the game, but his were so often of a darker and more menacing variety. "Anything I do," he finally expressed about the umpires, "they'll give me the worst of the breaks. I know what I am up against." Others sensed a double standard as well. "There is no question in my mind that the umpires are picking on Robinson," said Ford Frick, president of the National League. Robinson's clashes with umpires meant little to the umpires, but to blacks in the stands at ball-parks around the nation, he was now fighting back. It was apparent to Robinson that he would not get an umpire to change his mind about a call. But he also knew that hours after the game, a black father might be sitting someplace with his son or daughter and remark how important it was for Jackie Robinson sometimes to stand his ground in front of white people.

Robinson suffered a deep emotional loss in 1950 when Branch Rickey, his heroic benefactor, left the Dodgers to become general manager of the Pittsburgh Pirates. "It has been the finest experience I have had being associated with you," Robinson wrote to Rickey when news of his leaving the Dodgers became public, "and I want to thank you very much for all you have meant not only to me and my family but to the entire country and particularly the members of our race." Rarely had two men been so connected regarding the shifting and elevation of a particular sport upon the national mind-set of many in America. The big 1954 school desegregation ruling was still a few years away. The desegregation of the American military had happened only three years earlier, in 1948, but the military was almost like a closed society. The public at large hardly had to follow its lead. Baseball was another story. It was out in the open. It *was* America.

Shortly after the 1951 season was under way, Robinson, in Cincinnati for a game, was paid a visit by a couple of FBI agents. The local police and a Cincinnati newspaper had received letters vowing that when Robinson took the field, he would be assassinated by a sharpshooter positioned in a nearby building. The ominous letters were signed "Three Travelers." The entire Dodger team was made aware of the letters. They let Robinson know they were proud to be taking the field with him. The public heard about the threats as well. That day, standing at home plate in Cincinnati wondering if a rifle was aimed in his direction from an unseen location, Jackie Robinson reared his shoulders back, ferociously whipped his bat around, and sent the ball deep into the stands. A home run. The crowd went wild. The sniper, if there was one, went unseen.

At season's end the Dodgers found themselves in a three-game play-off series with the Giants; each team had 96–58 records. The New York

Giants had dazzled baseball fans by winning thirty-seven of their last forty-four games, catching their rivals across town. Baseball fans were thrilled by the combination of athletics and technology: It was the first baseball series to be nationally televised. After two games, the teams were tied, one game apiece. Robinson had homered in the second game, as did teammates Andy Pafko, Gil Hodges, and Rube Walker. On October 3 the teams squared off for the finale at the Polo Grounds. By the eighth inning the Dodgers looked unstoppable as Billy Cox hit a single, bringing Robinson across home plate, making the score 4–1 and sending Dodgers fans into ecstasy. (Don Newcombe was on the mound for the Dodgers.) In the bottom of the ninth, the Giants' Whitey Lockman connected on a Newcombe pitch and drove in a run; the score was now 4–2. Charlie Dressen, the Dodger manager, pulled Newcombe, believing him to be tiring. In the dugout, Jackie Robinson grumbled about the move. Newcombe was replaced by Ralph Branca. A nation on the edge of its seat was watching—either in the stands, or staring at a TV screen in their living rooms or in hotel lobbies or in department store windows. Bobby Thomson, the Giants' dangerous hitter, stood facing Branca with two men on base in the bottom of the ninth inning. The first pitch was a strike. Thomson sliced into Branca's next pitch, sending it whirring into the left field stands and rocketing the Giants into the World Series. The Giants hadn't won a pennant since 1937. It was a painful loss for the Dodgers, one that would be talked about and debated for, it seemed, eternity. Nevertheless, Jackie Robinson had a stellar 1951 season. His batting average was .338; he belted 19 homers and had 88 RBIs. He was also named an All-Star. That year another black player, Willie Mays of the Giants, was named Rookie of the Year. (The Robinson and Mays baseball cards became community totems, especially in black neighborhoods.) The inequality in baseball still remained painfully apparent, but five teams in the majors had at least one black player on their active roster during the previous season.

Jackie Robinson, to be sure, rolled about the country inside rarefied air. His mere presence was often fused inside a triple meaning: To blacks he remained a heroic and iconic figure. To many whites he remained an ongoing mystery in a country still obliging the laws of segregation in nearly all aspects of daily life. And to little boys who enjoyed baseball, he remained simply Jackie Robinson, the slugger pictured on baseball cards.

The Brooklyn Dodgers won the pennant in 1952 and made it to the World Series. The Yankees—still an all-white team—awaited them. The Dodgers won the fifth game, which went eleven innings, and then the Yankees won game six to tie the series. It was becoming a truism that where there were Brooklyn Dodgers, there was much drama. In the final game—the Dodgers down 4–2 in the seventh with the bases loaded— Jackie Robinson stood in the batter's box. Robinson connected on a ball down the middle, a hard crackling hit that lifted the crowd. But Billy Martin, the Yankees second baseman, stopped the ball's trajectory with his quick glove. Robinson was out. The Dodgers lost the series.

Athletes must count the years. Jackie Robinson was starting to mull his future. He lamented that he had not yet won a World Series title. Yet he also knew he had only so many playing days left. From his home in Connecticut during the off-seasons, he had begun investing in businesses in Harlem. He opened a clothing store in his name. Television execs in New York City also put him on TV programs, where he interviewed other celebrities.

During the 1953 season, even as he was sometimes idled with a knee injury, Robinson thought that he had "another two or three years to go as a full-time player." Nevertheless, he had a fine season, batting .329, besting his previous year's average of .308. In the coolness of mid-September, the Dodgers won the pennant. They were the first Dodger team to win 105 games. "If we don't win it this time," Robinson said of the looming World Series, "we'll never win it." It was déjà vu all over again because the Yankees, with Mickey Mantle and Billy Martin going on hitting sprees, took the series from the Dodgers in six games.

Between the 1953 and 1954 seasons, Jackie Robinson went around the country making a series of speeches on behalf of the National Conference of Christians and Jews. He was not a spellbinding orator, and his speeches were plain and void of any remark that might seem too radical. "Education must begin in the home and church and then in the public institutions," he said to one group.

In a nation where every black celebrity seemed to be breaking some kind of barrier by virtue of endurance, Robinson had forged to the head of the class. Other black celebrities of the time included, among others, Sammy Davis Jr., Eartha Kitt, Lena Horne, and Harry Belafonte, each making noise on the civil rights front.

When the clock ran out on his off-season and the speechifying, it was off to Florida for spring training. Being in Florida was always an ordeal because of the stiff and nasty segregation policies there. Robinson tolerated the customs of the South more easily than did his wife, Rachel. She never forgot the couple's first evening out at a white Miami nightclub: "Walter Winchell [newspaper columnist and radio commentator] had arranged it. He literally led the way, parted the waters, as Jack and I, Sugar Ray Robinson and his wife, followed him like sheep to his table. It was more tense than fun, but it was another barrier broken."

As the 1954 season got under way, something happened that gave black ballplayers—and blacks everywhere—a huge emotional lift. The meaning behind the Supreme Court's *Brown v. Board of Education* ruling on desegregation could not be separated from what they themselves, as black ballplayers, as men, had been so eager to prove: If given fair opportunities, their talents could prove the equal of any man.

As the seasons kept circling Jackie Robinson, who knew if he'd ever make it back to a World Series, let alone win one?

Robinson got off to a fine start in the new baseball season, hitting .368 in April. But it was a season of ups and downs; injuries plagued him. There was also an incident that happened in Milwaukee that he couldn't shake: After arguing with a plate umpire, Robinson was tossed from the game. He sulked, and as he walked back to the dugout he flipped his bat. Instead of landing harmlessly in the dugout, the bat soared into the stands, causing fans to duck and gasp. Robinson blamed the trajectory of the bat on the rain, which, he claimed, caused the bat to slip out of his hands. The umpire backed Robinson's account, but the damage was done. *Sport* magazine opined that, because he had thrown a bat, Robinson had suddenly become "the most savagely booed, intensively criticized, ruthlessly libeled player in the game." The magazine's assessment was harsh and seemed to be a rebuke of Robinson's often frosty relationship with many members of the white press, who considered his speaking out against racial injustice beyond his duties as a ballplayer. It was a fitful season, even as Robinson hit .311. Long feared as a base stealer, he stole only seven bases during the year. The year before, he had stolen seventeen. As well, the Giants won the pennant. "I would trade him," a Dodgers official said of Robinson.

Branch Rickey was now with the Pittsburgh Pirates organization, and rumors floated that Robinson might join the Pirates. Accustomed to epithets, Robinson began to hear one from fickle New York fans that had never been associated with him: Brooklyn Bum.

During the off-season, the most famous athlete in America—whose every season seemed to be a kind of dramatic, churning history lesson about race and American life—enjoyed time with his wife and three children in their new country estate in Stamford, Connecticut. There was a pond, and there were apple trees. Their integration into the community had not been without pain: The newspaper in Bridgeport ran a series of articles about segregated housing when it found out the Robinsons were initially being stymied in their efforts to purchase a home.

The Brooklyn Dodgers began their next training camp on March 1, 1955. Jackie Robinson was now fighting off younger players who wanted his spot. Grit and pride helped him endure as he held himself together, playing through nagging injuries and ailments. Sometimes, standing in the on-deck circle in the twilight, dust on his cleats, he looked beautiful: the old man and the dry earth. His batting average seesawed, but in June he hit .328. A *Pittsburgh Courier* writer, acknowledging that the Robinson of that season might not be the Robinson of old, wrote that he still possessed "a psychic, spiritual force" over the team, which served all well. The Dodgers won the National League pennant handily. The World Series foes—Dodgers and Yankees—might as well have been the Hatfields and McCoys; they were so familiar with one another.

At Yankee Stadium to open the series, the Dodgers fell behind two games to none. Dodger fans grumbled: the damn bums. Then it was over to Ebbets Field for a three-game home stand. Aided by power hitting, and Robinson's fearless base running, the Dodgers swept all three games, 8–3, 8–5, 5–3, thrilling their fans. "Aging Robinson Sets Dodgers Afire," pronounced one headline.

Jackie Robinson was a wily old pro now, a gray-haired eminence huffing around the bases.

The teams squared off for the sixth game. Whitey Ford had a fine game, and his Yankees won, 5–1. Now the series was tied. On Tuesday, October 4, the teams took to the grass at Yankee Stadium for the final game, which would decide the World Series champions. More than sixty-two thousand were in attendance. Figuring that Robinson was exhausted, Walter Alston, the Dodgers manager, decided to sit him. Gil Hodges was the Dodgers star that day; the Dodgers scored a run in the fourth inning on his single, then another run in the sixth when he sliced a sacrifice fly. There was a Yankee threat in the sixth inning when, with runners on first and second, Yogi Berra smacked a ball deep into left field. Dodger Sandy Amorós snatched the ball, rifled it to Pee Wee Reese, who threw quickly to teammate Gil Hodges, resulting in a crushing double play. The Dodgers went on to win their first World Series. Jackie Robinson was overwhelmed with the joy of being on a world champion team.

The following year the Dodgers won the pennant on the season's final day and made it back to the World Series, as did the Yankees. The Dodgers took the first two games. The Yankees roared back to take games three, four, and five. The fifth game of the series was scintillating: Don Larsen of the Yankees threw a perfect game, the only one in postseason history. It was Jackie Robinson's moment to shine in the sixth game: In the tenth inning, he laced a line drive into left field, scoring Jim Gilliam and giving his team a 1–0 win. During the seventh game the Yankee hits were unstoppable. Yogi Berra hit a two-run homer. His teammate, Bill Skowron, smashed a grand slam in the seventh inning. The Yankees ended the championship game on top, 9–0.

That year Jackie Robinson scored 61 runs and swatted 10 home runs. Playing in 117 games, he stole 12 bases. They were fine numbers for an "old boy" of thirty-seven, as he called himself. But the end had come. Jackie Robinson—traded ignominiously to the Giants—retired from baseball. His role in the great noble experiment that integrated baseball was finished. He had changed America. But now the legend had to find a job in the workaday world.

Robinson pined for a managerial job in baseball, and he was willing to start at the minor league level. But no offers came. He knew the reasons, or at least the primary reason. He imagined that baseball owners who might have considered him for a job talked themselves out of it, convincing themselves that white ballplayers would not follow his directions, or would question his baseball acumen. So Jackie Robinson would not have the same opportunities as white ballplayers who had enjoyed much less fame on the baseball diamond than he had. When it was finally accepted that Robinson would have no change of mind regarding the end of his playing days—other teams wanted him to extend his playing career—the tributes poured in. None were more poignant than the words from Brooks Lawrence, a pitcher with the Cincinnati Reds who had come up from the Negro leagues: "You opened the door for me and others who followed you and when you opened it you threw it wide open," he told Robinson. "You gave to us a new way of life for which we will be eternally grateful."

There was finally a breakthrough when Jackie Robinson was offered a vice president position with Chock full o'Nuts, a chain of coffee shops. William H. Black, the founder of the chain, had a progressive mind-set; his company had an integrated sales force. Soon enough, Robinson was working at the Chock full o'Nuts headquarters in Manhattan, a figure as rare in the white corporate world as he had once been on the baseball diamond. He was vice president for personnel, a job that gave him the opportunity to interact with company employees. He liked the work.

But beyond New York City, these were dangerous times for black America. There were civil rights murders and church bombings in Birmingham, Alabama, and other cities throughout the South. As Robinson put it, the church bombings were extremely shattering because "the Negroes are being hit in the one place where they have felt safe."

Politics was a way to address the nation's social ills, and it was the rare black celebrity who could avoid a connection to the politics of the times. Strong-willed politicians who wished to take on those who called for continued segregation often looked toward black celebrities to endorse them. Jackie Robinson supported both President Eisenhower and Vice President Nixon. Black identity with Republicans could be traced to Abraham Lincoln, a Republican. Nixon, like Robinson, hailed from Southern California. Because his family had roots in Georgia, Jackie Robinson had no illusions about the wrath southern Democrats felt toward civil rights and blacks. In time, Robinson became a stalwart speaker for the NAACP. He led marches for integration and began to write a column for the *New York Post*. His columns ranged from sports to international affairs. Like many, Jackie Robinson felt that civil rights legislation was not moving at all in America. The 1957 Civil Rights Bill was seen as a compromise piece of legislation that left much of the nation's segregation in place. With the 1960 presidential campaign under way, Robinson expressed an affinity for Minnesota senator Hubert Humphrey, but Humphrey lost the nomination to Massachusetts senator Jack Kennedy, who was later elected president.

The movement—as the civil rights crusade across America had come to be known—pulled Jackie Robinson deeper into its sphere. He went to look at a black church that had been burned out by Klansmen in Georgia. He consulted with Malcolm X in Harlem. Baseball executives decried him—even as he was being elected to the Hall of Fame in 1962—because he highlighted the lack of diversity in their front offices. Ordinary citizens were startled to see him on picket lines, holding signs aloft: HIRE US NOW—NOT TOMORROW NOT NEXT MONTH BUT NOW.

The "movement" for Jackie Robinson had meant newspaper articles, the written word. Now it was feet in motion, protesters marching and holding hands.

Martin Luther King Jr. battled with the Kennedy administration over the issue of civil rights. Against the concerns of the administration, he proceeded with his March on Washington. Ruby Dee, Sammy Davis Jr., James Garner, and Marlon Brando were among the Hollywood celebreties at the march. "I have never been so proud to be a Negro," Robinson expressed of his participation in the March. "I have never been so proud to be an American." Then came the dark and murderous days: President Kennedy's assassination; more church bombings in the South; Robinson's son, Jackie Jr., home from the Vietnam War and hooked on drugs; the assassinations of Martin Luther King Jr. and Bobby Kennedy.

Jackie Robinson confided to those who wanted to know that he considered himself a "Rockefeller Republican"—a class of Republicans considered to be more liberal and progressive than so-called county-club Republicans. In 1966, Robinson became a special assistant for community affairs to New York governor Nelson Rockefeller. But the turmoil persisted. He watched it all, the sadness engulfing the nation, the streets in flames. Then he split with the Republicans in 1968, incensed at Richard Nixon: "He's really prostituted himself to get the southern vote," he said of Nixon. Just after the Nixon family moved into the White House, Robinson and a group of other black leaders went there to meet with him. They didn't get beyond the front gates. Political commentators had begun talking more and more about Nixon's "southern strategy" and how it had snatched many voters from the Democratic Party and delivered them to the Republican Party by driving deeper division between blacks and whites. Conservative, suburban whites were given the impression that Nixon would save them from the aftermath of the civil rights revolution.

In 1971, Jackie Jr.—thought to be turning his life around—died in a car crash in Connecticut. Robinson and his wife, Rachel, endured the loss as best they could, which is to say they really couldn't. But they had other grown children, so they forged ahead.

Maybe it was nostalgia. Or maybe the nation was beginning to realize that there was indeed a black history that was grand and epochal. A great deal of attention began to turn in the direction of Jackie Robinson. There were testimonials and dinners in his honor. The further into the past the nation looked—and the bigger baseball continued to become—the larger Jackie Robinson, no. 42, loomed. Anyone could see he was aging. He was moving more slowly than ever. He had diabetes. With bad vision and an unsteady gait, he proudly reached for yet another plaque.

Sometimes he cried, tears falling down his face, swiveling his neck as he looked about the audience for his beloved Rachel. She'd also be overcome with emotion, listening to all the accolades about her Jackie. In 1972 he penned his autobiography, *I Never Had It Made*. On October 24 of that year, policemen were summoned to the house in Connecticut. His breathing was labored. The police supplied oxygen. It didn't help. Jackie Robinson died that morning. The funeral, held at Riverside Church in New York City, drew 2,500 mourners. Among the attendees were many Dodger players, and civil rights leaders Bayard Rustin and Jesse Jackson.

Bob Marsh, a young white junior high school teacher from the little farming community of Williston, Ohio, arrived in Columbus, Ohio, in 1966. There were no black students at the high school he had attended. In Columbus, he was assigned to teach at Monroe Junior High School, one of the city's all-black, still-segregated junior high schools; it was a feeder school for East High. Marsh, who had started playing baseball in Little League, asked for and got the head baseball coaching job at Monroe. He was bewildered when he found out that the school did not have its own baseball diamond. The players had to troupe a mile over to Maryland Park to practice and play their games. Marsh was also astonished when he saw how gifted the Monroe Junior High players were. He looked around the city and didn't see a Little League apparatus in place that might have nurtured them. How had they learned to play so well? What was inspiring these impoverished boys on the East Side of Columbus to play ball with such abandon? Then he realized what it was: "Baseball still had the impact of Jackie Robinson. His era was not far removed from the 1960s."

Jackie Robinson had integrated the National League, and Larry Doby was signed by the Cleveland Indians of the American League three months after Robinson joined the Dodgers. In the big cities and small towns of Ohio, Doby had also made a big impression. "You still had a lot of black role models, a lot of black pioneers," recalls Bob Marsh of baseball in the 1960s.

Over on Mount Vernon Avenue, inside those dark and smoky bars, one could still hear old-timers talking of the Negro leagues, crowing about the exploits of teams like the Indianapolis Clowns, Pittsburgh Crawfords, and Homestead Grays. Integration was the goal, but there were streams of unforgettable magic in that slipping-away world of segregation.

When Paul Pennell, the East High baseball coach, looked around at his assembled team in late March of 1969, he lamented that he did not have enough specific position players. He told the players some of them would have to play multiple positions. It was the kind of philosophy employed in the old Negro leagues—players were moved into different positions like pieces on a chessboard. Not a single player complained about Pennell's strategy.

So it would be a team—a season—of experimentation, of shuffling players around. Eddie Rat had just come off a triumphant championship season for the school basketball team. To him, the star pitcher, this baseball team did not have the same feel. Looking around, he did not see a great team. He did not even see a very *good* team. "No one expected us to win," Eddie Rat remembers.

11

Twilight at Harley Field

They wanted a dugout.

But just like last year, they were not going to have one. The school just couldn't afford to build one. So, once again, they would have to grab the old folding chairs from inside the school, haul them out to the parking lot, and load them into Coach Pennell's car. That would be their resting place between innings: a line of chairs ten or so yards away from the batter's box. It was all makeshift. There would be no cover from the rain that could come and go in springtime.

They also wanted new uniforms.

But also like last year, they were told they were not getting any. The players' shoulders slumped when they were told. A lack of school funds was the reason. As for cleats, the coach directed the players to a store where they could get them as cheap as possible. Some of the returning players would be retrieving their cleats from an earlier season.

Unlike with the basketball team, there was never a worry that too many players would try out for baseball. No matter how many bulletins were posted around the school ("Baseball Tryouts Today Harley Field"), or how many times the announcement went out over the school loud-

Tiger outfielders, left to right: Harry Williams, Tony Brown, Phil Mackey, Robert Kuthrell.
The team's five-game losing streak concerned everyone.

speaker, Pennell felt fortunate to get fifteen decent players to fill out his roster.

Actually, it was a stretch to say he was conducting "tryouts," because Pennell pretty much knew which fifteen players would make the team. There were no dazzling and heralded players who had come up from the junior high ranks in the spring of 1969. So, as baseball practice that season got under way, there were not a lot of expectations. There was just the sound of the bat and the whiz of the ball across the field, and the groans about the chilly March temperatures. Pennell could see he was going to miss the three seniors from last year's team. Mike Phillips and Will Britford, solid position players, were gone. So was star pitcher Erkie Byrd. Erkie was his real name; teammates always thought it sounded like something from a comic book. He didn't mind the teasing. Byrd had played multiple positions on the previous year's team. Off the field he had a quiet, unassuming personality. But on the field he was a demon, hitting and fielding and pitching. There were some around the city—especially aging black men who had seen Negro league baseball games—who thought Byrd had the stuff to make it in the big leagues. But professional baseball scouts didn't spend a heck of a lot of time in Ohio looking at high school players. They preferred locations such as California, Texas, Arizona, and Florida, where the players could play year-round. Those were the areas that tended to yield the better players. Pennell had at least hoped Byrd was going to go to college. A junior college in Iowa had showed a lot of interest in Byrd. Pennell felt a lot more colleges should have taken a look at him. But Erkie played in the inner city for an impoverished black school that was not known for producing baseball players. Erkie—and he never explained why to his coach—didn't attend that Iowa junior college. He joined the Marines. By the time Pennell and his team had begun practicing for the 1969 baseball season, Erkie Byrd had been in Vietnam for months, trying to stay alive in the middle of jungle gunfire. There was a lot of chatter about the war coming to a close in the early months of the Nixon administration, but the bombs were still exploding and the bodies still piling up. No one knew who to believe about the war anymore.

There was a rather spooky feeling among the returning players and Pennell when April 4, 1969, popped up on the calendar. They all remembered exactly where they had been on that day, a year earlier, when King was assassinated. They had been on spring break, with a game scheduled for April 5. Pennell reached every player—many phone lines were busy because families were calling other family members, especially those still living in the South—and told them to report to the school immediately. "I made up my mind to cancel everything," Pennell recalls.

At the beginning of the 1969 high school baseball season, and because of what had happened—and was still happening—around the country, Coach Pennell wanted a black coach on his staff. It was an obvious concession to the times, but it was also a move Pennell had been wanting to make. No time seemed as important as now. He found his new coach in Jim Henderson, a native of Columbus who had attended East High and played baseball for Pennell. Henderson had recently graduated from Kentucky State College. Henderson, like any assistant or head coach of the school, accepted the fact that he would receive only his teacher's salary and nothing for the extra hours spent coaching. (It wasn't until several years later that coaches across the city began receiving a little extra income for coaching. For now, they coached for the love of sports.) Pennell realized how lucky he was to have a head coaching job at such a young age. Columbus was a conservative town, and a conservative philosophy dominated the coaching ranks: Head coaches needed experience and mentors, but Pennell had become baseball coach when he was just twenty-six years old. In 1969, of the Jack Gibbs–Bob Hart–Paul Pennell troika, Pennell, at thirty years old, was still the youngest. He certainly deferred to both men, but he had forged his own identity as well.

Paul Pennell was born in Columbus in 1939 on the city's West Side, where racial clashes were most quick to erupt because of the mix of blacks and ethnic whites who had settled there at the turn of the century. Pennell's parents forbade Paul, his friends, or any visiting neighborhood adults or kids to use racial epithets. Paul desperately wanted to play sports in high school, but his father, Sam, wouldn't allow it. It was a blue-collar neighborhood, and kids who could work after school did so, to add funds to the family kitty. "I can't recall anyone in our neighborhood who had a college education," Pennell recalls. The fact that he loved sports and missed out on participating in high school only made him more eager to find some way into the world of coaching.

In 1957, Pennell enrolled at Ohio State University as a freshman. He rode the city bus back and forth from the West Side to the campus on the city's North Side. There was a lot of talk that fall—and a lot of images on the TV screen—of the Little Rock, Arkansas, school integration crisis. The Pennells followed the reports closely. "I remember my father rejoicing when Eisenhower sent in federal troops and made them enforce the law of the land," says Pennell.

As his graduation day neared, Pennell, an education major, didn't have a job lined up. He was worried. "Every Tuesday morning I'd call the board of education," he recalls. Finally, there was the offer to join the faculty of East High, where he was assigned to teach biology and driver's education.

One of Paul Pennell's passions growing up was baseball. He played and then coached various Little League teams on the West Side. He spent a lot of time around American Legion teams, made up of teenage boys with better-than-average skills who played during summers. A lot of the Legion teams were in the suburbs and in the rural, all-white towns that abutted Columbus.

Soon after joining East High, Pennell got the sole assistant basketball coaching position under Bob Hart. In 1963, John Rawn, the school's baseball coach, stepped down. No one was clamoring for the job. Because baseball was the forgotten sport of the school, young Pennell was handed the position. In those early years, Pennell's Tigers lost plenty of games. "The first couple years we got the mess kicked out of us," says Bobby Humphries, a member of Pennell's 1966 team.

But slowly things began to change. Pennell wanted the players on his teams to bond, and he wanted them to know they could trust him. America was afire; white coaches were looked on by some blacks with suspicion. Pennell and his wife, Sharon, didn't have any children. The players added a certain light to their lives. They would invite them to their home for backyard barbecues. For many of the players it was the first time they had been inside the home of a white family. "He didn't just coach us," recalls Humphries. "He mentored us." Then there was Pennell's way of introducing his baseball players to white baseball players during games and scrimmages. "In American Legion, he brought white players to play us," says Humphries. "He was letting us know we could play with anyone. We had played Little League against all-black teams."

Within three years of taking the job, Pennell had shown evidence of turning the team around. But still, they were playing on a subpar field, without a dugout. And it remained as difficult as ever to get anyone from the community—save for a very few stalwart souls—interested in the baseball team.

But Pennell realized something about his baseball players: They seemed to possess genuine talent. He had no idea about the history of the peculiar Little League team that had formed and shaped them on the segregated side of the city.

Before Paul Pennell had ever laid eyes on the Tiger baseball players warming up before him at the start of the 1969 season, those players had been

Coach Paul Pennell told his players to ignore the fact that they were attracting no Tiger fans to their away games.

dreaming of baseball for a long time. They had been helped in those dreams by four Columbus men: Gilbert Dodley, Garland Boffman, Ed Littlejohn, and Nate "Frog" Lawson. They were all self-taught Negro baseball coaches in their segregated America. They were determined not to allow Columbus—or its environs—to dim the baseball dreams of certain little black boys. Their god was Jackie Robinson.

They were blue-collar workers, good and dependable men who loved baseball. Sometimes, in the local watering holes over on Mount Vernon Avenue, the four men would get to regaling each other with stories about exactly which park it was that they had seen Jackie Robinson play in. Stories got tangled as the booze was consumed, but still, there were enough facts and moments laid out for nearby listeners to believe that the men had been there, that they had seen a great many unforgettable moments unfold in the Negro leagues. And when black sportswriter Hiram Tanner would join them the conversations would really take off because Tanner had actually *played* in the professional Negro leagues!

It was important to Dodley, Boffman, Littlejohn, and Lawson that the young black boys of segregated Columbus have a baseball league to play in, and they delighted in their 1953 founding and coaching of the Peers Club team. When the weather turned warm that year in Columbus, the Peers Club coaches could be found at Maryland Park, the East Side park where blacks congregated. It was also the park where the Columbus Royals, the all-black semi-pro team in town, played their games. The Royals were sponsored by a local gambler who loved baseball, and the team was made up of black players in their twenties. Peers Club players would watch the Royals play with wide-eyed excitement. If you were black and cared anything about baseball in Columbus, you had to get over to Maryland Park on Saturday afternoons. It wasn't that whites were forbidden to come; they just never did, because they were quite comfortable on their side of town in their own parks.

The Little League team was called the Peers Club because, although baseball was the anchor, the coaches wanted the boys to feel they were part of a special and unique club. They were little boys, peers for each other. The country was segregated, and that reality already assigned them to a certain club. But baseball made them all happy, the coaches as well as the players. "We had about a five-mile radius," remembers Dave Cole, a member of the Peers Club team in 1960, referring to the distance the team traveled for games. "If you went outside that radius in the city, you'd feel tensions. You knew there were white people who didn't want you around. So you'd pick your spots." Jim Henderson—the East High assistant baseball coach—had also been a Peers Club player. His mother, a maid, fretted that he might get hurt. "We went and played the white teams," he recalled decades later. "We smoked them."

To start a Little League team, you need uniforms. Team identity is manifest in those uniforms. So the Peers Club coaches fanned out up and down Mount Vernon Avenue. Each assigned himself a set of particular businesses—bars, clothing stores, drugstores, record shops—to go into and solicit. And when the players took to the field at Maryland Park, fans saw names on the back of their uniforms that were quite familiar: William McNabb Funeral Home, Tyler Drugs, Swan Cleaners, Tunie's Sunoco Gas Station. It was, of course, rather common advertising for the local businesses. But it was also how black America operated—on self-reliance and fortitude.

Peers Club players had a reverence for the coaches. "We listened to them like their word was gospel," Dave Cole says. "They kept us on the straight and narrow." Cole has never forgotten Coach Frog Lawson's constant admonition when he was playing the infield: "Cole, keep your butt down!"

After games, the coaches, who, needless to say, were never paid a dime, would sometimes just stand and marvel at the boys, how they came together as a team, year in and year out. And sometimes Ed Littlejohn—especially if the team had just had an unusually close victory—would yell for everyone to get into the cars. They were going over to the Dairy Queen to get ice cream! Once there, the young players—proud in their dusty uniforms, sitting in the shade out there on Sunbury Road with their ice cream cones, talking about Willie Mays or all the stories they'd heard about Jackie Robinson, or the game they had just won ("I can't remember losing many games," says David Cole)—would get to feeling that there was nothing better in the whole wide world than being a Peers Club baseball player. With their rumps planted on their battered gloves and their dripping ice cream cones in hand and the day rolling to a sweet close around them, they never felt happier, or safer.

In 1961, when twelve-year-old Eddie Ratleff arrived in Columbus from Bellefontaine, Ohio, with his family, he was intent on finding a Little League baseball team to play on. Growing up in Bellefontaine, he had been close to his grandfather, Richard Artis, who had played baseball and followed the Negro leagues very closely. He was a rabid Jackie Robinson fan. Artis taught Eddie Ratleff the rudiments of the game. "Baseball was my first love," says Eddie Rat.

As a new kid in Columbus, Eddie began asking around about local baseball teams. Someone told him about the Peers Club. He grabbed his glove and started out for the park, a couple of miles from his East Side home. Barbara, his mother, was sure to remind him to be careful, not to get lost, and to mind his manners. It was lovely summertime, and with his glove under his arm, he felt giddy and happy. Because he was confident of his own skills, Eddie was eager to see if this Peers Club Little League team was any good. As he approached the park, he saw a group of boys his age range who were playing. It made him feel good just to see them. They caught sight of him as he got closer; his height drew prolonged stares. He asked who he had to see to try out for the team. The boys pointed to one of the coaches, Mr. Littlejohn. Young Eddie made his way to the coach and started talking a little about himself, that he had just moved to the neighborhood, that he had played Little League in his hometown. Mr. Littlejohn cut the conversation short: "We don't have any more uniforms." Eddie was immediately dejected. But since he had walked all the way to the park, he decided to stick around and watch the practice. Just as it was ending, Eddie pulled aside a player and asked if he would catch some pitches for him. The player agreed. Eddie planted himself on a makeshift mound and started throwing pitches. Pitch after pitch after pitch. And he got stronger with each pitch. Some other players gathered around, watching wide-eyed. Eddie kept firing. Mr. Littlejohn came over to see what the commotion was about. The other coaches, Mr. Dodley, Mr. Boffman, and Mr. Frog (even he chuckled at his nickname), soon joined him. Littlejohn tried following Ratleff's thrown balls with his eyes, but the balls were coming out of young Eddie's hand so fast he could only hear them landing in the catcher's glove. The kid had a wicked fastball. Littlejohn began exchanging glances with his fellow coaches. No one knew who this kid was. Soon Mr. Littlejohn made his way toward young Eddie. "We just found another uniform."

Eddie Rat had found a team. It was almost as if he had been dropped into a kind of secret society—black kids, Little Leaguers. It was a scene unlike in Bellefontaine, where he was one of the few blacks playing on a white team.

In their own way, the Peers Club coaches were establishing a pipeline. They lifted these players on to their next hill to climb: junior high baseball. And these players—Garnett Davis, Leroy Crozier, Norris Smith, Tony Brown, Dave Cole, Eddie Ratleff, Lee Hawkins, Erkie Byrd among them—would never forget them. They'd never forget how their afternoon games would bring out the black community, and how sometimes after the games they'd be treated to grilled hot dogs, or be taken to get ice cream, or just sit in the shade talking about their heroes—Jackie Robinson and Willie Mays and Larry Doby—and how they were hoping they might get a new glove or baseball bat for their next birthday.

There were three all-black junior high schools on the East Side of the city. Some Peers Club players would be off to Monroe Junior High, others to Franklin, and still others to Champion. Tom Brown, in 1961, was named the baseball coach at Champion Junior High. And when the Peers Club players got to him, Brown was always grateful. They'd need more coaching and seasoning, of course, but he appreciated that they knew the rudiments of the game.

Brown was a native of Dayton, Ohio. When he was a kid, his dad had taken him to see the Cincinnati Reds play against the Brooklyn Dodgers—featuring Jackie Robinson. "I read every article about him," Brown says of Robinson. "When I read he had gone to UCLA, I said to myself, 'Damn, I gotta go to college.'" After excelling in both basketball and baseball in high school, Brown went to the historically black Central State University. There he became a small-college All-American in baseball. (He had also been a senior in 1958, when Martin Luther King Jr. addressed his graduating class.) After college, Brown signed with the Chicago White Sox, but he never made it up to the big leagues. He moved to Columbus and began teaching, first elementary school, then junior high.

When Tom Brown received the first group of Peers Club baseball players at Champion Junior High, he looked forward to coaching them. "We always stayed in the locker room the first two weeks of practice," Brown remembers. That was his ritual: he talked to the players about the mental aspects of baseball, and about society at large.

When Eddie Ratleff arrived at Champion in the fall of 1963, Brown had already heard plenty about him. And Ratleff did not disappoint. "Ratleff could throw smoke," remembers Brown. "And he could hit." Across three seasons at Champion Junior High, Eddie Rat threw five no-hitters. At the same time, at Franklin Junior High, onetime Peers Club

player Garnett Davis was making a name for himself in the City League
with his hitting and all-around skills as a catcher.

At Champion, the players found it easy to put their faith in Brown
because he had a pedigree as a player. Sometimes Brown would take
players to the downtown stadium in Columbus when a Negro league
team was in town. If they needed a local player, Brown would gladly
don a uniform; the kids got a kick out of watching him out on the field.
But Brown, for all the joy of coaching baseball, would not shy away
from what was roiling America—the continued struggle over race. "The
white cheerleaders were often warned not to come over to Champion
Junior High," he says, blaming it on stereotype and the school's East
Side location.

The better players fully intended to play high school baseball. They
were the ones who stayed late in Maryland Park participating in their
made-up home run derbies; they were the ones who sat watching the
black players on the Columbus Royals play back-to-back games so they
could learn as much as they could. Baseball was inside them. They loved
rubbing their mom's Royal Crown hair grease in the center of their baseball gloves to soften them; they loved racing out of their housing project
apartments with their cheap baseball cleats flung over their shoulders.
They loved being introduced to American Legion baseball. By the time
they got finished with Peers Club and junior high baseball, they were
ready for Paul Pennell, the East High Tigers' baseball coach.

Pennell could not give them a dugout. Or new uniforms. Still, he told
his wife, Sharon, season after season, these boys cared about baseball—
even if no one else at the school did—and he owed them the best of his
coaching ability.

For the past two seasons, the East High baseball team had had winning
seasons. A year earlier—the 1967–68 season—they shared a City League
title, although they were beaten in the district tournament. Some of the
old-timers in the city—those who had followed Peers Club players into
maturity—thought if there ever was an East High team that had the
gifts to advance and make some noise in the state tourney, it was the

Erkie Byrd team. Pennell bemoaned that that team hadn't gone further with the trio of Byrd, Mike Phillips, and Will Britford. He wasn't alone in wondering if the death of Martin Luther King Jr. that spring had troubled the psyche and equilibrium of the team and the individual players.

The Tiger baseballers assembled for the 1969 season consisted of Richard Twitty, first base; Kenny Mizell, second base; Garnett Davis, catcher; Roger Neighbors, shortstop; Norris Smith, center fielder–pitcher; Robert Kuthrell, right fielder; Phil Mackey, left fielder. Pitching duties fell to Eddie Rat and Smith, a southpaw. Pennell had already told himself that his nonstarters—Tony Brown, Ray Scott, Larry Mann, Harry Williams, Ron Harris, and Ernie Locke—would likely get good playing time because of the sheer individual talent the players who had left a season earlier took with them. There were three players from the state championship basketball team—Kenny Mizelle, Larry Mann, and Eddie Rat— who were now on the baseball roster. Pennell was impressed with the players who had successfully moved from varsity basketball to varsity baseball. The two sports required vastly different skill sets. Basketball was constant eruption and movement; so much of baseball was a stuttering time clock characterized by stillness, followed by lightning bolts of action.

When area high school baseball coaches gathered to talk before the start of the baseball season, a handful of city and county teams drew praise. Among those mentioned were Whitehall, Walnut Ridge, West, Brookhaven, Whetstone, London, Watterson, Grove City, and East High. A lot of the praise for East was owing to its two star players, Eddie Ratleff and Garnett Davis. None of the other inner-city teams, however, made anyone's list when it came to discussions of potential winning teams. The last team in the city to successfully navigate the tournament and win the state baseball crown was Columbus North High School. And that was way back in 1940—nearly three decades ago.

Paul Pennell knew he lacked the resources that other high school teams took for granted—fan and booster support, facilities—so he was

constantly thinking and imagining ways to make his inner-city baseball team better. The summer before the 1969 baseball season opened,
Pennell took the Tiger baseball team to Bainbridge, Ohio, site of Ted
"Big Klu" Kluszewski's Baseball Camp. Pennell had met Big Klu while
working summer baseball camps in earlier years. Kluszewski had played
Major League Baseball from 1947 to 1961, spending most of his career
with the Cincinnati Reds, where he had twice been named an All-Star.
The kids at the camp went through exercises and drills during the day,
and at night played a game against other campers. Pennell knew the
camp would benefit his players beyond baseball. "It exposed our kids to
other types of kids, and other types of coaching," he says.

East High's baseball team opened the 1969 season on April 1 against
Bishop Hartley High. Hartley's coaches conceded their team was in a
rebuilding year and that their squad was laden with underclassmen. The
weather was cool and the game tight. East's fleet-footed Norris Smith
scored two runs; four other Tigers scored a run each. It took every one of
those Tiger scores for the team to achieve a successful beginning to the
season, as they defeated Hartley by a single run, 6–5.

Next up on the docket was a match against Reynoldsburg High. The
suburban schools—better financed, with better facilities—had always
worried Pennell. It was another close game, but Reynoldsburg beat the
Tigers, 8–7. Pennell began to truly bemoan the lack of depth at the
pitching position. (It is a maxim of baseball coaches that you win games
with good hitting and two or three gifted pitchers on your team.) Pennell had another concern as well. In this early stretch of the season, the
game against Reynoldsburg was not on the official schedule. It was kind
of a shadow game. Suburban schools had sufficient money to send their
baseball teams to Florida to play several pre-season games before the
official season got under way. Thus, when the season officially started
in Columbus, those teams had a head start on the inner-city schools.
"Sometimes we played games and didn't report them," says Coach Pennell. "Playing games was important. We were limited to the number of
games we were supposed to play—as opposed to the suburban schools."

Because the baseball season—eight weeks, April through May—was far shorter than the basketball season, the games were squeezed into a tight schedule. There was no time for excuses. Ratleff started out pitching game three against Zanesville, but the competition was called because of the weather. There also was no time for Tiger players to lament the fact that hardly anyone ever came to their baseball games. There was always the issue of transportation, and the games started right after school let out: Parents who had jobs were still at work. Mothers had to be home to prepare dinner. The only time the coeds trekked over to Harley Field was during football season. "It was hard for the girls to come over to Harley Field and watch us play," says Eddie Rat. "Girls don't go for baseball guys. They go for basketball, football, and track." Ratleff had been on the varsity baseball team three straight years now. "I never heard a girl say, 'I watched you play baseball yesterday.'"

Every now and then a few winos would make their way down Mount Vernon Avenue, which led directly to Harley Field, and loll about watching the team. Some inebriated soul would always seem to corral another, and then there'd be two groggy figures leaning on the fence, watching the boys hit and round the bases. A teacher or two from the school would sometimes drop by, showing support. Principal Jack Gibbs was busy as ever at the school—especially with college decisions being made by students and with graduation in the near future—but he swung by Harley Field when he could. Even the April winds, or just a few raindrops, would shoo the scant onlookers away.

The Tigers played Linden-McKinley—their longtime basketball nemesis—and spanked them, 12–5. Norris Smith, small in stature and with a skinny build, pitched a complete seven-inning game—the standard number of innings in high school—throwing plenty of nasty curve balls. Richard Twitty and Robert Kuttrell each knocked in two runs. The team was showing flashes of power, which pleased Pennell and Assistant Coach Jim Henderson.

Pennell realized that there needed to be a player or two beyond Ratleff and Smith to take on pitching duties throughout the season. He figured such a player would emerge in the course of games and practices, but this early in the season, no one had. Many players were envious of the two pitchers. It wasn't because of the stature they held; it was because of the shiny Tiger baseball jackets they wore. Everyone would have liked a jacket, but the team simply could not afford to get one for every player. On a team that couldn't afford a dugout, or a team bus, a shiny jacket for each of the star pitchers was the only form of pampering.

Even though the 1969 season had been under way only a couple weeks, there was a lot of chatter about Northland High's team around town because they were undefeated in their first five games and were considered quite dangerous. Mike Kincaid, the Northland pitcher, had recently produced a 12-strikeout win against South High. Coach Pennell was delighted his Tigers would not have to face Northland until very late in the season.

Doc Simpson, who was doing his student teaching at East High in the 1968–69 school year—and whose uncle, Harry "Suitcase" Simpson, had been a Negro league and American League baseball player—was impressed with the talent on East High's baseball team. He knew that as the only all-black high school baseball team in the city, they faced specific challenges. "I had never seen black guys play baseball like that," he recalled. "Eddie could throw the ball eighty miles an hour. And Kenny Mizelle, at second base, was just a cold-blooded player."

Although it was rare, some of the white suburban schools had a black basketball player or two. But the suburban baseball teams remained, for the most part, all-white. A game that City League watchers were excited about was the upcoming East High versus Whetstone matchup. Whetstone, an all-white suburban school, had perhaps the finest and best outfitted high school baseball field in the city. They also had some highly touted players in pitcher Dwight Reinstettle, shortstop Steve Mirise, and Don Shields, their left fielder.

In the matchup between the two schools, the coaches of each team sent their marquee pitchers—Ratleff for East High, Reinstettle for Whetstone—to the mound. Ratleff remembered Whetstone from a year earlier: "They were really good." Fred Nocera, the Whetstone coach, was telling the local media he was disappointed his team had to come up against the Tigers so early in the season. Nocera wished they had played some more games. Pennell felt the complaint was just a ruse.

When they played games away from their home diamond, it would have been understandable if the Tiger players were disappointed by the fan turnout, which oftentimes approached a scant half dozen or so, and those were often volunteer faculty drivers. But the lack of fan support did not stop the momentum of the Tiger bats: the Whetstone pitcher, Reinstettle, gave up eleven hits in seven innings. Garnett Davis and Eddie Rat each smacked two hits, but Ratleff's fastball was bewildering to the Whetstone players. East departed the prettiest baseball facility in the city in a good state of mind, because of their pretty 6–1 victory.

Knowing just how quick the calendar pages turned during the eight-week season, Coach Pennell tried his best to keep his team primed and ready. During rainouts, Pennell's Tigers idled on their home field like shadows, in case the skies cleared. Before a contest against dangerous Mohawk High, they managed to sneak in two "unofficial" games against Newark Catholic High School, winning a game, 14–1, and losing another, 4–3. Pennell and his assistant coach, Henderson, took note of the shortcomings in the Tiger baseball team, which were to be expected this early in the season. They needed better defense and better hitting. The coaches were reluctant to appear too optimistic about just how good the Tigers could actually be.

It was widely acknowledged that Mohawk High's pitcher, Fred Saunders, a junior, and East High's Eddie Rat were the two best black pitchers in the city. Both were phenomenally gifted athletes, both had been groomed on the Peers Club team, and both players had completed celebrated three-year varsity basketball careers at their respective schools. Both of them were tall and rangy, and they both threw with power. "Ratleff had a harder curve than mine," Saunders recalled years later. "I had speed and control." Unfortunately, the two would not face each other in a game, because in an earlier contest Saunders had hurt his throwing arm. Charles Trimble, a southpaw, was announced as the Mohawk pitcher. Saunders would play first base, just as Ratleff usually did when he wasn't pitching.

Like Eddie Rat, Fred Saunders had fallen in love with baseball as a little kid. And when the Columbus Jets, the minor league team of the Pittsburgh Pirates, were in town, he'd beg his older sister to take him to the stadium. Not only would she take him, she befriended and then started dating Willie Stargell, who would, in time, become a genuine star of the Pirates. It was quite a thing for a kid to be able to tell other kids that he had spent time with Willie Stargell away from the baseball field.

As the Mohawk High Indians watched the Tigers warm up, they saw Eddie Rat on the mound. To those who followed Mohawk, they could be forgiven if they thought Eddie Ratleff—first basketball, now baseball— was haunting their dreams. The visiting Mohawk players heard the slap of the ball as Ratleff was warming up. He was so tall that his unwinding motion resembled a praying mantis suddenly erupting into motion. Through the first four innings not a single Mohawk player reached base or got a hit off Eddie Rat. Pennell and Henderson just nodded to each other and left him alone between innings. No one dares mention anything when a player is in such a groove, lest things get jinxed. Eddie Rat did quietly confide to others that his arm was feeling mighty good. Saunders watched Eddie Rat fan his teammates one by one, and he grew frustrated. "Dudes on my team just couldn't hit" Eddie Rat, Saunders later recalled of the game. (In his sophomore season, Eddie Rat had thrown a no-hitter against South High. So he well knew the sensation of such a building moment.) No matter which Mohawk player entered the batter's box, he left the same way, the victim of a strikeout. Meanwhile, Eddie Rat was also busy collecting a couple hits. East stretched a 1–0 lead into a 3–0 lead. Going into the final innings, tension mounted. When the final pitches whizzed into the glove of catcher Garnett Davis—who had called a beautiful game—Eddie Rat, a cool figure always, couldn't help shaking his head and pumping his fists. The final score: 4–0. He had authored the second no-hitter of his high school career, and his first perfect game, striking out twenty-one Mohawk batters. His teammates rushed him, jumping in the air, whistling, whooping, hollering; Pennell couldn't wait to report the win to the local reporters who hadn't bothered to come to the game. The Tigers knew, however, that there was nothing they could do about their anemic and nearly invisible fan following.

Often after big East High basketball victories, the basketball players could hear noise and lots of honking horns on Mount Vernon Avenue and throughout their East Side neighborhood. That was not something the baseball players experienced. When they got home, they shared the news with anyone in earshot. Eddie Ratleff particularly enjoyed sharing the news with his mother.

The day after the victory over Mohawk, there was no one in the hallways of East High saluting the Tiger baseball players. "No one talked about us," says Eddie Rat. Every now and then Bob Hart would come out to a baseball game to show his support for Pennell, his assistant basketball coach, and his former players Kenny Mizelle, Larry Mann, and Eddie Rat. He didn't always stick around for the entire game because, as a single dad, he had to get home and check up on his three daughters.

If only students had come out to Harley Field, they would have seen something spectacular: Kenny Mizelle fiercely scooping up hard-hit ground balls; Robert Kuthrell positioning himself perfectly under every fly ball hit to him; catcher Garnett Davis keeping Eddie Rat poised; Paul Pennell making all the right strategic moves and substitutions. They would have seen a baseball team that was extraordinarily steady under pressure.

When Paul Pennell glanced at the schedule going forward, he saw that there were some tough games looming. Marion-Franklin, Walnut Ridge, and Upper Arlington had long been fielding competitive teams. So had West High and South High. He was always worrying about the risk of leaning on the arm of Ratleff. Although the team sat atop the City League with two other teams, they also had two non-league losses that clearly exposed some of their deficiencies. There was also something else that Pennell could not possibly have felt as sharply as the players did. "Everywhere we went," Mizelle remembers, "the white boys called us all kinds of names."

The players had been preached to from parents and coaches that the names they were sometimes called at away games—"nigger," "coon," "darkie," "monkey"—sometimes by students in the stands, mostly by neighborhood ruffians who came to the games—were just names, and they had to rise above it all. Sometimes a white umpire, upon hearing the vicious language—none of the players could remember ever seeing a black umpire—would stop play and walk toward the name-callers, and that would be enough to stop the ugly language.

The Tigers had one simple antidote when they were in hostile all-white territory: Eddie Rat would start throwing his patented fastball just a little bit harder. And a little bit closer to the batter. Eddie had turned into a six-foot-six menace on the mound. When his teammates asked Eddie if he was making some kind of statement, he'd just grin. "The white boys were actually scared of Eddie," says second baseman Kenny Mizelle. "He threw the heat."

It was not lost on East High principal Jack Gibbs that all the new civil rights laws that had been passed were recent enough to still unleash deep resentment among a good many people. Only a few months before the beginning of the 1969 baseball season, the nation had passed the Fair Housing Act. The 1965 Voting Rights Act had been signed only four years prior, and the 1964 Civil Rights Act had been on the books for only five years. The narrative of America, when it came to race, had been as triumphant as it had been cruel. Blood was everywhere, both drying up and gushing anew. No one expected a single white neighborhood to be integrated overnight. America, in 1969, looked just as segregated as it had a decade before. Tiger players Garnett Davis and Tony Brown wanted one immediate change: They wanted the faculty members of East High to start talking more and teaching more about modern black heroes.

While it was certainly true that the most dramatic and horrifying moments of the civil rights movement had unfolded in the American South, there had been enough spasms of northern rioting to keep the whole of America on notice. And what the whole of America so often missed was the quiet tapestry of the movement, continuously alive in the conversations of black men. They missed Claude Willis, a local educator in Columbus—brother of NFL pioneer Bill Willis—jawboning with Amos Lynch, newspaper publisher, about some black kid who got straight As and was deserving of a write-up in the newspaper because that might help the kid to get a scholarship. And they missed John Combs, the managing editor of the newspaper, pulling out his pipe and striking a match and talking about some black politician up in Cleveland who was making noise and might be running for higher office. And Hiram Tanner, the veteran sports editor, pulling out a chair and telling everyone about this kid, Eddie Ratleff, and how great he was playing down the street at East High School, and that they just had to get out and see him.

The Tigers were a baseball team, sure enough. But they were also a group of boys in the throes of an America that had begun throwing harder and less gentle punches in the quest for equality. Campus protesters were rising up. But those punches were thrown alongside those who were counterpunching with their own aims of maintaining the status quo. The Nixon administration's constant espousing of the new law and order caused many blacks a great deal of worry. Jack Gibbs talked to his wife, Ruth, about the police, about the wider powers they suddenly seemed to possess. Sometimes he'd go to school board meetings just to remind the board how well his school was doing. He would look directly at some of the white board members and yet again invite them to a game, to come visit the school. His basketball players had made it through basketball season without getting into trouble with the police, which he considered a minor miracle. But with baseball season in progress, when there were more opportunities for the players to be outside where a confrontation might well take place, his concerns only grew. He constantly reminded the players not to lose their cool, even as rebellion was brewing and cresting all around them.

· 12 ·

Robert Duncan and
Richard Nixon's America

I t was as if an ax had been taken to the great American experiment of liberalism. Nixon's victory over Hubert Humphrey changed the political landscape of America. And that altering was felt inside the hallways of East High School.

In a strange twist, the destiny of the all-black school was tied up with Richard Nixon and Robert Duncan. Duncan was a black lawyer in Columbus who lived just a few miles from East High. He was raised into the judicial spotlight by President Nixon himself. The two men, while both members of the Republican Party, could not have been more different.

The town of Urbana, Ohio, lies a little less than fifty miles west of Columbus. A small rural enclave, its population in 1900 was a mere six thousand people. It was here in the summer of 1927 that Robert Morton Duncan was born to Benjamin and Wanda Duncan. His parents were respected among the small black populace. Benjamin had a factory job. Wanda, who consistently drew stares because of her beauty, was a homemaker. The couple did not have any other children. When it came to rural areas of Ohio and the issue of race, brutality periodically erupted. An incident that took place in Urbana thirty years before Bobby Duncan's birth proved that northern brutality against blacks could be just as savage as the injustices meted out in southern states.

In June of 1897, Charles "Click" Mitchell, a black man, was accused of raping and assaulting Elizabeth Gaumer, a white woman. She was much admired by the people of Urbana. Her late husband had been the town's newspaper publisher. In such a small town, everyone seemed to know everyone—from prominent person to derelict. When help finally reached her, she was seen to be badly bruised. Gaumer told authorities that she knew her assailant: Click Mitchell, the hotel porter. She said the attack happened because she wouldn't cash a check for him. Mitchell was located and arrested before nightfall. The evidence against him was strong; he was in possession of items that belonged to her. Word quickly leaked about the assault, inflaming townsfolk. The court bizarrely announced that the trial would take place that same week. Once inside the courtroom, Mitchell confessed and was sentenced to twenty years in the state penitentiary. The judge coldly told Mitchell that he wished he had the right to sentence him to death. Upon hearing the judge's wish for the death penalty, onlookers nodded with aggression.

Mitchell was led back to the local lockup. In the ensuing hours a mob began to form, and their numbers kept increasing. There were shouts that Mitchell should be hanged. Local authorities determined it best to make plans to get Mitchell over to Columbus, to the Ohio Penitentiary, to prevent a lynching by the determined and hell-bent mob. Deputy Sheriff Jesse Lewis figured that the mob would stop at nothing to get at Mitchell. He appealed to the mob, cautioning them against retribution, reassuring the people—among them Gaumer's son—that Mitchell had been sentenced to a lengthy term in prison, and exhorting them to obey the rule of law. He was hissed and booed. The deputy sheriff then appealed to Gov. Asa Bushnell to send in the militia. He did. When the small contingent of thirty-six men from nearby Springfield reached the town, they were stunned to find a throng of nearly two thousand people. Many in the mob were toting guns, sledgehammers, and other crude weapons. When the people faced off against the militia, shots were fired. Two men from the town fell dead; eight others suffered gunshot wounds. The scene was bedlam. Mitchell, alone in a cell, couldn't help but hear the gunshots. The militia, massively outnumbered, decided to retreat. The small contingent of law enforcement in Urbana was now quite vulnerable. The Ninth Ohio Volunteer Infantry was nearby. Deputy Sheriff Lewis thought to wire them, but then changed his mind: the Ninth was an all-black unit, and he imagined there would be a bloodbath should they come and take on the white townsfolk. Believing that Lewis and other deputies might try to sneak Mitchell out via the train tracks outside of town, members of the mob positioned themselves along the tracks. The following morning the mob stormed the jail and raced to Mitchell's cell. He was preternaturally calm, not uttering a word as he was belted and dragged out of the cell. He was taken to the courthouse square. There was no one to save him and he knew it. Raw fear now had him in its grip. A rope, looped over a sturdy limb, was tied around his neck. People cursed at him and spat in his direction. Men pulled the rope, raising his body up. His neck jerked, then snapped, killing him. The whooping and hollering began.

The news quickly spread of the lynching of a black man yanked from an Urbana, Ohio, jail cell in broad daylight. In a page-one story in *The Columbus Dispatch*, the reporter threw objectivity to the wind: "Click Mitchell, the negro brute, has paid the penalty of his foul crime with his life. An outraged people have taken the law into their own hands and meted out to Mitchell the punishment he so richly deserved."

Mitchell's body, in an open box in lieu of a casket, lay out in the open courtyard for several days for gawkers to peer at, sneer at, and spit at. The northern town of Urbana had joined the list of southern towns where blacks had been dragged from their cells and lynched. Many newspaper editorials from around the country weighed in. In one editorial titled "A Praiseworthy Lynching," the *Chicago Chronicle* wrote: "The negro was killed irregularly, but justifiably. He committed an offense far more heinous than simple murder." The New Orleans *Times-Democrat*: "The Ohioans of Urbana are not law abiding enough to allow a brute like 'Click' Mitchell to escape the noose, court or no court." And *The New*

York Times: "The whole story would be disgraceful if it were told of a mining-camp. But it is told of an old and settled town, fully equipped with schools and churches, which fairly represents the civilization of the Middle West of the United States. In that point of view it is extremely discouraging."

The hanging of Mitchell seemed to embolden other Ohioans who were in favor of lynching blacks. Following Mitchell's killing, a spate of hangings erupted across the state. In the years to come, no matter how much the town fathers and people of Urbana tried to avoid talk of Click Mitchell and the shameful event, there was no keeping the story secret. It was there, deep and searing, passed along in some form from generation to generation.

When Bobby Duncan was growing up in the 1930s in Urbana, the saga of Click Mitchell was sometimes told as an old ghost story to spook children. The small number of black families who had been in and around the town in 1897, however, knew very well that Click Mitchell was no ghost, but someone who once lived and was hanged right there in the courthouse square.

The Duncan family lived in the black section of Urbana known as Gooseville, where the streets were unpaved and city services were less than what they were in the white parts of town. The majority of blacks in Gooseville came from the South. Many had been born into slavery and benefitted by help from the Freedmen's Bureau, started after the Civil War, which helped them move into northern states in the intervening years.

Benjamin Duncan was a philanderer. His wife threatened to leave him more than once. And one day—when Bobby was just two years old—she announced she had had enough and left, leaving both husband and child behind. She could no longer take the embarrassment of being cheated on. There were no secrets in Gooseville. The boy pined for his mother. It was not rare for a man and woman to divorce in the 1930s, but it was certainly uncommon for a woman, after a divorce, to move away from her family. Wanda went first to Columbus, where she worked in a hotel that catered to blacks. A short while later she moved to Chicago. She sent her son letters, gifts, and money. Benjamin's parents moved into the house with him and his son, but there was a hole in Bobby's world—an absent mother—and the loss often tormented him.

Benjamin Duncan wanted his son to experience a bigger and more diverse world than Urbana. So he began taking his son to Columbus, the state capital, where the family had relatives. Bobby was quite excited about his trips to Columbus. He could visit the museum and the downtown library. "And I remember," Duncan would recall, "having my first ice cream soda here in Columbus at a drugstore at 17th and Long." He could walk around the downtown department stores, the likes of which they certainly didn't have in Urbana. But mostly in those years what Bobby Duncan began to look forward to, especially in the fall, was getting over to the football stadium at Ohio State University; over the years he had fallen hard for the Ohio State football team. He enjoyed nothing more than sitting inside that big stadium and watching the Buckeyes rush up and down the field, demolishing their opponents. He had a cousin—a teenager like him—he visited when in Columbus. She attended East High School and took him to the Maryland Park swimming pool, where the blacks swam. "That was the first time I had ever been in a swimming pool," he recalled. When his cousin went off to Ohio State, she told him about the excitement she felt being on campus. She made it feel almost exotic, even if the school was only a few miles away from the city's East Side.

During his senior year at Urbana High School, when Duncan started thinking about the college he wanted to attend, he didn't have to think long: he wanted to attend Ohio State University. His father, grandparents, aunts, and uncles all chipped in with tuition money. His mom sent what she could from Chicago. He was the first in his family to attend college. He had no idea what he wanted to study. There were not any black professionals in the town of Urbana, so there had been no one to mentor him, to sit him down and discuss professions.

It was 1945 when Bobby Duncan landed in Columbus to begin classes at Ohio State. Blacks were not yet allowed to live on the campus, but he was fortunate to have relatives who lived in town, on the city's

East Side; he could stay with them. Duncan would always remember the first day of classes. After his final class, he strolled over to the student union, a beehive of activity with a gaggle of white students. Because of his light-skinned complexion, some mistook him for a foreigner. They were all nice and friendly. (Bobby Duncan was always proud of his black heritage, and he informed fellow students he was not a foreigner.) He made a path over to the jukebox, scanned the selections, started grinning, rolling his head, swaying his shoulders. He dropped in some coins. His selection was "Route 66," sung by the Nat King Cole Trio. He made fast friends that day.

Because of the GI Bill—which gave veterans of all racial backgrounds the opportunity to attend college—Bobby Duncan met more black men pursuing higher education than he had ever met in his life. He enjoyed chatting up these black men on the streetcar—"the Big Yellow"—that clanged from the East Side of the city to the Ohio State campus. They were all squeezed into the streetcar and would talk about post–World War II America, civil rights, Negro authors, movies, and sports. No one on that streetcar had any inkling that onetime Ohio State University president William Oxley Thompson had played a major role in promoting and deepening racial segregation on the city's East Side in the early 1900s.

For the next few years Duncan lived in two worlds, the white world of the Ohio State campus, and the black world of the city's East Side. To be a black Ohio State student in the 1940s—the black student population was very small—was to be embraced by the city's black churches. The ministers and deacons in town were quick to invite the students to social events and dinners; the students' mere presence lifted community pride. Bobby Duncan further widened his world by becoming president of Kappa Alpha Psi, a black fraternity. Walking across the wide lawn of the campus oval, conversing with learned professors, hustling over to the football stadium on Saturday afternoons to watch the games, all made him feel like a lucky soul, even if there were shops on High Street, the main drag fronting the school, where he knew he was not welcome.

Bobby Duncan finished his studies in three years, graduating in the summer of 1948. He wanted to teach and expected his education degree to open doors. In Columbus, black would-be teachers at the time knew they were going to be directed to two schools on the city's segregated East Side: Champion Junior High and East High. He wanted to teach at the junior high school level, so Duncan applied for a job at Champion, the school where he had completed his student teaching. The competition among blacks for jobs at those two schools was fierce. Duncan was informed that no positions at Champion had opened up over the summer. He couldn't get in at East High, either. Effectively, there was no place in the city of Columbus for him to begin his teaching career. A return to small-town Urbana was out of the question. So Bobby Duncan phoned his mother, Wanda, in Chicago.

Wanda Duncan worked for the Spiegel Catalog company, a renowned mail-order business. She was industrious and beautiful and had a social circle of friends and suitors who adored her. When Bobby reached Chicago—their reunions were always a bit awkward—she reintroduced her son to her friends, showed him the same skyscrapers that he'd already stared up at before, took him down Michigan Avenue and to other places he had seen on previous visits. It was always hard to fill the gaps that had widened, because for years they had not been around each other.

The Chicago public school system offered him only substitute teaching work, and even that was sporadic. With a newly minted college degree from a good university, Bobby Duncan had expected better. After some months, he ditched the idea of teaching and took a job as a bellhop at a Chicago hotel. He wanted to make some money. He found himself dashing curbside and yes ma'am-ing women while he handled their luggage. "I made more money as a bellman than I was making teaching," he said, but he wanted a much better future.

Duncan decided to return to Columbus and apply to Ohio State's law school. In those days one did not have to take an admissions test to get into the OSU law school. Good undergraduate grades and strong references were all that was required. It was kind of a lark to Duncan: He looked upon the next stage of his education as a month-to-month wager. Maybe he'd stay in law school; maybe he'd drop out if something better came along. It all depended on his grades. When he did better than okay that first year, he realized he could do the work. He liked the challenge

Bobby Duncan as an OSU law school student. He became Columbus's first black federal judge. He would not forget the city's racial hypocrisy and was a crucial figure in ending the city's school segregation.

and didn't mind the long hours of studying. He even became president of his class. Then the kind of thing happened that has benefitted many a student everywhere: Bobby Duncan found a mentor.

William Saxbe was an Ohio State law graduate and a state representative who hailed from Champaign County, the same county that covers Urbana. On a few occasions back in Urbana, Saxbe had met the Duncan family. The politician was known as a candid, blunt-speaking sort. He hailed from that wing of the Republican Party that was quick to invoke the humanity of Abraham Lincoln. When Saxbe found out that Bobby Duncan was in law school at Ohio State, he invited the young student down to the statehouse. The rapport was immediate. Saxbe was starting to wield power in the statehouse and offered Duncan a part-time job in the Office of the Treasurer, a job he held during the remainder of his law school studies. The white, conservative Saxbe became a father figure to the ambitious young black man.

It was hardly unexpected that Bobby Duncan became a Republican. The Saxbe connection was one thing. Another was that blacks still held a fondness for the Republican Party. It had been mostly those southern Democrats who had blocked all the proposed anti-lynching legislation in the past.

Duncan now lived in a rooming house near the Ohio State campus. His roommates were former GIs. A couple had cars, and he'd bum a ride down to the statehouse after law classes. When he couldn't get a ride, he would walk straight down High Street. He was tall with long legs and could make the trek in less than an hour. Bobby Duncan thought he might, at long last, be getting a good foothold in the world. No more bellhopping for him.

He also met a girl.

Benjamin Duncan, Bobby's father, had a sly side to him. He knew his son was quiet around young ladies, so he hatched a plan. Shirley Thomas lived in nearby Piqua, and Benjamin knew her parents, William and Gwendolyn. Both families wanted to bring Shirley and Bobby together.

Shirley had very light skin, just like Bobby. When she enrolled at Defiance College in 1951, everyone on campus assumed she was white. Coming into the dorm suite one afternoon and hearing Shirley in the shower, one of Shirley's roommates yelled that she had heard the strangest thing on campus. "I said, 'What's that?'" Shirley recalls. "And my roommate said, 'I heard there's a colored woman somewhere on campus! I'd like to meet her.'" Shirley popped out of the shower. "I said, 'I'm colored! Didn't you know?'" The two roommates had a laugh, even if there was an awkward nervousness to it.

So that there would be no more doubt about her racial lineage, Shirley went around campus handing out issues of *Ebony*, the magazine that was popular throughout much of black America. Between the pages of that magazine was a world her white classmates knew little if anything about: the hard-fought stardom of actress Dorothy Dandridge; the brilliance of young writer James Baldwin; the musical odyssey of Duke Ellington; the swiftness of baseball player Jackie Robinson; the rising momentum of Rev. Martin Luther King Jr. There were so many stories—and plenty of glamour photos—pressed between those pages that Shirley imagined she was conducting her own ad hoc class on black life. And when she got her hands on copies of *Jet* magazine, another black-oriented publication—

albeit pocket size—she'd spread them around campus too. In time, Shirley's classmates came to adore her for her efforts to enlighten them.

The small dinner party that was arranged so that Bobby and Shirley could meet was held in a private home in Urbana. There were a dozen in attendance. Shirley remembers sipping on a rum and coke for the first time. While dinner was being served, she noticed someone staring at her: a shy, well-mannered young man. He was unable to take his eyes off her. "Bob was passing notes to me under the table," she revealed many years later. "I said, 'Lord, he's got some nerve!'" She was not going to give Bobby Duncan—never mind that he attended a respected law school—her family's phone number. The night ended quietly.

He pondered just how long it would take to get his nerve up to call her. It took a week to track down her number. When he reached Shirley, he invited her to a weekend dance in Chillicothe, a nearby small town. "I remember calling out asking my father if I could go to this dance," she says about the phone call. "He said, 'With who?' I said, 'Bobby Duncan.' He said, 'Bobby Duncan? Oh, yes, that's Benjamin Duncan's boy. Yes, you can go.'"

In Chillicothe, Bob and Shirley danced together. And smiled at each other, a lot. He wanted to go for a walk. Once outside, they spotted a big rock in the near distance and found themselves leaning against it, talking, glancing at the night sky. "Bob made me laugh so much that night," she remembers. "I said to myself that if a guy can make me laugh this much, he's not so bad after all."

Bobby Duncan was feeling like the luckiest guy in the world.

Then came the war.

In 1952, just as he finished law school, Duncan's military deferment ended. He had to report for duty and the Korean War. Shirley told him he must write letters, and he promised he would. She fretted he might forget her. And then he was gone.

When Bobby Duncan boarded the train in Columbus to report for duty, the train was integrated; not so once he reached Maryland. There he had to move to the Colored-Only section. The army sent Duncan to Officer Candidate School. The war was winding down and he did not fear being sent into harm's way. He eventually went to Fort Richardson,

Alaska, where he put his legal training to work handling an assortment of court-martial cases.

On May 17, 1954, Duncan and one of his barracks roommates, a white officer, were among the first on base to hear of the U.S. Supreme Court decision in the *Brown v. Board of Education* case, striking down segregation in public schools. Both began to feel one another out on the ruling. Duncan expressed to his fellow officer how important the ruling was, and that he believed it would bring about fundamental change in America, change for the good of equality. The white officer listened, then said that he saw mayhem and disaster on the horizon because of the court ruling.

As soon as he left Alaska and the Korean War behind, Bobby Duncan headed home to Urbana, where he spent time with Shirley and both of their families. From the start, he had two things on his mind: asking Shirley to marry him, and getting the hell out of small-town Urbana. When he asked for her hand, Shirley's eyes welled with tears, and she said yes.

There had never been a black lawyer in Urbana, and many people kept telling Bobby he should consider opening a practice there. But he was adamant about getting away. Bobby and Shirley were married in 1956. Then off they went to Columbus.

Shirley found a job teaching at an elementary school. Bobby faced challenges: No one would rent downtown office space to a black attorney. As well, not a single law firm employed black associates, so he went into private practice, working for Lawrence Curtis, a local black attorney. Their office was on the segregated East Side of the city. Duncan didn't really like the work—rental disputes, divorces, numbing lawsuits. Then one day his phone rang. It was William Saxbe, who had been elected attorney general of Ohio. Saxbe wanted to meet. He offered Duncan a job as assistant attorney general. The young lawyer couldn't wait to get started.

The hours were long, but Duncan liked the work. When Saxbe lost his post in the next election, Bobby Duncan was out of a job. But not for long. In 1958 he landed a position with the city attorney's office in

Columbus. When Saxbe won election again, he once again called for Duncan, who went back to the statehouse. He eventually became chief counsel in the attorney general's office, a plumb position. The Negro press around the country made note of Duncan's rise. He got to know James Rhodes, the Ohio State University dropout who had risen to the governorship. Governor Rhodes liked that Duncan was at his desk every morning by seven a.m., because Rhodes showed up around that time also. The more Rhodes interacted with Duncan, the more he liked him. He started telling others that Bobby Duncan was definitely going places.

When a vacancy opened on the Franklin County Municipal Court, Rhodes chose Duncan to fill the position. In 1966, Duncan had to run for the seat and won it outright. It was a first for a black man, as was his appointment by Rhodes to the Ohio Supreme Court in 1969. To local blacks, the moment felt like some kind of redemptive salve. Martin was in the ground, but Bobby Duncan was on the bench. There was pain, but also hope.

William Saxbe watched the rise of his protégé with keen interest. Saxbe was eventually pulled into the Nixon administration, and he did not forget Bobby Duncan.

In the succeeding years, there would be an array of jobs as Duncan swung between local, state, and federal positions, drawing praise from the national Negro press and becoming something of a local hero to the black community in Columbus. Duncan was forced to step out onto the campaign trail to outright win his Supreme Court seat, which he did in 1970. A year later, he was pulled into the Nixon orbit, as Nixon appointed him to the U.S. Court of Military Appeals, where Duncan rose to become chief judge. In 1974, Nixon appointed Duncan a federal judge for the U.S. District Court of Southern Ohio, a tenure that lasted eleven years. Every step of Duncan's rise had been historic, as he broke racial barriers all along the way.

Richard Milhous Nixon was born January 9, 1913, in Yorba Linda, California. (Many years earlier there had been slaves in the family: The patriarch, James Nixon, owned them and passed them down to descendants: "my Negro man named Ned" and "a Negro woman named Nance.") Richard Nixon's great-grandfather, George Nixon III, lived in Ohio during the Civil War. He joined the Ohio volunteers and was killed at Gettysburg. Richard Nixon's parents, Frank and Hannah, had six boys. They were Quakers, and Frank Nixon was a severe man who whipped his boys when he deemed it necessary. The neighbors thought him harsh. Hannah Nixon was peculiar. "In her whole life, I never heard her say to me, or to anyone else, 'I love you,'" Richard Nixon would recall about his mother.

In 1922, the family moved to Whittier, California, where Frank Nixon opened a gas station; later he added a little store. But the family was dragged down by tragedies. Their son, Arthur, died from tuberculosis. Then eight years later, another son, Harold, was stricken by the same disease and died. The young Dick Nixon wondered if the family was cursed in some way. Others were less mystical, fretting that the cause might lie in the unpasteurized milk that Frank insisted the family keep drinking.

Nixon went out for football in high school. He was awkward and it showed, but he made the team as a benchwarmer. People in the neighborhood snickered at his ungainliness. A reality emerged that, in the years ahead, would keep psychoanalysts and biographers busy: He was a boy with a stern father and a cold mother, a kid accustomed to death, a young man eager to please and worrying incessantly about what others thought of him.

He got into Whittier College, a small local school, where classmates once again thought him odd but also quite industrious. After classes, he would help his father with the family grocery store, driving at times into Los Angeles to pick up produce. It was in Los Angeles during the Depression that he saw the largest numbers of Negroes he had ever seen; they were crisscrossing the streets, idling, emerging from factories. It took stamina to get through classes, drive his dad's truck to pick up deliveries, and remain a member of the football team, even though he was used mostly as a fill-in player to be hit in practice. He didn't get a varsity letter because he didn't play. More than one classmate called him strange. "He was always apart," a cousin later remembered. "He didn't go helling around with the rest of us. He didn't approve of it. He used to scold me for wearing too much lipstick."

Strange individual or not, in 1934, Nixon was admitted to Duke Law School in Durham, North Carolina. It was a moneyed school, and it was his first time witnessing, up close, rigid racial segregation—blacks had to drink over there, couldn't use that bathroom, and dared not ask to try on any clothes in local department stores.

Nixon got his law degree, and in 1940 he found a bride. Pat Ryan, a smart and disciplined girl from rural California, had been an orphan yet possessed enough pluck to graduate from the University of Southern California.

Soon enough, Nixon turned his gaze to politics, stumping as a warm-up speaker for Republican candidates. He liked presidential candidate Wendell Willkie, but Willkie became just another victim of the titanic FDR's popularity. When World War II broke out, Nixon reported for naval officer training school in Rhode Island. And not long after that he was facing gunfire and shells on Guadalcanal, although he managed to escape injury. His fellow naval men never questioned his courage, but they too found him—that word again—strange: a morose figure, reluctant to engage in laughter and bonhomie.

When he emerged from the war, he had the credentials for politics: a law degree and military service. What Richard Nixon lacked in charisma he made up for in studiousness. He also had connections in his hometown. In 1946 he was elected to Congress, defeating Jerry Voorhis. Nixon's campaign themes were out of the playbook of fervent patriotism: ferret out communists wherever they are, challenge unions, and applaud the status quo. Voorhis thought he was a cunning and politically immoral man.

Then came a dark time in American history, roiling from the late 1940s to the mid-1950s, when men and women were maligned and destroyed if they were in any way linked to communism. Few denied that Communist aggressiveness was genuine, but when it was lathered with stateside paranoia and attendant smear campaigns—from the Truman White House to college campuses to Hollywood back lots, from union halls to civil rights organizations—the innuendos all but undermined the tenets of the U.S. Constitution. A letter, a photograph, attendance at a party in Greenwich Village, all could cause extreme personal and professional damage if there was even a hint of a link to communism. Congress formed the House Un-American Activities Committee, which held hearings and drew blood, hounding some admitted communists from public life. Wisconsin senator Joe McCarthy was the loudest accuser, and for that reason this period of witch hunts was named after him. He was a shabby man with an off-putting personality, a natural magnet for Congressman Richard Nixon, who became a like-minded sidekick. There were those who thought the HUAC was a joke; the committee believed that the popular child actress Shirley Temple had been compromised by unnamed Soviet provocateurs. But it would prove foolish to underestimate the committee. A group of Hollywood directors and writers who refused to answer the committee's questions were charged with contempt and jailed. They became known as the Hollywood Ten. The best known of the group were Dalton Trumbo, Ring Lardner Jr., and Edward Dmytryk. Clear-eyed observers raised eyebrows at the numbers of blacks and Jews who were hauled before the committee.

President Truman stunned the world by defeating Republican Thomas Dewey in 1947, a victory that only kept the HUAC alive and thriving. Truman could ill afford to seem weak on communism. Richard Nixon thrived, never more so than when Alger Hiss came into his life.

Hiss was a Harvard Law School graduate who had worked at the U.S. State Department, where he was known to be sharp and insightful. In 1948, Whittaker Chambers, a magazine writer, was summoned to appear before the HUAC and told the committee that the onetime State Department employee Alger Hiss had been a Soviet spy. Hiss and Chambers both had previously testified that they were not communists. Hiss sued Chambers. In the lawsuit, incriminating evidence revealed that Hiss had lied in his testimony to the committee. He was indicted on perjury charges, and in 1950 he was sent to federal prison. Nixon took a lot of credit for the strange, twisting, beguiling saga that played out in the hearing room. He sensed an opportune moment to make a political move, and set his sights on the U.S. Senate. Nixon zeroed in on the incumbent Democratic senator from California, Sheridan Downey. Nixon left Congress to run for the seat in 1950. Downey felt overwhelmed by the Nixon assault and dropped out of the race. Helen Gahagan Douglas, a staunch liberal, was left to battle Nixon. The contest drew nationwide attention.

Helen Gahagan Douglas was a native of New Jersey who had dropped out of Barnard College to study acting. She made a name for herself on Broadway in the 1920s by appearing in several plays, and she received fine notices. In 1930, she married the actor Melvyn Douglas. The two made a dashing couple. During an overseas trip she became alarmed at the rise of Nazism. When she returned to the States, she aligned herself firmly with liberal causes—women's rights, worker rights, the rights of disenfranchised blacks—and decided to enter politics. "The Daughters of the Confederacy . . . refer to her as a 'nigger-lover,'" her strategist once wrote. But she had powerful supporters, in particular President Roosevelt and, after his death, Eleanor Roosevelt. In 1944, Douglas was elected to Congress, where her record was unabashedly progressive. During his run for the U.S. Senate, Nixon corralled a cadre of aides intent on besmirching Douglas; they reintroduced her to California voters as "the Pink Lady," creating an association between her and the words "pinko" and "commie." From one of the first press releases sent out by the Nixon campaign:

> During five years in Congress Helen Douglas has voted 353 times exactly as has Vito Marcantonio, the notorious Communist party-line congressman from New York . . . Both Helen Douglas and Marcantonio voted against establishing the Committee on Un-American Activities and on four separate times they have fought appropriations for investigations by the committee, which, among many other meritorious services, disclosed "the seeds of treason" sown by Alger Hiss.

The name "Tricky Dick"—a reference to Richard Nixon—started being bandied about at this time, its use propelled by Manchester Boddy, a newspaper publisher who became an opponent of Douglas's in the primary.

When the Subversive Activities Control Act—another bill designed to thwart the spread of communism, it was partially written by Nixon himself—came up for a vote in Congress, Douglas could not betray her conscience. "I will not sacrifice the liberty of the American people on an altar of hysteria erected by those without vision, without faith, without courage, who cringe in fear before a handful of crackpots," she said, explaining her decision to vote against the bill. It took courage to make such a statement, because she surely knew it would doom her chances of beating Nixon, and it did. Nixon got 59 percent of the vote and an enduring reputation as a Machiavellian figure.

Two years later, Sen. Richard Nixon was chosen as Dwight Eisenhower's running mate in the 1952 presidential campaign. The Ike-Nixon ticket had a lot going for it: a war hero; two military veterans; a vice-presidential nominee from a state that was rich in electoral votes. They won handily and entered the White House with a rigid cockiness.

They did not see—or chose not to see—the civil rights revolution coming.

The first salvo unto the administration, in a literary sense at least, came in 1952, with the publication of Ralph Ellison's novel *The Invisible Man*. It was a civil rights novel writ large, brassy and bold and blunt, and it seemed to foretell a revolution on the horizon. Ellison's tome was about a man navigating the treacherous waters of a racist society. To a lot of whites, blacks were indeed invisible. Two years later came the 1954 *Brown* ruling. Ike was perturbed by the Supreme Court ruling, but now it was upon the land. In 1957, he made what some perceived to be a courageous decision when he dispatched army troops to Little Rock, Arkansas, where white mobs were trying to stop black students from entering Central High School. But he had needed a lot of persuading. Telegrams supporting the students inundated the White House. Martin Luther King Jr., A. Philip Randolph, and a few other civil rights leaders eventually talked their way into the White House for a meeting with Ike, where the plight of black Americans was at the forefront of their agenda. But the Eisenhower administration limited its involvement in civil rights causes. They could claim passage of the 1957 Civil Rights

Act, but the bill was weak and did not protect black voters from laws preventing them from getting to the voting booth. By 1960, only 3 percent more blacks had been registered to vote in southern states. It was evidence that states were still impeding blacks in their efforts to register as voters. Toward the end of the Eisenhower years, Richard Nixon was left standing: stiff, odd, and mercurial. He wanted badly to be president of the United States.

There were presidents who seemed to connect with black Americans on some level of decency—Abraham Lincoln, Theodore Roosevelt, Harry Truman, FDR, Lyndon Johnson, Jack Kennedy. Richard Nixon had one true chance to join that fraternity. Weeks before the 1960 election, Martin Luther King Jr. was arrested in Atlanta for joining a sit-in at a segregated restaurant. King might simply have been released with a fine, as had happened at times in some other cities, but there was an old outstanding traffic ticket, and the judge pounced on it. King was sentenced to four months at the notorious Georgia State Prison, and he was taken there in shackles. Aides to both Kennedy and Nixon urged them to phone Coretta Scott King to offer support. She was pregnant and deeply worried about her husband's imprisonment. Kennedy phoned. Nixon did not. To black America, Nixon's inaction felt like a rebuke. "I had known Nixon longer," Martin Luther King Jr. later said. "He had been supposedly close to me, and he would call me frequently about things . . . seeking my advice. And yet, when this moment came, it was like he had never heard of me, you see. So this is why I really considered him a moral coward and one who was really unwilling to take a courageous step and take a risk."

Eight years later, as a comeback candidate, Nixon didn't bother himself at all with the black vote. His "southern strategy" aimed at sweeping through the states below the Mason-Dixon Line and scooping up white votes. While campaigning, he incessantly talked about drugs and street crime. He let people know he admired the cops in Chicago who had severely beaten the demonstrators during the Democratic convention. A few weeks before the election, Nixon appeared in Columbus at the statehouse, standing next to Woody Hayes, the Ohio State football coach, a godlike figure in the football-crazed city. "Ohio State plays rock 'em, sock 'em football and that's what we're gonna do," Nixon cracked to thunderous applause.

The Machiavellian figure was in his element. Black parents could feel it. "My feeling," Nixon said, "is this: I think that busing the child—a child that is two or three grades behind another child—into a strange community . . . I think you destroy that child." He went on to explain that he felt the country should not "try to satisfy some professional civil rights group, or something like that, that we will bus the child from one side of the county over to the other."

Nixon made blacks downright nervous. His onetime ally, baseball legend Jackie Robinson, grew disgusted with him. "The Nixon campaign in 1968," Nixon aide John Ehrlichman later explained, "and the Nixon White House after that, had two enemies: the antiwar left and black people . . . We knew we couldn't make it illegal to be either against the war or black, but by getting the public to associate the hippies with marijuana and blacks with heroin, and then criminalizing both heavily, we could disrupt those communities. We could arrest their leaders, raid their homes, break up their meetings, and vilify them night after night on the evening news."

Politics, of course, can be a strange and unpredictable enterprise. In 1969, William Saxbe was elected U.S. senator from Ohio. In time he formed his bond with the Nixon White House. Back in Columbus, Saxbe's protégé, Bobby Duncan—sitting on the Ohio Supreme Court in 1969—was rising every morning, getting in his car, and driving to his downtown office. Oftentimes he'd think how life might have been different if he'd gotten a job at all-black Champion Junior High, or all-black East High, back in 1948. He might have become a teacher instead of a lawyer and judge. But life had turned out well. He and Shirley had three children, two girls and a boy. The Duncans subscribed to both city newspapers, the morning paper, *The Columbus Citizen-Journal*, and the afternoon paper, *The Columbus Dispatch*. Bobby Duncan had varied interests, but he always kept an eye on the sports pages. He thought it was wonderful that East High had just won a state basketball championship. Every now and then he'd hear something about the baseball team, mostly about its pitcher, Ed Ratleff, and catcher, Garnett Davis. When he drove out the driveway in the mornings, Bobby Duncan made a couple of turns and then there he was, gliding down East Broad Street and past the Greek columns and pilasters of the still segregated East High School. On one side of the front wall of the school was a quote from Socrates: WISDOM ADORNS RICHES AND SOFTENS POVERTY.

When he entered office, President Richard Nixon might not have been pondering the promises America had made to her black schoolchildren—and then broken. Far too many black schools in the nation still felt the residue of a separate-but-equal doctrine because of unfair school administration practices. But there was a judge in Columbus, Ohio, who would get a chance to weigh in on that undelivered promise. In order for him to get that chance, William Saxbe would have to do some cajoling on behalf of his protégé.

· 13 ·

The Catcher in the Storm

I f you asked anyone on the Tiger baseball team in 1969 who was the most gifted all-around player on the team, the response, without hesitation, would be Garnett Davis. Handsome, hazel-eyed Eddie Rat may have been the marquee player, but Davis was the one whom the players wished to measure themselves against. "Garnett was just a pure baseball player," says Coach Paul Pennell. "You just give him a ball and glove and he could practically play any position."

Davis, a co-captain of the team, was the full-time catcher, a position that took a combination of nerve, strength, and baseball intellect. He prided himself on being disciplined and staying focused. "I was a quiet leader with a noisy bat," he says. His batting average consistently stayed above .300. In some stretches of games, his average hovered near .400, a colossal batting average.

Garnett Davis never had to look around Harley Field to see if Gardenia, his mom, had come to see him play. "I don't ever remember my mother coming to a game," he says. She was off cleaning the home of some well-to-do white family. And he certainly didn't have to worry about his dad, Johnny Davis, showing up. He was lumbering around

in the South Carolina heat, on a chain gang, because he 'had been convicted of murder.

Johnny Davis was born in 1911 in Congaree, South Carolina. His wife,
Gardenia, was born nearby, in the town of Eastover. They met at a neighborhood get-together over red beans, rice, and sweet tea. They married
young, moved to Columbia, the capital, and started a family. Gardenia
gave birth to six children, four boys and two girls. Both of the girls died
in infancy, one a crib death, the other of undetermined causes. The young
couple were devastated. Gardenia could not tell if Johnny started gambling and staying out late at night because of the tragedies, but she imagined that was part of the reason. Garnett was the middle boy, coming
after Earl, whom everyone called "Spoon," and before Wali, the youngest.

Johnny and Gardenia were not well educated, being products of the
sharecropping era, when educational opportunities were limited for
blacks. Blacks in South Carolina seemed to be treated worse than blacks
in any of the other southern states after the Civil War; the mind-set there
bordered on feudalism. South Carolina governor Cole Blease served
from 1910 to 1915. He had a rather whimsical habit of issuing pardons,
often with attendant commentary. Newspapers considered him colorful
and quite quotable. When a black man named Sam Gaskins accidentally
killed the woman he planned to marry, Blease pardoned him. "It seems
to have been a very sad accident," Blease told the press, "however, after
a second thought, possibly it was for the good of humanity, for had they
married, no doubt they would have brought forth more negroes to the
future detriment of the State."

It was in Clarendon County—sixty-five miles south of Columbia—
that the roots of the epochal 1954 school desegregation federal lawsuit
led by Thurgood Marshall had been set. The stirrings of the lawsuit began
because James Gibson, a black farmer, approached R. W. Elliott, a white
man who was a powerful member of the school board, and asked him
to please get buses for the black kids. The children were getting rained
on going to school. Even in South Carolina, chilly winds unleashed on
some early mornings cut right through clothing. "We ain't got no money

to buy a bus for your nigger children," Elliott told the farmer. Gibson's only recourse was to report to other black parents what Elliott had said. They were outraged. So Thurgood Marshall of the NAACP Legal Defense Fund came to town and set the wheels of the lawsuit in motion. In the end, the case morphed into five combined federal desegregation lawsuits. The *Bolling v. Sharpe* case came from Washington, D.C.; the *Gebhart v. Belton* case from Delaware; the *Davis v. County School Board of Prince Edward County* from Virginia; the *Briggs v. Elliott* case from South Carolina; and the *Brown v. Board of Education* from Kansas.

The NAACP court victory at the Supreme Court was important, and wonderful, but Gardenia Davis couldn't see it changing her family's fortunes quickly enough. She thought life could be better in the North, so in 1955 the family headed for Ohio. Coincidentally, that was the year of the Emmett Till murder in Mississippi. There was something else that drove Gardenia's move. Her husband, Johnny, had already left the family to live up north. At the time, Garnett had no idea why his father had disappeared.

In Columbus, Johnny Davis finally reconnected with his wife and sons. She got work as a maid; she was employed by a job service that sent her around to various well-to-do families to clean their homes. Johnny Davis found work at the notorious Buckeye Steel plant on the city's near South Side, where the work was grueling and dangerous.

When he was old enough to join the Peers Club baseball team, Garnett Davis might have been the happiest kid in the neighborhood. He was always early for practice. He stayed late to hit balls. He was continually asking his coaches questions about the game. His keen interest in sports helped to take his mind off the family's dire economic straits. "We were on welfare," Garnett says. "I hated that. We went to Charity Newsies. I used to hustle up money cutting grass." The Davis boys were not only ashamed of the free clothing dispensed by Charity Newsies but also embarrassed about the commodity food they had to get from a government food center. There was peanut butter, cornmeal, oatmeal, rice, flour—just basic items. There never was meat.

When he entered Franklin Junior High, Garnett could hardly wait for baseball tryouts to begin. Coach Vernon Barkstall saw something special in the kid right away. A good many of those who had followed baseball in Columbus in the 1950s well knew the legend of Vernon Barkstall. He was the Jackie Robinson of baseball at Ohio State University.

A native of Cincinnati, Barkstall had a reputation for playing a number of sports in high school. After that, he went into the military, and when he got out, enrolled at Ohio State. In 1956 he became the Buckeyes' first black baseball player and the second black on the university's basketball team. There were taunts and epithets from opposing players. Barkstall credited his military service for imbuing him with the patience and grit it took to endure the racial slurs. "He would always say to me, 'You have to be cool,'" recalls Joe Roberts, who played on the basketball team at Ohio State with Barkstall. "When I was getting angry about some of the racial things, he'd day, 'Be cool, Joe. Be cool.'" Barkstall was so good—and cool—that his baseball playing teammates voted him team captain. "His age helped him get respect," says Roberts.

What Peers Club coaches didn't teach Garnett Davis, Vernon Barkstall did. Barkstall had applied for head coaching baseball openings at the high school level in and around Columbus, but despite his playing pedigree, not a single high school would hire him, including East High. He eventually left the state and settled in Illinois. There is now an elementary school in Champaign that is named after him.

When Garnett Davis arrived at East High, he was immediately tagged as an all-around athlete. He played varsity basketball, football, and baseball. But he let everyone know his favorite sport was baseball. Yet he wasn't—at least not yet—the most paid-attention-to athlete in his family. That honor belonged to Earl "Spoon" Davis, Garnett's older brother. Spoon was an enormously gifted basketball player. He'd go onto the local playground, pull a bottle of wine out of his back pocket, place it behind the basket, get chosen for a game of five-on-five, and proceed to dominate the game. Admirers would ooh and aah over his court moves. After the game, he'd retrieve his bottle of wine and bid everyone goodbye. Many believed that if Spoon went to class and quit all the drinking, he'd surely land a scholarship. "I used to drink that wine and didn't like to go to school," Spoon confesses all these years later. Spoon knew there was a budding rivalry between him and Garnett and that he wouldn't be able to keep up with his little brother. "He always went the right way," he says about Garnett. "I went the wrong way."

At the beginning of Garnett's junior year, in 1967, his father left the family again. Gardenia convinced Johnny to return to South Carolina and atone for what he had done before fleeing to Ohio. And this is what Johnny Davis had done: In a house in a black neighborhood of Columbia, he and others had been sitting around a table playing cards. Cigarette smoke was billowing and there was music on the radio. One of the players accused Johnny of cheating. The accuser walked around the table, in Davis's direction. There was yelling and pleas for both men to calm down. But as soon as the man reached Davis, he belted Davis, knocking him off the chair, sending his eyeglasses flying off his face. Davis, on his back, quickly reached for his hidden gun and shot the man. The shot was fatal. Davis fled for home and told Gardenia what had happened. He told his wife and children that he had to leave, right away. "He gave my mother the gun," Wali, another Davis son, remembers. There were a lot of tears with Johnny Davis on the run. Johnny Davis knew someone in Columbus, Ohio, who could help him start life anew there. He told the family he'd be in touch as soon as he got settled. He told them they would join him in due time, which they did.

So Johnny Davis was living in Columbus the entire time he was a fugitive. It was a black-on-black killing, and the South Carolina authorities made only a perfunctory effort to capture him. But as the years passed in Columbus, Johnny never stopped looking over his shoulder. He crept back into South Carolina a couple times, but never for long. Gardenia finally convinced her husband to return to Columbia and turn himself in. She said she could not stand it anymore, worrying whenever there was a knock at the door that it might be the police. He was sentenced to three years on a chain gang. "I remember him showing me the marks on his ankle," says Wali Davis of his father.

The night at the poker game was not the first time that Johnny Davis had been in trouble with the law. A few years earlier, there had been a nasty confrontation with a white man. Davis struck the man with a heavy stick. For that melee, he also served a prison stint.

.   .   .

Johnny Davis had left Columbus just as Garnett was going into his junior year of the high school baseball season. It was a time to start thinking about the future, about college, or maybe even the wild and beautiful dream of professional baseball. "It affected Garnett's psyche," his brother Wali says about their father's absence. "Every young boy wants to know his father is there for him. Garnett missed that father figure. He reached out to teachers." Wali himself suffered: "I went out into the streets," he says. Garnett adds, "When our dad left, the family started to unravel. I think that destroyed the family."

Johnny Davis's incarceration also created a financial burden for the family. They were now dependent on one income, and Gardenia's maid work was sporadic. There was always a panic at the first of the month, when the rent was due. "We'd move around a lot. The lights would get turned off," remembers Wali. "My mother would change her last name to get the lights turned on in another place." For much of Garnett's senior year, Gardenia was frantic. There were long stretches when she went without work. She wondered if she should move back to the South, a place she loathed but where living expenses were far less than in the North. There were also relatives who would help them out. But that thought always vanished as quickly as it had come. Her relatives in South Carolina were also living threadbare existences. And she knew how much baseball at East High meant to Garnett. But Johnny Davis was locked away, jangly chains rubbing his ankles raw in the South Carolina sun. Gardenia sent letters to her husband, telling him that the boys were doing all right. It wasn't the total truth. Spoon was out in the streets, drinking, worrying her something terrible. Wali hadn't gotten over his anger about the assassination of Martin Luther King Jr. Garnett was the bright spot in the family. "My father was proud of Garnett," says Wali. "I think he felt self-conscious because he wasn't around as much as he wanted to be."

At some point someone told school principal Jack Gibbs that the Davises were about to be evicted. Gibbs was not going to let that happen. He decided that East High School needed another all-around school aide to help out in the principal's office. And the cafeteria. And in the nurse's office. And the library. And, lo and behold, Jack Gibbs created just such a position, which is how Gardenia Davis got a full-time job at East High School that year.

All her life, Gardenia had cleaned up after people, washing and ironing clothes, scrubbing floors. Now she had a job working next to educators. She was nervous, no matter how much her sons told her not to be. The family didn't have a car, so she walked the half mile to school every morning. After some weeks passed, and she became comfortable in her multiple assignments, helping out wherever she was needed, she realized she loved it. She walked the hallways with great pride. When the maid service phoned her about a job, she told them she wasn't coming back, ever.

On the field, Garnett went out of his way to be courteous to opposing teams after the game, whether the Tigers had won or lost, exhibiting a maturity the coaches admired. (Eddie Rat could be pretty charming after games also.) And no one ever heard Garnett complain about the fact that team members had to wash their own uniforms. He took such great pride in being team captain. He had become the heart and soul of the East High baseball team. He was the first to get the chairs from the school to take out to the cars for the team's makeshift dugout down at Harley Field. But as Paul Pennell's Tigers began nearing the halfway point of the 1969 season, the coach couldn't help but hope for more settled, steady play.

The team had that emotional victory against Mohawk High. But on April 24, they had to face Marion-Franklin High. The Blue Devils of Marion-Franklin were respected as a well-coached, power-hitting team. Pennell sent his lefty, Norris Smith, to the mound, dispatching Eddie Rat to left field. No matter what Smith threw at the Blue Devils, they pounded him. It was a close game, but the Tigers went down, 7–6. There was no time to wallow in the loss, because there was another game the next day at Walnut Ridge High. Eddie Rat was back on the mound. Pennell shifted Larry Mann—who usually came off the bench—to short-stop, hoping that he would be more productive in that position. It did not seem to matter how fast Eddie Rat was throwing his fastball at the Walnut Ridge hitters; they kept hitting him. And it was yet another defeat, 8–3. And the team could not relax in light of their next foe either.

If there was a school in the greater Columbus area that represented academic and athletic achievement—not to mention money and status—it was Upper Arlington High School. F. Scott Fitzgerald would have salivated over this school's pedigree and image. For spring break the students' families went to the Caribbean or the pricey resorts in Mexico. They had summer cottages up in Michigan. In 1957, Upper Arlington's Jack Nicklaus led the school to the state golf championship. After he turned professional, he insisted he be known as the Golden Bear, because that was the name of his high school mascot. He just thought there was something powerful and gallant in the school team's name—the Golden Bears. Those who lived in that zip code had plenty of money; they paid lavishly for their homes and didn't mind paying high taxes; they had maids who came from the black side of Columbus. They expected their children to go to the best schools in the country—Stanford, Harvard, Yale, Cornell; Ohio State, right down the road, was a good choice for law school or medical school, but not for undergraduate study. The students were lavished with praise and much was expected of them. And although the school was rich and fancy, it was a mistake to think of the school's athletes as mere dilettantes engaging in the rough-and-tumble of contact sports. They had won the state titles in golf and football in 1968 and 1969—the year of East High's basketball glory. Trophies glistened in the school hallway. The school took pride in fielding championship-caliber teams across a variety of sports—track, football, tennis, golf, rowing, and baseball.

On May 2, 1969, the Tigers and the Golden Bears squared off. Norris Smith took the mound for the Tigers. Pennell sent Garnett Davis out to center field. Once again the bright spots for the Tigers were Davis, who got three hits, and Ratleff, who collected two. But it was hardly enough. The Golden Bears strutted away with a 10–5 victory. It was the defeat that hurt the most: The poor black kids had been pummeled by the rich white kids. Upper Arlington High's baseball team had already been getting high praise by those who were looking forward to the district, regional, and state baseball tournament. After their convincing defeat of East High, the praise heaped upon them only increased.

At the halfway point in the season, East High was suddenly in a downward spiral after three straight losses. The students at the school had always paid minimal attention to the baseball scores when they were announced over the loudspeaker; now they paid even less attention.

Pennell and his assistant, Henderson, knew they had problems. "It was midseason and we weren't clicking," recalls Pennell.

Pennell was lamenting anew that his players had not been able to play more games before the start of the official season. He and Henderson believed this was the main reason for the losses. Some of the teams they had lost to played with such poise and smarts. Those teams were jelling because of their experience. They had played plenty of games. Of course, some had even traveled south during school spring breaks to get in playing time.

The Tigers next faced West High. Norris Smith was on the mound once again. Pennell made another outfield move, sending Leroy Crozier to cover center field, replacing sometime starter Larry Mann. The always anemic fan base for East High's away games grew all but invisible following the string of defeats. "Many times I'd be the only fan at away games," says Sharon Pennell, the coach's wife.

West High sent East High to its fourth straight defeat, 2–1. West also went back to the top of City League standings.

Eddie Rat's alcoholic stepfather dismissed the baseball team from his concerns, taking a contemptuous pleasure in the losses. But Eddie Rat took pride in remaining calm and cool, and he reminded teammates that they were still playing for the league title. Garnett Davis took the losses hard. He hated losing. He was ultracompetitive and blamed himself for the team's losses. At such a time, a high school baseball player surely might benefit from the reassurance of a dad. Was there anything better than a father and son together in a baseball field, playing catch together?

Basketball coach Bob Hart got himself over to Harley Field to see the team play. Everyone knew they were in a tailspin. The next game

Garnett Davis's family depended on charity
and handouts to survive.

was against South High, Hart's alma mater. He knew how much the
players needed a victory. Pennell needed a fresh pitcher and found him
in sophomore Ernie Locke, a southpaw. The Tigers were competitive.
Locke pitched a nice game for a while, with Davis behind the plate.
Kenny Mizelle, the Tiger second baseman, broke out of an offensive
slump and smacked two hits. Davis also collected two hits and scored
two runs, Robert Kuthrell scored two, Richard Twitty scored two, and
Eddie Rat dashed across home plate for a score. But seven runs wasn't
enough. Locke lost his effectiveness and South High took the game, 8–7.

Now, they were in the throes of five straight defeats. Players were
angrily flinging their gloves into the dirt.

Paul Pennell began brooding. There had been a sense of pride about
the year, about this baseball team—and school year—being a tentacle of
the civil rights movement. The Tigers were meant to be more than just

a baseball team. "Walnut Ridge, Whetstone, North, the other schools, they're all white. We were really the only black kids playing baseball in the city," says Pennell.

Then, finally, it hit him.

He would have to reimagine how to play Garnett Davis, his most versatile player. He would have to think of Garnett the way the Dodgers had thought of Jackie Robinson, as a player with the unique talent to play practically any position on the field. "I went to Garnett," Pennell recalls, "and I said, 'I'm going to ask you to do something big.' I said, 'If we're going to turn this ball team around, you have to move away from being catcher.'" Garnett was taken aback. Ever since the Peers Club coaches had put him behind the plate, he had been a catcher. But it did not take him very long to come around to Pennell's reasoning. He too felt the team was in a perilous place and had to turn things around. Something had to be done.

Eddie Rat was surprised at the move. He had gotten used to Davis catching his pitches. But he also agreed with the plan, letting Pennell know that the important thing to him was making sure he didn't injure his arm before district tournament play rolled around. Just as with basketball, the baseball tournament was an open, round-robin affair. Every team, no matter their record, got into the tournament.

Don Laird, who was an American Legion coach in Columbus in the late 1960s, was following the Tigers' 1969 baseball season in the newspapers because he had once coached Garnett Davis. "When they lost those five games in a row," Laird recalls, "I said to myself that they weren't going to go anywhere in the tournament."

· 14 ·

Ghosts of the Blue Birds

Jack Gibbs asked Paul Pennell if there was anything he could do to help out the team. Pennell knew Gibbs had asked the question out of concern and kindness, but there really wasn't anything the principal could do. Pennell did mention—since his players couldn't get new uniforms or a constructed dugout—that it would be nice if he could get the maintenance crew to pay more attention to the upkeep of the field. Gibbs had someone out working on the field within days.

The players knew it was up to them to regain a sense of competitiveness. Their starting lineup versus Eastmoor, their next opponent, revealed that Coach Pennell had started to make his chess moves: Garnett Davis was now at third base; Richard Twitty was on the mound; Ray Scott was behind the plate. Pennell and his assistant coach, Henderson, hoped the moves would give the team a spark. Against Eastmoor, Richard Kuttrell came out swinging fiercely. He had two hits, including a triple, that knocked in four runs. Eastmoor was no pushover, but their ten hits produced only five runs, and at the end of the seventh and final inning the score was 6–5. The Tigers had escaped with a victory.

The Tigers faced off against Brookhaven in their next game. Norris

Smith was back on the mound. Some energy from the previous victory seemed to be lingering in the air. The Tigers scored two runs in the first inning and another in the second. Then two more in the fourth inning. Smith pitched a stellar 5–0 shutout.

The Tigers were still in the city title hunt, but Northland seemed in the best position to win it. Their team, the Vikings, was playing especially well.

All season long East High had been matched against only one Catholic League team, and that was Bishop Hartley, the team they had defeated in the first game of the season.

It was only at the beginning of the 1968–69 school year that it became noticeable around the greater Columbus area that Catholic schools were finally making a concerted effort to recruit black students. While there had been minor attempts in the mid-1960s—after the passage of civil rights legislation—it took the assassination of Martin Luther King Jr. to ignite a more noble effort. A year earlier, Bishop Hartley had two black players on its baseball team, the two brothers Dan and Michael Cunningham. They were talented athletes, but there was little doubt they were attending the parochial school only because their father, Oscar Cunningham, had a great reputation around town. He had also been a onetime Negro league baseball player.

Oscar Cunningham was born in Xenia, Ohio, in 1901. He did not have a high school career. He learned to play baseball on makeshift teams after high school. While he was sixteen and in high school, he met an older lady. She had three kids, but he fell hard for her and they married. The union didn't last long. He got himself into semi-pro baseball and in the 1920s and 1930s was playing in Negro leagues throughout the country, as well as on professional Latin American teams. The Cubans bragged about his wicked base-stealing abilities. When Jackie Robinson was just a kid, Oscar Cunningham was getting paid to play baseball, and wondering how high the dream might take him. Toward the end of the 1930s, his skills waning, Cunningham left baseball. In 1943 he landed a job in Los Angeles as director of recreation at the Good Shepherd Boys Club in Beverly Hills. The acting crowd in Hollywood adored him. Stars sent their children to him to learn to play tennis. He was a beautiful dresser, sporting tailor-made suits and fine shoes. By 1950, he was trainer for the Loyola Marymount University football team. Before the team traveled to play Texas Western College (now the University of Texas, El Paso), the Loyola Marymount coach wired the Texas coach, informing him they'd be arriving with three black players and a black trainer. Texas officials said they were looking forward to the game but suggested Loyola leave the blacks at home in California. Texas officials were not going to allow their players to take the field with black players. Loyola Marymount officials took a stand and cancelled the game.

Years rolled by, and Oscar Cunningham found himself back in the Midwest, hired as a football trainer for Ohio State University and, later, for the Cleveland Browns. (A black man needed a benefactor, and Cunningham's was Paul Brown, owner of the Browns.) Cunningham eventually settled on the East Side of Columbus. He wanted his boys—there were nine Cunningham children—to get a good education, and Bishop Hartley, a Catholic school, was on the East Side of the city, abutting the black community. Cunningham couldn't afford tuition for two boys at the same time, so the school cut him a deal: If he'd come aboard as a trainer, they'd wipe out the tuition costs, which he did and they did. The Bishop Hartley athletes adored him, the way he could rub down and limber up a body by giving massages. "He was a lovely guy," remembers Joe Eicenlaub, the left fielder on the 1969 Bishop Hartley team. "Everybody liked him."

Cunningham enjoyed watching his boys play baseball. And his boys—as well as other members of the Bishop Hartley baseball team—enjoyed listening to his stories about the Negro leagues and about all the gifted players from that era lost to history until recaptured years later in documentaries and books. He was telling anyone who cared to listen to him away from school grounds that there was a kid on the mound at East High, Eddie Ratleff, who had real talent. Despite East's not so great record, the team was to be feared because of this kid. And Oscar Cunningham, who had seen Satchel Paige and Josh Gibson play in the Negro leagues, knew talent.

·   ·   ·

On May 23, the Bishop Hartley Hawks traveled the short distance across the East Side of town to East High's Harley Field. The East High sophomore Ernie Locke had endured some tough innings of late, but he was back on the mound. Garnett Davis remained in his new position at third base. Bishop Hartley was seeking revenge for its early season defeat at the claws of the Tigers. It was a scoreless first inning, but the bats for both teams got hot after that. Each team scored four runs in the second inning. East shut Bishop Hartley down in the third, while notching another four for themselves, the score standing at 8–4. The Tiger momentum was not to be denied. Garnett Davis had a pair of hits, as did Robert Kuthrell. Eddie Rat had three. Locke suffered through four more Hartley scores, but the Tigers kept him out in front, 12–8, and claimed a third consecutive victory with that final score. Yet Mark Aprile, the Bishop Hartley shortstop, while giving East High credit for having a "really good" team, was not anointing them for any great success. "East would not have first come to my mind as the city's best baseball team," he says. "Northland was good, Marion-Franklin was good. But Whetstone was the city school that was really known for baseball."

In his previous years as baseball coach, Paul Pennell had not had an assistant coach. But Pennell was starting to appreciate Jim Henderson more and more. It was all the extra batting practice he was throwing. There were two areas where coaches felt the team needed to improve: defense, and better hitting deeper down the lineup.

Three days after the victory over Bishop Hartley, in another contest on the Tigers' home field, their bats—with the exception of Eddie Rat's—went silent against Central High. Norris Smith streaked across home plate—compliments of Eddie Rat's bat—giving the Tigers a sole score in the second inning. Fortunately, that proved just enough. In addition to Eddie Rat's two hits, he pitched another shutout. And East High had a fourth straight victory, 1–0.

Jack Gibbs had been encouraging some of the basketball players to get over to Harley Field to support the baseball team. "Me and Nick [Conner] would be at the games," recalls basketball player Kevin Smith. "I don't think anybody thought they had a prayer's chance of going any-where [during the season]." Robert Wright, another basketball player, also went over to a couple of the baseball games to offer his support. He was not surprised at the lack of turnout: "You'd go to a baseball game and there might be five or six old dudes there who lived in the neighborhood." (Some people might have been spooked that it was a tough neighborhood, and there was never any security at the games.) Even though she had known the seniors on the baseball team for three years, Alice Flowers, the school's Homecoming Queen, admits she never trekked over to Harley Field for a single game. "There just wasn't any hoopla" around the baseball team, she says.

In the next matchup against North High's Polar Bears—also played on the Tigers' home field—Pennell made yet another strategic move. To get more offense, he put Eddie Rat at third base, figuring he might be more productive not having to endure the stress of pitching. The move paid off because Ratleff smacked two hits. Jeff Kuntz, the North High pitcher, couldn't contain Garnett Davis, who exploded for three hits. The Tigers scored twice in the second inning, and again in the fifth. North could only manage one run, in the sixth inning. Their strong hitters, Tom Pappas and Dave Leatherman, managed a hit apiece. The Tigers handed the Polar Bears a defeat, 6–1. It was an important victory, because it set up the final game of the season for the Tigers before the start of state tournament play. There was no time for a practice session; the game was scheduled for the next day. If the Tigers managed a victory, they would have a chance to be in contention for the City League title— depending on what the other teams did.

Coaches Pennell and Henderson were concerned about Eddie Rat tir-ing his arm in the final game of the season and before the tournament. So prior to the Northland High matchup, Pennell informed Richard Twitty, the team's first baseman when Eddie was on the mound, that he would be pitching.

The Northland High baseball field was well designed and meticu-lously maintained, exactly the kind of field the Tiger players wished their school had. Northland also had Bob Lee, one of the finest high school pitchers in the region, and Northland stood at the top of the City League. And they made the early part of the game rough going for Twitty, the Tiger pitcher, scoring three runs in the first inning. Their fans were pumping their fists. Who did these inner-city kids think they were? Didn't they know that the suburban schools dominated high school baseball? In the fifth inning, the Tigers finally collected their first hit of the game. In the sixth, Ratleff, Mizelle, and Garnett Davis all got hits, and the Tigers scored their first run. But that was it. The Tigers lost, 5–1. "It was our last City League game of the season," recalls Pennell, "and the loss knocked us out of the running for the City League championship."

The Tiger players stewed on their ride back to the East Side. Eddie Rat told himself he now had to stay focused on the state tournament. Their disappointment had somewhat abated by the time they reached their part of town. But there was one Tiger player, Kenny Mizelle, who could never shed his emotions after losing. "He had a temper," remembers Ed Mingo, the Tiger student manager.

There were things that bothered Kenny—things that were old, even ancient, about families and blood, the kind of things that fester when kept hidden, sometimes for many years. Much of the mystery lay in an old black-and-white photograph hanging on a wall at East High School.

AN INTERLUDE

The "Dead" Man in the Photo

For years, a second-floor wall at East High was—and remains—adorned with large black-and-white framed photos. They are class photos and also photos illustrating the school's athletic history and honors across a variety of sports.

Ever since he entered the school as a sophomore, Kenny Mizelle, the Tigers second baseman, regularly walked past those rows of photographs as he went to and from classes. He was deeply connected to one of those photographs: the photo of the class of 1949. His father, Kenny Mizelle Sr., was in the picture because he was a member of that class. He was also the shortstop for the school's 1949 baseball team.

When Kenny Jr. was nine years old, his mother, Duckie Mizelle, told him that his father had died in California. He had abandoned the family, she said, gone to California to chase a crazy baseball dream, and had died under mysterious circumstances. But if Kenny Mizelle Sr. was dead in 1969, it would have been news to him. He was actually in Los Angeles, very much alive.

The elder Kenny Mizelle was born in 1932. From an early age, he showed a keen interest in baseball. He entered East High School in 1946, the year before Jackie Robinson broke the color barrier. Even before he took to the baseball diamond, Mizelle had earned varsity letters in both football and basketball, on his way to becoming the rare three-sport star. In baseball, Mizelle played shortstop; he was rabbit quick, and was also a feared base runner. He was also popular with his fellow high school teammates; he drove a car and seemed to be a magnet for the girls. Beneath his smiling senior class photograph, looking sharp in suit and tie, the handsome Mizelle was quoted as saying: "Girls bother me—I love to be bothered."

Bucky Walters was Mizelle's East High baseball coach. Walters was also a friend of Floyd Stahl, the Ohio State University baseball coach. Walters invited Stahl out to Harley Field one day. "Bucky, you got three good colored boys who can play at Ohio State," Stahl told Walters, according to Ray Humphrey, one of those three who were on the field that day. "But we don't play colored boys," Stahl said.

Mizelle—another of the three—graduated from East High in 1949. The rare white college or university that recruited black athletes at the time went after football or basketball players. Black baseball players were ignored. Mizelle surprised his teammates when he enrolled at Ohio Wesleyan University in nearby Delaware, Ohio. (East High's basketball coach Bob Hart graduated from Ohio Wesleyan three months before Mizelle stepped onto campus.) The school had become more welcom-

ing to a very small number of black students in part because of the fan-
fare around Branch Rickey, the former Ohio Wesleyan student who had
signed Jackie Robinson into pro baseball. It didn't take long for Mizelle
to make his presence felt on campus. He went out for the freshman
football team—known as the Baby Bishops—and became an immediate sensation playing multiple positions. "Ken Mizelle of Columbus is
the present tailback standout," the Ohio Wesleyan University *Transcript*,
the student newspaper, would write shortly into the season. A month
later: "Ken Mizelle, the Baby Bishops' starting left halfback, displayed
an accurate passing arm Saturday in the frosh's game with Mt. Union at
Selby Stadium. Mizelle had no trouble in hitting his receivers on most
occasions, but his receivers had a little difficulty in holding his passes."
The girls were bothering him on the rural campus, and he did love it.
He was a natty dresser; in a fraternity picture he is seen wearing a sharp
sport jacket and bow tie. The freshman football team played only three
games, and after the last game, against Bowling Green, Mizelle's name
again appeared in the headlines: "Baby Bishops End Season With 27–
20 Win Over Bowling Green—Mizelle, Day Lead Wesleyan's Passing
Attack; Season Record Stands at Two Wins, One Defeat."

After such a promising freshman season, the Ohio Wesleyan coaches
were expecting big things from Kenny Mizelle. But he stunned them
when he dropped out of school after that first year. There were financial
problems at home. College was a luxury the Mizelle family could no
longer afford.

Kenny Mizelle was now a college dropout, but still a gifted athlete. He
returned to Columbus. Even on a semi-pro level, he was too small for football. But baseball was another matter. There were times when he would
hear of a Negro league baseball team—the Birmingham Black Barons,
the Homestead Grays, the Kansas City Monarchs—coming through
Columbus on their barnstorming tours. Mizelle would hustle out to Red
Bird Stadium with Ray Humphrey, who had played with him on the
baseball team at East High. "If they were short a player or two," Humphrey recalled, "Kenny would get a little work substituting for a player."
Some of the managers of those teams took note of Mizelle's talents.

Mizelle started imagining a route to the big leagues. When the Kansas

City Athletics, impressed with his abilities, offered Mizelle a very modest baseball contract, he was ecstatic. He went off to train with the team. The Athletics liked him, his hustle and glove skills, but not enough to send him to the big leagues as quickly as he wanted. That didn't sit well with Kenny, and he abruptly left. "If he had been in a different era, he would have played for years in the majors," says Tom Brown, the onetime Champion Junior High baseball coach who had played in the Chicago White Sox farm club system and knew Mizelle. Brown was mesmerized by Mizelle's talent. "He was the only guy who I knew could drive up to the ballpark at the last minute and need no time to warm up. He'd get right out there on the field and play so well. Being an ex-pro myself, I knew natural talent."

Kenny Mizelle, cut loose by the Athletics, soon married. He had met Mildred Scott on the city's East Side. Everyone called her Duckie. Her family hailed from Champaign, Illinois; her father had come to Columbus to work as a doorman at a hotel. He wasn't crazy about his daughter carrying on with a baseball-dreaming smooth talker, but he couldn't stop them from marrying. They were a fiery couple, bouts of passion followed by arguments and the slamming of doors. Not long after they married, their son Kenny Jr. was born. Mizelle's friend Ray Humphrey recalls a time when he and Kenny Sr. were out carousing around Columbus, and Mizelle got to talking about baseball. He wanted to go to California and make a final stab at success playing the game he loved. "I took him home," Humphrey recalls. "Duckie came to the door and began screaming at him. He turned to me and said, 'Ray, you see what I have to put up with? That's why I'm leaving for California.'" Duckie exploded anew. Mizelle grabbed a few items and bolted from the house. She never saw him again. Nor did Kenny Jr.

Kenny Jr. was raised in the Bolivar Arms public housing projects. As a single parent, Duckie was loud, fiercely protective of all her children, and fastidious about keeping an immaculate apartment. To make extra money, she washed clothes for other residents of the housing project. The task involved her carrying large baskets of clothes to the local laundromat. She never once complained about the long hours of her days.

As the years rolled by, Kenny Jr. started asking about his dad. "My mother told me he was dead," Kenny recalls, sitting in a Columbus restaurant many years later. "She just said he went out to California and died."

Kenny Sr. was still alive, but his baseball dreams had died. Like so many Negro league–era players, he had simply been born in the wrong time. It was the curse of black ballplayers who had toiled in the Negro leagues that if they didn't have Jackie Robinson–like talent—or something close to it—white owners were often hesitant to give them an opportunity. Team owners would rather have a mediocre white player in the dugout than a good black player. Kenny Mizelle Sr. settled in Los Angeles in the early 1960s, and he worked odd jobs for years. He never returned to Columbus, never saw his son play Little League baseball or high school baseball at Harley Field, the same field where he himself had once played. An East High alumnus—from the Mizelle Class of 1949—was visiting friends in Los Angeles in the mid-1960s and had been given Kenny Sr.'s address by a classmate. When she appeared at Kenny Sr.'s home and he came to the front door and stepped onto the porch, the classmate was a bit confused by the conversation. Mizelle began talking about outer space and the CIA. "This classmate," Ray Humphrey recalls, "told me Kenny didn't look too well. He seemed kind of paranoid, too."

Humphrey tried unsuccessfully to reach his former classmate by phone. The old-timers said Kenny Mizelle Sr. was fierce on the diamond, so very gifted but with a temper.

The 1969 Tiger players said Kenny Mizelle Jr. was fierce on the diamond, so very gifted, but with a temper. "Kenny was a tenacious player," remembers Ernie Locke. Locke said that Kenny had an incredible sense of where to position himself on defense. He knew where the ball would be hit. "It was as if he had scouted [opposing] players himself." Locke adds one more thing: "But he had a temper."

Every day, inside the school, there was that picture: a baseball player from another time.

On the baseball diamond, Kenny Jr. was playing next to a ghost.

Kenny Sr. died in California in 2010. He never reconnected with his namesake and son.

———————————

Eddie Rat told his teammates that it didn't matter that they had lost the City League title; they had to retain their optimism about the days ahead. "I was going to be ready for the tournament," he recalled. Any team wanting to go far in tournament play had to face the treacherous trek of getting through the sectional tournament, then the district tournament, and finally the regional tournament, before making it to the finals of the state tournament.

Tournament games were played in different locations and ball fields around the state. Tournament officials scheduled only one game at East High School, and it was East's very first game. (The East High diamond was far from the best place to play, and other schools—fairly or not—would have balked at playing there.) When the tournament draws were announced, the Tigers were matched against Westerville South High School. It was a one-game elimination tournament.

Pennell's juggling of players continued. He placed Garnett Davis back at the catcher position. Norris Smith took the mound. Eddie Rat was at first base. The first three innings were scoreless, but then the Tigers came to life behind a solid offense. Roger Neighbors, Davis, Ratleff, and Kuthrell scored runs for East. Norris Smith allowed only three hits and one run, and the Tigers took their first tournament game, 4–1. The players were happy, but Pennell was cautious: "You have to play the games as they come up. And figure out your pitching rotation."

Any team facing East High in the tournament had to start paying attention to the Tiger bats. Garnett Davis was batting a fearsome .428. Ratleff wasn't far behind at .404. And Robert Kuthrell wasn't anyone's slouch, with a .315 average.

It would be up to Gahanna Lincoln High School, the Tigers' next foe, to try to tame the Tiger hitters. For those wondering why Ratleff

would not be on the mound against Gahanna, Pennell finally revealed
to the media that Ratleff had been nursing injuries from a base-running
collision in an earlier game. The sophomore, Ernie Locke, was starting.
He remained surprised he had been the only sophomore good enough
to make Pennell's varsity baseball team that year.

Ervin and Ernestine Locke could barely survive life in Birmingham, Alabama. There was never enough money. When Ervin was bamboozled
out of the little bit of land the family owned, his wife had had enough.
She told him she was leaving. Little Ernest was only two years old in
1952 when a relative in Columbus convinced his mother to bring her
kids and come north.

The only place she could afford was an apartment in the Lincoln Park
housing projects on the city's West Side. Her husband slipped into town
now and then to visit her and the kids. He'd leave, and nine months later
there'd be another baby. "They had an off-and-on-again relationship,"
says their son Ernie. Ernestine eventually had ten children. When she
heard about the new Bolivar Arms public housing projects on the city's
East Side, she applied and was accepted. It was a bigger apartment. "We
were one of the first three or four families to move in," says Ernie of the
family's second venture into public housing.

Ernie began playing Little League baseball. He was small and quick;
coaches were impressed with his speed. He made the team at all-black
Monroe Junior High, which sat just two hundred yards from their new
home. He was at Monroe Junior High the day Martin Luther King Jr.
was murdered. He got home from school that afternoon to find his
mother devastated. She had relatives in both Selma and Birmingham.
Over the years, Ernestine often told her children about Alabama relatives
who had seen King with their own eyes.

At Monroe Junior High, under Coach Bob Marsh, Locke mostly
played the outfield. But when he reached East High School, Coach Pennell saw something else in him: a nifty throwing arm. "I had no idea
I was even going to make the team," Ernie recalls. "Since I was left-
handed, they put me on the mound. I had a looping curveball that was

successful for me." Locke got so much attention before the season began, there were some who whispered that Eddie Rat—who was still busy with basketball at the time—had better watch out. "Of course that wasn't the case," Locke says, chuckling.

When basketball ended and Eddie Rat joined the baseball team, Locke realized he'd hardly be making anyone forget Eddie Rat's pitching prowess. But he made the team and was quite happy. He looked up to the players because they were so serious about baseball, and he began to study the sport as never before. He had read about Jackie Robinson, Willie Mays, Ted Williams, Mickey Mantle, Larry Doby. "I began to eat, drink, and sleep baseball." The Tiger road trips to the white schools amazed him. "Some of those white schools had fields that were like stadiums. They had concession stands. We didn't have that at Harley Field."

When the team suffered its five-game losing streak, Locke knew it rattled the players. "We had our heads down," he says. "But we went back to the drawing board. We had to re-evaluate."

Some of the Tiger players were more impoverished than others. Ernie Locke never told any of his coaches or fellow players that often he was hungry. He didn't like it when his stomach growled. "My mother had ten children and you didn't always get enough to eat," he says. He kept the after-school job he had at Carl Brown's grocery store, where he unpacked goods and stocked shelves. Right after baseball practice he'd bolt to the store on Mount Vernon Avenue. On his break out back, he'd think about baseball. "I really considered it an honor just to be on the team," he says. He wished he didn't have to work, but he had to and wanted to help out his mother at home.

Against Gahanna Lincoln, Eddie Rat got only one hit, but it was memorable: a soaring home run in the final inning, which brought two Tigers streaking across home plate. East bested Gahanna, 5–2, giving Ernie Locke a victory. The team now had back-to-back tournament victories.

Paul Pennell wore his warm-up jacket under his Tiger jersey those first two tournament games. He told his wife, Sharon, that he now believed it was a good luck charm and that he was going to wear it at every game—no matter how hot it got—as long as the team survived in the tournament.

On the loudspeaker the next day at East High, the Tiger victories were announced to yawns and voices yammering in classrooms. No one seemed to care. But Gardenia Davis, working inside the school, was mighty proud of her son and his team. She told a relative in South Carolina she hoped to get word to her jailed husband about their son's success.

As soon as Paul Pennell and his assistant coach, Jim Henderson, heard who the Tigers' next foe would be, they were concerned. And rightfully so. It was Bexley High School. As well, the winner of that game would go on to the regional tournament.

Bexley High wasn't just another good team, and Bexley wasn't just another community, either. This team was from another world; the school sat in a mostly all-white community just a short ride from East High. The student body at Bexley High School was 97 percent white; the fire department and police department were all-white. (Bexley didn't hire its first black police officer until 1996.) The community was moneyed, so was the school.

Aside from being baseball coach, Paul Pennell served as monitor of boys' attendance. (Principal Jack Gibbs had to get the most out of every teacher. Some teachers transferred to other schools because of the workload.) Part of Pennell's job also required issuing punishment to any boy—or girl—who went off school grounds without permission. Pennell took the job as seriously as he did all of his other tasks. He knew Gibbs expected nothing less. So the coach was quite curious when, the day before the game against Bexley High, he saw Roger Neighbors, his shortstop, loping back onto school grounds in the early afternoon. As Neighbors got closer to him, Pennell saw he was carrying a bag of Sandy's hamburgers, the red cursive insignia on the front of the bag known to everyone in the neighborhood. "I said, 'Roger, where have you been?'" Neighbors froze, speechless, his bag of hamburgers a clear giveaway. "So I had to bench Roger for the Bexley game," Pennell says.

Word spread throughout the team. The next game could propel them higher in the tournament. The player who played alongside Roger

Neighbors in the infield, Kenny Mizelle, was stunned that Neighbors would not be playing at such a critical time. "Neighbors was born to play shortstop," Mizelle felt. Neighbors's teammates attempted to console him, but he was beyond consolation, knowing he had let the team down. And Jack Gibbs was not going to overrule Pennell, even if it was a tournament game.

For Pennell and Henderson, it was back to the chessboard: The initial thinking was that they could move Mizelle to shortstop, but then who would play second base, a tricky and important position that required a lot of responsibility and mental agility? Pennell decided to keep Mizelle at his normal position and put Larry Mann at shortstop. Mann had come off the bench in previous games as a utility outfielder and had played well. Pennell trusted his talent. Pennell also decided to—for the time being—return Garnett Davis to the catcher's position.

It was a short ride for the East High Tigers to reach the site of their next game. The team's caravan of cars merely had to go east onto East Broad Street, keep straight past Franklin Park, on across Nelson Road, and right into Bexley. There had been numerous complaints over the years about the Bexley City Police Department and their brusque encounters with blacks passing through the community. The players, en route, couldn't help but gaze at the big shaded homes on both sides of the street. There was always a clear rule at play inside Bexley: Parents of East High students routinely told them how to conduct themselves if they were stopped by Bexley police—be courteous and answer their questions as politely as possible. Any other behavior could lead to serious trouble.

Even with the short distance between schools, East couldn't draw an appreciable crowd of supporters for the game: Their dozen or so fans were far outnumbered by the anxious Bexley fans rooting for their team, the Lions. Before the start of the game, Pennell donned his good-luck windbreaker under his uniform. Sharon, his wife, thought he was nuts because of the heat. But superstition had him in its grip. Eddie Rat didn't care how many supporters his school had; he was ready to play ball. His low fastball came zooming across the plate in the first two innings and he fanned all six Bexley players he faced. In the third inning, he smacked a

triple off Mitch Canin, the Bexley pitcher, bringing in two runs. Going
into the top of the final inning, Bexley held a one-run lead, 4–3. If they
were to survive, the Tigers needed some offense, and quickly. The next
batter up was Phil Mackey, one of the team's weakest hitters. But Mackey
trained his eyes on Canin's pitch and walloped it over the infield. Two
Tigers were on base and they both crossed home plate. The two-run single put the Tigers up, 5–4, and that was the final score of the game. Sharon Pennell howled with joy from the bleachers. Eddie Rat had struck
out ten of the Bexley batters in his complete game victory. Once again,
late-game heroics saved the day. The Tigers had vanquished the Lions.

It was a sweet ride back down East Broad Street for the caravan of
cars that took the team home. And the Tigers felt particularly happy for
Roger Neighbors. He would have taken a loss especially hard, given his
suspension. Now he would have a chance to play another tournament
game. Still, it didn't take his fellow Tigers long to start needling him
about going to Sandy's to get them some hamburgers.

The Tigers had now won three straight sectional tournament games.
They were now in the district tournament. Their announced foe: Whetstone High. The Tigers had knocked off Whetstone, 3–0, in the early
part of the season. But Whetstone had greatly improved since that outing; its team had knocked off Northland already in this season's tournament, with a 6–0 victory—the same Northland that had earlier knocked
East High out of the City League title competition. None of that mattered to Eddie Rat, even if he sensed the prognosticators were predicting
their elimination. "There was no one in the baseball tournament who we
were supposed to beat," he recalls.

The jiggering of East High's lineup continued in the game against
Whetstone. Pennell put Richard Twitty at first base, where Eddie Rat
usually played if he was not on the pitcher's mound. It was considered a
radical move, but he penciled Eddie Rat in as shortstop. Leroy Crozier
got the start in center field. And Norris Smith was back on the mound.

East High scored in the first inning. Whetstone came back to tie it
in the second. Neighbors—now playing second base because Pennell

decided to sit Mizelle—responded to his reinstatement with two hits. Smith's fastball confused the Whetstone batters; they swung wildly. East erupted for four runs in the third inning. Whetstone never scored again. At game's end, the score was 6–1 in favor of the Tigers. Whetstone had accounted for only two hits against the fiery pitches of Norris Smith. The Tigers had rudely knocked Whetstone out of the tournament. George Strode, the sportswriter covering the game for *The Columbus Citizen-Journal*, seemed a bit surprised when he wrote that the Tigers "are still alive."

The immediate gift to the Tigers after their victory against Whetstone was the chance to play another game. This one would be played at Jet Stadium against Bishop Watterson High.

Located in the shadow of downtown Columbus, Jet Stadium was one of the best stadiums in Ohio. It was kept in the finest condition because it was home to the Columbus Jets, the farm team of the Pittsburgh Pirates. The stadium held a deep and fond memory for many blacks in Columbus who remembered when it was home field for the Columbus Blue Birds, a professional Negro league baseball team that began play in 1933. Little Negro boys—and girls too—used to beg their parents to take them to see the Blue Birds play.

It took a hardy and enterprising soul to begin any kind of business operation in the 1930s. The Depression was gripping the country and stifling a good many plans. But not the plans of Gus Greenlee, who lived in Pittsburgh and made a lot of money from the city's gambling rackets. When the original Negro National League folded in 1931 because of financial woes, Greenlee began an effort to revive the league. He found investors and formed six teams for the 1933 season, the Baltimore Black Sox, Cole's American Giants, the Detroit Stars, the Nashville Elite Giants, the Pittsburgh Crawfords, and the Columbus Blue Birds. W. J. Peebles, who had made some of his money in the coal industry, was the primary investor in the Blue Birds. On Saturday and Sunday afternoons, blacks in Columbus would scrape their money together and hop the streetcars to get downtown to see the Blue Birds play. They played many of their games at Red Bird Stadium—later renamed Jet Stadium. Among the stars of the Blue Birds that year were Jabbo Andrews, Leroy Morney, Dizzy Dismukes, and Ted "Double Duty" Radcliffe. Double Duty would pitch one game and catch the next, usually on days when the team played a doubleheader. Several of the Blue Birds players had played with the Kansas City Monarchs, the Negro league team Jackie Robinson had played for. It disappointed many fans in the city when the team finished their first season with a lackluster 11–18 record and shortly thereafter abandoned the city. The team eventually merged with a Negro league team in Cleveland. But that hardly spelled an end to Negro league baseball in Columbus. Satchel Paige, the great pitcher, brought a group of Negro league All-Stars to town in the 1950s; they also played in the downtown ballpark. For the black residents of Columbus who were old enough to remember, Jet Stadium had very special meaning.

Eddie Rat was itching to get back on the mound. Inside Jet Stadium, he felt very strong throwing warm-up pitches to Garnett Davis. Mike Watson, a member of the Watterson High baseball team, had fully expected Whetstone to reach this phase of the tournament. Playing the Tigers was a surprise. Inside the stadium, he glanced over at the East players on the field. "When they were warming up," he says, "they didn't look all that impressive. They didn't look like world beaters. We thought we could beat them by just getting guys on base and then squeeze home some runs. The run-and-bunt game."

The Tigers had a different plan. As if anticipating a run-and-bunt game, Pennell installed the quick and powerful Garnett Davis at third and placed Ray Scott behind the plate. "I was ready," Scott recalls. "I thought it was an outstanding move. I was a defensive player. And I thought I was a good catcher."

Bunts plopped down the third base line, but Davis shut that strategy down cold. Scott kept signaling for Eddie Rat to throw fastballs, and he did. Bishop Watterson got one hit in the first inning. After that, the Tigers scored a run in the second, then two more in the third when Roger

Neighbors smacked a triple. Watterson collected another hit in the seventh, but it was meaningless. At the end of the game, Eddie Rat's wide smile told the story: He had pitched seven innings, striking out ten Watterson batters and shutting out the team, 4–0. And he had pitched his Tigers into the celebrated regional tournament. Watterson was stunned. "All our hopes got dashed," remembers Watson of Watterson High. "We were known to be a baseball school!"

When it was announced over the East High speaker system that the Tiger team had won a district championship and were now bound for the more illustrious regional tournament, there was finally some clapping and whistling. The enthusiasm dimmed, however, when students learned that the regional tournament game would be played in Gomer, Ohio. Few in the school had heard of the place. It was a small hamlet more than a hundred miles away. Since a good many Tiger families didn't have cars, there would be no contingent of fans making their way to rural Ohio to root their team on.

There were two games scheduled in Gomer, each billed as a semi-final game. East High's opponent was going to be Rossford High School.

Paul Pennell sat down inside the school and typed a letter that would be sent to the parent of each baseball player.

Dear Parent/Guardian:

Your son, as a member of the District Champion East High
Baseball Team, will be playing in the regional tournament
at Gomer, Ohio, this weekend. Gomer is located ten miles
northwest of Lima, Ohio.

We are scheduled to play at 4:00 p.m. on Friday. Upon
winning that game, we will stay overnight in a motel and play at
2:00 p.m. on Saturday. We will return home on Saturday evening.
Should we happen to lose on Friday, we will return home on
Friday night.

We will be traveling in cars driven by myself and other East

High School personnel. If you have any questions, feel free to contact me at school or at home.

Yours truly,
Paul Pennell

The day before the team took off, Pennell gave a pep talk to the team about conduct and manners and the need to get a good night's sleep. Henderson, the young black assistant coach, realized what Pennell really was trying to get through to the players: As black kids, they would be watched and judged with a heightened level of scrutiny. They would need to be on their best behavior, not because they were an unruly group, but because the world was unfair. So Henderson corralled the players and spoke to them more directly. The players' response was to implore Neighbors, with laughter, to stay away from Sandy's, the hamburger joint.

Even before the Tigers set off for their out-of-town tournament games, Ed Mingo, the team's student manager, could sense the skepticism spreading around Columbus about East High's chances. "There were actually people in the city going to the media saying that Northland should be in the tournament because they won the City League title and not us," he says. "It was incredible."

The town of Gomer boasted a lovely baseball diamond at the local high school. The school was in the smaller Class A division and had never come up against Class AA East High. Blacks were a strange and alien sight to Gomer townsfolk. When the Tigers stopped for a meal en route, there were plenty of stares. The whites in that part of rural Ohio had rarely seen so many black kids together, except on TV news broadcasts about the 1968–69 racial unrest and tragedies around the country. "It was culture shock," remembers Ernie Locke. "The whites were saying, 'Where did all of these black people come from?' "

The last time a major news event happened in Gomer had been back in 1939. Admiral Richard E. Byrd, the great Antarctic explorer, had left

Chicago, en route to Boston, where he planned to depart on another expedition. In Gomer, Ohio, of all places, the snow cruiser *The Penguin,* crucial to survival in bitter weather, suffered a broken steering system. It went careening through a railing on Old Lincoln Highway, right into the water. Fortunately, no one was injured, but it was a sight to see. Admiral Byrd was renowned enough that the incident brought the national media to Gomer. Townsfolk ate hot dogs while they watched the goings-on. It took three days to recover and fix the damaged vehicle. The mishap was so memorable to townsfolk that they began turning the anniversary of the event into a local festival.

Even before the East High Tigers reached Gomer, Jim Martz, who had lived in the town all his life, got a phone call. Martz was a "bird dog" scout, one of those guys from small towns across America who were hired by professional baseball teams to ferret out potential big league talent. He was the Gomer-area bird dog for the Baltimore Orioles. "This was a little Mayberry town out in the cornfields," Martz says. "Jim Frye was the Midwest director of the Baltimore Orioles. He calls me and says, 'Jim, there's a kid I'd like you to look at. His name's Eddie Ratleff. He's going to be playing over at Gomer High in a tournament game. I'd like you to go over there and scout him for me.'" So Martz made sure he had his notebooks and pencils in order. He had heard plenty about Ratleff during the high school basketball season. Now he looked forward to seeing the Tiger star pitch.

There was a reason Ohio High School Athletic Association officials wanted teams to come all the way to Gomer. Its field was a thing of beauty. Ed Sandy, the Gomer coach, had built one of the best baseball fields in the state, and word had spread. He looked on his baseball field as a work of art. "He'd put the batter's box in by hand," Martz recalls of Sandy. "He had a little two-wheeler, like a lawn mower, that he would use to draw lines around the batter's box. He would get up at four in the morning and do work on that field." He'd also tell the Gomer school principal that if he had some students who were interested in work study, they could come out to his field and help him out. Sandy had enjoyed a fine pitching career at Ohio Northern University. After that, the Philadelphia Phillies pulled him into their farm system, where he lasted a few years. Around Gomer, he wasn't above dining out on the fact that he had once struck out Hank Aaron in a minor league game in Billings, Montana. People snickered about him around town: Here comes Ed Sandy and that Hank Aaron story again. But they loved what he and his baseball teams meant to the community.

In 1969, the town still retained its Norman Rockwell–like feel, as if all the turmoil around America had skirted the place. It was beautiful, rustic, green, and everyone in town was white. "You never saw an all-black team in Gomer before East High," recalls Martz. "Now, I played a little semi-pro ball myself, so I played with black players. They weren't an unfamiliar sight to me."

When the Tigers walked onto the Gomer field, they, like so many others, were mightily impressed. Paul Pennell's wife, Sharon, sitting in the stands, was impressed with the beauty of the field. She also made up the entire Tiger cheering section.

The Rossford High Bulldogs, East's opponents, had been a big draw in their region during the season. Unlike East High, they had won their league championship and were crowned the 1969 Northern Lakes League baseball champions.

Eddie Rat was on the mound for the Tigers, and from the start he fired menacing fastballs. Nearly every Rossford High batter that faced Eddie Rat on the beautiful Gomer field was swinging—and missing. Sometimes they had the half-startled look of boys lost in the woods. Rossford got a meaningless hit in the second inning, then another in the fifth. They were unbowed, still confident going into the sixth inning as the game remained scoreless. But then came the sixth. All hell proceeded to break loose against Rossford as Eddie Rat smacked a three-run homer. The ball sailed out into the surrounding cornfields. Kids raced after it, and necks craned as Eddie loped around the bases. The Rossford partisans sat stunned as East scored six runs, three of those runs because of the Ratleff homer. The Tigers scored two more runs in the seventh, as if to put an exclamation point on the affair. The final score: East High, 8, Rossford, 0. It was the Tigers' most dominating tournament win. "They were superior to the Rossford team," Martz said years later. "Rossford was just overmatched athletically." But by game's end, Jim Martz could sense that the Rossford fans had become admirers of the all-black team. "It was unusual—and a great thrill—for us in Gomer to see athletes of that caliber," Martz says.

So the Tigers would not be returning to Columbus just yet. Eddie Rat had now pitched fifteen consecutive scoreless innings. Martz, the bird dog scout, was simply amazed. He had a lot to tell the Baltimore Orioles about this Ratleff kid.

When the Tiger baseball team reached their motel, they changed out of their uniforms to go get dinner in town. Coach Pennell called in the victory score and stats to the Columbus media. A couple of the players also made calls back to Columbus, telling their mothers they had won and would not be coming home that night. (In those days long-distance calls were costly, and the players who called asked their mothers to call the parents of the other players to save the expense of more calls.)

That night, the Tiger baseball contingent—mindful of the pep talks that had been given by Pennell and Henderson—stuck to their motel rooms. They tried to pick up some soul music stations on their motel room radios but weren't successful. Pennell did his best to prepare them for their next day's opponent, London High School.

London's Red Raiders had a renowned baseball pedigree. This was their fourth consecutive appearance deep into regional tournament play. Ray Chadwell's team had beaten Whitehall High, 2–0, at Jet Stadium in Columbus to garner their trip to Gomer. In Gomer, they defeated Mansfield Madison, earning their matchup with East.

No one was saying it aloud just yet, but every East High player had it in mind: If they won one more game here in Gomer, they were headed to the finals of the state tournament. "Just like in basketball, sometimes you get on a roll," Eddie Rat recalled. "And we were on a roll."

The next morning, however, the skies darkened in Gomer. Then it began to rain. Norris Smith was scheduled to pitch for the Tigers but began to wonder if he would make it to the mound. It kept raining. There was nothing magical that Ed Sandy—the legendary coach and groundskeeper—could do about the deluge. His field was soaked. Tournament officials huddled together. When the referees decreed that the field was unplayable, coaches and athletic officials reconvened and agreed that the game should be moved to Columbus, to a neutral field. The team assembled and thanked the Gomer officials. But inasmuch as they were riding a wave of momentum, the Tigers didn't know if they should feel spooked by the postponement, or if they should celebrate the extra rest they would be getting. They all packed and embarked back to Columbus.

Back in Columbus, Paul Pennell decided that if the game was scheduled for Tuesday, he'd stick with Norris Smith. But if the delay was longer, he aimed to put Eddie Rat on the mound.

The neutral site chosen for the game was Franklin Heights High School, located on the city's far West Side and boasting a top-notch playing field. On Tuesday, the rain fell on Columbus, causing another cancellation. On Wednesday, the weather finally cleared and the game was back on. Pennell told Eddie Rat he was going to be pitching. And, like a hardened card shark, Eddie Rat offered up only a tight grin.

Jack Gibbs realized that no matter how often it was mentioned over the school's loudspeaker that the Tigers were set to play another important game—one that could send them as one of four teams to play in the state finals—it would be an uphill task to get students to trek all the way across town to watch their team.

Leading up to the London game, Pennell decided to make yet another one of his endless chess moves: Garnett Davis was installed at third base, and Ray Scott was penciled in again at the catcher position. (Scott had two brothers serving in Vietnam. He couldn't wait to get word to them about what was happening with the team.)

The first four innings of the East-London matchup were scoreless. While Eddie Rat was striking out Red Raider batters, London's Dave Rutherford was doing the same thing to the Tiger hitters. The Tigers finally broke a scoreless game in the fifth inning when Ray Scott singled, scoring Robert Kuthrell. But the sixth inning for the Tigers was far more lethal and productive: Roger Neighbors banged a double, bringing home two Tiger runners. Eddie Rat got a turn at bat and also smacked a double, driving two more runners home. Now the score sat at 5–0, and the East High Tigers were one inning away from a ticket to the state tourney finals. In the final inning Neighbors hit another double; Davis and Kuthrell padded their batting averages, and it was a take-no-prisoners ending for the Tigers, a dynamic 9–0 victory. Eddie Rat had struck out nine London batters and pitched his third straight shutout. Pennell and Henderson rushed to embrace their players in a moment of giddy joyfulness. There were only a few Tiger fans on hand to join in a raucous field celebration, but that didn't matter to any of the team members. "You just can't describe it," Pennell bellowed afterward to a reporter.

The state championship baseball finals would take place at Ohio State University, with four teams playing on two fields. East High was going to face Cleveland St. Joseph. The winner would face the winner of the Miamisburg and East Liverpool game.

If there was any team across the state that struck fear into other teams bound for the tournament, it was East Liverpool. Their team was loaded down with veteran players and power hitters. "Liverpool was probably the state tournament favorites going in," Pennell remembered.

Now, more than ever, East High principal Jack Gibbs considered it vitally important to rally fan support both inside and outside the school for this baseball team.

There was no way that the Columbus city school system was going to fork over money to transport East High students to the Ohio State campus, even when the team was playing in the state championship finals. So just days before the East–Cleveland St. Joseph matchup, Gibbs got in his car and drove the short distance over to Mount Vernon Avenue and he walked into business after business, telling the owners: He needed money to rent school buses to take students to the baseball state finals. If an owner went all miserly on him, he remained there and started talking again about the past year, about Martin Luther King Jr., about what had happened across America, about the pride these black kids had brought to the whole city, black and white alike. He would thank them when they went back into their pockets and forked over another $10 bill. Then he rolled over to Long Street and did the same thing. After he was finished with the businessmen and businesswomen on Long Street, he rolled over to East Main, where, once again, he solicited money. "He loved those kids," says Ruth Gibbs of her husband. "He would do anything for them."

Senior Prom was the day before the four teams clashed at Ohio State. Members of the senior class had been thinking about and planning this event for a long time, including the seniors on the baseball team. On the day of the prom, Pennell gathered not his players who were going to the prom—Ray Scott, Roger Neighbors, and Eddie Rat—but their dates. Too much was at stake. "I said, 'Ladies, we've got a semi-final game Friday. It's very important,'" Pennell remembers. "They all said, 'Coach, we'll have them home in time.'"

Even if he could have afforded a rental tux and the other accoutrements needed, which he couldn't, Garnett Davis wouldn't have gone to the prom. "I was focused on that baseball game." He didn't even bother to broach the subject with a female classmate. Ray Scott looked forward to going. He had fussed about which tux he was going to wear.

The prom unfolded at the Imperial House Hotel on the city's North Side. The ladies looked beautiful in their silk gowns, corsages pinned on, and high heels. The young men looked suave in their tuxedoes and patent-leather shoes. They all aimed to put the political turmoil of their city and nation behind them for one special night. Inside the ballroom, they danced to sweet soul music and sipped punch. They complimented one another on how fine they looked, and they chatted about the college choices they had made. Some couples moved quietly to corners and kissed, discreetly. Eddie Rat was having a wonderful time. Then, he remembers: "I told my girlfriend, 'I have to go.' She said, 'Let's stay a little while longer. No one will know.'" Eddie Rat remembers what he said next: "I would know."

So he left. Soon after, so did Ray Scott and Roger Neighbors.

.   .   .

In the early afternoon of May 30, the Tiger baseball players gathered their belongings inside their homes and their apartments in the low-income housing projects. The night before, some of their mothers had washed their uniforms by hand. Some of the players had washed their uniforms themselves. They still had mismatched belts and worn-down cleats.

Leroy Crozier came out the door at 1152 East Rich Street; Garnett Davis from 1629 Oak Street; Robert Kuthrell from 421 Chatfield; Ernie Locke out the door at 980 Caldwell Place, Apt. 21. Phil Mackey said good-bye to his mother at 1447 Fair Avenue; Larry Mann emerged from 1586 Tiffin; Kenny Mizelle exited from 980 Caldwell Place, Apt. 24. Roger Neighbors stepped into the daylight from 453 Eldridge; Norris Smith from 216 N. Garfield; Richard Twitty from 309 Linwood; Harry Williams from 2483 Brocton Court; Ray Scott from 364 N. Garfield; Tony Brown from 1200 Author Place. Eddie Rat emerged from 1201 Bryden Road, passing an alcoholic stepfather who was already mumbling nonsense. In every one of their homes, either on a wall or atop a mantelpiece, sat the visage of Martin Luther King Jr., dead thirteen months now. They were Tigers, and they didn't just have an appointment on the North Side of the city. They had a dream. They were going to meet a group of baseball players from Cleveland St. Joseph High School who aimed to stop their journey, and they were intent on not letting that happen.

Jack Gibbs met them as they walked onto the Ohio State University field. As they looked at him, and then beyond him into the bleachers, they saw a sight they had not seen all season long: hundreds and hundreds and hundreds of East High Tigers, whistling and yelling and waving pom-poms. Gibbs had corralled a few bus drivers and gathered some students. From the bleachers, that old Tiger chant erupted:

> I went down to the river
> Oh yeah . . .

The local news folk had been talking and writing about the fact that a Columbus school hadn't won the AA state baseball crown since 1940. And that no AA school had ever won *both* a state basketball and

Hiram Tanner, in the middle wearing glasses, had played baseball
in the professional Negro leagues. For years he was the only black sportswriter
in Columbus, writing for a Negro publication.

a state baseball title in the same year. Such a twin feat seemed unimaginable—until now. The white press throughout Ohio completely avoided writing about the cultural potency of the East High team and their journey. It was left to Hiram Tanner—who made up the entire local Negro sportswriting press and who followed the black athletes with cultural insight—to remind his readers that something special seemed to be happening with this team in this year of so much pain and blood. Tanner had been following the exploits of both Davis and Ratleff since they were junior high players. "My father was especially taken with Garnett Davis because he could hit," Hiram Tanner's son, Hiram Jr., recalled.

In the stands there were several men who had played for the all-black Peers Club team. There were also a few Peers Club coaches who had coached Eddie Rat and Garnett Davis and other Tigers. When they saw each other, they gathered and embraced.

The Vikings of Cleveland St. Joseph sent Al Zdesar to the mound; unsurprisingly, Eddie Rat got the call for the Tigers.

Terry Thomas, the Cleveland St. Joseph coach, stood watching the action unfold: Eddie Rat singled. Then he stole second. Richard Twitty, an anemic .155 hitter, suddenly found his groove and walloped a triple, knocking in Eddie. Robert Kuthrell and Norris Smith drove in two more runs. St. Joseph infielders made two costly infield errors. Tiger fans were screaming; Cleveland St. Joseph fans were shaking their heads. The score at the end of the first inning: East High, 4, Cleveland St. Joseph, 0.

"We jumped on them real quick," recalls Ed Mingo, the Tigers' team manager.

Eddie Rat took the mound. Through the first five innings, he mowed the Vikings down. He did not give up a single run, and St. Joseph's Doug Mervar was the only batter to get a hit. In the sixth, Coach Pennell, with two innings to go, pulled Eddie Rat. He sent the versatile Garnett Davis to the mound in his place. But Eddie Rat still wanted to play, so Pennell installed him at third base: That hard grin of the card shark lined Eddie Rat's face. The Vikings thought their starting pitcher, Zdesar, had had enough. He was replaced by Frank Lopuszinski, a senior; the Tigers ruined the waning days of his high school pitching career when they belted five hits off him, resulting in four more runs. The Vikings managed three runs off of Garnett Davis in the final two innings, but by then the Tiger fan noise told the story: East High, 9, Cleveland St. Joseph, 3. The Tigers had turned in another virtuoso performance. Hiram Tanner was tapping the white sportswriters on the shoulders: Told you so. He was referring to all those times he had been jawboning about the Tiger baseball team. It was hardly lost on the St. Joseph coach that his players had simply dropped too many catchable balls during the game. The Tigers were now headed to their first-ever state final baseball game. "That first inning was it for us," confessed St. Joseph coach Terry Thomas. "If we would have caught the ball we would have been out of the inning without East scoring. We didn't catch it, and East's momentum went up 50 percent and ours dropped."

Paul Pennell was overjoyed by the way his team had performed. Jack Gibbs was also beaming, especially when the Tiger players went over to the stands and buses to thank their fellow students for coming to the game.

East Liverpool High defeated Miamisburg, 5–4, that same day, and the stage was now set for the state championship finale.

East Liverpool, nudged up against the West Virginia and Pennsylvania borders, sat in a valley in the northwestern region of Ohio. The locals referred to it simply as "the valley." All through the early and middle part of the twentieth century, many of the men in the area worked in the big steel mill, called Crucible, just across the state border in Midland, Pennsylvania. The mill was still going strong in the 1960s. It was no surprise that the men who worked in those mills raised their sons to be tough. Sports became a huge draw in the valley. Football etched character, but baseball had been played in the valley since the 1800s, when all the mining camps had teams. Fathers worked and dreamed and nursed beers and buried their own fathers in the valley. Their sons came bounding through the doorway with gleaming football and baseball trophies. But even in the time-warped valley, the residents couldn't escape change.

In the fall of 1968, when school began at East Liverpool High—the sole high school in the community—the teachers could feel immediate tension between blacks and whites. The aftermath of the King assassination hung in the air. "I remember we athletes had to line up for something," says Bill Montgomery, an East Liverpool senior that year and a pitcher on the baseball team. "Well, the black athletes lined up on one side, by themselves. It was a protest. Something like that had never happened before."

A new day had dawned.

When budget cuts caused the high school to disband its baseball team in 1967, there was outrage. So some of the deep-pocketed individuals in the community decided such a foolhardy thing would be remedied. The baseball team was back on the diamond in 1969. It was a tribute to the athletic program and community. And that year the East Liverpool High baseball team earned their way to the final game of the state tournament. Their team was loaded with seniors. Their team batting average was a potent .337. "We were running with the big dogs," says Montgomery, their best pitcher. "We were not in fear of East," he says of the Tigers from Columbus.

East Liverpool athletes and students were known as the Potters. The unique name stemmed from the fact the region boasted a good many pottery refineries, giving the town's brawny image an artistic touch.

The excitement for East Liverpool's baseball team was not lost on Frank Dawson. There was not a bigger booster of Potter athletics than Frank, who owned the biggest funeral home in town. Beginning in the early 1960s, Dawson kept scrapbooks of all the football, basketball, track, and baseball team activities. He was never a notable athlete himself, but he was the kind of soul who kept a community's history alive, who knew that high school so often held emotions that were complex, rich, and enduring. Every summer he invited the school's athletes out to his farm, where he and his family hosted cookouts. There was a lot of bonding, and pledges to get an elusive state title—it didn't matter which sport. That is what gnawed at everyone in the valley: Up to the beginning of the school year in 1968, no East Liverpool team had ever won a state championship title. So with the warm breezes of 1969, they were putting their hopes on their baseball team, a team that boasted several two-sport athletes who were already holding big-time scholarship offers in football and baseball.

In Frank Dawson's mind, it just wouldn't do for the team to travel down to Columbus in an old school bus. So the funeral director went to his parking lot and buffed up his two limousines. He told baseball coach Jim Potts that he was going to take care of the team's travel.

It was a three-hour drive, and all the way down to Columbus the East Liverpool boys talked about their intent to win the school's first-ever championship trophy. The folks out on the highway thought the limousines carried a group of dignitaries. Nope, just an all-white baseball team with a lot of swagger, bound for Columbus in a funeral-like procession. "The school's athletic director, Bob McNea, installed that swagger in that team," Dawson said. "They thought they could beat the Marine Corps at Guadalcanal." The team knew that East High had won the basketball championship a couple months earlier. But they had never heard anyone boasting of the school's baseball team. They hadn't heard of any of the Tiger baseball players aside from Eddie Ratleff. It mattered not at all to them, however, who the East High Tigers sent to the mound.

When Jack Gibbs got home from East High's victory over Cleveland St. Joseph, he told his wife, Ruth, that he now needed more buses. He wanted to gather up more kids to take to the championship game. He wanted a bigger turnout, so Gibbs called the soul radio station, WVKO—where East High student Kirk Bishop was still spinning records—and implored him and anyone on air to say as much as they could about the next day's game. Then Jack Gibbs went about commandeering more school buses.

The following day, when the Tigers of East High walked onto the varsity field at Ohio State University, there were more than twenty-five hundred fans, howling, jumping up and down, and a good many of them were Tiger fans. "I remember that crowd, and all those buses," recalls the pitcher Ernie Locke. "It was really something."

When the East Liverpool team reached Ohio State, Frank Dawson and his other driver parked the limousines behind the fence near the varsity baseball field. The players got dressed. Then they made their way onto the field, wearing their sparkling white uniforms. They looked like world-beaters.

The Tigers were warming up, throwing the ball around. Frank Dawson caught sight of the East High players. "They weren't wearing the best-looking uniforms," he recalls. "They [were clearly] on a budget."

East Liverpool's coach was sending Jim Musuraca to the mound. Musuraca was a three-sport star and already the proud recipient of a football scholarship offer from Notre Dame. It was tricky for Musuraca to play baseball and run track, since both were spring sports, but he managed. Musuraca practiced his pitching using a shot put, which he was thoroughly convinced made his fastball all that much faster.

The East Liverpool players saw East High's pitcher warming up. It was Norris Smith, a leftie. (Eddie Rat had pitched the day before and was starting at first base.) Norris Smith stood all of five foot eight and weighed only 130 pounds. "We looked at that little Norris guy," Dawson says, "and we all said, 'We're gonna jump all over that guy.'" Both Dawson and Liverpool's Coach Potts were licking their chops imagining what Tom Chambers, their center fielder with a garish .417 batting average, would do to little Norris Smith.

Of the four teams who had played a day earlier in the semi-finals, East Liverpool had amassed the most hits, thirteen. East Liverpool's batting lineup was referred to as a "Murderers Row" lineup. "If we were worried about anything," says East's Ray Scott, "it was their batting average." The Potters, all season long, always seemed to have runners on base.

Musuraca was angry with himself an hour or so before game time. He had forgotten his shot put. So he ran around the baseball field area and found a cinder block. He came back with it and made sure that the Tiger baseball players saw him with it. "I'd throw it, then would go get it. And I'd throw it again. I was probably scaring the hell out of the East High players," he says.

Neither pitcher gave up a hit in the first inning. In the second, Musuraca yielded a single to Kenny Mizelle. The hit pumped up the Tiger crowd. The Tigers got another hit in the second inning, but neither hit led to a score. In the bottom of the third, Jim Massey faced Smith. Massey eked out an infield hit. An error got him to second. Liverpool's Bill Montgomery came up to bat, and with his teammate in scoring position, smacked a single into left field. The Liverpool crowd erupted; Frank Dawson could hardly contain himself, poking at those around him. This was how they played baseball down in the valley!

East Liverpool, 1, East High, 0.

Pennell later confessed that his Tigers were "a little tight for the first time this season during the early innings" of the game.

In the fourth inning, Norris Smith came up to bat with Robert Kuthrell on second. Smith connected on a Musuraca pitch, and Kuthrell scored. Now the score was tied, 1–1.

In the sixth inning, Smith confessed to his coach that his thumb was sore—even though he insisted on staying on the mound.

In the top of the seventh inning, Musuraca walked Ray Scott. Next up, Kenny Mizelle. The second baseman got the signal and bunted, doing his job perfectly and sacrificing Scott over to second. Phil Mackey stepped into the batter's box. He had not come close to a hit all game. The Musuraca pitch came toward the plate; Mackey swung: *bam!* Scott took off as Pennell, coaching at third base, furiously waved his arms in a windmill motion. Scott scored standing up and the Tigers were, for the first time all game, ahead. The Tiger crowd exploded.

With his team down by one run in the bottom of the seventh and final inning, Liverpool's Jim Massey smacked a ball deep into the center field. Robert Kuthrell took off in pursuit. "I remember watching that ball," recalls Sharon Pennell, "and saying, 'Oh please catch it! Please catch it.' "

Kuthrell caught it.

After the second Liverpool out, the Tigers just needed to retire one more batter and the game, and championship, was theirs. The Liverpool batter bounced a ground ball toward Garnett Davis at third. Davis scooped the ball up and fired it, right into the waiting glove of Eddie Rat. The ref called it with a flourish of his arm: Runner out!

It was over.

And this was how they played baseball in the inner city of Columbus, Ohio.

The players rushed to surround their coach and hoisted Pennell onto their shoulders. Sharon Pennell and Jack Gibbs made their way down to the diamond, along with the throng of Tiger fans. "When that last out was made," recalls Sharon. "I said, 'I can't believe this.' I was twenty-nine years old and I thought, 'Look at what I've just experienced.' It was a gift from God." As he was walking away from the stadium, Ed Littlejohn, who had coached many of these Tiger players on the Peers Club team, looked back over his shoulder at their field celebration. He was still beaming. His son, Ed Jr., had driven him to the game. "I have contributed something to the world," the father told the son, pointing at the champion Tigers.

It was the first time a school had won the state championship in basketball and baseball in the same year since the inception of the Ohio High School Athletic Association in 1919. Columbus also now had its first state baseball champion since 1940 who hailed from the city league.

Norris Smith had pitched a mighty fine game. "Norris was on target," says Scott, his catcher. "He made very few mistakes. He followed what I wanted him to do." Lou Berliner, *The Columbus Dispatch* sports writer, conceded that Smith had been "the complete master over a determined East Liverpool Club." Musuraca, the Liverpool pitcher, admits he and his teammates had been bewildered by Smith. "He didn't throw very hard," Musuraca says. "He threw junk. He got us out of our rhythm. We were used to flamethrowers. Their little guy just threw us off."

Musuraca believes, to this day, that East Liverpool could have won were it not for the absence of Sonny Clark. Clark—who would have been the only black on the team's roster in 1969—had been the team's catcher the year before. "Just a great athlete," says Musuraca. But Clark hadn't gone out for baseball his senior year. He was feeling the political vibe of the times. He had begun talking about the need for whites to respect blacks. Ultimately, he said "no thanks" when baseball practice got under way.

Eddie Rat was overcome with joy following the victory. "No way did I think we could win the state going into the season," he recalled years later. Garnett Davis had a similar feeling: "There was no way in the world I thought we were going to win the state." Ernie Locke had heard a lot about East Liverpool. "We heard rumors that they were some tough cats," he says. "But the stuff we had to go through on a daily basis— being poor and black—we figured was tougher than what they went through." Still, he recalls sitting in the dugout thinking: "There was the real possibility we could lose. We said, 'We can't give up.'"

Norris Smith was engulfed by fans after that last out. He knew there were many who had wondered why Eddie Rat wasn't starting. But Pennell had been determined to stick with his rotation. "It was the greatest display of courage I have ever seen from a youngster," Pennell said of Smith after the game. "He had a job to do and he simply went out and did it." Then Paul Pennell broke down, crying as he saw his wife, Sharon, approach.

When Jack Gibbs reached the players, he hugged them all, one by one. He wasn't just hugging them as school principal; he'd been a father figure for them for a long time. Eddie Rat got a special bear hug. Then Gibbs let him in on a secret: "We won't be able to have a parade," he whispered to Eddie Rat. Gibbs told him it was because of all the extra money for the school buses. Eddie Rat's smile quickly faded. "Just kidding!" the principal quickly shouted. They broke into laughter together.

The baseball players of East Liverpool—after exchanging handshakes with the Tigers—trudged across the baseball field to their waiting limousines. "It's like it was yesterday, it hurt so much," Bill Montgomery recalled years later about losing the game. As well, years later Frank Dawson couldn't stop himself from saying, "We couldn't hit that little Smith kid," referring to Norris Smith.

Every Tiger player kept his uniform on when they got back to their neighborhood. As they walked by houses and tenements, folks came rushing out to congratulate them. Some windows had been quickly painted orange and black, the school colors. "It was a special feeling," says Ernie Locke, "walking through our neighborhoods with our uniforms on. And knowing the news was being broadcast all over WVKO. I'll never forget it."

The next morning, the Tiger baseball team and coaches rose early and together attended a church service at First African Methodist Episcopal Zion Church on Bryden Road in Columbus. After the assassination of Martin Luther King Jr., and in the midst of the street uprisings in Columbus in that summer of 1968, the church's minister, Rev. John Frazier, had been hand chosen by Mayor Sensenbrenner to join a commission to recruit blacks to apply for positions in the city's 94 percent white police department. The bylaws of the First AME Church state: "The African Methodist Episcopal Church has rejected the negative theological interpretations which rendered persons of African descent second class citizens." Reverend Frazier was also one of the black ministers in the city who had trekked over to Ohio State the previous day to watch the championship game. "Because baseball is a game where the skills of the coach are always on display," he told the congregation, "it was a joy to watch Paul Pennell directing the game from the third base coaching box. The response of the players to his strategy was almost professional in its execution. You just should have been in the stands."

Immediately after church, the players were whisked over to the Novelty Food Bar on East Long Street for an early dinner. The Novelty was so identified with East High supporters that sometimes Pennell and basketball coach Bob Hart would receive mail there. The eating establishment had been founded by Otto Beatty Sr., who had been involved in the fight for civil rights in the city for a long time. In addition to Rev. Phale Hale's home, Martin Luther King Jr. had also stayed at Beatty's home on North Monroe Avenue. (King had his pick of black homes to stay in when he visited the city, often making mental notes of which family had served the best soul food meal during a previous visit.) The cooks had been inside Beatty's restaurant since early morning preparing the food for the victorious Tigers. When the players and coaches arrived, their eyes widened at the sight of the expansive buffet: green beans, chicken, mashed potatoes, macaroni and cheese, cabbage, corn bread, apple pie, sweet potato pie. The Tigers feasted. Beatty was one of the men Jack Gibbs always went to when he needed a little extra money for some school function. While they were all eating, Beatty kept talking about *two* championships, and how he couldn't believe it, and how amazing it was. Ernie Locke, who never got enough food at home, not with nine brothers and sisters, couldn't stop eating. They had to pull him away from the buffet.

After their meal, everyone gathered over at East High, where the parade began. More than a thousand students and alumni showed up. The baseball players couldn't help but wonder: Where were these people when the season was unfolding?

The players rode in convertibles as the parade looped around East Broad Street, glided up Long Street, then circled back around to the front of the school. There was a makeshift stage erected there. Pennell climbed up onto it. He and his players looked like kings of the world. The sun was shining brightly. Pennell's voice cracked as he started talking. "I guess these kids decided to gobble up the title this year," he told the crowd. Jack Gibbs was overcome with emotion. He so wished the entire world could witness this inspiring moment. For weeks afterward, Jack Gibbs would receive letters and telegrams from alumni around the country, and also from fans far and wide who had heard about what the teams had accomplished. *The Columbus Dispatch*—its editorial page so often viewed as being at odds with the black community—weighed in

The second half of the miracle was now complete.

with an editorial. "Sports reporters agree that this unprecedented feat of winning both championships in one year showed a dedication seldom equaled in any level of sports from Little League through professional." It went on: "The team members, the coaches, the faculty, and the student body of East High School have . . . shown the world that they are champions in the true sense of the word."

They had—the East High basketball team and the baseball team—made history. But they were well aware that not all was right with the world around them. There was the night when Garnett Davis had gotten locked out of his home and phoned Coach Pennell. Davis thought it wise to have a white man standing in front of the house in case a police officer drove by and saw a black kid trying to break in. Coach Pennell got in his car and drove right over, all the way across town. So the team players were all astute to the temper of the times. They had gone into neighborhoods where they were not welcome, and they had come out victorious. They had—most of them—missing fathers, and mothers also who were doing their best just to hold on, but they were mothers who were not about to stop demanding their civil rights. They had brought black and white together in a city still grappling with school segregation and inequality. They gave people a reason to look backward—if only to look forward. They made old Negro Little League coaches think about the meaning of their attempts to rally the little black boys on the city's East Side to play Jackie Robinson's game. They made people think of the long-gone all-black Columbus Blue Birds, who used to play downtown in a city that didn't welcome the players into its downtown hotels. They had shown the world they could win without money, or deep-pocketed boosters.

The dreamer, King, who had walked these very streets, who had paraded down East Broad Street, was now gone. But they had forged on. They were the 1968–69 mighty Tigers of East High School. And they were among the best America had to offer, even if America didn't quite realize it. "We were," says Eddie Rat, "just a black school with players who loved each other."

And now, their futures were in front of them.

15

Off into the World

In the spring of 1969, Eddie Ratleff was one of the most highly sought after high school athletes in America. He was an All-American in basketball and had made many baseball All-Star teams. He told professional baseball scouts that he intended to go directly to college. That did not stop the Pittsburgh Pirates from drafting him in the fifth round that year.

But Eddie Ratleff was determined to go to college, and basketball was his ticket to get there.

Ohio State, once again, proved its disdain for local black athletes. Fred Taylor, the basketball coach, had an affinity for recruiting white suburban and rural basketball stars over inner-city black stars. Other Big Ten basketball coaches outpaced him in the recruitment of black athletes. The university's lack of interest in Ratleff, Nick Conner, and Bo-Pete Lamar—homegrown stars—infuriated Jack Gibbs. "I remember Gibbs called an assembly at the school and really lit into Ohio State for not going after Ratleff and Conner especially," recalls Scott Guiler, the volunteer assistant basketball coach.

Before basketball season ended, Ohio State football coach Woody

Hayes summoned Ratleff to meet with him. Hayes knew the disappointment and anger blacks in the community felt toward Fred Taylor. "I got
close to Woody Hayes. I always saw him at banquets," Ratleff says. "One
day Hayes had someone come get me. Woody said, 'If you come to Ohio
State to play for Fred, I'll take care of you. I'll watch out for you.'" That,
of course, was but a telltale sign—the football coach having to vouch for
the basketball program.

Ratleff came to the conclusion that he still loved baseball, even if he
was willing to turn his back on a professional contract. He began looking for a good college that had strong basketball and baseball programs.
If he chose a midwestern school, the weather would not be as good for
baseball. Like the other East High basketball players, he had sworn
off the South because of its racial history. But he was also impressed
with the rising career of Skip Young, his onetime basketball foe from
Linden-McKinley High School in Columbus. In 1967, Young became
the second black basketball player to receive a scholarship at Florida
State University. Young had also become the first black to start a varsity
basketball game; Lenny Hall, the first black recruited to the school in
1966, played in one varsity game in 1967, damaged his knee, and never
played again. Young said nice things to Ratleff about Hugh Durham, his
Florida State coach. The same year, 1967, Charlie Scott, another player
in the Atlantic Coast Conference, became the first black player to play at
the University of North Carolina. In the following two seasons, Scott led
his team to the Final Four of the NCAA tournament. He was considered
a shoo-in for Player of the Year both seasons but never won the honor.
Both years it went to a white player. Some white sportswriters simply
refused to place Scott on their ballots.

With Skip Young, Ratleff figured the South was changing, so he
decided, after some hard thinking, to go to Florida State. Eddie signed
his scholarship offer in Columbus with both his mother and Florida
State coach Hugh Durham by his side. Soon thereafter, Ratleff made
his first visit to the school. He met the coaches and members of the
basketball team. While there, he was invited to an off-campus party by
a couple of black students. He was excited to go. "It was a nice party,"
Ratleff remembers. "But then somebody on the street called the police.

The police came to the house. The black student who answered the door said, 'There are a lot of parties on this block. How come y'all are always coming to this house?' And right then and there, I saw something I didn't want to see. So I said to myself, 'I'm not coming down here.'" Ratleff began toying with the idea of going to a smaller school. He liked what Long Beach State (much smaller than Florida State) coach Jerry Tarkanian had said to him: that he could come there and play both basketball and baseball.

Eddie Ratleff didn't care that the Columbus media had already printed stories about him having signed with Florida State. His fears about the South had been confirmed. His mother, Barbara, wanted him to be happy. Jack Gibbs told him to follow his gut. Eddie Ratleff stunned people in Columbus when he announced he was not going to Florida State, but to Long Beach State, on the other side of the country.

Jerry Tarkanian had been at Long Beach only a year when Ratleff arrived. Tarkanian, a funny, intense, smart man, was not afraid to recruit black players. At the time, freshmen could not play varsity; they had to wait until their sophomore year, so Ratleff had to play for the freshman basketball team. In one early-season scrimmage against the varsity team, Ratleff torched the older players for 30 points. He was constantly dazzling the Long Beach coaches. "You guys know me; I'm a player's coach," Tarkanian said to his players one day after practice. "If you give me 100 percent on the court, I don't have a lot of rules. But from now on, there are two rules that everyone in this program must follow. When you are on the floor with Ed Ratleff, get him the ball. The second rule is not to forget the first rule." Ratleff averaged a whopping 39 points a game for the freshman team. After the season, he pitched on the freshman baseball team, but a hand injury the following year brought his baseball playing days to an end. In basketball, he led Long Beach State to the NCAA tournament each one of his varsity seasons. In his three-year career there, he was named Conference Player of the Year twice, and an All-American twice. Jack and Ruth Gibbs hopped a plane a couple times to go see Eddie play. When people asked Ratleff if there was any special reason he wore no. 42 on the basketball team in college, he told them there was indeed a reason: It was the number Jackie Robinson wore during his baseball career.

Ratleff was named to the 1972 Olympic basketball team. So was Bill Walton, UCLA's All-American center. But Walton begged off, citing health reasons. Others saw it as a political statement, given Walton's opposition to the Vietnam War. Hank Iba, who had coached the Americans to Olympic gold in 1964 and 1968, was named coach again.

Following their grueling training camp in Colorado Springs—where the team was winnowed to its final twelve players—the team flew off to Munich, Germany, site of the Olympics. "When we got to Munich," Ratleff recalled, "they put us up on the second floor of one of the buildings in the Olympic Village. You could come and go, and you didn't think anything was going to happen . . . It wasn't like anybody was going to come into the village and get you."

One of the thrilling moments for Eddie Rat was to look up one day and spot Phyllis Cooley and Vivian Crisp. They were teachers at East High and had traveled all the way across the Atlantic just to see him play.

The basketball Olympians won seven straight games before the world seemed to stop. On the evening of September 5, a group of Arab terrorists, members of the Black September group, jumped a fence and entered the Olympic Village. Wearing athletic clothing, their assault rifles hidden in duffel bags, they went directly to the dorm where the Israeli athletes were staying. They shot and killed a weightlifter and wrestling coach who tried to stop them, then took nine other athletes and coaches hostage. The basketball players were in a nearby building; some heard the gunshots but thought they were hearing firecrackers. The next day a shootout took place at the airport between the terrorists and West German police. Nine Israeli athletes died in the shootout; five of the terrorists were killed. Many thought the games would be suspended, but they went on, although their luster was lost. The Olympic basketball players reached the final game, against the Soviet Union. It was no surprise, as every USA Olympic basketball team before them had won gold. In a widely disputed call by a referee, in the last seconds the ball got turned over to the Soviet team. The Soviets won, 51–50, on a last-second shot. The Americans were stunned. There were immediate cries of cheating. It was like a bad dream to the American athletes—the killings, the ending of the final game—so surreal as to be unbelievable. As a team they decided not to accept their silver medals.

In 1973 Eddie Ratleff was drafted by the NBA's Houston Rockets. He had a fine five-year career, but it was cut short by persistent back ailments. After his pro career ended, he did some teaching and then became a successful insurance salesman. He continues to live in the Long Beach area, where he stays in shape playing golf. In 2017, he returned to Columbus, where he was inducted into the Ohio High School Hall of Fame. Bo-Pete Lamar got down to the ceremony to join him.

Nick Conner may have played in the shadow of Eddie Ratleff at East High, but he was a star in his own right, a fierce rebounder and an unselfish player. He was pursued by many colleges. Many in Columbus thought he might attend Marshall University in Huntington, West Virginia, because his family had roots in the state. Ohio State, having lost Ratleff, made a halfhearted attempt to woo Conner, but neither he nor his mother felt the effort was genuine.

In the early 1960s, a group of black businessmen in Columbus formed the Cavaliers Club, a men's club where black businessmen and educators gathered. In a way, it was their answer to the white downtown Athletic Club. The Cavaliers Club was wood-paneled, carpeted, and featured a lovely bar. Its one-floor squat building was located right off East Long Street, a five-minute walk from the offices of the black newspaper, the *Call and Post*. Amos Lynch, the newspaper's editor, was a proud Cavaliers Club member. The club held jazzy dances, bestowed scholarship money upon gifted minority students bound for college, commiserated about the heartache flowing across black America, and gathered there on the day King was shot. They also allowed their club to be used for important announcements. So that's where Nick Conner revealed his college choice. Conner phoned his coach, Bob Hart; his running buddy, Eddie Rat; and Ann Ward, his favorite teacher at East High, and asked them to join him. His decision: the University of Illinois, a Big Ten rival of Ohio State. Conner took time to mention both Ohio State and Michigan State by name, wanting all in attendance to know he had spurned them.

Such was Conner's leaping ability, that at only six foot six, he starred at the center position for Illinois, usually playing against players three and four inches taller. He played alongside Nick Weatherspoon, the great Canton-McKinley player whose team the Tigers defeated in the 1969 high school tournament.

During the 1971–72 basketball season, the Illini bested Ohio State in a game played at Illinois, 64–63. The Illinois team later came to Columbus to play Ohio State. Many Tigers were on hand to watch Conner and cheer for him that day, among them Jack Gibbs. While warming up, Conner engaged in a dunking contest with a fellow teammate. He cupped a ball in each hand, soared toward the basket, went up, and dunked both balls coming down from above the rim. There was such pandemonium in the arena that security personnel wondered if something untoward had happened. Conner seemed to be sending a vivid message to Ohio State fans, reminding them of his talent. The Buckeyes got the best of the Illini, however, 103–70. Between those two games Conner averaged 7 rebounds and 8 points. The following season Illinois beat Ohio State in Columbus, 79–68, then lost, 65–64, back on the Illinois campus. In those two games Conner amassed 29 points and 25 rebounds. The civil rights movement in the early 1970s had hardly manifested fully in college athletic departments. Even in a fairly diverse state such as Illinois, the University of Illinois had only two black players during Conner's senior season. The next year the basketball team was all white.

Conner was drafted into the NBA by the Buffalo Braves. His lack of height undermined him at the NBA level. He bounced around the European league for a while but was plagued by knee problems. He returned to Columbus and took a factory job with General Motors. In 2005, Conner was spotted walking around Columbus using a cane. He was ill; it was lung cancer. He died that year. He was fifty-five years old.

Of all the players from the 1969 basketball team, Dwight "Bo-Pete" Lamar had the most uncertain journey to college. Eddie Rat tried to get Long Beach State to take a look at Lamar, but they were not interested.

"I tried to get Western Michigan to offer him a scholarship," says Joe Roberts, the East High alumnus and assistant coach at Western Michigan. Ohio State showed absolutely no interest. During his summer after high school, Lamar would sometimes go to the Ohio State campus to play in one of their indoor gyms. It was mostly high school kids wanting to play hoops. But sometimes, Ohio State varsity basketball players would be there as well. One afternoon Lamar found himself flying down court and facing Luke Witte, Ohio State's seven-foot varsity center. Lamar went skyward and dunked on Witte. On that particular day, OSU Coach Fred Taylor was watching. Taylor rose from his seat and strode out to the court. "He threw us out," Lamar recalls. The seven-footer had been embarrassed.

In 1969, all the basketball guards who came to Ohio State on scholarship were white. Many in Columbus wondered if Lamar's so-called rebel reputation (that Afro!) from North High had somehow infected the minds of college recruiters. As Jack Gibbs knew all too well, it did not take much scurrilous gossip for a black high school athlete's fortunes to turn in a wayward direction. Lamar sat at home waiting for a scholarship offer to come from a big-time university. He had submerged some of his explosiveness to fit in with the East High team, and he was happy about the state championship, but now he wondered if that tactic—scoring less on behalf of the team—had hurt him. He finally began telling family and friends he was going to go to Federal City College, in Washington D.C. It seemed a peculiar choice. Federal City was an open-enrollment school, meaning anyone with a high school degree could get in. The school had just opened in 1968—growing out of civil rights protests— and had suffered financial woes from its beginning. It also lacked a home gymnasium for its basketball team. A player of Lamar's caliber deserved better opportunities than what Federal City College could offer. The school had absolutely no athletic history.

When Beryl Shipley, the coach of the University of Southwestern Louisiana, had come into Columbus to visit Eddie Ratleff and watch him play, he found himself also paying attention to Dwight Lamar on the court. He liked the way Lamar shot and the confidence with which he carried himself on the court. So when Shipley found out Lamar was thinking about going to unheard-of Federal City, he called Jack Gibbs and asked if it was true. Gibbs told him yes, and he also told him Lamar deserved a better scholarship offer. He vouched for Lamar's character and praised him to the skies. Gibbs had persuaded Lamar to come to East for his senior year of high school, so he had a special concern about the direction his former student's future might take. Shipley decided to offer Lamar a scholarship, figuring he just might become a nice role player on his team. Lamar thought long and hard about the offer. He was petrified of going into the Deep South.

Southwestern Louisiana had been notable for being the first university in the South to welcome black students—a small number of them—following the 1954 *Brown* desegregation ruling. The first black basketball player arrived there in 1966. It made national news. By 1969, the flagship university in Louisiana, Louisiana State University, had still not integrated its all-white basketball team.

AN INTERLUDE

Down in Dixie

Beryl Shipley grew up in rural Mississippi. He knew and heard of that world of Negro maids and Negro sharecroppers. He knew of red-eyed former slaves sitting in town squares, old men and women, swollen ankles and arthritic limbs, the life drained from them. He knew of married white men who carried on affairs with Negro women. He knew that Mississippi's William Faulkner and Robert Penn Warren were fascinating figures and writers. And like most who were living in Louisiana in the latter part of the 1950s, as he was then, he knew the name Mack Charles Parker.

On February 23, 1959, June Walters, white, married, and pregnant, was sitting in a Dodge sedan just off U.S. Route 11, a few miles outside of Lumberton, Mississippi. The car had broken down. Her four-year-old daughter was with her. Jimmy, her husband, had gone to get help. Mack Charles Parker, a black man recently out of the army, was in the area, coming from a Negro juke joint not far away. He was in a car with four black friends. They had consumed some moonshine. They came across Walters and left after she informed them her husband was returning. A day later, Walters claimed Parker, having sent his companions onward, had circled back, kidnapped her and her daughter, taken them to a nearby creek, and raped her. Walters picked Parker out of a lineup. Parker vehemently denied the charge. Walters said Parker had a gun. A gun linked to Parker was never found. Parker was jailed a day after the charge. On April 13, he was indicted on charges of rape and kidnapping. On April 25, hooded men broke in to the Mississippi jail where Parker was being held, beat him, and dragged him out, bleeding badly, to a waiting car. The men raced across the state line into Louisiana. Just inside the state, they stopped the car, pulled Parker out, stood him up, and fired bullets into his chest at point-blank range. They then threw him into the Pearl River. Word of the jailhouse abduction hit the newswires. Martin Luther King Jr. notified the U.S. Department of Justice and the FBI. J. Edgar Hoover, FBI director, sent upwards of sixty agents into Mississippi to investigate. Parker's swollen body was pulled from the river on May 4. The FBI agents, in what was widely believed to be a serious and thorough investigation, got confessions from three of the Parker murderers. The agents also identified the other members of the kidnapping-lynching party. The FBI wrote an extensive report and turned it over to the Mississippi prosecutor, expecting indictments. But the prosecutor refused to hand down any indictments. Brave FBI agents then volunteered to testify before the state grand jury themselves. The prosecutor quashed that plan. A federal grand jury also refused to indict the men identified in the Parker killing. To this day, the murder of Mack Charles Parker remains unsolved and the perpetrators unpunished.

Beryl Shipley had been in Lafayette, at the University of Southwestern Louisiana, for two years when the Parker killing occurred. It was the talk of Louisiana. Shipley had been raised in that stark and corrupt world where blacks were terrorized and faced a cruel and indifferent justice system. The South's political heroes were men like George Wallace of Alabama, Strom Thurmond of South Carolina, and Leander Henry Perez of Louisiana. "Bad ones are niggers and good ones are darkies," Perez once said about the black populace of his state. Perez was a lawyer, a liar, a bully, a bigot, and a political intimidator. In 1965, less than 5 percent of the blacks who lived in Perez's Louisiana parish were registered to vote. He routinely sent goons to intimidate would-be black voters.

It was into this racial history and political brew that Bo-Pete Lamar traveled in 1969 to play basketball for the Ragin' Cajuns of the University of Southwestern Louisiana. Before leaving home, he promised his mother, Lucy—who remained frightened of the South—that he would not travel alone after dark if he could help it. Lamar remembers the first evening in his dormitory, settling in, then going to watch TV in a common area. "I was watching TV. And on the channel, they started playing 'I Wish I Was in Dixie.' I said to myself, 'What the hell?'"

He was definitely in Dixie.

It may have had "University" affixed to its name, but the school played in the small college division. As soon as basketball practice got under way, it took Shipley and his coaches little time to realize that Bo-Pete Lamar had come south to make his mark. He stunned onlookers with his offensive prowess, tossing in jump shots from all over the court. He made Houdini-like passes. Shipley couldn't wait for the season to start. He asked his coaches and himself: How did the Ohio colleges not see this kid's talent? Lamar averaged 22 points a game in his freshman year; in the small college division, freshman could play varsity. He was a shoo-in and won Freshman of the Year in the league conference.

By the middle of his sophomore season, Lamar—his Afro now grown to epic proportions—was all the rage for the Ragin' Cajuns: He was leading the *entire* nation in small college basketball scoring, averaging 36 points a game. With no Eddie Rat around, the reins had come off the small stallion. He was unanimously voted first team All-Conference

Bo-Pete Lamar of Southwestern Louisiana and
Eddie Ratleff of Long Beach State. The former East High teammates
were both named UPI first team All-Americans in 1973.

selection. In his sophomore season, on February 25, 1971, Lamar evis-cerated a school record, scoring 62 points against Northeast Louisiana. In Lamar's junior year, the school moved into Division 1. They would be playing bigger schools, against bigger and better basketball players. Lamar didn't care: He scored at a 30-plus clip in the early part of the season. They were the Ragin' Cajuns of Southwestern Louisiana, and Shipley kept telling the kid nobody wanted out of high school to just keep shooting the daggone ball, which he jubilantly did.

Fans couldn't wait for that year's Bayou Classic tournament, which was going to be hosted by the University of Southwestern Louisiana. The teams that were invited included Texas El Paso, Pan American, and Long Beach State, which featured Eddie Ratleff. Jack Gibbs had jour-neyed from Columbus and was in the stands, along with Lee Williams,

East High's track coach. The games shook out in a dream fashion, with Southwestern Louisiana pitted against Long Beach State in the final. Ratleff's team was blisteringly hot, shooting 68 percent, and led at the half, 41–36. Lamar had a frigid first half, making only six of eighteen shots. The game seesawed in the second half, but Lamar stepped up. He had poured in 22 points by the time the Ragin' Cajuns pulled the game out, 90–83. Eddie Rat had 26 points and 8 rebounds. Bo-Pete Lamar and Eddie Rat were named Co-MVP's for the tournament. They stood at midcourt, their cool Afros abloom, to accept their awards. The moment was magical for Jack Gibbs, like something that had been beautifully scripted. He joined his fellow Tigers for an after-game celebration.

That same year, Lamar led all major colleges in scoring with a 36.3 per game average. He was the first player in history to lead the nation in small college scoring one year, then to lead the nation in major college scoring the next. It was an astonishing feat. On the hardwood courts of college basketball, Bo-Pete Lamar was unstoppable. The Cajun fans loved his flamboyant game. Sometimes on campus he was seen sporting a purple leather jacket. Before home games the crowd chanted "Dwight Lamar Superstar," as the band played "Jesus Christ Superstar." Dixie grew on him. But he still wouldn't drive around the Cajun countryside at night alone. In his senior year, Lamar finished sixth in the nation in scoring, and he led the team, once again, to the NCAA tournament, where they lost in the second round to Kansas State, 66–63. That year, Bo-Pete Lamar made the UPI first team All-American squad. The other members were Bill Walton of UCLA, David Thompson of North Carolina State, Doug Collins of Illinois State, and Eddie Ratleff of Long Beach State. Ratleff and Lamar thus became the first two players in NCAA Division 1 college history to have played on the same undefeated high school team and gone on to become first team All-Americans in the same year.

Drafted by the Detroit Pistons, Lamar instead chose to play in the American Basketball Association (as did fellow All-American David Thompson) and, in 1973, signed with the San Diego Conquistadors. First things first: He took care of his mother, Lucy. She never had to scrub another bathtub, save her own. He couldn't make the migraines go away, though she did get better medical attention. The ABA was an enigmatic league with outsized personalities. The league's game ball was red, white, and blue; the Conquistadors' coach was Wilt Chamberlain; and the team's organization was a mess. The team owner had signed Chamberlain as player-coach, but a court battle with Chamberlain's former NBA team, the Lakers, allowed him only to coach. Lamar had a stellar rookie season, averaging 20 points per game. On January 13, 1974, Lamar set the team scoring record, pouring in 50 points against the Indiana Pacers. He played two more years in the ABA, then went to the Los Angeles Lakers. His first season there he suffered a host of injuries, most severely a dislocated bone in his hand. The Lakers let him go after one season, and his basketball career ended.

He returned to Lafayette, became a sales distributor for a beer company, married, and had two daughters. When Hurricane Katrina struck New Orleans in August of 2005, the aftermath affected businesses all across the state. The economic suffering drove Lamar to move back to Columbus. Michael Coleman, the city's first black mayor, helped him get a job in recreation. Coleman thought that players who had gone off and had success in the professional ranks and then returned to the city should have an opportunity to work with inner-city kids.

In 1973, the year Lamar finished college, the NCAA suspended the basketball program at his former college (now known as the University of Louisiana at Lafayette) for two years, citing a slew of NCAA violations when he was there. It remains a painful subject for him, and he says he had no idea how the program was run administratively during his career there. There were supporters of Beryl Shipley who believed it was all about revenge by other white southern coaches who resented Shipley for defeating them with his black players. Shipley's team was penalized for doing things those coaches had been doing with white players for years, Shipley's supporters howled.

In 2016, Bo-Pete Lamar retired from working for the recreation department in his hometown.

Roy Hickman and Larry Walker, the other two starters on the 1969 basketball team, ventured out west, like Eddie Rat, getting scholarships to play basketball at Citrus Junior College. They both had fine careers. Hickman returned to Columbus after two years. "I met a woman, got married." He began rehabbing houses. He'd show up at a Tiger reunion, then he'd go five or so years before attending another one. He still has a bull-like physique, though he has a noticeable limp: the knees sometimes get to throbbing. Walker finished his education at Central State University in Ohio. He didn't play basketball, but he caught the coaching bug. He wound up coaching the boys basketball team at his alma mater, East High, and in 1979 he led the team to a state championship, the first championship since the 1969 Tigers won it all. He now resides in Indianapolis.

Robert Wright, a role player who came off the bench on that 1969 team, went to a business college and still works as a consultant. His business takes him around the world. Sometimes in his travels he'll run into someone who knows someone who went to East High. Then the memories start to swirl. Kevin Smith got a scholarship to George Washington University. Knee problems curtailed his basketball career. He came back to Columbus and finished his degree requirements at Ohio Dominican University. He currently works as a car salesman in the city.

When Bob Hart stepped down from coaching East High in 1971, the school hired Tom Fullove. (He was the school's first black head basketball coach.) Hart became the athletic director at Walnut Ridge High School up until his retirement. He married Millie Cooper, who had been a longtime neighbor. During horse racing seasons, he'd ride out to Scioto Downs Racetrack, where he continued to work in the evenings as he did in many previous years. Whenever a Tiger alumnus appeared at his ticket window and recognized him, they'd start a conversation about his teams. It made him feel good to be remembered. Some of the ticket holders in line would get to grumbling because they wanted to place their bets. One day he arrived home and told Millie he wanted to return to the battlefields of World War II. It caught her off guard, but she was game. He dipped into his savings, got two plane tickets, and off they flew. As they walked the battlefields where he had fought, Millie could tell how meaningful it was to him to be there. He stared quietly out over the terrain and summoned names of the dead. He was an old soldier tasting the salt air and remembering the bloody cost of freedom.

It began to upset Bob Hart that no one called him for induction into the Ohio High School Athletic Association Hall of Fame. Coaches with less stellar records than his were being inducted. He'd been voted Ohio Class AA coach of the year three times. And that was the top high school division in the state. What more did it take? He'd heard what was said behind his back: That those teams he coached on the segregated East Side were just naturally gifted; that it didn't take a genius to coach them. The more astute coaches knew otherwise. "He kept saying to me," recalls Paul Pennell, "'I don't want to go in posthumously.'" But Bob Hart died in Venice, Florida, in 2005, and his Ohio Hall of Fame induction didn't come until two years later, in 2007. Even with the Hall of Fame honor, Hart's daughters have never thought their father was properly appreciated, especially for his progressive racial outlook. "I can remember," says Sherri, "me and Dad sitting at the counter of the Novelty Food Bar. We'd be the only white people in there."

There was little doubt that Garnett Davis would be drafted by a professional baseball team. The scouts had been eyeing him since his junior year of high school. He had also become something of a local legend playing American Legion summer ball. He had made first team All-State in Ohio as a catcher and was named to several All-Star teams. So it was a joyful event for Davis and his family when he was drafted in the third round, in June of 1969, and signed by the New York Mets, the team that was racing to a World Series championship that year. Lloyd Gearhart was the Ohio scout who had pushed for Davis. In the 1940s, Gearhart had played in the minor leagues for the Atlanta Crackers of the Southern Association. Blacks knew to steer clear of the all-white Crackers and their ballpark. After his playing days were over, Gearhart did some scouting around Ohio and Kentucky for the Mets, and Davis caught his attention.

Garnett Davis received a $15,000 signing bonus. To a poor kid on the

East Side of Columbus, it was a princely sum. He was very proud that he was now able to help out his hardworking mother.

The Mets assigned him to one of their AA minor league teams and he reported to Marion, Virginia. Garnett had little understanding of how difficult it was to ascend the ladder in professional baseball. Less than 10 percent of drafted players actually make it to the big leagues. Garnett, unwittingly, added to his long odds. The team had another player slated to start at the catcher position on their Virginia minor league team, and they told Garnett he'd be playing third base. "They didn't want to waste his speed as a catcher," Paul Pennell says of the Mets. But the switch confused and upset Garnett. He kept telling anyone in the organization who would listen that he was a catcher. But professional baseball coaches aren't in the business of bending to bruised egos; there are simply too many players in any organization who are willing to do whatever is asked of them. He had a decent enough rookie campaign, and the following season, Garnett Davis made the twenty-seven-man Mets roster for the Florida Instructional League. The team played in Pompano Beach, Florida. It didn't take long for his complaints to start up again. He wanted to catch. But there was already a catcher in Pompano Beach, and the Mets liked him. In the eyes of Mets officials, Garnett became a malcontent. The next season, he made the self-defeating move of asking the Mets organization for his unconditional release, imagining such a request might force the team to yield to his demands. But on April 5, 1972, Garnett received a Certified Letter in the mail. At the top of the letter from the Mets, in bold print, was written: OFFICIAL NOTICE OF DISPOSITION OF PLAYER'S CONTRACT AND SERVICES—National Association of Professional Baseball Leagues.

In the middle of the letter there were four words, surrounded by a lot of white space, as if to starkly emphasize the point the team wished to make: "You are released unconditionally."

Garnett couldn't help but be surprised by the suddenness of the Mets' reaction. But he had, in effect, cut himself out of the organization. Pennell, his high school coach, was bewildered that Garnett had demanded his release after a little more than two years. "There are ten- and twelve-year minor league players," Pennell says, pointing out that players who stay in the league for their entire careers can still make a good living.

There were discussions between Garnett and the Cincinnati Reds about getting into their minor league system, but the talks went nowhere. He was adrift. Garnett attended some baseball games back in Columbus; people listened to his long spiel about what had happened. He began saying that he had been "blackballed" by the Mets, a term connoting underhanded banishment. He began losing sleep. All his life, he had played baseball. In 1975, he enrolled at Central State University, in Wilberforce, Ohio, and majored in recreation. One day, on campus, in his dorm room, he began wondering if he had been too impatient, if he had foolishly tossed away the dream he had possessed since junior high school. So he swallowed his pride and wrote to Joe McDonald, the Mets general manager. It was a one-page typed letter. At the outset, he explained how much he missed baseball. But then the letter quickly took on an accusatory tone, saying that the Mets had misused him by putting him at third base. He also said he had not received "proper compensation" for having been a third-round draft choice, and he wondered if his race had anything to do with his treatment. The letter finally swooped back around by its conclusion with a plea. "May I have a second chance," he asked the Mets general manager. "I am ready to play baseball the way you want it played. I want to be a pro. I want to supplement my baseball dreams with reality."

Joe McDonald might have thought of tossing such a letter away. But he had grace, even empathy, and wrote back. His letter, dated May 23, 1975, reached Garnett in Wilberforce. It started out with McDonald warmly and personally recalling Garnett as a Mets draft choice. But it quickly veered back to answering Garnett's charges against the Mets. "The New York Mets gave you every opportunity to show your ability, but, unfortunately, the potential which we initially saw in you as a player never fully developed," McDonald wrote. "We certainly did not resent the fact that we were wrong or you did not succeed. We fully understand when we sign a player he only has one chance in ten of making it to the Major Leagues. It is a long and difficult road." McDonald went on, intent, in a very down-to-earth manner, to defend the character of the

Mets. "Garnett, you know as well as I how we worked with you and tried to get you to the Major Leagues. Neither the color of one's skin nor the bonus he receives for signing have any bearing on the outcome. It is strange that four other players who made it to the majors were mentioned. . . . namely John Milner, Dave Schneck, George Theodore and Bob Apodaca. If we were to combine their aggregate bonuses, they would not approach the amount you received for signing." A young man sitting in a dormitory room in Wilberforce, Ohio, reading such a letter, might certainly have reeled from the directness of it, but he would also have had to appreciate the respect and reasoned tone it conveyed. "Regardless," McDonald concluded, "we just have to concentrate on signing younger players in the hopes we come up with a Major Leaguer. I hope you can understand and we wish you nothing but the best in the future." Garnett Davis never heard from the Mets again.

Davis got his college degree in 1977 from Central State University, then took a job with the American Electric Power company in Columbus. He worked there for seventeen years, mostly answering emergency calls about downed power lines. Most weekends he found a baseball game to play in. He continues to live in Columbus and has started a small baseball training camp for kids. It's a modest endeavor; he does all the printing for the brochures himself. On a recent visit to his home, I spotted a brand-new baseball sitting idly on the dining room table. At sixty-seven years old, he still looks fit enough to belt a couple balls into the bleachers.

Ray Scott, who periodically took over the catcher position when Coach Pennell moved players around, enrolled at the Columbus College of Art and Design after high school. It's a well-regarded school and a pricey one. He lasted less than a year because of money woes. He then joined the Air Force. The Vietnam War was still going on, and he got orders to go. Then someone in the Air Force was smart enough to realize he already had two brothers, Ken and Jesse, who were Marines serving in Vietnam, and the Air Force determined maybe that was enough sacrifice for the Scott family. His Vietnam orders were rescinded at the last minute, although he spent a career in the Air Force. Afterward, he returned to Columbus. He now works for the city's bus company on a specialized route, picking up and taking seniors where they need to go. Ray Scott's wife, Cynthia, is the daughter of the late Hiram Tanner, the onetime sports editor of the *Call and Post*.

As gifted and fearless as Norris Smith was on the Tiger mound, he could not garner the attention of professional baseball scouts. But that didn't much matter to him, because Capital University in Columbus offered him a scholarship. In his freshman year, he pitched a no-hitter. He retired as a Columbus schoolteacher.

In the mid-1990s, Roger Neighbors, the Tiger shortstop that victorious year of 1969, was walking across East Broad Street—near East High School—and by the time he saw the bus, it was too late. The impact left him severely injured, forcing him to go on disability. Every now and then Coach Pennell would go pick him up and they'd go out to Jet Stadium to watch the Columbus Clippers minor league team play. His health deteriorated. When he died in 2000, his friends later told stories at his funeral of what a great high school shortstop he had been.

In high school, it was hard not to envy Robert Kuthrell, the right fielder, just a little: He could make it home to dinner before every other Tiger after baseball practice. His family lived in a white house on a hill above Harley Field; he could get there in less than seven minutes. Sometimes he'd race up the hill, reach his porch, and turn around and wave at the players going by. He played baseball at Miami University, in Oxford, Ohio. He later moved to Illinois, where he worked for many years. When his father, William, died on March 28, 2005, Robert returned to Columbus for the funeral. While in Columbus, on April 2, Robert himself suffered a heart attack and died. He was fifty-three years old. His mortified family had to hold a double funeral.

Erkie Byrd, the star pitcher on the 1967–68 East High baseball team, who had gone off to Vietnam right after high school (actually completing two tours), made it back home. The old-timers in the neighborhood who would see him out and about after his military service told him he was as good as Eddie Rat on the mound. He would just chuckle. He worked in Columbus seventeen years for the Ohio Bureau of Workmen's Compensation, helping veterans with their paperwork about Agent Orange, the chemical spray that was used to defoliate the forests in Vietnam but that entered the respiratory system of American soldiers with devastating effects. Byrd died in 2008 at age fifty-seven. He had been suffering for years from his own exposure to Agent Orange.

Coach Pennell, in later years, always took time, when someone asked about that 1969 baseball team, to mention the juniors on the squad. "When we came down the stretch," he says, "those juniors were really important. They stepped up." Those juniors were Phil Mackey, Robert Kuthrell, Richard Twitty, Leroy Crozier, Larry Mann, Tony Brown, and Kenny Mizelle. They all returned for their senior season.

When he was a high school senior, Kenny Mizelle dreamed of going to California to play college baseball. "I thought I could play for UCLA." The ghost, his father, was out in California, supposedly dead, only not really. Instead of going to the West Coast, Mizelle remained in Columbus and went to Ohio Dominican College, now Ohio Dominican University. He played point guard on the basketball team and set some school assist records. After college, he married Cynthia Chapman, his sweetheart from East High, went to work in banking, had a son, later divorced, and became a fairly popular deejay in the city. He's retired now and living in a suburb of Columbus.

Ernie Locke, the lone sophomore on the baseball team that year, abruptly left baseball behind in his junior and senior years of high school. His decision surprised and disappointed Coach Pennell. A seemingly promising career simply ended. "My girlfriend didn't want me to play," Locke says. "And, well, so I didn't." She was his first serious girlfriend. He continued to work at the grocery store on Mount Vernon Avenue. After high school, he enrolled at Ohio State. Walking around campus his freshman year, the fall weather sweet, the World Series on television, a thought came to him: He wondered if the Ohio State baseball coach might be interested in a onetime pitcher who had played for the East High School state championship baseball team three years earlier. No, he was not. He worked some blue-collar jobs but decided he wanted more for himself. He got admitted to the police academy and became a police officer. In thirteen years on the force, he never fired his weapon and was grateful for that. But the job wore him down. "I once got a call to the West Side of town. A home had been burglarized. The white lady standing at the door wouldn't let me come in and investigate. She said, 'You're not coming inside my house. I want a white officer.'" He left the force after thirteen years. When he thinks of the baseball championship, he often thinks of the day the entire team was standing tall together in front of the school during the celebration. "Standing up there with the team," he says, "was so inspiring to me. I think that's the reason I never got in trouble as a teen." Ernie is also retired now.

Paul Pennell eventually left East High and became a coach at Briggs High, also in Columbus. In 1991, he took Briggs to the final four of the state basketball tournament. They didn't win, but it was a proud moment. He has amassed a shelf full of honors and awards for his coaching and community service. He and Sharon get out to all the East High reunions. At the reunions, they don't even have to ask; he insists on singing the Tiger fight song. And there he stands, white man, crew cut, contorting himself:

> I went down to the river
> Oh yeah
> And I started to drown
> Oh yeah
> I started thinking about them Tigers
> Oh yeah
> And I came back around

They crack up. They're crazy about him. Every now and then, Sharon Pennell—lifelong teacher and community volunteer—will be in the kitchen in the early morning, brewing coffee. There's a knock at the back door. Garnett Davis. "We'll just sit and talk," she says. At one of the 1969 baseball banquets, Garnett had singled Sharon Pennell out, telling the audience that at the away games that final baseball season, she often was the only Tiger supporter in the visitors' section. She got tears in her eyes.

Throughout much of 2017, Sharon was in and out of the hospital with kidney problems and other ailments. Sometimes, back at home, in her special hospital bed, Paul would hear her cackling on the phone. It was Eddie Rat, calling from the West Coast. Sharon died on September 3, 2017.

In 1971, Jack Gibbs announced he was leaving East High. He wanted to try something new after having been in the Columbus school system for twenty-seven years. There was a dinner and testimonial for him at East High. He was given many gifts, and the school auditorium was renamed in his honor. Hampton Kelley, a singer and East High graduate, flew in from South Carolina just to sing "If I Can Help Somebody."

Gibbs subsequently got a lot of speaking invitations. He liked to tell audiences that the 1968–69 school year at East High was quite special to him because of its unforgettable twin championships, yes, but also that it was the first full class to graduate following the King assassination— and that year the school had the highest number of graduates go on to two- or four-year colleges in the school's history. "At least 30 percent that year went on to some kind of college," says Roger Dumaree, the vice principal at the time.

One day not long after he had left East High, Jack Gibbs was riding downtown, going to a meeting. Phillip Pool, a young white teacher Gibbs had hired at East High in the fall of 1968, was in the car with him. Gibbs wanted to discuss future business opportunities but also wanted Pool to catch him up on what was going on at East High. Through the car window, Gibbs spotted a haggard and disheveled figure pushing a grocery cart. It wasn't his first time seeing this man downtown. Pool half glanced at the man as the car slowly kept rolling. "Jack turned to me," Pool recalls, "and said, 'Phil, did you see that man pushing that cart?' I said, 'Yes.' Jack said, 'That's my father.' I didn't know how to respond. It was one of the most shattering things that ever happened to me."

Clarence Gibbs, Jack Gibbs's father, was staying at the Faith Mission, a homeless shelter in downtown Columbus. Every year the Gibbs family had a family reunion in Harlan, Kentucky. And every year Clar-

ence Gibbs showed up—in suit and tie. He always looked more like a
tired businessman in a tired-looking suit than a homeless figure. Jack
Gibbs was amazed at how his father always pulled himself together for
these reunions. Clarence told whoppers about how well he was doing in
Columbus. The truth was, no matter how much his son tried to help his
father, he couldn't keep Clarence away from the bottle. Jack Gibbs continued to spot his father in downtown Columbus, pushing the grocery
cart, shambling about like some Stagolee figure.

Jack Gibbs took a steady job directing a program called Educational
Resources, under the umbrella of the Model Cities program, a nationwide antipoverty program. From a tiny office on Bryden Road, not far
from East High, he helped college-bound minority kids get scholarship
money. They were overwhelmingly first-generation college students. He
still worked long hours. Ruth kept on him about his weight, and his
blood pressure medication. He nodded and basically ignored her. Every
year he went back to Harlan, Kentucky, to put flowers on the grave of his
little sister. Sometimes, looking around Harlan, he couldn't believe how
far he had come, both from the town and in life. Everyone in Harlan
was proud of him.

One day, Jack Gibbs decided Columbus should have a career center
for high school students, something that would incorporate the arts and
vocational learning. It would be akin to New York City's High School
for the Performing Arts, but even more ambitious than that because
it would offer many innovative challenges; he envisioned more than a
dozen one- and two-year intensive programs. Gibbs poured every brilliant idea he ever had about education into this concept. The school
opened in 1976 and was labeled a magnet school. It's now known as
the Fort Hayes Metropolitan Education Center, and it has a national
reputation.

On June 22, 1982, Ruth Gibbs was rushing about because she had to
get out the door for church. Jack wasn't going; he wanted to catch up on
some reading. "I said, 'Honey, give me some money to put in the church
basket,'" she recalls. He did and off she went. She came home to get his
supper going, then went right back out to get to Bible study. That evening, when she arrived back home, Jack Gibbs was in a coma; he'd had

a massive stroke, from which he would never recover. He'd always found it hard to stick to the routine of taking his prescribed medication. His death, at age fifty-one, shocked the community.

In the 2016–17 NCAA college basketball season, those who rapaciously followed the sport heard the name Jack Gibbs quite a bit. He was one of the highest-scoring guards in the nation for the Davidson College basketball team. He is the namesake and grandson of Jack Gibbs.

16

Blood in Ohio

The sixties seemed to fight very hard to prevent coming to a close. It often felt like the social protest war on the home front was endless.

Anyone waking up in Columbus, Ohio, on July 21, 1969—six weeks after the Class of 1969 graduated from East High School—could tell it was going to be quite a warm day. But there was also a great feeling of hope and joy in the air. The Apollo 11 moon landing, a day earlier, had been successful, causing the nation to celebrate. President Nixon announced that government offices would be closed the following day in honor of the landing. But in Columbus, when that next day came, something else happened that added yet another bloody scar to the city and the racially haunted sixties.

Dave Chestnut was a white businessman who owned the Pad and Pillow Place, a dry-cleaning operation on East Main Street. Not many people in the community knew much about Chestnut, except that he was stern, constantly scolding children—no matter their race—who ran and played around his establishment. His yelling and berating of black children touched an especially raw nerve among parents in the black community. They warned him to be mindful of their children. Chestnut was sixty-nine years old, set in his ways, and mean. He took up the habit of breaking bottles and sprinkling the shards of glass around his yard, cackling when barefooted children cried out from the pain of their bloody feet. Tony Johnson was a four-year-old black child who lived near Chestnut's establishment. The boy ambled into Chestnut's business that morning. In no time, he was dashing from the store, fleeing home, where he told his stepfather, Roy Beasley, that he had been struck by the man behind the counter—Dave Chestnut. Beasley, twenty-seven, was a sanitation worker for the city, and he had the day off because of the moon landing. He walked over to the dry-cleaning store. Words were quickly exchanged as Beasley stood in the doorway. Shots suddenly rang out. Beasley slumped to the floor; two bullets had hit him directly in the heart. "Have you had enough?" Chestnut shouted at the bleeding and dying black man. The police and an ambulance raced to the scene. When they arrived, Chestnut was standing, gun in hand, casually smoking a cigarette. It was too late to save Beasley. Blacks started to congregate. Many hissed when Chestnut was escorted to the police cruiser, without handcuffs, sauntering as if he didn't have a care in the world. Martha Beasley, wife of the slain man, came upon the scene. She started wailing; neighbors rushed to her side. Hours later, the rebellion started. During the next two days, forty fires were started. The community was under siege. Rocks and bricks flew through windows. Stores were looted. George Stultz, fifty-three at the time, cared about the neighborhood. He was white, had friends in the area, and was a member of a crime watch group. During the intense melee, he realized that someone needed to direct traffic, so he stepped out into the street and proceeded to do so. A sniper's bullet struck and killed him. The police presence got heavier. Gov. Jim Rhodes called out the National Guard. More than twelve hundred guardsmen eventually arrived. Thirty-six people suffered injuries of varying degrees. Violence broke out in other parts of the city as well. A year later, Chestnut, the shooter, was acquitted of all charges.

The shooting of Beasley—and subsequent acquittal of Chestnut—also woke up many students at Ohio State University, who were not only continuing to protest the Vietnam War but also were assailing police brutality in the city. Mayor Sensenbrenner, the city's East High Tigers self-appointed mascoting cheerleader, expectedly positioned himself firmly on the side of law and order.

On February 16, 1970—seven months after the Beasley shooting—six hundred people stood before the Columbus City Council to talk about police brutality. Mayor Sensenbrenner presided. His words hardly soothed the gathering. "We will not make changes just because some militant groups make demands to suit their own self seeking interests," he said. Many wondered: Was the mayor so tin-eared he couldn't hear what was going on around the country, out on the streets, on college campuses? Having only attended Bible college out west for a brief time, Sensenbrenner saw college kids much the same way as he saw high school kids: They should be taking orders from parents, listening to and obeying their elders. His senselessness began to grate. With good reason, Sensenbrenner considered the campus of Ohio State hostile territory.

Beginning in the mid-1960s, Ohio State students—even if schools on the West and East Coasts received more attention for their activism—had been staging their noisy protests against the war in Vietnam and inequality. Now the Nixon administration had emboldened their ire.

On April 29, 1970, at a noon rally, two thousand white and black students massed on the OSU campus in a show of protest. They held signs aloft: "On Strike; Close It Down"; "100 Years of Racism." Strike leader Lorraine Cohen told the gathering, "Apathetic students are finally getting together and showing their power together on campus." She cautioned against any use of violence. But hours later, along Neil Avenue on the campus, violence erupted. A group of Ohio Highway Patrolmen, bolstered by two hundred Columbus police officers outfitted in riot gear, fired teargas into a group of marching students. The police made arrests, swinging their batons. Students threw bottles at buildings. That evening, a National Guard riot battalion stormed the campus. The next day, April 30, upwards of five hundred National Guardsmen were on the Ohio State campus. The guardsmen had eight-round clips in their rifles. Now more than four thousand students gathered themselves on the campus Oval. The guardsmen, on orders from superiors, told the students to disperse. Then they unleashed the teargas. The yelling and running began. But some of those running stopped, picked up the tear-gas canisters, and flung them back at the guardsmen, who began coughing and suffering from burning eyes. They had to quickly don gas masks.

On May 1, a nation's attention suddenly turned to downtown Kent, Ohio, where a melee erupted. Kent, 139 miles from Columbus, was home to Kent State University. The confrontation was between local police, bar patrons, and students. It began as an anti-Vietnam protest, then turned unmanageable. Someone lit a bonfire; a brick went flying through a bank window, setting off an alarm. Before the evening ended, teargas was used to disperse the crowd. On Friday, May 2, the Kent State University ROTC building was burned to the ground. Campus officials panicked, unsure how to react. On May 3, Gov. Rhodes flew to Kent to assess the situation. He was, at the time, running for a U.S. Senate seat. Now was time to strut his law-and-order bona fides. At a press conference, he referred to student protesters as "the worst kind of people we harbor in America . . . I think that we're up against the strongest, well-trained, militant revolutionary group that has ever assembled in America." He went on: "We're going to eradicate the problem, we're not going to treat the symptoms." Rhodes sent an order for the Ohio National Guard to descend upon the town of Kent and Kent State University. On May 3, a Sunday, an uneasy peace descended on the campus, marred by small bursts of teargas being thrown. Then the troops arrived the following day, when the students, now more defiant than ever, vowed to hold another rally. More than two thousand students, unarmed, gathered. At midday, without warning, a volley of shots rang out from the guardsmen. Within seconds, four students—Jeffrey Glenn Miller, twenty; Allison Krause, nineteen; William Schroeder, nineteen; Sandra Scheuer, twenty—lay dead. Two of them had been part of the protest, while two others had simply been trying to get to class. It was a shocking, horrific, and bloody scene. Nine others were injured by National Guard gunfire. News of the killings quickly spread across the country. Colleges and high schools closed. Students at New York University hung a banner: "They Can't Kill Us All." Mississippi Highway Patrol officers, responding to rocks being thrown at motorists, fired into a dormitory on the campus of Jackson State University ten days after the Kent State shootings. Phil-

lip Gibbs, twenty-one, a Jackson State student, and James Green, a high
school student, were both killed. There were no charges in the Jackson State shootings, although the President's Commission on Campus
Unrest concluded that the shootings were unjustified.

In the fall of 1970, a presidential commission issued a report also pro-
claiming that the Kent State shootings were unjustified. Eight guardsmen who had been at Kent State were indicted on civil rights charges.
All the charges were later dismissed.

Jim Rhodes lost his bid for a U.S. Senate seat. (He would win re-
election to the governor's office in 1974.)

Amos Lynch, editor of the *Call and Post*, was not known for taking
on the local police department in his newspaper. But in 1971 something
happened that changed his mind: William Allen, a World War II vet
and a local doctor, was beaten by police in a restaurant. Mayor Sensenbrenner would not condemn the beating. The day before the mayoral
election, the *Call and Post* landed in stores and newsstands around the
city. Taking up a full page was a searing montage of all the recent victims
of police brutality with their disfigured faces, swollen jaws, and busted
lips. Sensenbrenner lost his re-election bid.

Hiram Tanner retired from newspaper writing in 1976. However, he
continued contributing columns to Amos Lynch's newspaper. One of his
last columns was about the forlorn journey of Kenny Mizelle Sr. to make
it onto the Kansas City Athletics baseball roster in the 1950s.

17

Sins Laid Bare

Columbus activist Sam Gresham felt that mistreatment of blacks by police would have far-reaching reverberations. "It was the issue of police brutality that gave people the courage to take on school segregation," he said.

For so many years, teachers in Columbus knew that the schools that served their children were poorly funded. Their textbooks were often outdated. Everyone knew when the school board assigned black teachers—even those who lived in modestly integrated neighborhoods and had enough seniority to work in those neighborhoods—they would assign them to black schools on the East Side. It was a pernicious pattern. More often than not, the black teacher would then choose to move his or her family to the East Side, thus reinforcing the city's segregation. "The thing that most of us black teachers realized were the inequities in the facilities, and the school materials," says Catherine Willis, who began her teaching career in 1955 in Columbus at all-black Beatty Elementary School. "It wasn't about going to school with white children."

If one wanted to examine how the American government abetted racial real estate segregation, all one needed to do was study what hap-

pened in Levittown, New York, after World War II. Following the end
of the war, there was a hunger for housing and an extreme shortage
of it. William Levitt came from a building family. At the end of the
war, Levitt scooped up a thousand acres of potato farmland in Long
Island, New York. In 1947, he finally broke ground with an intention of building seventeen thousand homes. He imagined the building
process would move fast, like General Motors and their car building
machinery. Lumber was cheap because Levitt bought a whole forest
in Oregon. A two-bedroom house sold for $7,900. The government
joined the enterprise because the Federal Housing Administration provided loans. Levitt played into the politics of the times. "No man who
owns his own house and lot can be a communist," he said. "He [has]
too much to do." Thus began the explosion of the American suburbs.
There was something else about what would come to be known as Levittown: it was all white. The Levitt housing contracts forbade resale
to blacks. "We can solve a housing problem, or we can try to solve a
racial problem," Levitt said. "But we can't do both." In Columbus, as
elsewhere, all-white suburbs grew; blacks were squeezed into the inner
city and into housing projects.

Catherine and Ed Willis came to Columbus in 1955 to teach. They
were lured to the city by J. Arnett Mitchell, the principal of Champion Junior High School. Mitchell was born in Gallipolis, Ohio, a river
town just across the Ohio border from West Virginia. Blacks in Gallipolis attended Lincoln High School. Now and then, a black applied
to the all-white Union High School, only to be denied. Mitchell finished fifth in his senior class, which numbered eighty-seven students. He
went off to Maine in 1909 to attend Bowdoin College. He was only the
fourth black student the school had ever admitted. He graduated a year
early, in 1912. During summers back home in Gallipolis, Mitchell was
befriended by Edward Alexander Bouchet, the new principal at Mitchell's old high school. Bouchet saw brilliance in Mitchell and became
his mentor. Bouchet had been recruited to Lincoln from Philadelphia's
Institute for Colored Youth. He had taught chemistry there for more

than two decades. He was a Yale man, the school's first black graduate in 1874. He was also the first black to earn a doctorate from Yale, which he was awarded in 1876, in physics. When he arrived in Gallipolis, Bouchet brought astounding credentials with him and a desire, in spite of the deep-rooted segregation in America, to get the best out of his charges. When Bouchet met J. Arnett Mitchell, he was reminded of his younger self. While at Bowdoin, Mitchell got a Phi Beta Kappa key (the highest of academic honors); he graduated cum laude. "I stood among them but not one of them—and yet at heart I was," Mitchell forlornly remarked beneath a class photo of himself.

Following graduation, Mitchell went abroad to study in Germany. Back in the United States, white institutions considered him nearly freakish: a Negro with a Bowdoin degree, international study behind him, and a Phi Beta Kappa key to boot. White academic officials nodded at his potent credentials and wished him well. All-black Tuskegee Institute in Alabama finally gave him a job teaching English. It was not his field of expertise, but he was brilliant and could adapt. He most certainly needed the income. His next step was becoming a dean at all-black Southern University in Baton Rouge, Louisiana. In 1921, Mitchell received a job offer from up north, from Columbus, Ohio. He was lured to all-black Champion Junior High School to become its principal. A tall man with a deep voice, at first he was snickered at by kids who wanted to mock his authority. He ignored the mockery and established a commanding presence. He knew he was the most accomplished black academic the city had ever seen. He wore his Phi Beta Kappa key around his neck because he wanted the black parents, teachers, and students to be inspired by the honor he had received. And for decades he inspired those teachers in Columbus, dining with the likes of Jack Gibbs and others who cared about the fate of the city's black children. Mitchell remained at Champion—watching less qualified whites take up principal positions all over the city—constantly battling for better resources and materials, which rarely came. He died in 1969, living long enough to feel the stirrings of the civil rights movement and sense the glory East High had given the city. "He was absolutely brilliant," teacher Catherine Willis recalls of him.

When she arrived in Columbus with her husband, Ed, from Cleveland to begin teaching, Catherine Willis was assigned to Beatty Elementary School; Ed to Champion Junior High. Both were surprised at the lack of black political voices regarding education. "They weren't as militant," she says of Columbus blacks, comparing them to blacks in her native Cleveland. "Ed and I would say that the further south you go in the state of Ohio, the more docile blacks would become. Once you got to Cincinnati, you were in the South."

Columbus was not Greenville, Mississippi, or Baton Rouge, Louisiana, or Selma, Alabama. Columbus was a northern city, a state capital, quite conservative, and the power brokers liked it that way. School officials systematically orchestrated a violation of the 1954 *Brown* school desegregation decision. That was why Beatty Elementary, Felton Elementary, Franklin Junior High, Monroe Junior High, Champion Junior High, and East High all remained black schools in spite of laws that had been passed to ensure black children received an equal opportunity education. Jack Gibbs had seen this system at work, had witnessed its churning gears. He was an educator, not a lawyer, and the only way he imagined he could effect change was to get inside the system and work from the inside, demanding the most from his teachers and students. What the parents of Columbus schoolchildren needed was a voice that would hammer the city with the virtuous might and weight of the Fourteenth Amendment. And they needed a judge who would hold the city accountable for its sins against equal education. President Richard Nixon, of all people, was about to give the black parents of Columbus just such a judge.

The East High School Class of 1969 was the first class at the school to graduate during Nixon's presidency. His campaign had made them nervous, and the first six months of his presidency only magnified that unease. There was not a single black serving in the Nixon cabinet. The administration's tone was stark, a law-and-order mandate aimed at the inner cities. There was talk of many millions of dollars added to the war on drugs, which meant sending police en masse into urban areas, targeting blacks. Such coded words were well understood throughout the urban ghettos of America. The reality of all this frightened Jack Gibbs, and it was one of the many things that hastened his exit from East High School: He felt it was time to do more to get black students into colleges.

Nixon won re-election in 1972 by a walloping margin, carrying forty-nine states. His opponent, George McGovern, won only Massachusetts and the District of Columbia. But Nixon's past—of paranoia, lying, and engaging in unethical behavior—was about to catch up with him.

On June 17, 1972, a group of burglars broke in to the offices of the Democratic National Committee at the Watergate complex in Washington. They were soon linked to the Nixon White House. Before long, it turned into a scandal that would unleash dark moods and ravings inside the White House. "Never forget, the press is the enemy," Nixon screeched to his aides. "The press is the enemy . . . The establishment is the enemy. The professors are the enemy." Senate investigations and probes were begun. Some were televised. Aides started to turn on one another inside the White House. "We're being blackmailed . . . people are going to start perjuring themselves very quickly that have not had to perjure themselves to protect other people," John Dean, a Nixon aide, warned the president. The pressure became hotter by the day inside the White House. Days felt like months. With so much of the White House's attention devoted to enduring what became known as Watergate, it was a good time to get a judge nominated to the federal bench, and that is exactly what Attorney General William Saxbe intended to do.

Saxbe had been named Nixon's attorney general in January of 1974. Nixon's previous two attorneys general had been linked to Watergate and had to go. The third attorney general entering the quagmire, Elliott Richardson, quit when Nixon sought to diminish the scope of the Watergate special prosecutor. There were resignations throughout the Department of Justice. In June, with the Nixon presidency in a death spiral, Saxbe helped move the wheels to get Robert Duncan an open federal judgeship in Columbus. The Senate approved Duncan, making him the first black federal district court judge in Columbus. Two months later, in August, Nixon resigned.

Throughout the 1940s, 1950s, and 1960s, even as blacks knew the

Columbus school system was segregated, they lacked the proper muscle to do much about it. While there were a few brave souls, such as David Hamlar, a dentist elected to the school board, and William "Wild Bill" Davis, an attorney, they were too few and seen, by most whites, merely as nuisances. The NAACP in Columbus—unlike aggressive branches of that civil rights organization in Dayton and Cleveland—found it hard to exert power. "Dayton had the black unions. Cleveland had angry people. The soft people stayed in Columbus," says Sam Gresham, referring to the black migration into Ohio's cities. Gresham arrived in the city in 1974 by way of Chicago and Mississippi. He knew how to protest. He became an activist, aiming to focus on the segregated school situation.

In 1969, a parallel narrative was rising. Teachers were holding secret meetings in homes, advocating that something must be done about school segregation. The Tiger athletic teams were winning; the Tiger debate team was winning. But teachers and parents were losing the battle for school integration. All eyes focused on East High, and Sam Gresham, the activist, knew why. "East had given the community such pride," he says. "And it *was* the focus of the black community." Catherine Willis realized as much as well. "East High had the same kind of thing that people felt about black colleges: You wanted to show it to the world. You wanted to show that black kids there were as good as anybody. East High was a source of pride for everybody."

The school board was flexing its attitude, and it was vehemently opposed to busing. The white members of the board listened heartily to the anti-busing chorus in the city. "There will be no busing strictly for racial balance if I can help it," said Virginia Prentice, who won a school board seat in 1972 and played to the fears of whites in the city. The cries about the need for some kind of remedy took on a higher volume all around. Blacks announced runs for political office. (A black candidate ran for mayor and lost.) Business leaders began to get nervous: The state capital had an image to maintain.

The school board, under intense pressure, finally announced a plan called the Columbus Plan—which was, more or less, a voluntary transfer plan. Critics pounced on it, rightfully concluding that since it would allow no money to move students around on buses, it would hardly assure authentic integration. School board member David Hamlar was incensed. He had gone to Virginia's segregated schools in his youth. He did not want the black kids of Columbus to continue enduring the same fate. "I'm almost willing to bet my life savings that we will get a suit within two years," Hamlar predicted.

Black parents in the city needed help, and some of it came from NAACP attorneys outside the city. In 1973, along with three other groups—the Columbus Area Civil Rights Council, the Northwest Area Council on Human Rights, and the local NAACP—parents planned their legal assault. They were going to sue the city. Bill Davis, one of the attorneys, saw no other option. Referring to the city's pattern of building schools in segregated areas, "Wild Bill" said, "We're getting ready to build edifices which could set the pattern of attendance for two generations or more. If the board doesn't start doin', we'll start suin.'"

The local black publication, the *Call and Post*, accused the school system of backing "a construction program covertly planned to continue, forever, racial segregation of Columbus schoolchildren." Amos Lynch, a longtime Republican, usually adopted a reserved tone on his editorial page, owing to the advertising dollars he counted on. But the school board had gotten his goat. He accused its white members of playing "sadistic racial games" with the black community and its schools.

On June 21, 1973, the pro-integration forces filed a complaint with federal judge Carl Rubin, asking him to stop the board from its school building program because it was promoting segregation. Months later Rubin convened a hearing to determine if it was necessary to issue an injunction. Witnesses testified all morning. Rubin made his announcement, all but telling the plaintiffs they were aiming too low, that they should take the entire school system to court. The case, in his mind, was far more insidious than just the construction of buildings. "If plaintiffs are willing to file an amended complaint," he told them, "that issue may be adjudicated in court." Between the legalese, Rubin was telling the plaintiffs: You have a case.

John Ellis, the Columbus schools superintendent, tried to nudge the

white members of the school board away from their intransigence, but
it didn't work. They turned on him. "It was obvious," Ellis later said,
"that there was a move at the time to do something to me—maybe fire
me." The white members of the school board would not budge. "We are
dealing with four dangerous white men and women," the *Call and Post*
fumed.

When the NAACP and their activist groups in Columbus filed suit,
the case became known as *Penick v. Columbus Board of Education.* (Penick
was Gary Penick, a thirteen-year-old student whose family allowed his
name to be used.) When the lawsuit finally landed in federal district
court, it was on the desk of Robert Duncan, the newly appointed federal
judge. Maybe it was kismet. Maybe it was just a coincidence. If it was
anything other than a judge's turn at a case on the court's docket, Duncan himself wasn't thinking too much about it. White judges routinely
got cases from white plaintiffs. "The case landing in front of Duncan,
well, that proved to me there was a God," says Sam Gresham.

This was the same Bobby Duncan who couldn't get a job at all-black
Champion Junior High or East High School when he graduated from
Ohio State back in the mid-1950s because, while they were the schools
black teachers were sent to, they had no openings at the time. This was
the same Bobby Duncan who used to ride down East Broad Street on
his way to work every day, past East High School, one of the schools
prominently mentioned in the suit.

As the trial was set to begin in Columbus, the town's citizenry felt rattled. There had been riots and extreme violence in Boston and Louisville
over the issue of busing and school integration. Walter H. Rice, who
would become a United States district judge in Dayton, followed the
Columbus school case as it was unfolding. "By the late 1960s," he says
of the school integration battles and black parents, "patience was gone.
We started seeing a tremendous number of school segregation cases in
the North." But Rice also saw the overwhelming burden faced by black
parents and lawyers in the North when it came to desegregation cases.
"The northern cases were harder to win than the southern cases because

the southern cases were de jure," he says of the willful segregation in southern states.

There were armed guards on April 6 when arguments for *Penick v. Columbus Board of Education* began downtown. Federal judges are often anonymous figures, but Judge Robert Duncan knew this case was about to all but evaporate his anonymity. Reporters from national publications came in droves. "He didn't have the reputation of a Wild Bill Davis," teacher Catherine Willis says of Duncan. "He was known as a fair-haired boy who could get the attention of white people."

The trial went on for nearly two months. Passionate witnesses testified for both sides. The final transcript stretched to 6,322 pages. The closing arguments wrapped up on September 3, 1976.

On March 8, 1977, Judge Robert Duncan issued his decision. In tones both measured and direct, he ruled for the plaintiffs, agreeing to their charge that the Columbus public school system was not only segregated but that city leaders had knowingly perpetuated the situation. "As I understand [their] argument," Duncan wrote of the school board, "they claim that they would have investigated had Columbus school officials so requested. This position borders on the preposterous. It cannot reasonably be expected that those who violate the Constitution will be anxious for an investigation in order that a remedy may be leveled against them." In another part of the ruling, Duncan harkened to the *Brown* decision. "The Brown principle [is] still quite valid today," he wrote, "that unlawfully segregated schools are inherently unequal. Because black children are expected and required to grow up, live and work in a majority white society, it is not only unlawful, it is unfair for public officials, by their actions or their inaction, to promote with segregative intent racially imbalanced schools." Duncan, who had known great black educators like J. Arnett Mitchell and Jack Gibbs, who might have become a schoolteacher himself, who had felt the sting of racism in the city, left little doubt that he knew how much this case meant to the plaintiffs. "The evidence in this case harkens back to a previous era in the history of Columbus: a time fresh in the memory of some who testified at trial, when black parents and their children were openly and without pretense denied equality before the law and before their fellow citizens." As for semantics when it came to "de facto" and "de jure" segregation—shrewd application versus intentional—Duncan gave no comfort to the wily school board defendants who had been operating there for years. "In Columbus, like many urban areas, there is often a substantial reciprocal effect between the color of the school and the color of the neighborhood it serves," he wrote. "The racial composition of a neighborhood tends to influence the racial identity of a school as white or black . . . The racial identification of the school in turn tends to maintain the neighborhood's racial identity, or even promote it by hastening the movement in a racial transition area." He went on: "The interaction of housing and the schools operates to promote segregation in each."

Duncan blew a cold and harsh wind over all the Levittowns of America, exposing the racially motivated thought process that went into building them and how that affected—and continued to affect—education in America.

The school board reacted as expected and voted, 4–3, to appeal Duncan's ruling. When Justice William Rehnquist issued a stay soon after—meaning the U.S. Supreme Court was interested in hearing the appeal—it sent shudders through the desegregation advocates, black and white, in the city. Clifford Tyree was director of the Columbus Youth Services Bureau at the time. The Rehnquist stay sent him into a tailspin. "I experienced feelings that I had felt only on three previous occasions— the deaths of President John Kennedy, Dr. Martin Luther King Jr., and Senator Robert Kennedy—the feeling of anger, disbelief, and frustration," he said.

Sam Porter, the lead attorney for the Columbus school board, traveled to Washington that spring. On April 24, 1979, he stood before the United States Supreme Court, defending the school board's opposition to the Duncan ruling. It was his first time arguing before the Supreme Court. Porter gave himself high marks for his testimony. "When we left," he later said, "they carried me out on shields."

During the summer—and bolstered by the Supreme Court injunction—anti-busing whites made a series of threats should the appeal fail: They were going to boycott the schools; they were going to home-school their children; they were going to move to the suburbs. Many of the threats felt hollow. Still, they were disturbing and disruptive.

On July 2, 1979, the Supreme Court's *Penick* ruling was announced. Sam Porter, who had exuberantly proclaimed that after the conclusion of the initial hearing he had been carried out of the courtroom on shields by his so-called troops, saw those shields fall to the ground. The high court stated:

> From the evidence adduced at trial, the Court has found earlier in this opinion that the Columbus Public Schools were openly and intentionally segregated on the basis of race when Brown [vs. Board of Education] was decided in 1954. The Court has found that the Columbus Board of Education never actively set out to disman-tle the dual system . . . The Columbus Board even in very recent times . . . has approved optional attendance zones, discontiguous attendance areas and boundary changes which have maintained and enhanced racial imbalance in the Columbus Public Schools.

Penning the decision for the court's majority, Justice Byron White added that before and since the 1954 *Brown* ruling, the Columbus School Board had been conducting "an enclave of separate, black schools on the near East Side of Columbus."

On the black side of town, many still called him Bobby. But now, more than ever, his title was uttered with reverence: Judge Duncan. Peo-ple celebrated the high court's decision up and down Mount Vernon Avenue and inside the summer recreation centers. Shouts went out over the airwaves of WVKO, the soul music radio station. Catherine Willis, the black schoolteacher, cried along with many of her teacher friends. "These are the decisions that determine which century modern America celebrates, the post-Reconstruction abandonment of black Americans, starting in the 1870s or the birth of liberty heralded by the 1770s," *The New York Times* wrote on its editorial page. "Columbus showed a pattern of segregative choice that the justices could not condone."

.   .   .

Some of the threats made by whites leading up to the beginning of the
1979 school year and, finally, the start of local busing turned out to
be anything but hollow. Two brothers, Edward and John Gerhardt, led
the Columbus faction of the American White Nationalist Party. They
were violent operatives, and the Columbus police and FBI had files on
them. Both brothers were livid about Duncan's landmark desegregation
ruling. They found out that Tracey Duncan, the judge's ten-year-old
daughter, went to Olde Orchard Elementary School. They decided to
bomb it. Edward got an acquaintance to buy the materials. They were
going to give this upstart black judge the kind of grief he'd never recover
from. The acquaintance dispatched to buy the bomb materials was actually a police informant. The brothers were sentenced to lengthy prison
sentences.

Ed Willis followed Jack Gibbs as principal at East High School.
    The national media came to East on the first day of school in 1979,
the first day that busing and integration were official policy. This was the
school that symbolized the struggle; this was the school of the champions. The media lights shone all day. A school that had been all black in
1978, the year before, now was 55 percent white. Ed Willis, standing six
foot five and weighing 250 pounds, had a quiet and cool cockiness that
had developed during his years in Cleveland. "I don't want to hear the
word 'nigger,' and I don't want to hear the word 'honky,' or I'm going to
deal with it," he told an assembly of nervous black and white students
that first morning.
    There were fissures along the way. The KKK—local members and
recruits to the city—staged a demonstration at the state capitol. Pro-
busing advocates received death threats. Mayor Tom Moody, a Republican who remained against busing, announced it was his sworn duty now
to simply uphold the law. "Fight if you want in the courtroom," he said,
"but not in the streets. The minute you begin to fight . . . black or white,
I will lock you up and put you both in the same jail cell."

.   .   .

In time, Columbus proved to the nation that its citizenry could adapt to legally enforced integration. In time, the city received plaudits from local business leaders and even the Department of Justice in Washington.

In time, as the years rolled outward, local citizens would look back, swiveling against the memories of 1968–1969, when a group of high school basketball and baseball players had created their own legend. They had helped to bring hope to a city, giving it a reason to cheer and also proving that there was more than one route to Dr. King's mountaintop.

Epilogue

Still Standing

I t was to be expected that with the beginning of busing in Columbus, white flight accelerated.

In the years following Judge Duncan's ruling, black teachers and administrators got jobs that were never before available to them, but the city also closed three high schools. White flight drained the population. Upwardly mobile black families also fled the inner city, taking their children to the suburbs, too.

When East High closed for renovations in 2006, frantic gossip raced along that ever present inner-city grapevine. People worried that once the school closed, it might never reopen. According to one theory, it was going to become a city municipal building. Education officials vowed, and kept vowing, that the school would reopen, and, in 2008, it did. The city has taken care through the years to be mindful of the school's historical significance. At the school's reopening, dignitaries trooped over to East Broad Street to celebrate with parents, students, and alumni. They all gushed at the work that had been done. There was a shiny new gymnasium with many more seats. There were new skylights. A new technology lab had been built, and throughout the halls and classrooms there was new carpentry and stonework. It all amounted to the most significant improvements to the school in more than half a century.

Ernest Wood, the East High principal during the 2016–17 school year, had arrived in Columbus nine years earlier from Syracuse, New York, where he had worked in education. He had first been assistant principal at Briggs High School, and then he was promoted to principal at East. Wood loved rushing about the building with a handheld walkie-talkie, communicating with staffers throughout the school day. In that 2016 school year, East High enrolled 450 students. In 1968–69, 1,200 students were enrolled at the school. Many of today's East High students need transportation; the school could not be filled by the number of high school students who live within walking distance. Eight buses are sent out to get students to and from school. The tearing down of the low-income Poindexter Village housing projects—where so many blacks had lived following their arrival during the Great Migration—cut deeply into the school's population. The site where Poindexter once sat now has multifamily units and senior citizen housing.

The city's school system, in addressing diversity, has also adopted new programs, such as school choice, much of which is carried out by a lottery system. Still, none of that has stopped East High from—once again—becoming a 98 percent black school.

On April 11, 1985, Judge Robert Duncan, who set the busing plan in motion, released the city of Columbus from his judicial order. "There are no perfect remedial Court orders," he wrote. "All racial problems in the Columbus School District have not been eliminated by this litigation. Although the Court is satisfied that the remedy ordered in this case has substantially accomplished its objective, racial problems persist."

Robert Duncan died November 2, 2015. There were many fine eulogies given. He had made a city pay attention to its deprived, wounded, and educationally mistreated.

East High is no longer an athletic powerhouse. But Ernest Wood knows the school's athletic pedigree and is always quick to show off its trophies, along with those black-and-white photographs that still line the walls on the second floor. Following the renovations, it was discovered that some of the memorabilia were missing. "We've looked everywhere," Wood says. Some of the missing items were treasures from the twin championship year of 1968–69. Alumni from that year banded together and began donating their own keepsakes to the school. Visitors come by the school and want to see pictures of Eddie Rat, Bo-Pete, Garnett Davis, and Norris Smith.

Rev. Joel King is the city's living touchstone to the MLK era. He came to the city to minister at Union Grove Baptist Church, recruited by Martin Luther King Jr.'s friend Rev. Phale Hale. Reverend King is Martin Luther King Jr.'s nephew. He has gone to East High to talk during the city's MLK Day event.

Every now and then a seemingly ageless man can be seen gliding through the hallways of East High School. Principal Wood has tracked down several of the 1968–69 sports heroes, inviting them to come talk to the students about perseverance and resilience. "I had to reach back to the past to bring the school forward," Wood says. That ageless man is Garnett Davis. He returns to talk to the kids about baseball, to tell them stories about Willie Mays and Jackie Robinson, and also about Norris Smith and Eddie Rat, how they had to come from behind in some of those tournament games the year they won it all. The students walk up and give him high fives.

Garnett Davis thinks a lot about baseball and its place in society. The numbers of black players on major league rosters have been declining. It is a vexing problem for the league. On opening day in 2015, only 8 percent of players on major league rosters were black. That same year, the Major League Baseball Players Association and Major League Baseball joined forces and announced a $30 million plan to foster youth development programs in the United States and Canada. The hope is that the initiative will attract inner-city youngsters to the game.

In 2016, Northwestern University hired Spencer Allen as its baseball coach. He became the first black head baseball coach in the Big Ten.

Recognizing the decline of baseball in the inner city, Garnett Davis started his own baseball camp. It's quite modest, a dozen kids most years. He prints his own brochures, scours the city for talent, talks to parents

Garnett Davis after he was drafted by the New York Mets.

in gritty neighborhoods about the beauty of the game. The fact that he played for East High, and in the New York Mets farm system, gets the attention of parents. He often gets bigger bursts of excitement when recalling his playing days at East High than he does recounting his professional career. Some of the kids he takes on don't have fathers.

On some May afternoons, Garnett Davis will hop in his car and drive over to Harley Field to catch a varsity baseball game. Sometimes, he'll wear a New York Mets jersey. Other times he'll amble through the gates in one of his East High shirts with the Tiger emblem. He buys his Tiger outerwear at alumni events. Except for the Tiger coaches—and the few who recognize an old high school legend—he pretty much goes unnoticed. The Tiger baseball team hasn't been good in years. Their last great glory year was 1969. The scruffy diamond needs an upgrade. But when there's the threat of rain, Garnett Davis doesn't have to feel sorry for the players. They've got a dugout now.

Acknowledgments

Many high school stories are both poignant and complex. When they flow out of the 1960s—one of the most volatile decades in modern American history—those stories can be mesmerizing. The story of the 1968–69 East High Tigers struck me as a quintessential American saga rich in drama that encompasses politics, race, sports, and history. Many stories above the Mason-Dixon Line got lost in the hard roiling of southern history. The 1968–69 Tigers represents one such story.

Peter Gethers, my longtime editor at Alfred A. Knopf, was in Europe when I first told him about the idea for this book. By the time he landed back in America, he had made up his mind that he wanted to publish *Tigerland*. During the years of my researching and writing, he deepened my understanding and appreciation of this story. His line editing was crucial; his knowledge of baseball a saving grace.

Also at Knopf, I'd like to thank Sonny Mehta, Janna Devinsky, Jenna Brinkley, Kathy Zuckerman, Victoria Pearson, Madison Brock, Paul Bogaards, Emily Murphy, Maggie Hinders, and Tyler Comrie.

Esther Newberg, my indomitable literary agent, has been an important and indispensable figure through the years of my writing life (now eight books together!). She has my deep gratitude.

I was fortunate in 2017 to receive the Patrick Henry Writing Fellowship, bestowed by the Starr Center for the Study of the American Experience at Washington College, in Chestertown, Maryland. It is given for a writing project that addresses "the nation's founding ideas." That the Starr Center had faith in this project was wonderful; that they supplied me with a home and collegial atmosphere to work in was an added gift. I would like to thank those affiliated with the center, among them Adam Goodheart, director; Pat Nugent, deputy director; Jean Wortman, assistant director; and Michael Buckley, program manager. Also at Washington College, my gratitude extends to Patrice DiQuinzio, Amanda Ceruzzi, and James Allen Hall.

At Miami University, in Oxford, Ohio, I'd like to thank Gregory Crawford, Richard Campbell, Ron Scott, James Tobin, Claire Wagner, Patti Newberry, Ted Pickerill, Donna Boen, and Susan Coffin for their unending support while I was working on this book.

This book is dedicated to Phyllis Callahan, provost at Miami University, and to Paul Pennell, retired Tiger coach. Their gracious and humbling spirits are inspiring. The names Jack Gibbs and Bob Hart also appear on the dedication page of this book. They gave so much to East High School.

There were many, beyond the writing, who offered encouragement and warmhearted gestures along the way. My thanks to Peter Guralnick, Bill Orrico, Tina Moody, Carol Tyler, Larry James, Faness Haygood, Greg Moore, Tom Martin, Tony Stigger, Pam Williams, Rick Momeyer, Naomi Shavin, Frank Hurst, Ron Peleg, Michael Coleman, Bob Davis, Sue Momeyer, Alex Shumate, Donna James, Sherri Geldin, Michelle Fee Smith, Lynn Peterson, Robert Lewis, Kat Bogel, Beth White, Ellen Hurst, Larry Young, Mary Jo Green, Sabrina Goodwin Monday, David Hodge, Professor Serena Williams, Warren Tyler, Patricia Pfeiffer, Valerie Hodge, Marty Anderson, Steve Flannigan, Vic Pfeiffer, and Bob Miller. Shane Cagney and the folks at Politics & Prose have my gratitude as well. Steve Reiss's lessons about the craft continue to resonant.

Notes

In addition to personal interviews, this book has also benefitted from the help of librarians and archival repositories. I would like to thank Tim Stried and Andrea Heiberger of the Ohio High School Athletic Association. I'm also grateful to Pat Losinski, director of the Columbus Public Library, and his dutiful staff for their assistance in tracking down old newspapers. Ernest Wood, former principal of East High, allowed me to spend as many hours poking around the school for records and photos that I needed to. Of the books cited in the bibliography, a few deserve special mention for increasing my understanding of certain events and personalities. These books are *Getting Around Brown* by Gregory S. Jacobs, *Jackie Robinson: A Biography* by Arnold Rampersad, *I Never Had It Made: An Autobiography* by Jackie Robinson, and *Jackie Robinson and the Integration of Baseball* by Scott Simon.

When I told Ruth Gibbs that I was going to travel to Harlan, Kentucky, to piece together Jack Gibbs's life, she immediately insisted on going with me, never mind her advancing age. The trip was unforgettable, and I was grateful for her company, as well as that of her son, Jack, and daughter, Cheryl.

Sherri Hart saved quite a bit of memorabilia from her father's life, three trunks of materials that proved indispensable to my research. Lynne Hart and Bobbi Hart also gave freely of their time in sharing memories about their father.

Paul Pennell not only remains, thank goodness, a pack rat—he allowed me use of his basketball and baseball memorabilia saved from

1968–69—but he possesses a remarkable memory. He would recall which Tiger baseball player got a game-winning run in which game, sending me to a newspaper clipping for confirmation. His memory was rarely wrong.

Greg Winbush, himself a former Tiger athlete, helped open many doors.

I'm also grateful to John Stanford, Gary Baker, and Ed O'Reilly of the Columbus City Schools for understanding the scope of this project.

To all the Tiger athletes, faculty, and students from 1968–69 who gave me their time, helping me grasp that one year—and the years surrounding it—I am beyond grateful. Their names appear here, as well as many others in Ohio and elsewhere around the country who aided my effort. Thanks to : Ed Ratleff, Larry Walker, Robert Wright, Kenny Mizelle, Ed Mingo, Garnett Davis, Roy Hickman, Ernie Locke, Kevin Smith, Henry Johnson, Calvin Ferguson, Wali Davis, Scott Guiler, Joe Roberts, Sam Gresham, Earl Davis, Phil Pool, Romeo Watkins, Skip Anderson, Mollie Pool, Roger Dumaree, Brian Mizelle, Roseanne Bell, Theresa Barnes, Mike Gordon, Jim Musuraca, Frank Dawson, Jim Henderson, Shirley Duncan, Ray Scott, Terry Holliman, Dave Hanners, Sandra Moody, Keith Young, Cheryl Johnson, Hal Thomas, Mark Corna, Bob Marsh, Charles Richardson, Andrew Ginther, Mark Mahan, Cynthia Scott, Hiram Tanner Jr., Dwight "Bo-Pete" Lamar, Fred Saunders, Al Harris, Jerry Saunders, Millie Hart, Jim Martz, Mike Watson, Dick Linson, Mike Curtin, Karen Caliver, Joel King, Chris Dawkins, Mel Griffin, Tracy Brown, Velda Otey, Alice Flowers, Cynthia Chapman Kasey, Stan Rubin, Robert Vincent Duncan, Pop James, Don Tishman, Jr., Harvey Alston Jr., Bob Whitman, Curt Moody, Zita Moses, Ann Walker, Lynn Carter, Ozark Range, Steve Fields, Sandra Montgomery, Tom Brown, Ray Humphrey, Dave Cole, Ed Littlejohn Jr., David Reid, Lee Hawkins, Ed Stahl, Terry Holliman, Nick Saunders, Dave Hanners, Greg Olson, Bob Marsh, Jim Cleamons, Skip Young, Bert Kram, Mary Lazarus, Nancy Jeffrey, Hilton Hale, Gene Caslin, Mel Nowell, Janice Hale, Louise Williams, Bob Martin, Vonzell Johnson, and Tom Fullove.

Prologue

6   "Basketball in the '60s": *The Columbus Dispatch,* March 23, 1983.

1 Down to the River

12   "He said she was the most beautiful girl": Sherri Hart interview by author.
13   "Hi Sweetheart": Bob Hart Papers (private collection held by Sherri Hart), letter dated June 21, 1941.
14   "James Robert Hart": BHP, letter dated June 21, 1941.
14   "James Robert Hart": BHP, *The Columbus Dispatch,* undated.
14   "My Dearly Beloved": Bob Hart to Jean Woodyard, February 21, 1944, BHP.
14   "As far as we know": Ibid.
15   "Get up, there's Krauts all over the place!": Connelly, *The Mortarmen,* 145.
15   "The approximately 62 hours spent": Privately published history/field report of Bob Hart's battalion, BHP.
16   "There has never been any rest": Ibid.
16   "This might sound funny": Bob Hart to Jean Woodyard, April 13, 1944, BHP.
17   "I am convinced": The college term paper is dated February 18, 1946, BHP.
19   "She was the one": Romeo Watkins interview by author.
21   "Bob should have gotten the job": Paul Pennell interview by author.
21   "We were just like a misguided missile": Bob Martin interview by author.
23   "They knew his system": Paul Pennell interview by author.
24   "One of the things I remember": Bobbi Hart interview by author.
24   "I'd get off the bus": Ibid.
25   "Mom was this little farm girl": Ibid.
25   "I remember people telling Dad": Ibid.
26   "If I'd been playing'": Bob Martin interview by author.
27   "He is the best sixth man": Undated clipping, scrapbook, BHP.
27   "You have devoted a lot of time": *The Columbus Dispatch,* March 28, 1963.
28   "Now let's see you make one last layup": Ibid.
29   "ON BEHALF OF THE FIRST COLUMBUS EAST HIGH SCHOOL BASKETBALL TEAM": Telegram dated April 2, 1963, BHP.
29   "I'm sorry, we can't do it": Bobbi Hart interview by author.
29   "It crushed my grandmother": Ibid.
30   "At the outset": *The New York Times,* February 15, 1963.
31   "I say to you today": Marable, *Freedom: A Photographic History of the African-American Struggle,* 326.
32   "James Baldwin, the gifted Negro writer": *The Columbus Citizen-Journal,* August 29, 1963.
33   "a rebuilding year": Paul Pennell interview by author.
34   "Larry Jones set me straight": *The Toledo Times,* March 24, 1969.

36 "I was Robin and he was Batman": *The Columbus Dispatch,* March 21, 2007.

36 "I had a big Angela Davis Afro": Sandra Montgomery interview by author.

36 "Brothers and Sisters": Hayes, *Smiling Through the Apocalypse,* 397.

37 "Brothers and Sisters, don't let them separate you": Ibid.

39 "a half-step up from homelessness": Sides, *Hellbound on His Trail,* 145.

40 "The black people's leader": Ibid., 190.

40 "No man spoke harder against violence": *Life,* April 19, 1968.

40 "I'm shocked": Sides, *Hellbound on His Trail,* 225.

41 "A shot killed the dreamer": *The Columbus Dispatch,* April 8,1968.

41 "We have to leave Mississippi": Zita Moses interview by author.

42 "I will not send one of my white officers": Lynn Carter interview by author.

42 "The X-Ray would like to express": *The X-Ray,* April 1968, Vol. 1.

2 Eddie Rat Meets the Afro-Wearing Bo-Pete

48 "Athletes are on the field": *Newsweek,* July 15, 1968.

48 "I feel it's outside influences": Ibid.

48 "It seems a little ungrateful": Ibid.

49 "Why Run in Mexico": Ibid.

50 "She had three or four houses": Bo-Pete Lamar interview by author.

50 "She had that southern mentality": Ibid.

51 "Bo looked like Spiderman": Jim Cleamons interview by author.

51 "Bo understood the game": Ibid.

51 "No one just ever thought": Roseanne Bell interview by author.

51 "Bo had a free hand": Curt Moody interview by author.

52 "American couple Win and Joyce Wilford": *Look,* January 17, 1969.

52 "I played the whole season": Bo-Pete Lamar interview by author.

52 "We didn't know what Bo was going to do": Curt Moody interview by author.

53 "Kloman didn't know": Donnie Penn interview by author.

53 "It was disappointing": Ibid.

55 "Man, we'd really like you to come": Bo-Pete Lamar interview by author.

57 "There is division in the American house now": Kearns-Goodwin, *Lyndon Johnson and the American Dream,* 348.

57 "With America's sons in the fields": Ibid.

58 "'a new way to say 'Nigger'": *Life,* August 23, 1968.

58 "If you've seen one city slum": Kaiser, *1968 in America,* 250.

58 "I'm Lucy Lamar": Paul Pennell interview by author.

59 "I said, 'Are you sitting down?'": Ibid.

59 "We were looking for him to fit in": Karen Caliver interview by author.

59 "It was up to Bo": Kevin Smith interview by author.

61 "It's going to be Eddie's team": Bo-Pete Lamar interview by author.

61 "Everybody knew everybody": Ed Ratleff interview by author.

62 "He was the best basketball player": Gene Caslin interview by author.

62   "We all knew": Curt Moody interview by author.

62   "Our coach said": Ibid.

62   "All week in school": Ibid.

63   "Ratleff was the last guy": Ibid.

64   "I had tunnel vision": Roy Hickman interview by author.

64   "My mom would say": Ibid.

64   "King was everybody's hero": Ibid.

65   "Seniors tend to be disgruntled": Paul Pennell interview by author.

66   "My mother worried": Larry Walker interview by author.

67   "We were precocious enough": Robert Wright interview by author.

67   "He told me": Ibid.

67   "We were, for the first time": Ibid.

67   "We saw what was going on": Ibid.

68   "We didn't look at King": Ibid.

68   "I felt like I wanted to go out": David Reid interview by author.

69   "The rules changed": Robert Wright interview by author.

69   "They beat us": Kenny Mizelle interview by author.

69   "Before practice, I'd play": Scott Guiler interview by author.

70   "He just hated black people": Sides, *Hellbound on His Trail,* 380.

70   I can raise a lot of money": Ibid.

72   "Basketball color is an intangible quality": Undated typed note card by Bob Hart, BHP.

72   "Mohawk will be a serious threat": Paul Pennell, personal scouting report of Coach Hart typed by the assistant coach.

73   "It was designed for you": Al Harris interview by author.

73   "I'm like, shut up and play": Ibid.

74   "I put 'em back in": *The Columbus Citizen-Journal,* December 14, 1968.

76   "an unconditional war on poverty": Updegrove, *LBJ in the Presidency,* 147.

76   "It will not be a short or easy struggle": Ibid.

77   "give every American community": Ibid., 148.

3   The House That Jack Built

82   "Whether it is because I belong": Deutsch, *You Need a Schoolhouse,* 96.

83   "You do not know what joy": Ibid., 120.

84   "I knew he liked me": Ruth Gibbs interview by author.

85   "That's when he wrote me a love letter": Ibid.

88   "That play turned the game around": Ibid.

89   "This was the second period": *The Columbus Dispatch,* November 21, 1954.

90   "Segregation of white and colored children": Haygood, *Showdown,* 77–78.

93   "The world of high school principals": Paul Pennell interview by author.

93   "It's a good question": Ibid.

93   "His whole life": Ibid.

94   "He wanted East High to be the best": Mike Gordon interview by author.

94   "This is what he said to me": Ibid.

94   "He ran a tight ship": Scott Guiler interview by author.

95   "Jack would call me": Pop James interview by author.

95   "He understood the black psyche": Robert Wright interview by author.

96   "After school,": Roger Dumaree interview by author.

97   "Gibbs held 'women assemblies'": Zita Moses interview by author.

97   "The assembly hall is the principal's classroom": Jennings, *The 1971–1972 Jennings Scholar Lectures,* 229.

97   "Have you ever worked on community problems": Ibid., 230.

98   "What made East different": Zita Moses interview by author.

98   "You can't imagine": Gibbs family scrapbook, undated clipping. (Jeanie Strand, Central State University public relations official, covered Gibbs's appearance at Central State University and sent his remarks in to the *Xenia Daily Gazette.*)

98   "I tell them it's just the same": Ibid.

98   "The same thing goes for the police reports": Ibid.

101   "Jack said, 'Hey, it's not only'": Phillip Pool interview by author.

101   "That was his way": Zita Moses interview by author.

101   "We called her 'Ms. East'": Phillip Pool interview by author.

101   "Went to Dottie": Ibid.

101   "We had to run around": Ibid.

103   "I bought me a pair of pants": Calvin Ferguson interview by author.

104   "Oh man, we had beautiful uniforms": Ibid.

104   "I did what I had to do": Ibid.

104   "East had beautiful girls": Ibid.

104   "Pimps just hung around the school": Cynthia Kasey interview by author.

105   "He was condemning Calvin Ferguson": Skip Anderson interview by author.

105   "Bo listened to me": Calvin Ferguson interview by author.

105   "A friend of mine": Ibid.

106   "One of the secretaries": Ruth Gibbs interview by author.

106   "Whatever those kids needed": Ibid.

107   "Why didn't you tell me": Vonzell Johnson interview by author.

107   "Our neighborhood is classy": Ibid.

109   "We pulled him out of that back row": Jennings, *The 1971–1972 Jennings Scholar Lectures,* 233.

109   "They loved him": Louise Williams interview by author.

4 Momentum

112   "I remember we were standing around": Larry Walker interview by author.

112   "We're gonna kick their asses": Ibid.

114   "We really wanted Ratleff and Conner": Joe Roberts interview by author.

114   "My mother was afraid": Vonzell Johnson interview by author.

119 "so everyone can see": Michaeli, *The Defender: How the Legendary Black Newspaper Changed America,* 325.

119 "It would appear from this lynching": Ibid.

119 "Mississippi hasn't got any law": Ibid., 332.

120 "It didn't make no sense": Anderson, *Emmett Till: The Murder that Shocked the World and Propelled the Civil Rights Movement,* 198.

120 "Can't you make it $150": Ibid., 191.

120 "It will add to the drama": Ibid.

120 "a black pygmy": Roberts and Klibanoff, *The Race Beat,* 99.

121 "It is true": Anderson, *Emmett Till,* 191.

121 "I rode into this gas station": Joe Roberts interview by author.

122 "We've got 18 groups": Jennings, *The 1971–1972 Jennings Scholar Lectures,* 226.

124 "It was the hottest thing": Terry Holliman interview by author.

124 "Everything would have to go right": Ibid.

125 "If you had one turnover": Larry Walker interview by author.

125 "Coming into our senior season": Ibid.

125 "There was racial tension": Mike Stumpf interview by author.

125 "I remember at halftime": Ibid.

126 "We had a full-court press": Larry Walker interview by author.

126 "They were structured": Mike Stumpf interview by author.

127 "That's the reason": Dave Hanners interview by author.

127 "They'd win by fifty": Ibid.

127 "I wanted to find": Ibid.

127 "There was no one": Ibid.

127 "He never got tired": Ibid.

128 "Bo-Pete was a better shooter": Ibid.

128 "It was still quite a segregated mess": Ed Stahl interview by author.

128 "We had such great respect": Ibid.

128 "This was during the late 1960s": Greg Olson interview by author.

128 "He was probably the most prolific": Ibid.

129 "I remember being in the three-second lane": Ibid.

129 "If you looked at them": Ed Stahl interview by author.

131 "It didn't matter who scored": Ed Ratleff interview by author.

132 "Their enrollment was fluid": Paul Pennell interview by author.

133 "We knew they were jailbirds": Larry Walker interview by author.

137 "That was a real coup": Paul Pennell interview by author.

138 "Time has stood still": *The New York Times,* April 1, 1980.

138 "a kind of all-round super combination": Ibid.

5 Keeping Food in the Pantry

142 "He was so determined": Tracy Brown interview by author.

143 "What was the guy gonna say": Dan Tishman interview by author.

6 So Many Dreams in the Segregated City

148 "The most common": Kluger, *Simple Justice*, 75.

148 "We consider the": Ibid., 80.

148 "If laws of": Ibid., 82-83.

149 "No people ever": Jacobs, *Getting Around Brown*, 12.

150 "Such separation of": Ibid., 14.

150 "The Negroes are": Ibid., 7.

151 "Directly and indirectly": Ibid., 69.

152 "The outcome of": Kluger, *Simple Justice*, 684.

153 "We conclude": Ibid., 707.

154 "There wasn't any": Jacobs, *Getting Around Brown*, 16.

154 "There were 'black'": Ibid., 18.

155 "I knew this": Ibid., 19.

155 "How many schools": Ibid.

157 "His wife was": Ann Walker interview by author.

164 "People have always": Nancy Jeffrey interview by author.

165 "I had a different": Ibid.

165 "The discrimination was": Ibid.

165 "The rumor was": Ibid.

165 "They wouldn't have": Ibid.

166 "The city was": Mary Lazarus interview by author.

166 "East Broad Street": Ibid.

166 "I thought it": Ibid.

166 "The Wolfes were": Ibid.

166 "The Athletic Club": Bert Kram interview by author.

166 "tensions were very": Ibid.

168 "It's a bad": *Saturday Evening Post*, May 3, 1952.

169 "My mother called": Bo-Pete Lamar interview by author.

7 Panthers and Tigers, Oh My

172 "When I started": Larry Mays interview by author.

174 "he worked so hard": Bo-Pete Lamar interview by author.

174 "Mike Owens": Itinerary, private collection, BHP.

175 "He'd knock it into the stands": Scott Guiler interview by author.

176 "It was going to be speed": Larry Mays interview by author.

176 "It's always been a game": *The Spectator*, December 19, 1968.

176 "I don't believe there is a team": *The Columbus Citizen-Journal*, March 18, 1969.

177 "I didn't even figure on him": Ibid.

177 "Gibbs said, 'Somebody get an electric razor'": Kevin Smith interview by author.

177 "He was not overrated": Larry Mays interview by author.

8 The Church Where Martin Luther King Jr. Preached

180 "There were a lot of pretty girls": Kevin Smith interview by author.

181 "I remember those pies": Bob Whitman interview by author.

184 "My father instead took a job": Janice Hale interview by author.

186 "Every member of Dexter": Branch, *Parting the Waters*, 116.

187 "It was like double Easter": Janice Hale interview by author.

187 "Is this Martin Luther King Jr.?": Branch, *Parting the Waters*, 243.

187 "I've been after him": Ibid., 243.

188 "I remember in 1960": Janice Hale interview by author.

188 "To sit and listen": Ibid.

189 "Ray's Judge Admits Case Baffles": *The Columbus Dispatch*, March 17, 1969.

189 "I would truly like to know": Ibid.

9 St. John Arena

191 "Zanesville does a lot of things well": *The Spectator*, March 13, 1969.

191 "And we were pretty even": *The Columbus Citizen-Journal*, March 11, 1969.

191 "Good team spirit and morale": Notecard, BHP.

192 "That new floor is a big difference now": *The Columbus Dispatch*, March 24, 1969.

194 "You've got to throw all kinds of bouquets": *The Columbus Citizen-Journal*, March 14, 1969.

195 "on your side": *The Spectator*, January 23, 1969.

197 "It was a great game": *The Columbus Citizen-Journal*, March 17, 1969.

197 "They wouldn't go in": Ibid.

197 "Tell the folks": *The Columbus Dispatch*, March 16, 1969.

200 "I didn't want to split up": *Toledo Blade*, March 5, 2006.

200 "the best basketball player": *The Columbus Dispatch*, March 23, 1969.

200 "They're real physical": *The Spectator*, March 20, 1969.

201 "He said, 'Hey Mr. James'": Pop James interview by author.

203 "Libbey looked every bit": *The Columbus Dispatch*, March 22, 1969.

204 "That one will haunt me": Ibid.

205 "Why didn't they call a foul": Ibid.

205 "I can still see it": Ibid.

205 "We did a good job": Ibid.

205 "Two inches": Ibid.

205 "The way [the Canton McKinley team members are]": Ibid.

205 "It'll probably go right down to the wire": Ibid.

207 "We had five thousand": Stan Rubin interview by author.

207 "Our fans traveled everywhere": Ibid.

208 "We were concerned about Bo-Pete": Stan Rubin interview by author.

208 "keep a hand in his face": *The Columbus Dispatch*, March 23, 1969.

209 "We told him": Ibid.

209 "two shots to our one": *The Columbus Citizen-Journal,* March 24, 1969.

210 "We gotta win": *The Toledo Times,* March 24, 1969.

211 "This team is of a different era": *The Columbus Citizen-Journal,* March 24, 1969.

212 "James had on a blanket": Kevin Smith interview by author.

212 "I finally met someone shorter": Larry Walker interview by author.

212 "He was wearing lifts": Cynthia Chapman interview by author.

212 "Look at them": Larry Walker interview by author.

10 The Ballad of Jackie Robinson

219 "You learned to respect": Ed Ratleff interview by author.

220 "Once East High became a black school": Jim Henderson interview by author.

221 "You're about the sassiest nigger": Rampersad, *Jackie Robinson,* 15.

221 "Sometimes there were only two meals": Ibid., 23.

222 "had been the outstanding athlete": Ibid., 39.

223 "created a sensation": Ibid., 42.

223 "one of the most successful": Ibid.

223 "the greatest base runner": Ibid., 54.

223 "Geez, if that kid": Ibid., 55.

226 "Do we, by any chance": Ibid., 120.

226 "I didn't like the bouncing buses": Ibid., 117.

227 "I was thrilled": Ibid., 126.

228 "I'm looking for a ballplayer": Ibid., 126.

228 "I had to do it": Ibid., 127.

228 "of the carpetbagger stripe": Robinson, *I Never Had It Made,* 36.

228 "Mr. Rickey": Rampersad, *Jackie Robinson,* 142.

229 "Of course I can't begin": Simon, *Jackie Robinson and the Integration of Baseball,* 85.

230 "And high up in the press box": Carson, Garrow, Kovach, and Polsgrove, comp., *Reporting Civil Rights, Part One,* 76.

230 "Make no mistake": Rampersad, *Jackie Robinson,* 150.

230 "converted his opportunity": Ibid., 150.

230 "Thus the most significant sports story": Ibid., 150.

230 "Hey, Jackie": Robinson, *I Never Had It Made,* 49.

231 "It was probably the only day": Rampersad, *Jackie Robinson,* 157.

231 "The Brooklyn Dodgers today purchased": Ibid., 167.

232 "the Negro first baseman": Ibid., 177.

232 "Hey, snowflake": Robinson, *I Never Had It Made,* 58.

232 "They're waiting for you": Ibid., 59.

232 "You'll see something": Rampersad, *Jackie Robinson,* 183.

233 "I've played a": Ibid., 186.

234 "He can win": Ibid., 210.

234 "They'd do their best": Ibid., 214.

234 "Every single Negro": Ibid., 214.

235 "You must admit": Ibid., 217.

235 "For Bigger's": Baldwin, *The Price of the Ticket,* 33.

236 "I simply don't want": Robinson, *I Never Had It Made,* 102.

236 "Anything I do": Rampersad, *Jackie Robinson,* 235.

236 "There is no question": Ibid., 229.

237 "It has been the finest experience": Ibid., 231.

239 "If we don't win it this time": Ibid., 259.

239 "Education must begin": Ibid., 262.

240 "Walter Winchell": Ibid., 266.

240 "the most savagely booed": Ibid., 269.

241 "I would trade him": Ibid., 275.

242 "Aging Robinson Sets Dodgers Afire": Ibid., 285.

242 "old boy": Ibid., 285.

243 "You opened the door": Ibid., 308.

243 "the Negroes are being hit": Ibid., 323.

245 "I have never been so proud": Ibid., 379.

246 "Baseball still had the impact": Bob Marsh, interview by author.

246 "You still had a lot of black role models": Ibid.

11 Twilight at Harley Field

250 "I made up my mind": Paul Pennell interview by author.

251 "I can't recall anyone": Ibid.

251 "I remember my father": Ibid.

251 "Every Tuesday morning": Ibid.

252 "The first couple years": Bobby Humphries interview by author.

252 "He didn't just coach us": Ibid.

252 "In American Legion": Ibid.

254 "We had about a five-mile radius": Dave Cole interview by author.

254 "We went and played": Jim Henderson interview by author.

255 "We listened to them": Dave Cole interview by author.

255 "Cole, keep your butt down!": Ibid.

255 "I can't remember": Ibid.

255 "Baseball was my first love": Ed Ratleff interview by author.

256 "We don't have any more uniforms": Ibid.

256 "We just found another uniform": Ibid.

257 "I read every article": Tom Brown interview by author.

257 "We always stayed in the locker room": Ibid.

257 "I coached life": Ibid.

257 "Ratleff could throw": Ibid.

258 "The white cheerleaders": Ibid.
261 "It was hard for the girls": Ed Ratleff interview by author.
261 "I never heard a girl": Ibid.
262 "I had never seen black guys": Doc Simpson interview by author.
262 "They were really good": Ed Ratleff interview by author.
263 "Ratleff had a harder curve": Fred Saunders interview by author.
264 "Dudes on my team": Ibid.
265 "No one talked": Ed Ratleff interview by author.
265 "Everywhere we went": Kenny Mizelle interview by author.

12 Robert Duncan and Richard Nixon's America

270 "Click Mitchell, the negro brute": *The Columbus Dispatch,* June 4, 1897.
270 "The negro was killed": *The Literary Digest,* June 19, 1897.
270 "The Ohioans of Urbana": Ibid.
271 "The whole story": Ibid.
272 "And I remember": Robert Duncan, Ohio State University Oral History Program, Ohio State University, 3.
272 "That was the first time": Ibid., 3.
274 "I made more money": Ibid., 11.
276 "I said, 'What's that?'": Shirley Duncan interview by author.
277 "Bob was passing notes": Ibid.
277 "I remember calling out": Ibid.
277 "Bob made me laugh": Ibid.
280 "my Negro man"; "a Negro woman": Farrell, *Richard Nixon,* 43.
280 "In her whole life": Ibid., 47.
281 "He was always apart": Ibid., 62.
283 "The Daughters of the Confederacy": Ibid., 131.
283 "During five years in Congress": Ibid., 151.
284 "I will not sacrifice": Ibid., 152.
285 "I had known Nixon longer": Ibid., 289.
286 "Ohio State plays": Shkurti, *The Ohio State University in the Sixties,* 279.
286 "My feeling is this": Farrell, *Richard Nixon,* 329.
286 "try to satisfy some professional civil rights group": Ibid.
286 "The Nixon campaign in 1968": *Harper's,* April 2016.

13 The Catcher in the Storm

288 "Garnett was just a pure baseball player": Paul Pennell interview by author.
288 "I was a quiet leader": Garnett Davis interview by author.

288 "I don't ever remember": Ibid.

289 "It seems to have been": Litwack, *Trouble in Mind,* 269–70.

289 "We ain't got no money": Kluger, *Simple Justice,* 4.

290 "We were on welfare": Garnett Davis interview by author.

291 "He would always say to me": Joe Roberts interview by author.

291 "I used to drink": Earl Davis interview by author.

292 "He gave my mother": Wali Davis interview by author.

292 "I remember him showing me": Ibid.

293 "It affected Garnett's psyche": Ibid.

293 "When our dad left": Garnett Davis interview by author.

293 "We'd move around a lot": Wali Davis, interview by author.

293 "My father was proud": Wali Davis, interview by author.

296 "It was midseason": Paul Pennell interview by author.

296 "Many times I'd be the only fan": Sharon Pennell interview by author.

298 "Walnut Ridge, Whetstone, North": Paul Pennell interview by author.

298 "I went to Garnett": Ibid.

298 "When they lost those five games": Don Laird interview by author.

14 Ghosts of the Blue Birds

301 "He was a lovely": Joe Eicenlaub interview by author.

302 "East would not have first": Mark Aprile interview by author.

303 "Me and Nick [Conner]": Kevin Smith interview by author.

303 "You'd go to a baseball game": Ibid.

303 "There just wasn't any hoopla": Alice Flowers interview by author.

304 "It was our last City League game": Paul Pennell interview by author.

304 "He had a temper": Ed Mingo interview by author.

305 "Bucky, you got three good colored boys": Ray Humphrey interview by author.

306 "Ken Mizelle of Columbus": Ohio Wesleyan *Transcript,* October 12, 1949.

306 "Ken Mizelle, the Baby Bishops'": Ibid., November 2, 1949.

306 "Baby Bishops End Season": Ibid., November 23, 1949.

306 "If they were short a player": Ray Humphrey interview by author.

307 "If he had been": Tom Brown interview by author.

307 "I took him home": Ray Humphrey interview by author.

308 "My mother told me": Kenny Mizelle interview by author.

308 "This classmate told me": Ray Humphrey interview by author.

308 "It was as if": Ernie Locke, interview by author.

309 "I was going to be ready": Ed Ratleff interview by author.

309 "You have to play the games": Paul Pennell interview by author.

310 "They had an off-and-on-again relationship": Ernie Locke interview by author.

310 "I had no idea": Ibid.

311 "Of course that wasn't the case": Ibid.

311 "I began to eat, drink": Ibid.

312 "I said, 'Roger, where have you been?'": Paul Pennell interview by author.

313 "Neighbors was born to play shortstop": Kenny Mizelle interview by author.

314 "There was no one": Ed Ratleff interview by author.

315 "are still alive": *The Columbus Citizen-Journal,* May 16, 1969.

316 "When they were warming up": Mike Watson interview by author.

316 "I was ready": Ray Scott interview by author.

317 "All our hopes": Mike Watson interview by author.

317 "Dear Parent/Guardian": Letter in Paul Pennell private collection.

318 "There were actually people": Ed Mingo interview by author.

318 "It was culture shock": Ernie Locke interview by author.

319 "This was a little Mayberry town": Jim Martz interview by author.

319 "He'd put the batter's box": Ibid.

320 "You never saw an all-black team": Ibid.

320 "They were superior": Ibid.

321 "Just like in basketball": Ed Ratleff interview by author.

323 "You just can't describe it": *The Columbus Citizen-Journal,* May 22, 1969.

324 "He loved those kids": Ruth Gibbs interview by author.

324 "I said, 'Ladies'": Paul Pennell interview by author.

324 "I was focused on that baseball game": Garnett Davis interview by author.

324 "I told my girlfriend": Ed Ratleff interview by author.

326 "My father was especially": Hiram Tanner Jr. interview by author.

327 "We jumped on them real quick": Ed Mingo interview by author.

327 "That first inning was it": *The Columbus Dispatch,* May 31, 1969.

328 "I remember we athletes": Bill Montgomery interview by author.

328 "We were running with the big dogs": Ibid.

329 "The school's athletic director": Frank Dawson interview by author.

330 "I remember that crowd": Ernie Locke interview by author.

330 "They weren't wearing the best-looking uniforms": Frank Dawson interview by author.

330 "We looked at that little Norris guy": Ibid.

331 "If we were worried ": Ray Scott interview by author.

331 "I'd throw it": Jim Musuraca interview by author.

332 "I remember watching that ball": Shirley Pennell interview by author.

332 "When that last out was made": Ibid.

332 "Norris was on target": Ray Scott interview by author.

333 "the complete master": *The Columbus Dispatch,* June 1, 1969.

333 "He didn't throw very hard": Jim Musuraca interview by author.

333 "Just a great athlete": Ibid.

333 "No way did I think": Ed Ratleff interview by author.

333 "There was no way": Garnett Davis interview by author.

333 "We heard rumors": Ernie Locke interview by author.
333 "It was the greatest display": *The Spectator,* June 5, 1969.
333 "We won't be able": Ed Ratleff interview by author.
334 "It's like it was yesterday": Bill Montgomery interview by author.
334 "We couldn't hit that little Smith kid": Frank Dawson interview by author.
334 "It was a special feeling": Ernie Locke interview by author.
334 "Because baseball is a game": Reverend Frazier's remarks in Paul Pennell private letter collection.
335 "I guess these kids": *The Columbus Citizen-Journal,* June 2, 1969.
336 "Sports reporters agree": *The Columbus Dispatch,* June 3, 1969.
337 "We were just a black school": Ed Ratleff interview by author.

15 Off into the World

338 "I remember Gibbs called an assembly": Scott Guiler interview by author.
339 "I got close to Woody Hayes": Ed Ratleff interview by author.
339 "It was a nice party": Ibid.
340 "You guys know me": Brewster and Gallagher, *Stolen Glory,* 45–46.
341 "When we got to Munich": Ibid., 193.
344 "I tried to get": Joe Roberts interview by author.
344 "He threw us out": Bo-Pete Lamar interview by author.
347 "Bad ones are niggers": *Time,* December 12, 1960.
347 "I was watching TV": Bo-Pete Lamar interview by author.
351 "I met a woman": Roy Hickman interview by author.
352 "He kept saying": Paul Pennell interview by author.
352 "I can remember": Sherri Hart interview by author.
353 "They didn't want": Paul Pennell interview by author.
353 "OFFICIAL NOTICE OF DISPOSITION": Garnett Davis, personal collection.
353 "There are ten- and twelve-year minor league players": Paul Pennell interview by author.
354 "May I have a second chance": Garnett Davis, personal collection.
354 "The New York Mets gave you": Ibid.
357 "When we came down the stretch": Paul Pennell interview by author.
357 "My girlfriend didn't want me to play": Ernie Locke interview by author.
358 "I once got a call": Ibid.
358 "We'll just sit and talk": Sharon Pennell interview by author.
359 "At least 30 percent": Roger Dumaree interview by author.
359 "Jack turned to me": Phillip Pool interview by author.
360 "I said, 'Honey'": Ruth Gibbs interview by author.

16 Blood in Ohio

363 "Have you had enough?": *The Columbus Dispatch,* July 21, 2009.
364 "We will not make changes": Shkurti, *The Ohio State University in the Sixties,* 311.
364 "Apathetic students": Ibid., 314.
365 "the worst kind of people": Ibid., 324.

17 Sins Laid Bare

368 "It was the issue of police brutality": Sam Gresham interview by author.
368 "The thing that": Catherine Willis interview by author.
368 "No man who owns his own house": *Time,* December 7, 1998.
368 "We can solve a housing problem": Ibid.
369 "I stood among them": *Bowdoin Daily Sun,* April 25, 2011.
369 "He was absolutely brilliant": Catherine Willis interview by author.
370 "They weren't as militant": Ibid.
371 "Never forget, the press is the enemy": Farrell, *Richard Nixon,* 499.
371 "We're being blackmailed": Ibid., 506.
372 "Dayton had the black unions": Sam Gresham interview by author.
372 "East had given the community": Ibid.
372 "East High had the same kind of thing": Catherine Willis interview by author.
372 "There will be no busing": Jacobs, *Getting Around Brown,* 72.
373 "I'm almost willing": Ibid., 38.
373 "We're getting ready": Ibid., 46.
373 "a construction program": Ibid.
373 "sadistic racial games": Ibid.
373 "If plaintiffs are willing to file": Ibid.
374 "It was obvious": Ibid., 50.
374 "We are dealing with four dangerous white men and women": Ibid.
374 "The case landing in front of Duncan": Sam Gresham interview by author.
375 "He didn't have the reputation": Catherine Willis interview by author.
375 "As I understand [their] argument": Jacobs, *Getting Around Brown,* 57.
375 "The Brown principle": Ibid., 60.
375 "The evidence in this case": Ibid., 61.
376 "In Columbus, like many urban areas": Ibid., 63.
376 "The interaction of housing and the schools": Ibid.
376 "I experienced feelings": Ibid., 97.
376 "When we left": Ibid., 103.
377 "From the evidence": Ibid., 104.
377 "an enclave of separate": Ibid.
377 "These are the decisions": *The New York Times,* July 8, 1979.

378 "I don't want to go in posthumously": Paul Pennell interview by author.
378 "Fight if you want in the courtroom": Ibid., 92.

Epilogue

381 "There are no perfect remedial Court orders": Jacobs, *Getting Around Brown,* 157.
381 "We've looked everywhere": Ernest Wood interview by author.
382 "I had to reach back to the past": Ibid.

Selected Bibliography

Anderson, Deversy S. *Emmett Till: The Murder that Shocked the World and Propelled the Civil Rights Movement.* Jackson: University of Mississippi Press, 2015.

Branch, Taylor. *Parting the Waters: America in the King Years 1954–63.* New York: Simon and Schuster, 1988.

Brewster, Mike, and Taps Gallagher. *Stolen Glory: The U.S., the Soviet Union, and the Olympic Basketball Game that Never Ended.* Los Angeles: GM Books, 2012.

Carson, Clayborne, David J. Garrow, Bill Kovach, and Carol Polsgrove, compilers. *Reporting Civil Rights, Part One: American Journalism, 1941–1963.* New York: The Library of America, 2003.

Deutsch, Stephanie. *You Need a Schoolhouse: Booker T. Washington, Julius Rosenwald, and the Building of Schools for the Segregated South.* Evanston, Ill.: Northwestern University Press, 2011.

Farrell, John A. *Richard Nixon: The Life.* New York: Doubleday, 2017.

Goodwin, Doris Kearns. *Lyndon Johnson and the American Dream.* New York: St. Martin's Press, 1976.

Hayes, Harold, ed. *Smiling Through the Apocalypse: Esquire's History of the Sixties.* New York: Crown, 1987.

Haygood, Wil. *Showdown: Thurgood Marshall and the Supreme Court Nomination that Changed America.* New York: Vintage, 2015.

Jacobs, Gregory S. *Getting Around Brown: Desegregation, Development, and the Columbus Public Schools.* Columbus: Ohio State University Press, 1998.

Jennings, Martha Holden (foundation). *The 1971–1972 Jennings Scholar Lectures.* Cleveland: The Educational Research Council of America, 1972.

Kaiser, Charles. *1968 in America: Music, Politics, Chaos, Counterculture, and the Shaping of a Generation.* New York: Grove Press, 1988.

Kluger, Richard. *Simple Justice.* New York: Alfred A. Knopf, 1976.

Litwack, Leon F. *Trouble in Mind: Black Southerners in the Age of Jim Crow.* New York: Knopf, 1998.

Marable, Manning, with Leith Mullings. *Freedom: A Photographic History of the African American Struggle.* New York: Phaidon, 2002.

Michaeli, Ethan. *The Defender: How the Legendary Black Newspaper Changed America.* New York: Houghton Mifflin Harcourt, 2016.

Rampersad, Arnold. *Jackie Robinson: A Biography.* New York: Ballantine, 1997.

Roberts, Gene, and Hank Klibanoff. *The Race Beat: The Press, the Civil Rights Struggle, and the Awakening of a Nation.* New York: Knopf, 2006.

Robinson, Jackie. *I Never Had It Made: An Autobiography.* New York: HarperCollins, 1995.

Shkurti, William J. *The Ohio State University in the Sixties: The Unraveling of the Old Order.* Columbus: Trillium, 2016.

Sides, Hampton. *Hellbound on His Trail: The Electrifying Account of the Largest Manhunt in American History.* New York: Anchor, 2010.

Simon, Scott. *Jackie Robinson and the Integration of Baseball.* Hoboken, N.J.: Wiley, 2002.

Updegrove, Mark K. *Indomitable Will: LBJ in the Presidency.* New York: Crown, 2012.

Index

Page numbers in *italics* refer to illustrations.

ILLUSTRATION CREDITS

A NOTE ABOUT THE AUTHOR

Wil Haygood has had notable careers in journalism and book writing. As a reporter for *The Boston Globe*, where he was a Pulitzer Prize finalist, he reported from around the world, including stops in Somalia—where he was taken hostage by warring rebels—and South Africa and India. While at *The Washington Post*, he covered Hurricane Katrina for thirty-three straight days, and the presidential campaign of Barack Obama. It was at the *Post* where Haygood wrote the story about White House butler Eugene Allen, later adapted into director Lee Daniels's award-winning film which starred, among others, Oprah Winfrey, Forest Whitaker, David Oyelowo, Vanessa Redgrave, and Jane Fonda. Haygood has written seven nonfiction books, among them acclaimed biographies of Adam Clayton Powell Jr., Sammy Davis Jr., Sugar Ray Robinson, and Thurgood Marshall. Among his honors are the Deems Taylor Music Biography Award, the Zora Neale Hurston–Richard Wright Award, the Scribes Book Award, and the Ohioana Book Award. The Boadway Distinguished Scholar-in-Residence at Miami University, Ohio, Haygood is also the recipient of writing and research fellowships from the John Simon Guggenheim Memorial Foundation, the National Endowment for the Humanities Foundation, the Alicia Patterson Foundation, and the Starr Center for the Study of the American Experience at Washington College, where he was the 2017–18 Patrick Henry Writing Fellow. He resides in Washington, D.C.

4296